David Doty's
A Field Guide to Carnival Glass

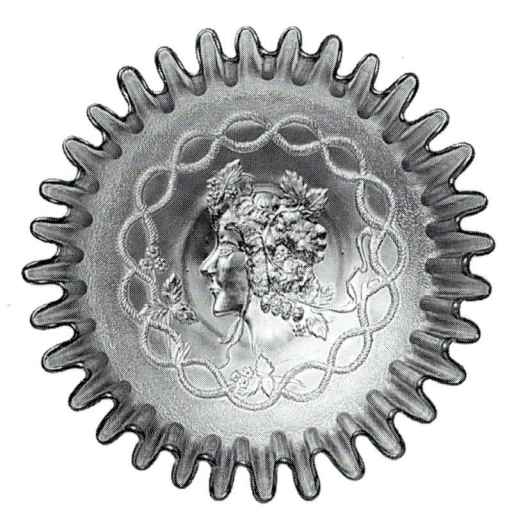

Fenton's Goddess of Harvest bowl in amethyst with tight crimped edge. This rare bowl is one of the few patterns in carnival glass that shows a representation of the human figure.

About the cover

Indeed, why would a common pattern in a common color sell for so much—repeatedly? There are several reasons, all typical of the carnival glass experience. While the pattern is common, the shape—a low ruffled bowl, almost a plate—is unusual in Imperial Grape. In addition, the color blue (that's the glass color, not the iridescence) is quite rare in most Imperial patterns, certainly in this shape. Furthermore, the iridescence is of top quality with reflections of reds, blues and yellows—an effect referred to by collectors as multicolor. Finally, the piece is quite rare; no other example has been found. A piece that many collectors would gladly sacrifice for. Will it sell for more next time? Stay tuned.

© Copyright 1998

ALL RIGHTS RESERVED

The Glass Press, Inc.
dba Antique Publications
P.O. Box 553 • Marietta, Ohio 45750

ISBN 1-57080-051-0

No part of this book may be reproduced, stored in a retrieval system or transmitted in any form or by any means—electronic, mechanical, photocopying, recording or otherwise—without the prior permission of the publisher.

Yet another book on carnival glass?

As we approach the one-hundredth anniversary of the advent of carnival glass, the fascination with this extraordinary product of a unique era continues to draw the interest of collectors and students.

There have been many books written about carnival glass, of course, and many are quite good. Most deal with the products of a specific manufacturer and are excellent in providing background and detail.

None, however, approach carnival glass from the point of view of the newer collector—those with the greatest need to understand the basics of what makes carnival collectible. I feel that need should be addressed.

When I decided to produce this book I knew it had to be portable (collectors like to carry around their reference material), organized for easy searching (several categories have their own sections), thorough (virtually every significant pattern is represented), and accurate (the prices are based on an analysis of my database of sale prices—now in excess of 37,000 different carnival items).

There are other price guides, of course, but from examining those I don't understand how the prices were determined. In some cases the figures are so far out of the range that they can trap an inexperienced buyer into spending far more than common sense would otherwise dictate.

Granted, some pieces of carnival do achieve astronomical prices at auction. And there are reasons for that: Some are truly great examples of the pattern, shape, and color and may be quite rare in that combination. In other cases it is obvious that a couple of deep-pocketed buyers were attempting to outbid each other. I've seen this happen at auctions time and again.

Does this mean that auctions generally bring higher prices than, say, what you find in malls? Not necessarily. Ten percent of items at carnival auctions sell for $25 or less. Many, many times I've seen good examples of auction glass sell for well under the market because no one was interested or someone didn't realize what a bargain they were passing by.

Auctions, of course, are not the only place to buy carnival. Flea markets, malls and antique shops abound. Many offer astounding sales—for either the buyer or the seller. Seldom for both. I hope this book helps even the playing field.

David Doty
August 1998

How this book is organized

Classic patterns, A-Z   1
These represent the bulk of this book and includes most standard shapes such as bowls, plates, compotes, rosebowls, water sets, and so on. These are from the classic era of carnival, about 1907 to 1925 or so, although I include a few patterns from the depression era. Also included here are the non-US patterns, generally produced from the early 1920s on.

Lettered carnival   259
Here we show most patterns with molded-in lettering. This includes advertising premiums, commemoratives, and Elks pieces. The principal exception is the Good Luck pattern—which remains in the above section.

Vases   269
For the most part vases have unique patterns; only a few are extensions of other pattern lines. Where vases are appropriate to list in this section as well as the classic section, I duplicate the entry.

Novelties and miniatures   309
I'm convinced that one of the reasons most conventional guides are hard to use is that these highly interesting pieces distract from visually sorting the patterns of more ordinary shapes such as bowls and plates. Plus, it's really interesting to see these gathered together where they can be studied as a group.

Special color section begins on page 153
Index for color section is on page 367

Decorated carnival 325
When enameled pieces are mixed in with non-decorated patterns and shapes, they receive little of the attention they deserve. This section provides an overview of this colorful category and shows a number of unusual pieces.

Lamps and shades 333
This sections includes kerosene and electric lamps and chandeliers as well as the shades used on them.

Hatpins 339
It's strange how much attention these little pieces attract. More than 80 are shown here and a few more are listed. That makes it among the most extensive references available for hatpins.

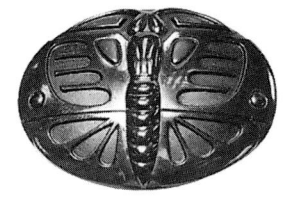

Contemporary carnival 349
Knowledge about newer carnival is important for two reasons: Those who specialize in the classic period glass need to know whether the glass they're buying is authentic; and the more recently produced glass has become collectible in itself. While of necessity this section is somewhat abbreviated, it is one of the few places where so many reissues, reproductions, and fakes are shown.

Acknowledgments

A reference work such as this field guide cannot be the work of just one person. The number of people who lent their knowledge and perspective is almost too many to count; it would take a book to do it. I am particularly indebted to the late John Britt for the example he set of combining words and photos to illustrate the detail and beauty of carnival glass.

My thanks could not be complete without acknowledging the enormous help and encouragement given by my wife, Joan.

I am also indebted to the staff at The Glass Press for their ideas, skill, support and understanding.

Below are listed many of those who graciously allowed me to photograph their glass or gave me the benefit of their experience.

David and Amy Ayers
Beck and Dorothy Bechtel
Dee Bekemeier
Carl and Eunice Booker
Gary and Donna Braden
John and Lucile Britt
Maxine Burkhardt
Tom Burns
Marie Capps
Richard and Carol Cinclair
Betty (and the late Smokey) Cloud
David Cotton
Harold Cox
Jerry and Carol Curtis
Bob and Sherrie Cyza
Barton and Sue Dooley
Don Doyle
Gale Eichhorst
Wayman and Nilah Espy
Frank Fenton, The Fenton Museum
the Fortneys (Jackie, the late Glen, and Harold)
Clint Fox
Dean and Diane Fry
Bob Gallo
Roger Gladson
Rick and Debbi Graham
Bob Grissom
Don and Linda Grizzle
Jack and Eleanor Hamilton

Don and Becky Hamlet
Dennis and Denise Harp
Roy Hieger
Bruce Hill
Richard Houghton
Dick and Jennie Hostetler
Richard Jarnig
Galen and Kathi Johnson
Don Kime and the late Roland Kuhn
Rick and Jackie Kojis
Janet Knechtel
Ed Kramer
Chuck Kremer
Todd and Susan Kuwitsky
Steve Lauer
Bob and Geneva Leonard
George and Mavis Loescher
Steve Long
David Malick
Lee Markley
Marie McGee
Bertie Metzger
John Mikkonen
Charles and Eleanor Mochel
Tom and Sharon Mordini
Steve Morrow
John Muehlbauer
Ken and Aileen Oppenlander
Ken and Bev Osbon
John and Ruth Phillips

Alan and Lorraine Pickup
Brian Pitman
Randy and Jackie Poucher
Elvis Randell
Mickey Reichel
Bill and Sandy Reyan
Bill and Carole Richards
Billy Richards
Grace (and the late Byron) Rinehart
John and Jeanette Rogers
Nola Schmoker
Carl and Ferne Schroeder
Joyce Seale
Jim and Jan Seeck
Karen Skinner
Bob Smith
Ingrid Spurrier
Randy and Joyce Stenback
Fred Stone and Ann McMorris
Bob Stremming
Daryl and Norma Strohm
Stephen and Glen Thistlewood
George Thomas
Swede Tilberg
Dick and Emma Tilton
Alphonse Tvaryanas
Harold and Dolores Wagner
Floyd and Cecil Whitley
John Woody
Larry Yung

Acquiring carnival glass

No matter how one starts the carnival collecting habit, finding sources to fulfill the fascination is high on the list.

Just where is this market? Surprisingly, a tremendous amount of glass changes hands each year. Much of that is at public auction, of which there are some three dozen held at various sites around the United States. Those sales account for perhaps 15,000 items, so you can see that quite a bit changes hands. A list of auctioneers who specialize, or at least have occasional sales, in carnival glass is included at the back of this book. While most of these auctioneers accept mail bids, I recommend that you attend the auction. That way you can see the glass you're interested in and can check it for damage, quality of iridescence, and nuances of shape that may not have been conveyed in the auction catalog.

A new method of buying and selling antiques—including carnival—is through the Internet. There are a number of websites that offer carnival glass. Use one of the common search engines and specify "carnival glass." As with ordering sight unseen at regular auctions, buying on the Internet poses some risks. Most auction or sale sites do give you the opportunity to ask the owner about details of pattern, color, shape, iridescence, and damage. Don't be in too much of a hurry to buy something. An extraordinary amount of carnival—no doubt hundreds of thousands of pieces—are out there. A similar or better piece will show up later.

Antique stores and malls also account for a huge amount of carnival sales. I probably don't have to tell you, though, that it's the rare shop or mall that has much of a selection of better-than-average glass. This sort of shopping is pretty much a chancy undertaking—requiring a lot of time to come up with a small amount of good glass.

Perhaps the best place, though, to buy carnival, is at conventions. There are about a dozen clubs around the US that are large enough to sponsor annual conventions and some draw folks from around the world. Just seeing room after room of glass on display and sale is enough to stun the first-time attendee. These are good places to simply see a lot of glass and to meet others with like interests. You need not be a member to visit a convention or attend their auction, but you will probably want to join. A list of carnival clubs and associations appears in the back of this book.

Although few attendees go to this length, Dennis and Denise Harp of Michigan cleared everything out of their hotel room to set up an elaborate display of their glass at the 1996 International Carnival Glass Association convention.

How to use this book

The bulk of this book is devoted to photos and descriptions of carnival glass and accompanied by prices for virtually all of the known shapes and colors. Pattern names are arranged alphabetically, with an alphabet key at the top of each right-hand page.

If you know the pattern name, flip through the pages until you come to the right place in the alphabet and then check for that pattern.

If you don't know the name of the pattern, the photos included should help. Finding a pattern this way may not be easy, but it *is* a good way to learn more about other patterns along the way. After all, this book is intended to be a learning experience.

Under each pattern name and photo there are listings of the shapes found in that pattern. Following those are a list of colors found in that shape accompanied by a price range.

The prices were determined by an extensive analysis of a database of carnival glass sales at auction. The database contains more than 37,000 listings.

Strawberry, Fenton

The design incorporates two sprigs of strawberries. Some pieces have an additional berry in the bottom center and are slightly more valuable.

Bonbon or card tray shape

Amber	60–100	relatively common color
Amberina	200–350	or reverse amberina
Blue	55–90	most common color
Blue	70–100	berry in bottom
Green, rare		
Lime green opal	300–400	scarce color
Marigold	20–30	scarce color
Marigold	60–115	berry in bottom
Red	400–500	rare color
Vaseline	60–115	scarce color
Vaseline opal	250–300	rare color

A typical listing. The right column is used to show relative scarcity, variations in that color, or miscellaneous information about unusual shapes or sizes.

By using auction prices, I was able to determine a fair actual sales price for a given piece, not an estimate or a guess inflated to "cover the ground." For many examples, the actual range of prices was often quite wide, i.e., the top price may have been four or even 10 times the lowest. Consequently, during the analysis of the data, I narrowed down the range to where the top end was no more than twice the bottom end—reflecting the healthy middle of the price range.

That meant eliminating many of the very highest prices—as well as the lowest prices. The lowest figures often represent poor quality or damaged examples; the highest are often a result of a couple of people fighting over a piece—to the auctioneer's delight.

The price ranges are intended to serve only as a guide, of course. If you can buy a good or better quality piece at the low end of the range, great! If you find an outstanding example and can afford it, there is nothing wrong with paying at the top of the range—or even more. It's your choice.

General shapes, A–Z

Included here are bowls, plates, compotes, bonbons, water sets, punch sets, table sets and most other mainstream carnival shapes. Lettered pieces, vases, lamps and shades, hatpins and novelties/miniatures are found in separate sections. Reissued and reproduced items are found in their own section but patterns made late in the carnival era or Depression era are listed in this section.

ABC Stork
See Stork ABC

Acanthus, Imperial

Found only in bowls and plates made from the same mold. Plates are usually 10 inches so are considered chop plates. This is a different pattern than the Beaded Acanthus found in pitchers, but also made by Imperial. Imperial made another pattern called Acanthus in the 1970s—with the design on the exterior. Fenton has made club souvenirs from the original molds of this pattern in recent years.

Bowl, about 8"
Green/helios	70–120	
Clambroth	110 (1998)	
Marigold	50–90	most common color
Purple	110–170	very common color
Smoke	60–100	scarce color

Chop plate, 9½"–10½"
Clambroth reported but very rare
Marigold	125–175	most common color
Smoke	150–275	scarce color

Acorn, Fenton

Acorn can be confused with a similar Fenton pattern, Autumn Acorns. Acorn, however, does not have a leaf in the center. The eight-inch plate above, in blue, is one of the few plates known (and only in blue). It is owned by Floyd and Cecil Whitley.

Bowl, 7–9", ruffled, round, or ice cream shape
Amber	90–180	scarce color
Amber opal	325 (1996)	
Amberina	500–700	rare color
Amethyst	150–250	rare color
Amethyst, black	110 (1994)	
Aqua	75–150	fairly common color
Blue	40–60	common color
Green	35–55	scarce color
Lavender	60 (1998)	6¼" round, marigold irid.
Lime	55 (1998)	
Marigold	15–30	common color
Mar/moonstone	200–300	rare color
Peach opal	200–300	rare color
Red	400–900	most common color
Red slag	375–600	rare color
Vaseline	100–200	rare color

Acorn, Millersburg

Only a handful of examples are known of this compote—found in amethyst, green, marigold, and vaseline. This marigold one is owned by Harold and Dolores Wagner. Another marigold one—round rather than ruffled—sold at the 1996 Heart of America club auction (Jim Seeck) for $1,600.

Acorn Burrs, Northwood

Although chestnuts are realistically depicted, the pattern is known as Acorn Burrs. Above are two pieces from a marigold eight-piece berry set that sold in 1994 for $200.

Berry set, 7 piece
Amethyst/purple 350–600
Green 750 (1995)
Marigold 250–400

Bowl, large berry
Amethyst/purple 145 (1994)
Marigold 75–125

Bowl, small berry or sauce
Amethyst/purple 35–50   most common color
Green 15–25
Marigold 15–25

Punch set (usually 6 cups)
Green 1,900–2,900

Ice blue 3,750 (1996)   specks in glass
Ice green 5,250 (1995)   broken tip
Ice green 8,000 (1996)   small crack
Marigold 1,200–2,500
Purple 1,400–2,100
White 4,500 (1997)   bruise inside bowl

Punch bowl and base
Aqua opal 21,500 (1993)   minor chip on collar

Punch base only
Green 30–50
Purple 35–60
White 60–80

Punch cup
Amethyst/purple 15–25   most common color
Blue 70–130
Aqua opal 2,050 (1997)
Green 25–40   common color
Ice blue 145 (1997)
Ice green 60–140
Marigold 30–50   scarce color
White 60–90   fairly common color

Table set, 4 piece
Amethyst/purple 500–800
Green 500–900
Marigold 600–1,100

Butter dish
Amethyst/purple 175–325
Marigold 150–250

Creamer
Amethyst/purple 75–125
Marigold 75–100

Spooner
Amethyst/purple 75–100
Green 100–200
Marigold 85–140

Sugar, covered
Marigold 115 (1996)
Purple 200–275

Water sets take up a lot of room so many collectors settle for a pitcher and a tumbler. Others assemble their own sets so that the colors match better.

Water set, 7 piece
Amethyst/purple 800–1,200
Green 900–1,300
Marigold 900–1,700

Pitcher, water
Amethyst/purple 350–700
Green 400 (1993)
Marigold 350–400

common color
base bruise

Tumbler
Amethyst/purple 25–45
Green 55–90
Green 40
Marigold 40–70
White, one reported

most common color
fairly common color
Etched "Bertha–1914"

Ada

This marigold tumbler was identified as Ada and listed as being made by the Ohio Flint Glass Company at the 1995 auction where it brought $110.

Adam's Rib, Dugan/Diamond

Both the pitcher and tumbler in this rare pattern are pedestalled and have handles. The sides have a subtle fluting.

Tumbler
Ice green 55 (1994)

Amaryllis, Dugan

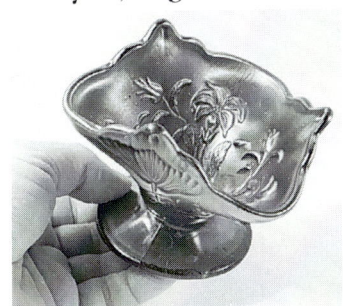

As you can see, this is a rather small compote. Found in a variety of shapes, including a small plate made from the compote. This tricorner amethyst example sold for $225 at the 1993 Great Lakes Carnival club auction (Tom Burns). A white whimsey plate exists and blue has been reported but not confirmed.

Compote, tricorner
Amethyst/purple 200–325
Marigold 150–250

Compote, deep round
Marigold 200–400

Plate, from compote mold
Amethyst 600 (1992)
Marigold 300–425

electric iridescence

American, Fostoria

Although produced in a variety of uniridized shapes, few examples of this pattern are found in carnival. This marigold rosebowl brought $350 in 1994 but another sold for just $155 in 1996.

Toothpick holder
Marigold 140 (1994) extremely rare

Tumbler, 4½" high, footed (or pedestalled)
Teal 50 (1993)

Juice tumbler
Aqua 35 (1993)

Perfume
Marigold 50 (1993)

Apple Blossoms, Dugan

The pattern has a wreath of apple blossoms around a central blossom. Seen mostly in small marigold bowls, round or ruffled, and worth $15 to $25. Occasionally found in rosebowl shape. A ruffled bowl in lavender slag sold on the www.cga web site in 1998 for $240. It may be the only one.

4 A Field Guide to Carnival Glass

Apple Blossom Twigs, Dugan

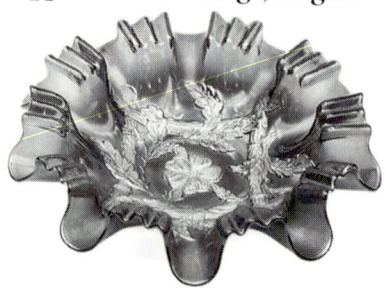

The pattern has an apple blossom bordered by four twigs. Bowls can be found with a variety of ruffles, the exaggerated three-in-one above perhaps the most interesting. Some pieces have sawtooth edging rather than the smooth shown here. Some pieces are found with Dugan's version of the basketweave pattern on the back, others with a plain back.

Bowl, 8–9", ruffled, ice cream shape, or 3/1 edge
Amethyst/purple	100–200	common color
Amethyst, black	95 (1997)	
Blue	175–250	rare in bowl, low ruffled
Lavender	120–175	ice cream shape
Lav. smoke	350 (1993)	low ruffled
Marigold	40–55	scarce color
Peach opal	90–150	most common color
Purple	300–400	3/1 edge
White	100–150	scarce

Bowl, banana bowl shape (2 sides up)
Peach opal	100–200

Plate, 9–9½"
Amethyst/purple	200–350	common color
Blue	200–350	fairly common in plates
Lavender	300–400	
Marigold	100–150	
Peach opal	175–350	most common color
White	100–200	scarce color

Plate, variant (smooth edge)
Amethyst/purple	250–350	
Amethyst/purple	725 (1998)	great example
Peach opal	300–500	

Apple Panels

Found only in a marigold breakfast set (small creamer and sugar) for $40 to $60.

Apple and Pear, Dugan
See Peach and Pear for this oval-shaped bowl.

Apple and Pear Intaglio, Northwood

Has heavy intaglio details and iridescence on the outside only—and no collar base. In strong marigold, this example is 9¾" wide. Few sales records available; an estimate of value would be between $75 and $100. Similar prices would apply to the related strawberry pattern.

Apple Tree, Fenton

Found only in water set pieces in marigold, blue, and white. The pitcher is known in a rare vase version; there are at least three examples without the handle.

Water set, 7 piece
Blue	825 (1997)
Marigold	200–350

Water pitcher
Blue   1,000–1,500
Marigold   150–250
White   400–500
Tumbler
Blue   60–90
Marigold   20–35
White   150–250

April Showers, Fenton
See Vases

Asters, Brockwitz (Germany)

This small rosebowl sold at Jim Seeck auction in March 1993 for $350. A small plate (5⅝" wide) from which the rosebowl was made is shown below. A similar one sold in 1998 for $125. Also known are vases and large berry bowls in blue.

Rosebowl, small (also known in blue)
Marigold   200–350
Chop plate, 12"
Marigold   165 (1996)

Compote
Marigold   50–65

Athenia, US Glass

This pattern is sometimes called Panelled 44 because of the distinctive design near the top. Few shapes have been spotted in carnival. This sugar bowl is 3¼" high and is courtesy of John and Lucile Britt. A toothpick holder in marigold brought $450 in 1995.

Australian Daisy, Jain

This unusually shaped pattern was made in India in spite of its name (it was found in Australia). The thin blown glass is typical of Jain items. These pieces were sold at a 1995 Mickey Reichel auction. The pitcher brought $85, tumblers $80 and $85—all marigold.

Australian Carnival Glass

A considerable amount of carnival glass was made in Australia, most of it by Crown Crystal. While the shapes may be familiar to us—mostly bowls, compotes and the occasional water set or vase, the patterns tend to reflect indigenous Australian flora and fauna. Colors seem to be limited to the marigold much like US glass, a deep purple that some characterize as black amethyst, and a few rare pieces on aqua base glass with marigold iridescence. A number of patterns are marked with a registration number on the front—which has no effect on value.

Australian carnival was made somewhat later than in the US, generally beginning in the early 1920s. Australian pieces, particularly the dark color, generally bring good prices.

6 A Field Guide to Carnival Glass

An excellent source for information on Australian carnival glass is *Carnival Glass of Australia*, by the Australian Carnival Enthusiasts Association.

Australian Banded Diamonds (also called Heavy Diamonds)

This marigold tumbler sold at the 1995 Lincoln-Land auction (Tom Burns) for $600. Water sets in purple and marigold have also been reported. Made by Crown Crystal Glass Company of Sydney, Australia.

Tumbler
Marigold   200–300
Purple   300–400

Bowl, 8½"
Purple   70–90

Australian Blocks and Arches

This pattern is very similar to the European pattern called Ranger. In fact, I photographed this marigold milk pitcher (6½" tall) at a carnival meeting where it had been identified as Ranger. I would estimate the value to be between $50 and $90 based on general demand for such shapes. Matching tumblers exist.

Australian Butterfly Bush, Butterfly and Bells, Butterfly and Flannel Flower, Butterfly and Waratah

This ruffled compote, 9½" across, sold at the 1994 Heart of America auction (Jim Seeck) for $300. Many Australian compotes are seen in the flattened salver or cakeplate shape or in this low ruffled shape. There are a number of similar patterns with much the same design. The Butterfly Bush has a stylized butterfly in the center and butterflies in the encircling groups of flowers. If the design has a group of bell-shaped flowers in the middle it's called Butterfly Bush and Xmas Bells. If it has a Zinnia-type flower in the middle it's called Butterfly Bush and Waratah; if the central flower has 10-pointed petals it's called Butterfly Bush and Flannel Flower. Such patterns are valued similarly.

Compote, round or ruffled
Marigold   200–350
Purple   300–500

Cakeplate or salver shape
Marigold   300–400
Purple   350–550

Cakeplate, miniature
Marigold   300–400

Australian Covered Panels

Although this simple pattern has been attributed to a number of US makers, we think it is Australian in origin. These pieces sold at a 1997 Mickey Reichel auction for $30 for the sugar and creamer together and $25 for the covered butter. Two low covered sugar bowls or powder jars sold for $15 each.

Australian Diamond Cut

This 9" bowl has a satiny marigold finish and sold for $250 at a Mickey Reichel auction in 1996.

Australian Emu

The Emu is a flightless, ostrich-like bird. The design shows the bird within a floral wreath or band. Found in five- and nine-inch bowls and a compote. Rare.

Bowl, about 9"
Marigold   250–400
Purple   300–500

Small bowl or sauce, about 5"
Marigold   100–150
Purple   150–200

Compote
Purple   750–1,000

Australian Kangaroo

Known in both nine- to ten-inch (2 versions) and five-inch bowls, this design has a Kangaroo sitting among grass and trees. The marigold nine-inch bowl shown sold for $500 at the 1994 Heart of America auction.

Bowl, 9–10"
Marigold   200–350
Purple   500–700

Bowl or sauce, about 5"
Marigold   100–150
Purple   150–200

Australian Kingfisher or Kookabura

The Australian Kingfisher and Kookabura pieces are similar, with a small large-billed bird sitting on a branch in the middle of a floral design. They are seen in the five-inch and nine-inch bowls as well as an eleven-inch float bowl. There are several pattern variations, but prices are similar.

Bowl, 9–10"
Marigold   100–150
Purple   250–450

Small bowl or sauce, about 5"
Marigold   80–150
Purple   100–200

This 10½" Kookabura float bowl in dark purple brought $750 at the 1998 Lincoln-Land convention auction (Tom Burns). Also known in marigold. The tumbler shows how large the bowl really is.

Australian Kiwi

As with several several patterns, the Kiwi (a small flightless bird) bowl is found in both nine- and five-inch sizes. The design shows two birds within a garland of ferns. A rarely seen pattern.

Bowls, about 9"
Purple   900–1,200

Small bowl or sauce, about 5"
Marigold   200–300

8   A Field Guide to Carnival Glass

Australian Magpie

The Magpie pattern is found in both large and small bowls. The bird sits on a branch against a stippled background. This purple bowl sold for $400 at the 1994 Heart of America convention auction (Jim Seeck).

Bowl, 9–10"
Marigold   125–250
Purple   250–400

Small bowl or sauce, about 5"
Marigold   100–150
Purple   150–200

Australian Panelled

This purple sugar, identified as "Diamonds," a similar Australian pattern, sold for $50 at a 1996 auction.

Australian Swan

Again, found in nine- and five-inch bowls. This purple bowl with 16 ruffles sold for $225 at the 1993 International convention auction (Jim Seeck).

Bowl, 9–10"
Marigold   150–250

Purple   200–350

Small bowl or sauce, about 5"
Marigold   100–180
Purple   110–200

Australian Shrike

A truly spectacular design, this pattern is often called Thunderbird in the United States. Found in nine- and five-inch bowls. This purple 12-ruffle bowl brought $290 at a 1993 auction. Such pieces have almost doubled in price since.

Bowl, 9–10"
Marigold   150–225
Purple   300–500

Bowl or sauce, about 5"
Marigold   90–160
Purple   150–250

Australian vase (Gum Tips)
See Vases

Autumn Acorns, Fenton

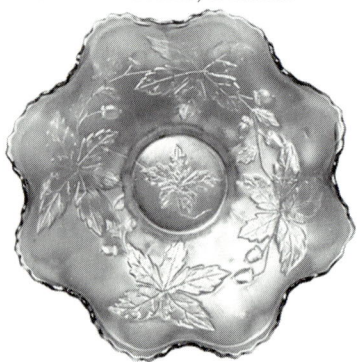

This pattern is sometimes confused with another Fenton pattern, Acorn. However, Autumn Acorns has a leaf in the center of the design—Acorn does not.

Bowl, about 9", ruffled, 3/1, or ice cream shape
Amethyst   70–130   fairly common
Blue   45–60   most common color

Green   50–100   fairly common
Lime   105 (1993)
Marigold   25–40   common color
Persian blue known
Red reported
Vaseline   200–250
Plate, 9", rare
Blue   1,400 (1998)
Green   1,500–1,700

Aztec, McKee
A rare pattern occasionally seen in a pitcher, tumbler, rosebowl, sugar, and creamer. May be marked "PresCut."

Banded Grape

Creamer, miniature
Marigold   15–30
Tumbler
Marigold   15–30

Banded Rib, Imperial

This is a Depression era water set seen only in marigold. The above 5-piece set sold for $30 at a 1997 auction. A 7-piece set sold for $70 in 1994.

Band of Roses
As the name suggests, this pattern has a narrow band of roses encircling the pieces. In addition, there are vertical flutes above and below the band.
Cordial set with decanter, 6 cordials, and tray
Marigold   575 (1998)
Tumbler
Marigold   185 (1998)

Band of Stars

A rare pattern, this wine set has 4-inch tall glasses. It is in the collection of John and Lucile Britt.

Barbella, Northwood

These tumblers are very hard to find, this being the only one I've seen at auction. It is vaseline (the usual color, I understand) and it sold for $110 at the 1995 Lincoln-Land convention auction.

Basket of Roses, Northwood

Often confused with Fenton's Wreath of Roses bonbon. This is the rare one. Note the basketweave exterior. Also found unstippled.
Bonbon
Amethyst   400–500
Marigold   300–400
Purple   200–350

Basketweave Open Edge
See Open Edge

Beaded Acanthus, Imperial

Although made by Imperial, this pattern is unrelated to Imperial's other pattern called Acanthus—which is found only in bowls and plates. This milk pitcher is the only shape known and usually found in marigold for $100 to $150, although some examples have sold for more than $300. Also reported in smoke.

Beaded Basket, Dugan

This pattern is similar to Dugan's Big Basketweave and has two handles rather than one that loops over the top. It's about five inches tall. Usually the top flares as in the example shown, but those with the top straight up are less common and more desirable.

Basket
Amethyst/purple 50–100
Amethyst/purple 260 (1994) not flared (sides straight up)
Aqua 425 (1996)
Blue 80–125
Lime green 150–250
Marigold 20–40 most common color
White 80–100 scarce color

Beaded Bullseye
See Vases

Beaded Cable, Northwood

With many colors available, Beaded Cable has formed the core of many a rosebowl collection. Most have a plain interior, some a rayed interior—which is slightly more desirable. Some have ribbed feet, other plain. One of the most common colors in this pattern is aqua opal—quite rare in most patterns. The example shown above is peach opal (rare for Northwood) and is one of two known. It sold for $8,500 at the 1997 Lincoln-Land convention auction (Tom Burns).

Rosebowl
Amethyst/purple 75–135 common color
Aqua 425 (1997)
Aqua opal 300–500 butterscotch iridescence
Aqua opal 400–700 pastel iridescence
Blue 150–250 common color
Blue, electric 200–400
Green 100–200 common color
Ice blue 500–800 scarce color
Ice green 1,200–1,500 rare color
Lavender 115 (1995)
Marigold 80–150 most common color
Mar/custard 5,250 (1996) 8,000 (1997)
Peach opal 8,500 (1997)
Persian B opal 500 (1996) cracked
Powder B opal 435 (1996)
White 300–500 scarce color

Candy dish or nut bowl shape (ruffled or flared)
Amethyst 40–75
Marigold 25–40

Beaded Panels, Dugan

This pattern, known only in a compote, is distinguished by its unique open stem. It was also made in opal glass prior to the Carnival era. The pattern is sometimes called "Opal Open." I can't recall seeing any that weren't like the crimped tricorner example shown here. All that I have seen were peach opal. Valued in the $50 to $80 range.

Beaded Shell, Dugan

An enormously charming pattern, Dugan's Beaded Shell pattern dates from before the Carnival era. Shown are a spooner and a sauce or small berry. Water set and table set repros have been reported.

Berry set, 5 piece
Marigold   100–150
Small berry
Amethyst   25–50
Butter dish, covered
Known in amethyst/purple and marigold. Rarely sell.
Creamer
Amethyst/purple 40–60
Marigold   20–30
Creamer and sugar
Purple   60 (1995)   creamer damaged
Spooner
Amethyst/purple 60–100
Marigold   30–60

Always popular and desirable, Beaded Shell mugs have a twig-style handle. Shown here are white and marigold mugs that brought $300 and $105 in 1994.

Mug
Amethyst/purple 40–70   most common color
Blue   80–150
Horehound   125 (1997)
Marigold   100–200
Violet   75 (1998)   pastel iridescence
White   500–900   rare color

The marigold pitcher above, with six tumblers, sold for $850 at the 1993 American auction (Tom Burns).

Water set, 7 piece
Marigold   500–800
Purple   575 (1995)   chip on pitcher
Water pitcher
Marigold   100 (1998)   light color and iridescence
Tumbler
Amethyst/purple 50–80
Blue   120–150   rare color
Marigold   20–35

Beaded Spears, Jain

This tumbler can be found in many sizes and several variations, including some with flared rims. Blown of thin and fragile-feeling glass, this pattern is rather typical of the output of the Indian company, Jain. Rarely seen.

Tumbler, lemonade, 4½" tall
Marigold   140–150
Tumbler
Marigold   150–200
Pitcher, water
Marigold   300–400

12 A Field Guide to Carnival Glass

Beaded Stars, Fenton

Beaded Stars was an early carnival pattern. It consists of 6 six-pointed stars on the exterior of small compotes, rosebowls, card trays, and an occasional plate.

Compote
Marigold   10–20

Rosebowl
Marigold   20–30

Plate
Marigold   70–100

Beads and Flowers, Dugan

Usually seen on the back of small plates. The beads are like those on the back of Fishscale and Beads with addition of flowers extending out from collar base. The front is plain. Found in purple, marigold, and peach opal for $40 to $75.

Bellflower

See Bells and Beads

Bells and Beads, Dugan

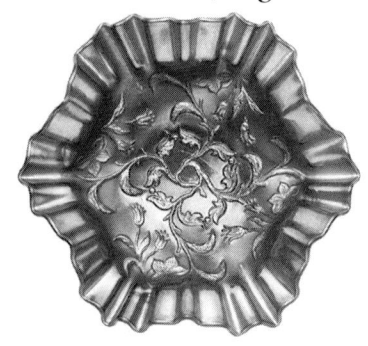

This Dugan pattern is often referred to as Bellflower, the name given it by Rose Presznick.

Bowl, about 7", ruffled, tricorner, and/or crimped
Amethyst/purple 80–150
Peach opal   40–75   most common color

Bernheimer Brothers–Many Stars

See Lettered section

Berry Band and Ribs

Distinguished by a band of berries and vertical ribs and a slight hour-glass shape to the body. This marigold set sold for $500 in 1994.

Big Basketweave, Dugan

This is similar to the identically named pattern that was also made into vases (see Vases).

Basket
Marigold   25–40

Big Butterfly (or Butterfly)

This is the only known marigold example and is courtesy of Cecil Whitley—who also owns one of the four known in green.

Big Fish, Millersburg

The pattern is very similar to Millersburg's Trout and Fly, but without the fly. This example is unusual in that it is exactly as it came from the mold, without ruffling or other modifications to the shape. Courtesy of Harold and Dolores Wagner. One large marigold rosebowl whimsey is known along with a green crimped oval bowl whimsey.

Bowl, 8–8½", ruffled, 3/1 edge, or ice cream shape
Amethyst	600–800	most common color
Green	500–900	ruffled or 3/1 edge
Green	800–1,500	ice cream shape
Marigold	400–600	
Vaseline	6,000 (1996)	6 ruffles, crimped

Big Thistle, Millersburg

Two of these punch bowls are known, both amethyst. The other, flared and with a chip on the collar base, sold at a Tom Burns auction in 1996 for $11,000.

Birds and Cherries, Fenton

Found in handled bonbons, stemmed compotes, and rare bowls and chop plates in marigold and blue.

Bonbon or card tray shape
Amethyst	75–125	scarce color
Blue	50–80	
Green	60–100	most common color
Marigold	25–40	scarce color in this pattern

Compote
Amethyst	35–60	scarce color
Blue	65–120	
Green	85–150	
Marigold	30–50	scarce color in this pattern

Bowl, ice cream shape
Blue	675 (1993)

Chop plate
Blue	2,700 (1997)	one known

Birmingham Age Herald
See Lettered section

Blackberry, Fenton

These miniature compotes are found in a number of shapes, including a tricorner version not shown here. These three are courtesy of Carl and Eunice Booker.

Compote, miniature
Amethyst/purple	100–135	rare color
Blue	50–70	most common color
Green	125–250	
Marigold	50–90	
White	350–400	scarce color

Plate, miniature, about 4¾" dia., from compote
Blue	300–400

Blackberry, Northwood

There can be some confusion here as the Northwood Raspberry compote is sometimes listed as Blackberry. The raspberries around the edge of the compote—

elongated by stretching—do resemble blackberries. See Raspberry.

Blackberry Banded, Fenton

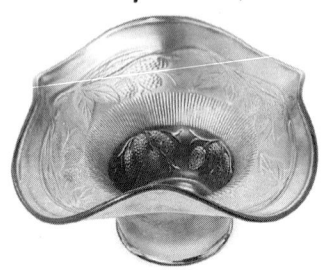

Similar to Fenton's Blackberry Spray but with a band of short vertical lines around the middle of the inside.

Hat, ruffled
Marigold	15–25
Mar/moonstone	70–90
White	130–150

Blackberry Block, Fenton

Found only in tankard-style pitchers and tumblers, the pattern is defined by the berries wandering over the squarish blocks.

Water set, 7 piece
Amethyst	1,900–2,500	
Blue	1,000–1,800	most common color
Green	3,750 (1994)	
Marigold	1,000–1,300	

Water pitcher
Amethyst	1,000–1,500
Blue	1,200 (1994)
Green	1,050 (1994)
Marigold	300–400
White reported but not confirmed	
Vaseline, one known	

Tumbler
Amethyst	85–105	
Blue	40–70	most common color
Green	60–100	
Marigold	25–40	
White, rare		

Blackberry Bramble, Fenton

Blackberry Bramble is found only in compotes.

Compote
Amethyst	30–45	
Blue	30–40	scarce color
Green	40–60	most common color
Marigold	20–30	

Blackberry Open Edge, Fenton

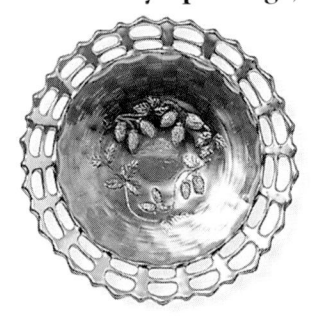

Very similar to Fenton's other pattern, Open Edge, but slightly larger. This pattern has a blackberry design in the center of the interior. Like Open Edge, it has a basketweave exterior and is seen in a variety of baskets/hats, bowls and an occasional plate. There are also rare vases whimsied from the bowl (see Vases) and one each of blue and marigold spittoon whimsies. Watch for red as quite a few pieces were made in this color—about the same quantities as amethyst, blue, green, and marigold.

Bowl, about 7", 2 sides up
Red	500–700

Basket or hat, ruffled or 2 sides up
Amberina	150 (1995)	
Amethyst	50–90	common color
Aqua	80–130	
Blue	50–80	common color
Celeste blue	900 (1994)	some edges closed
Green	80–150	common color
Marigold	20–40	common color
Red	300–500	fairly common color
White	60–100	scarce color

Plate, 7½"
Blue 4,000 (1993)
Marigold 125 (1994) damaged lattice
Ice blue reported
White, one known

Vase whimsey, 7–8"
Blue 1,400 (1994)
Marigold $1,500–2,000

Blackberry and Rays, Northwood

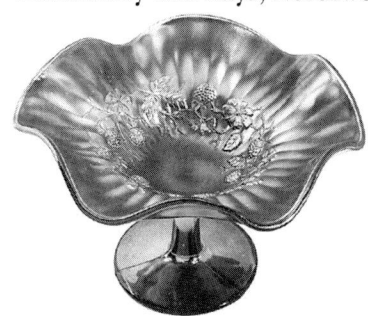

Extremely rare. Rays distinguish the pattern from other berry compotes. Purple examples sell for about $300. A marigold sold for $500 in 1994 and a green for $175 in 1996.

Blackberry Spray, Fenton

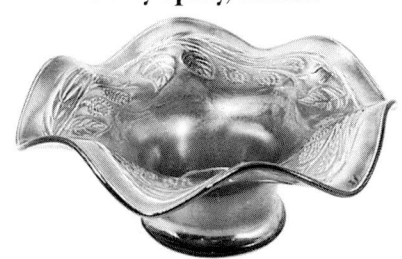

These Fenton hats are usually found in this ruffled shape or a jack-in-the-pulpit (usually crimped as well) but occasionally are seen in a two-sides up style. The blackberry pattern circles the edge of the interior. Most have four sprays of blackberries, some examples just two. The exterior is plain. Note that red is the most common color in the pattern.

Hat, ruffled
Amberina 300–400 rare color
Amberina, rev. 300–500 (reverse amberina)
Amberina opal 700–1,100 very rare color
Amethyst 120 (1997)
Aqua 70–125 scarce color
Aqua opal 500–800 rare color
Blue 30–50 scarce color
Blue opal 275 (1993)
Green 60–90 scarce color
Lime 30–45 scarce color
Lime green opal 150–300
Marigold 15–30 common color
Red 250–450 most common color
Red opal 600–800
Vaseline 45–90 scarce color

Hat, jack-in-the-pulpit
Amber 60–80 scarce color
Amberina 400–600 (reverse amberina)
Amethyst 150–200 scarce color
Aqua opal 1,750 (1994)
Blue 60–100
Green 350 (1994)
Horehound 80–100 rare color
Lime 85 (1994)
Marigold 20–30 common color
Red 300–500 most common color
Vaseline 70–100 scarce color

Hat, 2 sides up
Amethyst 295 (1997)
Amethyst opal 175–225
Aqua 70–100
Red 300–400 most common color
Vaseline 70–100

Hat, square (4 sides up)
Amethyst 75 (1997)
Aqua 50–80
Green 70–90
Red 250–400 most common color
Vaseline 50–90 scarce color

Blackberry, Wild
See Wild Blackberry

Blackberry Wreath, Millersburg

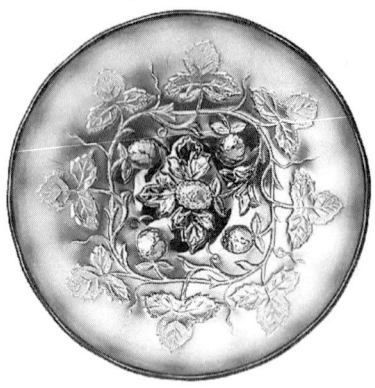

While the overall design is similar to the Grape Wreath and Strawberry Wreath patterns, the Blackberry Wreath is the only one with a central berry that has three leaves. A rarely seen variant has four leaves attached to the center berry. The sauce above (in blue, a rare color for Millersburg) is courtesy of Fred Stone. There are one known 7" rosebowl in marigold, one green 8" plate, three spittoons in marigold and one in amethyst, and a 7" ice cream shaped bowl in blue.

Sauce, about 6", ruffled, 3/1 edge, or ice cream
Amethyst	80–130	
Green	45–85	
Marigold	30–55	
Marigold	100 (1994)	tricorner
Marigold	195 (1995)	tight crimp

Bowl, small, about 7", ruffled or 3/1 edge
Amethyst	60–90	
Amethyst	200 (1998)	tricorner
Green	70–120	
Marigold	40–60	
Marigold	50–80	ice cream shape

Bowl, large, (8–10"), ruffled or 3/1 edge
Amethyst	80–160	
Blue	800–1,200	rare color
Green	60–100	
Marigold	50–90	

Bowl, large, ice cream shape
Amethyst	150–250
Blue	1,700 (1993)
Green	150–300
Marigold	50–90

Bowl, large square shape
Marigold	150–200

Plate, 6–7"
Amethyst reported
Marigold	1,900–2,200
Green	2,700 (1996)

Chop plate, two known
Marigold	7,000 (1995)

Blaze, Imperial

Another of Imperial's many geometric patterns. This one has hobstars and fan designs. The hexagonal design in the base is unique. Blaze has often been mistaken for Crabclaw. This 9" bowl sold as a clambroth Crabclaw (no pun intended) for $75 in 1996. A purple bowl brought $235 in 1998.

Blossom Band

An infrequently seen pattern, this marigold sauce has the pattern of blossoms and rayed beads only on the exterior. Courtesy of Carl and Eunice Booker.

Blossomtime, Northwood

Not as scarce as some people would believe, this pattern has a theme of blossoms and overlapping arcs. The easiest way to confirm the pattern is its unique threaded stem. Found only in a ruffled compote.

Compote
Amethyst/purple	300–500	most common color
Amethyst/purple	600–700	electric iridescence
Green	400–600	scarcest color
Marigold	200–350	

Blueberry, Fenton

Pitchers in this pattern are quite hard to find and the electric blue is a spectacular piece of carnival. The last complete blue water set to sell was in 1992, for $750.

Water set, 7 piece
Marigold   900–1,200
Pitcher
Blue   800–1,200
Blue, electric   1,300 (1993)   crack near handle
Marigold   500 (1994)
Tumbler
Blue   60–90   most common color
Green   100 (1997)
Marigold   25–40
White   80–100   rare color

Bo Peep, Westmoreland

Child's cereal bowl (rare)
Marigold   800 (1993)

Mug
Marigold   80–150

Border Plants, Dugan

A hard-to-find item, Border Plants is usually seen in the handgrip plate. This one brought $550 at a 1997 Jim Seeck Auction.

Bowl, 8¾", 3/1 edge, dome-footed
Amethyst/purple   500–600
Plate, handgrip
Peach opal   200–400
Purple   400–500

Bouquet, Fenton

A delicate design with daisy-like flowers spread rather evenly over the surface. Note the crimped top on the pitcher—typical of the pattern.

Water set, 7 piece
Blue   1,000–1,500
Marigold   275–325
Pitcher
Blue   350–500   rare color
Marigold   200–300   common color
Tumbler (see page 182)
Blue   70–130
Marigold   20–35   common color
Persian blue   600–700

18 A Field Guide to Carnival Glass

Boutonniere, Millersburg

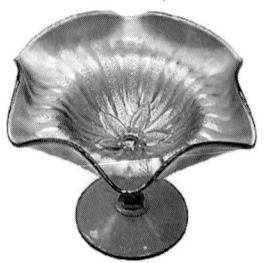

A modest Millersburg pattern, Boutonniere is found only in ruffled compotes in about equal quantities of amethyst, green, and marigold.

Compote
Amethyst	80–140
Green	90–150
Marigold	55–100

Briar Patch, Fenton

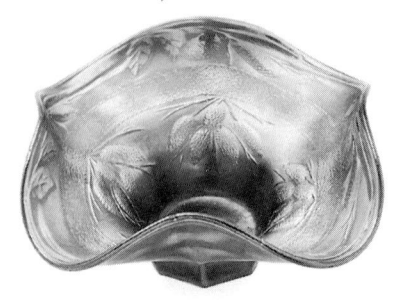

A seldom-seen pattern, Briar Patch gets little attention because few people recognize it. It it much like Fenton's other berry hats, but has four groups of berries at the very edge and four groups toward the center—separated by a subtly textured band. It has an octagonal base that rises to flutes on the back. When you find one it will probably be identified as another Fenton pattern—often Blackberry Spray. Seen only in blue. You should be able to pick one up for around $70 to $100.

Britt

This rare tumbler, in light blue, is named for John and Lucile Britt. It is in a private collection.

Brocaded patterns, Fostoria

While some collectors do not consider Fostoria's brocaded patterns to be mainstream carnival, they *are* iridized, were produced about the same time as classic carnival and often come up at auction, so we list them here. The effect was achieved with an acid etching process, producing the brocaded look that gives them the name. Found only in pastel colors.

Brocaded Acorn
Bowl or bonbon, 2 handles
Ice blue	40–70
Pink	25–40

Bowl, divided, with lid
Ice blue	50–70

Candlesticks
Ice blue	80–140	short, 3"
Lavender	50–70	tall

Console set (bowl & candlesticks)
Ice blue	300–500
Lavender	300–400

Console or centerpiece bowl
Ice blue	100–200

Ice bucket
Ice blue	95	
Ice blue	275	miniature
Lavender	400	

Mayonnaise pail, metal handle
Ice blue	125

Oyster cocktail glass
Lavender	90

Tumbler
Ice blue	100 (1997)

Vase
Ice blue	75 (1993)

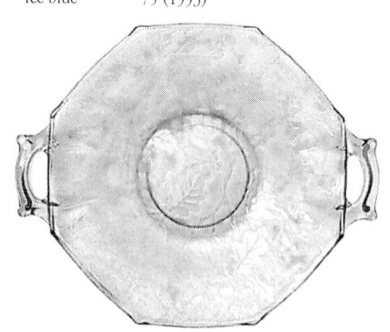

Plate, two handles, 7", 8½" or 12½"
Ice blue	30–50
Lavender	225 (1997)
Pink	45

Brocaded Daffodils

This white with gold decoration creamer and sugar on tray is courtesy of Carl and Eunice Booker.

Bonbon or card tray, 2-handled
Ice green 30–45

Bowl, 6" handled
Ice green 45

Bowl, divided, 8", oval
White 18

Cake plate, large, handled
Ice green 45

Cookie tray, handled
Pink 85

Plate, 7" handled
Ice green 50

Brocaded Palms

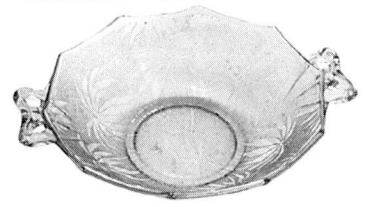

Bonbon or bowl, 2-handled
Ice green 70–150
Pink 80

Bowl, centerpiece
Ice green 95

Candy dish, covered
Ice green 200

Console set (bowl and candlesticks)
Pink 105 one candleholder cracked

Console bowl, 12", 3-footed
Ice green 145

Nappy
Ice green 35

Planter, with flower frog
Ice green 75

Relish, stemmed, oval
Ice green 100

Tray, handled, 12"
Ice green 100

Vase
Clear, blue 50 11"
Ice green 140 8", melon ribbed
Pink 200 8¼", bulbous, pinched in

Brocaded Poinsettia

Compote
White 30

Brocaded Poppy

Ice bucket
Ice green 45

Brocaded Roses

Bowl, 10" banana boat shape, handled
Pink 70

Sandwich tray
Pink 160

Brocaded Rose and Birds

Relish, stemmed
Ice green 100

Brocaded Summer Gardens

Console bowl, 10½", flared
Clear 20

Serving tray, large, handled
White 50

Sweetmeat, covered
Clear 120

Broken Arches, Imperial

Easy to remember because the arches are divided into several smaller pieces, much like stones in an arched doorway.

Punch set, 8 piece
Marigold 500–900
Purple 1,000–1,500

Punch bowl and base
Marigold 325 (1993) ruffled (rare)
Purple 800–1,200

Punch cup
Amethyst/purple 30–40
Marigold 10–20

Broecker's Flour
See Lettered section

Brooklyn Bridge
See Lettered section

Bullseye and Beads
See Vases

Bullseye and Leaves, Northwood

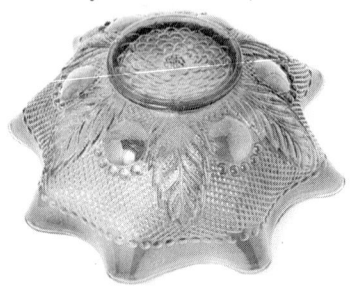

An exterior-only pattern made up of bullseyes and leaves. Because the bullseyes are beaded, the pattern sometimes is called Bullseye and Beads, but that's the name of a vase pattern. Mostly seen in green in the $30 to $40 range. Marigold reported at about $20.

Bushel Basket, Northwood

These baskets must have been very popular during the classic Carnival era as there are so many of them around. The basket on the right shows the rarer version with smooth handles where they connect to the bowl. It should be noted that these baskets are occasionally found in noniridized glass.

Round, ribbed handles
Amethyst/purple	85–160	common color
Amethyst, black	160 (1994)	
Aqua	350–500	scarce color
Aqua opal	300–450	very common color
Aqua blue opal	750 (1996)	
Blue	100–200	common color
Blue, electric	300–350	
Blue, lavender	300 (1997)	
Blue, Persian	650 (1996)	
Blue, smoky	400 (1995)	
Celeste blue	400 (1995)	repaired foot
Gold-flashed	250–300 (1998)	not iridized
Green	300–450	scarce color
Green, emerald	600 (1993) 910 (1996)	
Horehound	400–700	scarce color
Ice blue	400–700	rare color
Ice green	175–300	common color
Lavender	200–400	scarce color
Lime green	300–450	scarce color
Lime green opal	2,300 (1993)	one known
Marigold	85–150	very common color
Sapphire blue	1,400–2,000	rare color
Smoke	500–700	rare color
Vaseline	2,400 (1995)	
Violet	150–250	scarce color
White	125–200	average availability

Round, smooth handle variant (rare)
Amethyst/purple	275–350
Green	400–700

The 8-sided versions are exactly like the round except that they were spread slightly with a special tool that made the distinctive flare.

8-sided
Amethyst/purple	150–200	common color
Aqua	1,700 (1996)	
Blue	125–200	common color
Blue, elect	200–300	
Blue, Renninger	410 (1996)	
Green	300–500	common color
Horehound	275 (1996)	
Ice blue	400–600	fairly common color
Ice green	300–500	fairly common color
Lavender	255 (1994)	
Marigold	100–180	common color
White	90–150	common color

8-sided, smooth handle variant
Amethyst	400 (1996)

Butterflies, Fenton

Fenton's bonbon can be distinguished from the similar Northwood design by its ring of butterflies.

Bonbon or card tray shape (shown above)
Amethyst	30–50	common color
Blue	40–60	scarce color
Green	30–50	most common color
Marigold	25–40	

Bonbon with Horlacher advertising on base
Amethyst	80–150
Green	105 (1996)

Butterfly, Northwood

Northwood's bonbon has a single butterfly with stippled rays radiating from the center. The version with fine rings on the back is referred to as "threaded" and seen much less often than the plain one.

Bonbon, plain back
Amethyst/purple 50–80
Green 100–175
Marigold 35–55
Smoke, rare

Bonbon, threaded back, rare
Amethyst/purple 200–350
Blue 500–800
Green reported
Ice blue 3,000–3,500
Marigold 650 (1997)

Butterfly ornament
See Novelties/miniatures section

Butterfly tumbler
See Big Butterfly

Butterfly and Berry, Fenton

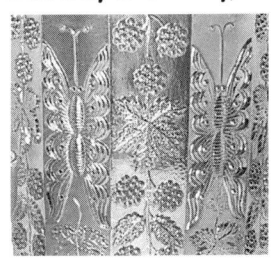

Butterfly and Berry was Fenton's most popular pattern. It was made in a large variety of shapes but not in many colors. The pattern was used as the exterior for several other Fenton large bowls: Heart and Trees, Fantail, and Panther. Imported fake large berry bowls are known in white and amethyst.

Berry set, 6 or 7 pieces
Amethyst, green, and white
Blue 250–300
Marigold 100–200 most common color

Bowl, large berry
Amethyst 125–200
Blue 85–150
Green 150–200
Marigold 45–80 most common color
Nile green, one known
White, very rare

Bowl, small berry or sauce
Amethyst 40–60
Blue 20–30
Green 40–70
Marigold 20–30 most common color
Red 500 (1997)

Whimsies
This blue whimsey bowl with no interior pattern and feet raised almost to where they leave the surface sold for $250 in 1993. A similar bowl in green with the feet entirely off the surface is also known as is a sauce in marigold with similarly raised feet. There is a whimsey spittoon in cobalt made from a sugar bowl and a similar spittoon in amethyst from a small sauce. In addition, there is a hair receiver made from a marigold sauce that has been cupped in like a rosebowl but then flattened down.

The Butterfly and Berry fernery (although some think it is a rosebowl since it is slightly cupped in) is a dramatic piece fashioned from a large berry bowl. This example, in blue, is from a private collection. Mickey Reichel auctioned a blue example in 1998 for $725.

Table set, 4 piece
Table set pieces have also been reported in amethyst and green
Blue 250–350
Marigold 200–300

Butter dish, covered
Blue 85–100
Marigold 80–150

Butter dish, base only
Blue 50–80
Marigold 30–50

22 A Field Guide to Carnival Glass

Creamer
Blue   65–110
Marigold   55–100
Spooner
Blue   60–100
Marigold   50–80
Sugar, covered
Marigold   50–90

On the left is the standard footed Butterfly and Berry hatpin holder. The piece on the right is whimsied from the tumbler mold with a different ring cap.

Hatpin Holder
Blue   1,600–2,400
Marigold   1,500–2,000
Whimsey hatpin holder from tumbler (2 known)
Marigold   850 (1993) 1,650 (1996)

Note that the tumbler was reissued by Fenton in the early 1970s in amethyst.

Water set, 7 piece
Amethyst, rare
Blue   600–900
Green   1,500 (1994)
Marigold   200–350
Pitcher
Green   300 (1995)   some roughness
Marigold   150–250
White, one known

Tumbler
Amethyst   50–70   scarce color
Blue   20–35   most common color
Green   80–150   scarce color
Marigold   15–25
Vaseline   325 (1995)
Vase
Amber   100–150   rare color
Amethyst   75–125   scarce color
Blue   50–75   most common color
Green   85–150   common color
Marigold   25–45   common color
Red   1,600–2,200   rare color
Red slag   700–1,000   rare color
Vase, crimped top
Blue   75–100
Marigold   40–60
Red   425 (1993)

Butterfly and Fern, Fenton

The pitcher in front was probably a prototype with the fern pattern added later. Such examples are very rare and none have sold in recent years. Courtesy of Carl and Ferne Schroeder.

Water set, 7 piece
Amethyst   800–1,000   scarce color
Blue   750–1,100   most common color
Green   850–1,200   rare color
Marigold   525–600
Pitcher
Amethyst   300–500   scarce color
Blue   350–650   most common color
Blue, electric 600–900
Green   500–800   rare color
Marigold   250–350   fairly common

Tumbler; most have manufacturer-ground base, variant does not
Amethyst	30–50	
Blue	40–70	most common color
Green	60–90	scarce color
Marigold	40–70	

Butterfly and Plume
Another name for Butterfly and Fern

Butterfly and Tulip, Dugan

A large butterfly hovers in the center of a spray of tulips. The exterior pattern is Inverted Feather and Fan, also used on Dugan's Grape Arbor fruit bowl. These large bowls are often squared like this one and bring excellent prices in amethyst/purple.

Bowl, square
Amethyst/purple	1,800–3,000
Marigold	250–350

Bowl, round
Marigold	200–300

Bowl, two sides up, rare
Marigold	200–300

Buttermilk Goblet, Fenton
These are the same as the Fenton Iris goblets, but without the Iris pattern on the interior.

Goblet
Amethyst	40–60
Green	40–60
Marigold	20–30
Red	80–150

Buzz Saw, Cambridge

Although known by the name Buzz Saw, these cruets are actually the pattern known as Double Star. Bear in mind that the stopper is the most difficult part to find and may be worth more than the cruet.

Cruet, small
Green	400–600	with stopper
Green	180–250	no stopper
Green	300–400	damage to stopper

Cruet, large
Green	400–500	with stopper
Green	125–200	no stopper
Marigold	450–500	with stopper
Marigold	175–250	no stopper
Marigold	250–300	damage to stopper

Buzz Saw and File

Buzz Saw and File pieces are known only in marigold. These two juice glasses are courtesy of John and Lucile Britt.

Goblet, two known
Marigold	35

Water set, 7 piece
Marigold	150	2 tumblers have base check

Pitcher, water
Marigold	400 (1998)

Tumbler
Marigold	145 (1998)

Juice glass
Marigold	70 (1998)

Cambridge Cologne

Although commonly referred to as the Cambridge cologne or barber bottle, this piece is part of the Cambridge Wheat Sheaf family. It stands 8½" high and is seen most often in green—although it is also known in marigold. The value in green is $300 to $400 but less than one third of that with no stopper.

Cane Panel

An infrequently seen pattern, this example is a tumbleup, a set that consists of a small water container and a tumbler for use on a night stand. This marigold set sold for $175 in 1998.

Cape Cod, Imperial

This pattern has been identified from old Imperial catalogs. It is sometimes called Heritage. The cruet in marigold brought $225 at a 1998 Reichel auction; the amethyst tumbler belongs to Lee Markley.

Captive Rose, Fenton

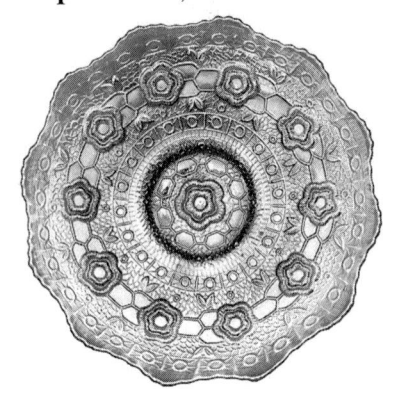

Captive Rose imitates embroidery stitching. It is sometimes confused with other similar patterns such as Northwood's Embroidered Mums and, because of its rose design, Dugan's Double Stem Rose. Interestingly, the most common shape in Captive Rose is the plate.

Bonbon (or 2-handled card tray)
Amethyst	70–100	scarce color
Blue	35–70	most common
Green	90–140	rare color
Marigold	20–35	scarce

Compote, ruffled or 3/1 edge
Amethyst	45–75	most common color
Blue, electric	475 (1997)	
Blue, powder	100 (1994)	
Green	60–100	common color
Marigold	75–125	scarce color
White	90–150	

Bowl, 7–9", ruffled, 3/1, or crimped
Amethyst/purple	60–100	most common color
Blue	75–125	common color
Green	60–100	common color
Marigold	60–100	scarce color

Plate, about 9"
Amethyst/purple	400–700	scarce color
Blue	300–600	most common color
Blue	1,000 (1997)	electric iridescence
Green	700–1,200	
Marigold	250–450	scarce color

Carolina Dogwood, Westmoreland

Not to be confused with a Dugan pattern, Dogwood Sprays. This one, though, has an overall design of petals and leaves punctuated by a large five-petal flower in the center.

Bowl, about 9", ruffled
Amethyst/purple 75–100
Blue opal 250–450 most common color
Marigold 75–100
Mar/milk glass 175–300
Peach opal 100–150

Plate, deep flared (or low bowl)
Blue opal 250 (1996)
Peach opal 160 (1996)

Caroline, Dugan

The interior rayed effect on Caroline is quite distinctive. The exterior pattern is a subtle arrangement of foliage radiating out from the base.

Basket, handled
Peach opal 200–250
Peach opal 350 (1997) lavender handle

Bowl, 8–9", ruffled or crimped, some tricorner
Peach opal 50–80

Bowl, 9", handgrip
Peach opal 65–100

Cathedral
See Curved Star

Chain and Star, Fostoria

Known in a handful of marigold tumblers and just one creamer and sugar set. The pattern, repeated on two sides of the tumbler, is a whirling star encircled by a chain. The base is ground and has a diameter of 2½ inches. Also known as Virginia or No. 1467. This tumbler is courtesy of Lee Markley.

Chatelaine, Imperial

This is a very rare Imperial pattern and the pitcher seldom comes up at auction. Known only in purple. This one, which is cracked, brought $195 in 1994.

Tumbler
Purple 150–250

Checkerboard, Westmoreland

Another rare pattern, seldom offered for sale. Pitchers and tumblers were reproduced by L.G. Wright using the old molds, so buy with caution.

Water set, 7 piece
Amethyst   2,000 (1998)
Pitcher, water
Amethyst   900 (1994) 3,500 (1995) 3 or 4 known
Tumbler
Amethyst   200–300
Marigold, rare
Goblet
Amethyst   70–125
Punch cup
Marigold   50–70

Checkers

Depression era pattern available in several shapes. Most can be purchased for $20 or less. This rose-bowl is from a private collection.

Cherries, Dugan

This pattern is found in both three-footed and collar base bowls as well as a small mold used for the 6" plates and sauces. Purple pieces like the one above generally are worth the most—especially with strong iridescence.

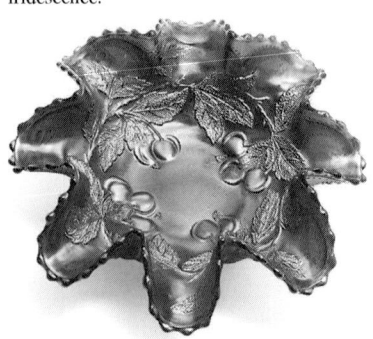

This is the collar base version of Dugan Cherries. It has the Jewelled Heart exterior—as opposed to the Cherries pattern on the exterior of the footed version. This example is one of the few that have eight ruffles (most have six) and is courtesy of Carl and Ferne Schroeder.

Bowl, footed, about 9"
Marigold   60–90
Peach opal   70–100   most common color
Purple   125–200
Bowl, footed, 2 sides up (banana bowl)
Peach opal   80–125
Bowl, large, about 10", collar base, Jewelled Heart exterior, ruffle or 3/1 edge, occasional ice cream
Peach opal   150–250
Purple   300–500
Purple   525 (1996)   electric irid., ice cream
Purple   950 (1997)   3/1 edge, spectacular color
Plate, 6–7" generally crimped, some ruffled (collar base), Jewelled Heart exterior
Amethyst/purple 150–300   most common color
Peach opal   125–200
Sauce (made from plate mold)
Purple   80–150
Peach opal   40–70   most common color

Cherries, Panelled, Dugan

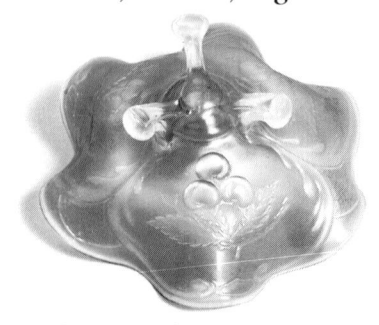

Similar to Dugan Cherries but with a smooth interior. Versions with enameled flowers on the front are worth more.

Bowls, 3-footed, ruffled
Marigold 50–70
Peach opal 50–70
Purple 80–100

Panelled Cherries bowl with enameled flowers
Peach opal 160–200

Cherries, Fenton

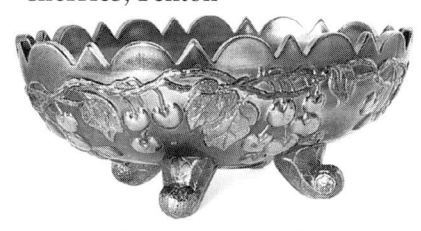

Not many collectors are aware that Fenton made a pattern much like Millersburg's Hanging Cherries. The only shape known is a small banana boat (about 9½" long). This blue one sold for $2,700 at the 1998 Lincoln-Land auction (Tom Burns). Three other blue examples have been reported plus a marigold piece with a floral interior.

Cherry and Cable, Northwood

There are only three known pitchers in this pattern, and this may be the only complete set. It's in marigold and is courtesy of Grace Rinehart.

Pitcher, water
Marigold 1,200–2,000
Tumbler
Marigold 150–200
Bowl, large berry (some with gold trim)
Marigold 60–100

Bowl, small berry
Marigold 25–30
Table set, 4 piece
Marigold 350 (1998)

Butter dish
Marigold 275 (1995)
Creamer, table size
Marigold 300 (1997)

Cherries, Millersburg
See Hanging Cherries

Cherry Chain, Fenton

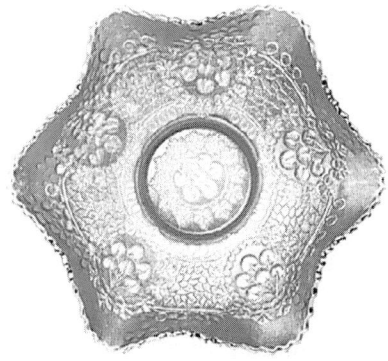

This pattern can be distinguished from Cherry Circles by the grouping of six cherries in the center. It has the same looped chain motif around the edge as Leaf Chain. The back pattern is Orange Tree. It is found only in bowls and plates. Amethyst and green items are particularly desirable in this pattern. The pattern has been reissued by Fenton in several colors and shapes including a chop plate.

Small bowl or sauce, ruffled or ice cream shape
Blue 35–50
Marigold 20–30
White 20 (1997)

Large bowl (9–10"), ruffled, 3/1 edge, or ice cream shape
Blue 70–100
Clambroth 60–100
Green 250–350
Marigold 60–90   most common color
Vaseline 50 (1995)
Red reported 7,000+
White 90–140   scarce color

Chop plate, 11"
Marigold 1,900–2,200
White 550–900

Small plate, (6–6½")
Amethyst 800 (1996)
Blue 90–150   common color
Marigold 70–125   most common color

Cherry Circles, Fenton

Cherry Circles is found only in the bonbon shape, sometimes in the card tray variation (two sides pulled down). Note the scale band around the outer part of the pattern. Several red examples are known.

Bonbon or card tray
Amethyst	150 (1998)	
Aqua	300–400	
Blue	50–90	
Blue, powder	130 (1998)	
Green	125–225	
Green, emerald	650 (1996)	fabulous iridescence
Marigold	30–50	most common color
Red	5,600 (1996)	
Red	1,900–2,700	damage

Cherry Smash

Cherry Smash is a Depression era tumbler known only in marigold. Also called Cherryberry. Not many around. Courtesy of Carl and Eunice Booker.

Cherry Wreath
See Wreathed Cherry

Chesterfield, Imperial

In his 1996 book on Imperial glass, Carl O. Burns points out that the difference between the Chesterfield and similar fluted patterns is the flat portion at the top of the handle. This mug sold for $12.50 at a 1995 auction where it was identified as a Colonial lemonade mug. A red compote brought $265 at a 1998 Mickey Reichel auction. Chesterfield pieces are sometimes identified as Wide Panel or Colonial.

Christmas Compote, Dugan

On everybody's favorites list. Admired because of its elegant shape and pattern of holly spread over all surfaces. Usually great iridescence. In 1997 the original molds were uncovered—clearly showing the Dugan/Diamond mark. Dave Richardson has reissued this compote in three Fenton colors: ruby, topaz, and green opalescent

Compote, original
Marigold	2,800–4,000
Purple	4,000–8,000

Chrysanthemum, Fenton

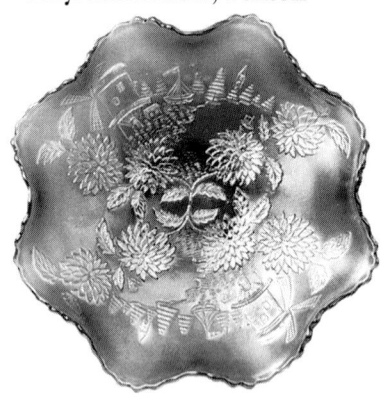

Sometimes called Chrysanthemum and Windmills, the pattern has sailboats in addition to the title flowers and windmills. Found in large, about 11", ball footed bowls and about 9" collar-based bowls. There are also scarce spatula footed bowls usually a little under nine inches. Alan and Lorraine Pickup report white ball-footed bowls.

Bowls, large ball-footed, ruffled or ice cream
Amethyst	150–250	
Blue	150–250	
Blue	900 (1997)	spectacular example

Green	175–300	
Marigold	45–80	most common color
Vaseline	200–300	

Bowl, small, collar base, all are ruffled
Amethyst	90–150	
Blue	90–150	
Green	110–175	
Marigold	40–70	most common color
Red	2,500–4,000	
Red	7,000 (1998)	spectacular example
Teal	200–300	

Bowl, spatula footed, about 8"
Amethyst	35–50
Marigold	30–45

Chrysanthemum, Imperial

A large flat plate dominated by a large blossom. Often, but not always, marked with the NuArt logo near the bottom edge of the design. This piece has also been reproduced in marigold, smoke, blue, and white. The repro should have the IG mark.

Chop plate, about 10½"
Amber	1,500–2,000
Clambroth reported	
Green reported	
Honey amber	800 (1994)
Marigold	550–700
Purple	1,500–1,900
Smoky blue	1,600 (1994)
White	800 (1994)

Circle Scroll, Dugan

Most often seen in a hat shape, the large bowl above is very rare in purple. Courtesy of Carl and Ferne Schroeder. Pitchers are reported in marigold and purple, but rarely are sold. Marigold pitchers would probably be priced in the $800 to $1,000 range, purple $1,000 to $1,500.

Berry set, 5 piece, rare
Marigold	70–100

Berry, small
Amethyst	25–40
Marigold	15–25

Butter dish
Known in marigold and purple

Creamer
Marigold	40–70
Purple	95 (1997)

Spooner
Marigold	35–50
Purple	200 (1995)

Sugar
Marigold	60–80

Hat, ruffled, JIP, or tricorner, from tumbler
Amethyst, black	110 (1998)	tricorner
Marigold	45–70	
Purple	100–175	

Tumbler
Amethyst/purple	300–400
Marigold	50–90

Vase, swung from tumbler shape, 6–8", see also Vase section.
Marigold	95–135
Purple	200–300

Classic Arts

The Classic Arts pattern is characterized by a frieze of nude figures playing musical instruments. While the body of the pieces is always marigold, the frieze has a greenish patina that looks like tarnished bronze. A similar pattern, Egyptian Queen, has Egyptian-like figures. The tall piece shown is thought to be a short vase or tall tumbler. Probably made in Czechoslovakia.

Rosebowl
Marigold   200–350

Vase or tumbler
Marigold   160–300

Powder jar
Marigold   280 (1998)

Cleveland Memorial ashtray
See Lettered section

Cobblestones, Imperial

Has an overall pattern of small raised dots. The back pattern is Arcs, unique to Imperial. Mostly seen in purple in ruffled bowls like that above for $140 to $250. As sometimes happens with thinly traded patterns, the price range can be enormous: purple examples sold for both $45 and $850 in 1998—as well as prices in between. It is sometimes called Pebbles, although there is a Fenton pattern by that name—which is often seen in small green sauces. There is one known purple chop plate. Carl O. Burns, in his 1996 book on Imperial carnival, reports amber, marigold, helios, and blue bowls.

Coin Dot, Fenton

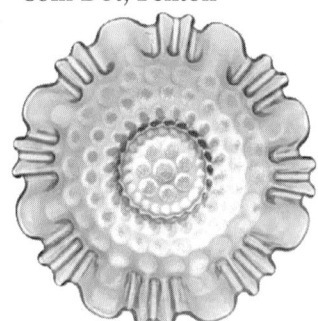

A commonly seen pattern, seldom selling for much (except in red). This pattern has stippled dots. If the dots are smooth, it's probably Westmoreland's Pearly Dots pattern. The three-in-one edge shown above is unusual but not rare. Some collectors think Fenton's Feather Stitch pattern was made by adding detail between the dots in the mold for this pattern. See also Inverted Coin Dot, a similar pattern that includes pitchers and tumblers.

Bowls, 7–9¼"
Amethyst	20–35	
Blue	25–40	not a common color in pattern
Green	40–60	most frequently seen color
Marigold	15–25	
Red	1,100–1,800	
Vaseline	135 (1996)	

Plate, 6"
Amethyst   70–110

Rosebowls. Coin Dot rosebowls are found in several sizes. The larger sizes, 6–7" bring $30 to $50 in amethyst, green, or marigold. The smallest and least often seen, about 5", bring $10 to $15 more. A lime green example sold for $70 in 1998.

Coin Spot

Usually attributed to Dugan although some collectors feel Westmoreland made them, these compotes have an exterior pattern with columns of stippled thumbprints. Unusual colors such as celeste and cobalt are highest in demand. A few of these have been reported in the goblet shape.

Compote
Aqua opal, one known		
Blue	80–120	
Celeste	700–850	
Cobalt	650 (1994)	
Ice green	275–300	
Marigold	15–25	
Peach opal	45–80	most common color
Purple	80–120	
Purple	300 (1997)	electric iridescence

Colonial, various makers

Virtually all glass factories made at least one variation of the pattern called Colonial. More confusing, the pattern is sometimes called Flute or Double Loop.

Candlesticks, pair

Ice green	200	probably Fenton, 10¼"
Marigold	80	probably Fenton, 10¼"
Marigold	95	9"
Marigold	100	8½"
Red	205	9", one has open bubble
Red	295	probably Fenton, 10¼", single
Sapphire blue	105	
Smoke	45	
White	100	

Covered Candy dish
Olive   25 (1994)

Goblet
Marigold   15–25
White   18 (1995)   stretch iridescence

Lemonade mugs, footed
Marigold   15–25

Tumbler
Marigold   40–60

Colonial, Imperial

Toothpick, 2-handled, Iron Cross mark
Marigold   125–250

Water set, 7 piece
Marigold   50 (1997) tumblers have Iron Cross

Colonial, Northwood
See Double Loop

Colonial Flute, Imperial

Colonial Flute is the name given this pattern in Imperial catalogs—although some collectors refer to it as Flute and Honeycomb. This marigold 9" bowl is courtesy of Tom Townsend. Carl and Eunice Booker have a purple sauce in the pattern.

Colonial Lady
See Vases

Columbia, Imperial

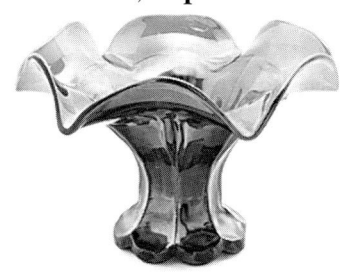

There was only one mold for this pattern, but it yielded many shapes. There are variously shaped compotes, vases, and a few rare rosebowls. I've seen two plate whimsies sell in marigold for $25 each and a third for $250. Why the difference? Who knows?

Compote
Marigold	35–60	common color
Purple	200–300	rare color
Smoke	80–120	

Vase
Marigold	25–45	common color
Purple	100–175	
Smoke	85–125	rare color

Compote Vase

This doesn't seem to be either a compote or a vase but collectors know it by this name. At the 1998 auction where this green piece sold for $42.50, it was identified as a Westmoreland tulip-shaped plain compote. It's usually attributed to Dugan. Similar shapes in other common colors would probably be worth about what this one brought.

Concave Diamonds, Northwood

Said to date from the 1917 era, Concave Diamonds has a soft quilted effect—often with a stretch glass-like finish. Water sets in celeste blue sell for between $300 and $500 for 10- to 14 piece sets. Note that complete sets will include coasters and a lid for the pitcher. As tumblers are found in russet/olive and vaseline, it's possible there are sets in those colors.

Tumbler
Celeste   20–30
Russet/olive   50–70
Vaseline   100–200

Tumble up (guest water bottle and tumbler)
Celeste   175–225
Russet/olive   60–100
Vaseline   300–400

Tumble up, tumbler only
Blue opaque   80 (1998)
Celeste   80 (1997)
Russet/olive   115 (1997)
Vaseline   115 (1996)

Vase
Celeste   100–150
Russet/olive   185 (1997)
Vaseline   250 (1997)

Concave Flute, Westmoreland

Concave Flute has nine plain panels—each finished off with a rounded scallop. In addition to the rose-bowl, the same mold was used to make vases and banana dishes—the latter of which are quite scarce.

Rosebowl
Amethyst   60 (1996)
Marigold   40–70
Teal   70–100   rare color

Vase, straight
Amethyst   25–40

Blue opal   150–300
Marigold   35–50
Teal   45–70

Vase, jack-in-the-pulpit shape
Blue opal   210–350
Mar/moonstone 150–200

Concord, Fenton

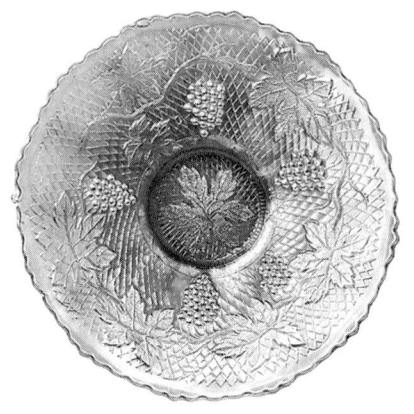

Concord is the only grape pattern with a latticed background. It appears to be the Fenton Vintage pattern to which the lattice design has been overlaid. Bowls are seen about equally in three-in-one edge and ruffled, with an occasional ice cream shape showing up.

Bowl, 7½–9"
Amethyst   375–500
Blue   200–300   rare color
Green   250–450   most common color
Green   500–800 brilliant or electric iridescence
Marigold   200–350

Concord Plate
Amethyst   1,500–2,500
Green   2,500–4000
Marigold   1,500–2,000

Cone and Tie, Imperial

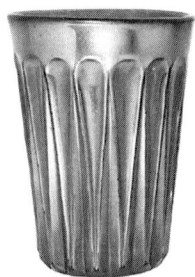

Slightly taller than the average tumbler, this stylish pattern is only found in purple and no pitchers are known. Very rare; none have sold publicly in recent years. This example is courtesy of Lee Markley.

Constellation, Dugan

This small compote is the only shape in the pattern. It was made from the S-Repeat goblet mold. The interior has a beaded star. White is most often seen.

Compote
Amethyst/purple	300–500	very rare
Lavender	600 (1997)	
Marigold	90–140	
White	80–130	

Coral, Fenton

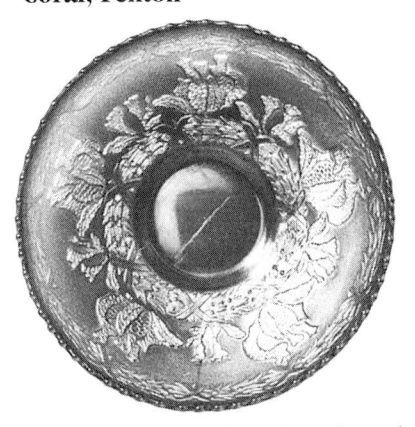

The two bands of wrapped wreaths are also used in Fenton's Little Fishes and Peter Rabbit patterns. This one, though, has leaf-like designs that apparently reminded someone of coral. The pattern is found only in plates and bowls and is quite scarce.

Bowl, about 9", ruffled, 3/1, or ice cream shape
Blue	500–700	rare color
Green	180–250	scarce color
Marigold	100–200	common color
Marigold	300–500	spectacular examples

Plate, 9"
Marigold	900–1,500

Corinth, Westmoreland

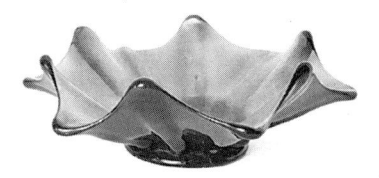

A rather stark pattern with no design on the interior and 12 exterior ribs. The Corinth mold was often pulled up into vases, many of those in jack-in-the-pulpit style. See Vases for photo. This is a bowl.

Banana dish shape (two sides up)
Amber	25–45
Amethyst	25–45
Marigold	20–30
Teal	30–50
White	25–40

Bowl, about 8"
Amethyst	15–25
Blue opal	250 (1996)
Mar/milk glass	25–35
Peach opal	20–30

Corinth vase, straight
Amber	70–90
Amethyst	25–40
Blue opal	150–300
Green	25–40
Mar/moonstone	75 (1995)
Teal	60–100

Vase, jack-in-the-pulpit shape
Amber	75–105
Amethyst	70–100
Blue opal	150–300
Marigold	25–50
Mar/moonstone	80–150
Teal	125–225

Corn bottle
See Novelties/miniatures section

Corn Vase
See Vases

Cornucopia, Fenton

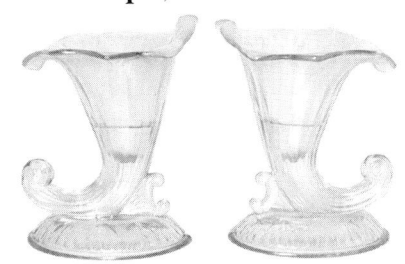

This pair of ice blue candlesticks sold at the 1998 Lincoln-Land auction (Tom Burns) for $225.

Cosmos, Millersburg

Found only in green, a large flower dominates the pattern. Small (6"–7") bowls, either ice cream shape or ruffled are valued at $50 to $80. Plates from the same mold are reported but difficult to find.

Cosmos variant, Dugan

Because of the similar names, this pattern is often confused with the above Millersburg one. If it's larger than 7 inches and not green, it's probably this one.

Bowl, about 10"
Amethyst   25–40
Blue   100–200   rare color
Marigold   20–30   most common color

Chop plate (flattened from bowl)
Amethyst   210 (1998)
Marigold   120–140

Cosmos and Cane, US Glass

The pattern has two styles of flowers repeated alternately around the shape. The cane design is lower on the pattern. The honey amber coloring—a soft mellow amberish on clear base glass—was unique to US Glass products. Lots of interesting whimsies in this pattern.

Berry sets, 5–7 piece
Honey amber   150–250
White   200–300

Bowl, small, or sauce
Honey amber   15–30
White   10–20

Bowl, large (7–10")
Honey amber   70–120
White   70–110

Bowl, headdress interior
Honey amber   460 (1997)   square
White   150–250

Bowl, whimsey
White   255 (1998)   5¼" square

Chop plate, 10–10½"
Honey amber   625 (1996)

Breakfast set (creamer and sugar)
Honey amber   100–150

Table set, 4 piece
Honey amber   200–350
White   500–900

Butter dish
Honey amber   160–175
Marigold   130–160
White   350 (1996)

Creamer
Honey amber   50–70
Marigold   35–50

Spooner
Honey amber   40–70
Marigold   35–50

Sugar
White   140 (1996)

Rosebowl, from small bowl
Marigold   150–300   Headdress interior
Honey amber   300–500

These three marigold Cosmos and Cane rosebowls sold at the 1997 Lincoln-Land auction for prices below what many observers thought they should have brought. The spittoon-shaped rosebowl on the left brought $550, the goblet-shaped rosebowl in the middle $350, and the volcano shape at right, $475. All are from the mold used for the regular compote.

Rosebowl, spittoon-shaped
Honey amber   450–800
Marigold   1,000–1,200

Volcano rosebowl whimsey
Purple   1,450 (1995)
Honey Amber   475 (1998)

Compote, dome-footed, ruffled
White 275 (1998)

Compote, stemmed
White 1,000 (1998) from Don Moore collection

Some Cosmos and Cane tumblers have advertising for J.R. Millner, Lynchburg VA, molded into the base.

Tumbler
Honey amber 50–80
Honey amber 100–150 with advertising
Marigold 60–100
White 300–500

Water pitcher
Honey amber 500–900
Marigold 700–1,000
White 1,200–1,500

Country Kitchen, Millersburg

Country Kitchen is a difficult pattern to recognize as it looks like many other cut-style patterns. While there is no easy way to remember it, note the series of adjoining 16-pointed star medallions separated by arc panels. Marigold milk pitchers are known and there is one amethyst spittoon whimsey made from the spooner. The spooner, by the way, was sometimes swung into a vase. The pattern was also used as the exterior design on Fleur de Lis bowls.

This peculiarly shaped bowl is in marigold and about 10 inches on a side. It sold for $575 in 1994.

Table set, 4 piece
Amethyst 325 (1996) no butter base
Marigold sets known

Butter dish
Amethyst 325–450
Marigold 350 (1995)

Creamer
Green 650 (1994) electric irid

Spooner
Amethyst 175–300
Marigold 350 (1995)

Sugar, covered
Marigold 75 (1997)

Courthouse
See Lettered section

Covered Hen, Sowerby

This pattern is heavily sculpted, with chicks along the side. Chic was the Sowerby name. Sowerby was an English company that made a considerable amount of carnival glass.

Butter dish
Blue   70–100
Marigold   60–90

Covered Swan, Sowerby

The covered swan has been reproduced. Note the filled-in neck on the newer version on the left, while the older has no glass between the neck and body. More scarce than the covered hen.

Amethyst   100–150
Blue   200–300
Marigold   100–150

Crabclaw, Imperial

Crabclaw is another of those confusing Imperial patterns. The key to spotting it, however, is to look for the shape of the crab's claws, pointing down. Found only in pitchers and tumblers. Blaze bowls are sometimes mistaken for Crabclaw even though there are none of the distinctive crabclaw designs on them.

Water set, 7 piece
Marigold   200–300
Water pitcher
Marigold   100–150
Tumbler
Marigold   10–25

Crackle, Imperial

The Crackle pattern dates from the Depression era. Shown above are candlesticks and a spittoon. The patterns known as Tree of Life and Soda Gold are sometimes identified as Crackle—and vice versa.

Candlesticks, pair
Marigold   15–25
Candy jar with lid
Marigold   5–10
Fan vase
Marigold   5–10   clear base
Lamp, oil, miniature
Marigold   43 (1994)
Spittoon
Marigold   25–30
Salt shaker
Aqua   50 (1995)   marigold overlay

Found only in marigold, the Crackle water set brings less than $40.

Tumbler
Marigold   7–10
Wall or car vase with or without bracket
Marigold   10–15

Crosshatch, Sowerby

A rarely seen pattern, Crosshatch was made in a variety of shapes—although few were iridized.

Curved Star, Brockwitz (Germany)
Curved Star was produced in a wide variety of shapes in marigold and blue by Brockwitz. Some shapes were also produced by Eda of Sweden. The pattern is also seen in vases.

Bowl, 9½", Headdress interior
Marigold   40

While sometimes referred to as Cathedral chalice, there is nothing of religious significance about this shape. It's the Curved Star celery vase.

Celery
Blue   60–100
Marigold   40–60

Child's dish
Marigold   175 (1998)

Creamer
Blue   60–90
Marigold   40–60

Butter dish
Two different butter dish shapes are known

With such an easily confused pattern, pieces are often misidentified. These two marigold Curved Star epergne lilies were sold at a 1993 auction as Star and Fan candlesticks. They brought $205.

Punch bowl, one piece
Marigold   70 (1994)   Headdress interior

Rosebowl, small
Blue   80–150
Marigold   125 (1994)

Although this piece is an open sugar, it was identified as a compote. Inverted, it does double duty as the base to a two-piece fruit bowl. For the interior pattern, see Headdress.

Sugar, ruffled, Headdress interior
Blue   60–110

Cut Cosmos

An unusual pattern with the flowers cut into the six panels. No pitchers are known. The maker is unknown. Tumblers are found only in marigold and sell in the $130 to $170 range.

38   A Field Guide to Carnival Glass

Cut Ovals, Fenton
This pattern is found on six-sided candlesticks in which circular portions of the juncture of the vertical sides have been cut out—forming ovals. A pair of 10" marigold candlesticks sold at a 1997 Tom Burns auction for $375.

Dahlia, Dugan

A unique design with a large, highly detailed flower dominating fluted panels. White pieces often have the flower or edges trimmed in gold, red, or blue. Some of these painted pieces can be quite expensive as there are so few and people want complete sets. The berry set (above) has the flower on the inside of the bowls as well as outside.

Berry set, 6 or 7 pieces
Amethyst/purple 175–250
Marigold   110–170
White   200–350

Bowl, small berry or sauce (5")
Amethyst/purple 50–80
Marigold   20–35
White   60–110

Bowl, large berry
Amethyst/purple 100–150
Marigold   50–90
White   150–200   some with red and gold trim

Table set, 4 piece
Amethyst/purple 400–700
Marigold   300–500
White   500–800

Butter, covered
Amethyst/purple 150–200
Marigold   75–105
White   210 (1995)   gold decoration

Creamer
Amethyst/purple 55–85
Marigold   40–70
White   90–125
White   135 (1995)   gold decoration

Spooner
Amethyst/purple 60–90
Marigold   50–80
White   70–100

Sugar, covered
Amethyst/purple 60–100
Marigold   60–100
White   70–125

Both pitchers and tumblers have been reproduced. The rule of thumb for determining the difference between new and old pitchers is that new pitchers, made from the original molds, were iridized on the underneath of the base; the old version was not—although it's not a guaranteed method of determining the age. New tumblers have three flowers around the sides and a plain base bottom while old tumblers have four flowers around and a starred base.

Water set, 7 piece
Amethyst/purple 1,000–1,500

Pitcher, water
Amethyst/purple 600–900
Amethyst/purple 70–150   reproduction
Marigold   350 (1994)
White   900 (1997)   gold painted flowers

Tumbler
Amethyst/purple 70–125
Marigold   80–150
White   215 (1997)   gold painted flowers
White   90–125   some original gold paint
White   150 (1995)   blue decor is light

Daisy, Fenton

These blue bonbons are quite scarce and are generally quite attractive. Valued at $150 to $200.

Daisy, Imperial

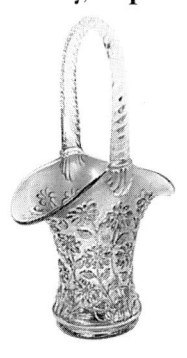

The Imperial Daisy basket has much the same shape as other Imperial baskets such as Imperial Grape. The Daisy basket was reproduced and should carry the IG mark.

Basket
Marigold   30–50
Smoke   50–90

Daisy Block Rowboat, Sowerby
See Novelties/miniatures

Daisy Cut Bell, Fenton

A favorite among collectors. This example sold at the 1994 Heart of America club auction (Jim Seeck) for $375. Known only in marigold. Usually sells in the $250 to $400 range. A marigold whimsey with a ruffled skirt is in a private collection.

Daisy and Cane
See Tartan

Daisy Dear, Dugan

Daisy Dear is another of those simple, low-relief Dugan flower patterns frequently found on the exterior of small ruffled bowls. As with the two other very similar Dugan patterns—Single Flower and Triplets—the pieces are usually peach opal with no interior pattern. Generally valued at $10 to $20.

Daisy and Drape
See Vases

Daisy and Lattice
See Lattice and Daisy

Daisy and Plume, Northwood

The three-footed rosebowl (left) is the most commonly seen shape but the pattern was also made as a stemmed compote and rosebowl (right). Most three-footed pieces have a plain interior but others have a raspberry or rayed interior. Some pieces were made by Dugan. The stemmed pieces are sometimes opened into a compote, some with fern interiors.

Daisy Squares

Most often seen in the rosebowl style above, the pattern was occasionally flared and ruffled into a compote. Generally attributed to Westmoreland. Known in marigold and a light green variously identified as lime or vaseline. In either color the rosebowl typically sells in the $300 to $450 range. The flared compote or tricorner version usually brings a bit more. The ruffled compote on the right, in light green, sold for $200 in 1998.

Daisy Web, Dugan

Dugan's Daisy Web basket (some call it a hat) is a rarely seen pattern. The electric purple example above sold at a 1994 Jim Seeck auction for $1,800.

Basket or hat shape, some 2 sides up
Marigold   200–300
Purple   200–250

This whimsied version of Daisy and Plume is by Dugan. It is peach opal and courtesy of Larry Yung.

Candy dish, 3 footed
Amethyst/purple	100–175	berry interior
Ice blue	450–800	berry interior
Ice green	600–1,000	
Green	40–70	
Lime green	600–900	berry interior
Marigold	25–45	
Marigold	45 (1997)	tricorner whimsey
Peach opal	80–100	Dugan
White	300–450	

Rosebowl, 3 footed
Amethyst/purple	95–150	berry interior
Aqua	1,100 (1997)	polished flake on foot
Aqua opal	17,000 (1997)	three known
Blue	300–400	berry interior
Green	65–90	common color
Green	75–135	rayed interior
Ice blue	500–700	berry interior
Ice green	800–1,100	berry interior
Lavender	175 (1993)	berry interior
Marigold	50–80	most common color
Marigold	60–100	berry interior
White	500–900	berry interior

Rosebowl, stemmed
Amber	115–200	scarce color
Amethyst/purple	50–75	
Green	50–75	
Green	85–105	fern inter., opened to compote
Marigold	30–45	most common color
Marigold	40–60	fern inter., opened to compote

Daisy and Scroll

This small marigold tumbler (2⅝" tall) was probably intended as a shot glass or small wine as it has been found with a decanter of the same design. From the John and Lucile Britt collection.

Daisy Wreath, Westmoreland

Usually found in bowls but occasionally as a plate. A rare vase in marigold is known to have been whimsied from this mold. Both blue opalescent and marigold on milk glass are very desirable.

Bowl about 9", ruffled or ice cream shape
Blue opal   200–350
Marigold   75–125
Mar/milk glass   150–250
Peach opal   150–200

Plate
Blue opal   350 (1996)

Dandelion, Northwood

The Dandelion mug is another of those patterns in which a lot of aqua opal pieces were made. Blue opal and a noniridized custard with nutmeg have been reported. The Knights Templar mug has the Knights Templar insignia and the words "Pittsburgh May 27, 28, 29, 1912" molded into the underside of the base.

Mug
Amethyst/purple 150–250   fairly common color
Aqua opal   400–550   most common color
Blue   400–500   scarce color
Blue, electric   600–750
Green   400–600   scarce color
Lavender   300 (1994)
Marigold   200–300

Mug, Knights Templar
Ice blue   500–700
Ice green   700–900
Marigold   250–400   most common color

The flower depicted here is a sunflower but the pattern is known as Dandelion. The pattern on the tankard and tumblers bears no resemblance to the pattern on the mug.

Water set, 7 piece
Amethyst/purple 1,000–1,200
Green   2,000–3,000
Marigold   500–700

Pitcher, water
Amethyst/purple 400–700
Green   1,000–1,500
Horehound   650 (1994)
Ice blue known, rare
Marigold   300–500
Violet   200 (1994)   crack by handle
White   3,000–5,000

In addition to the standard tumbler shown here, there is a rare variant with vertical ribs on the interior found in amethyst, ice blue, ice green, and white.

Tumbler
Amethyst/purple   45–80   most common color
Amethyst, black   70 (1998)
Green   65–95
Ice blue   200–300
Lavender   65 (1997)
Lavender, smoky   180 (1995)   slag effect
Marigold   35–60   common color
White   100–150

Davidson's Society Chocolates
See Lettered section

Deep Grape, Millersburg

A highly desirable compote pattern known in ruffled, square, and round flared shapes. There is one known rosebowl shape (in green). This flared marigold version sold for $1,600 at the 1994 John and Lucile Britt auction. A couple of blue examples are known, one selling for $7,500 in 1998.

Compote, round flared
Amethyst   2,300 (1998)
Green   1,500–2,000
Marigold   1,400–1,600

Compote, square shaped or 4-sided top
Amethyst   1,500–2,200
Marigold   1,900 (1998)

Compote, ruffled
Amethyst   1,500 (1998)   12 ruffles, rough edges
Amethyst   3,000 (1998)   CRE, starred base

Diamond Block, Imperial

A pattern consisting of raised triangles arranged so they form an overall pattern of diamonds. Found in marigold pitchers, tumblers, rosebowls, and vases for modest prices.

Diamond and Daisy Cut, US Glass

A late 1920s—Depression era pattern also called Floral and Diamond Band. A few shapes; tumbler, pitcher, butter, and compote are found in marigold.

Tumbler
Marigold   40–70

Pitcher
Marigold   65 (1994)

Diamond and Fan

Also known as Washboard (because of the pattern under the spout), this creamer or small pitcher has diamonds and fans around the trunk. Known only in marigold and worth $50 to $75.

Diamond Fountain

A rare pattern, this marigold vinegar cruet sells in the $350 to $450 range.

Diamond Lace, Imperial

One of Imperial's more popular and frequently seen patterns—at least in the pitchers and tumblers. The bowls are quite scarce but seldom bring high prices because the pattern is on the exterior only.

Bowl, large, 9", ruffled or ice cream shape
Clambroth   20–35
Green   110–200
Purple   60–90

Bowl, small berry or sauce, about 5"
Green 20–30
Marigold 20–30
Purple 20–30

Berry set, 7 piece
Marigold 50–70

Usually exhibiting spectacular color and iridescence, the purple pitcher or water set is seen quite often at a fair price and can form the basis of an excellent collection. One of the few patterns in which purple is common and marigold rare. No marigold pitchers are known and only a few marigold tumblers exist.

Water set, 7 piece
Purple 400–600

Pitcher, water
Purple 200–350

This marigold rosebowl whimsey, made from a tumbler, sold at the 1995 ACGA auction (Tom Burns) for $1,850 (with a heat check in the base). The variant tumbler, shown above) has no collar base.

Tumbler
Marigold 100 (1993) cracked, 3 known
Purple 45–75

Diamond Points, Northwood

A very scarce pattern, always bringing a good price if iridized (some were not) and in good condition.

Basket, handled
Blue 1,800–2,300
Marigold 1,200–2,000

Vase
Vases are a different pattern. See Vases.

Diamond Point Columns, Hazel Atlas

This pattern has alternating vertical strips of small diamonds and plain panels. It has, unfortunately, the same name as the better-known Fenton vase pattern. See Vases. Found in a small range of shapes including large and small bowls and table set pieces. None are worth more than $10 or $15 individually.

Diamond and Rib, Fenton

These rather large pieces are called jardinieres. Both are from the same mold, but the one in front was flared and ruffled. Vases were also swung from the same raw shape as well as smaller vases from smaller molds (see Diamond and Rib in Vases section). These marigold examples are courtesy of Carl and Ferne Schroeder.

44 A Field Guide to Carnival Glass

Jardiniere
Green   1,100 (1995)   chips
Marigold   1,250 (1997)   not ruffled

Diamond Ring, Imperial

The diamond design at the top of oval-shaped rings gives the pattern its name.

Bowl, 8–9" ruffled
Marigold   25–35
Smoke   15–30   most common color in bowl

Bowl, large in metal brides basket
Smoke   200 (1998)

Sauce or small bowl
Purple   30–45
Marigold   10–30

Berry set, 6 piece, ruffled
Smoke   40 (1995)

Rosebowl
Marigold   50–80
Smoke   275–350

Diamond and Sunburst, Imperial

The pattern is a favorite among those who collect wine and cordial sets. This marigold six-piece set sold for $185 at a 1994 Tom Burns auction.

Wine set, 10 piece
Marigold   170–250

Wine set, 5–7 piece
Marigold   120–200
Purple   425 (1996)

Decanter, wine
Marigold   80–120
Purple   400–600

Decanter stopper
Amethyst   40 (1993)

Wine glass
Marigold   20–40
Purple   30–50

Diamonds, Millersburg

A startlingly simple design but executed very well. The most common color is green.

Water set, 7 piece
Amethyst   450–600
Green   400–600
Marigold   300–500

Pitcher, water
Amethyst   200–350
Aqua   325 (1996)
Green   300–400
Marigold   125–200

Tumbler
Amethyst   55–90
Aqua   120 (1993)
Green   50–80
Marigold   40–65

Apparently Millersburg never got a chance to roll out its line of Diamonds in the punch sets. No cups are known and only three complete punch bowls with bases are known; marigold, green, and purple. The purple one sold at the 1995 American Carnival Glass Association auction (Tom Burns) for $3,700.

The only such piece known, this marigold spittoon whimsey made from a Diamonds tumbler brought $7,000 at a 1994 Jim Seeck auction.

Diamonds, unknown maker

This tumbleup, of unknown origin, is marigold and 8 inches high. Tumbleups, also called guest sets, were a small jug and a glass that fit over the neck of the jug. They were kept on the night stand next to the bed. The pattern is similar to that of Forty Niner.

Diving Dolphins, Sowerby

A very recognizable design with three dolphin feet and a floral exterior. The interior has the Sowerby version of Scroll Embossed. Occasionally flared into a candy dish (which may be called a bowl or compote).

Candy dish, bowl, or compote, 8–8½" diameter
Amethyst   200–300
Aqua   375 (1997)
Marigold   125–200

Rosebowl
Amethyst   400–500
Marigold   200–300

Dogwood Sprays, Dugan

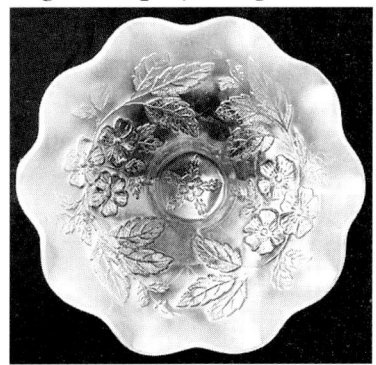

Dogwood Sprays has two sprays around the bowl and a small blossom medallion in the center. All examples have the typical Dugan dome-footed base.

Bowls are almost always ruffled but seldom pulled up as much as this deep example. Tricorner examples are occasionally found and a bit more desirable.

Bowl, about 9"
Amethyst/purple   90–150
Amethyst/purple   140–170   deep ruffled
Amethyst/purple   300 (1997)   tricorner, electric iridescence
Marigold   40–50   scarce color
Peach opal   65–100   most common color

Dolphins, Millersburg

Three dolphin feet (one is hidden behind the stem) support a bowl with Millersburg's Rosalind pattern in the interior. Blue is very rare.

Compote
Amethyst   2,000–3,000
Blue   5,250 (1996)
Green   4,500 (1996)

Double Diamonds, Josef Inwald

Double Diamonds has two diamond shapes arranged horizontally within a oval. This tumbleup set is courtesy of Bob Smith. Also known in small bowl and powder jar with lid, in addition to the shapes below.

Perfume atomizer
Marigold   120 (1998)

Cologne bottle
Marigold   115 (1994)

Pin tray
Marigold   55–60

Ring Tree
Marigold   80 (1994)

Double Dolphins, Fenton

Most often seen in stretch glass, this pattern is occasionally found in carnival. This example sold for $60 at a John Woody auction in February 1993.

Compote/vase
Purple   60 (1993)
Tangerine   1,000 (1993)   stretch

Candlestick
Ice green   175 (1996)
Pink   55 (1998)

Double Dutch, Imperial

Similar to Imperial's Windmill pattern, this one has two windmills and a fisherman in a boat. In fact, some collectors consider this to be part of the Windmill line, so you may find some Double Dutch bowls identified as Windmill. These bowls have three feet and Floral and Optic exterior. The above bowl, in purple, sold at the 1995 ACGA auction (Tom Burns) for $180. A marigold spittoon whimsey made from a bowl is in the Carl and Ferne Schroeder collection.

Bowl, about 9"
Marigold   20–30
Purple   180 (1995)
Smoke   150 (1996)

Double Loop, Northwood

This pattern is sometimes identified as Colonial. Shown are an open sugar (sometimes referred to as a chalice) and a creamer. The creamer is scarce in blue and very rare in other colors.

Creamer
Blue   350–425

Open sugar
Aqua opal   125–200
Blue   40–65
Green   45 (1998)
Marigold   25–35
Purple   55–90

Double Scroll, Imperial

A distinctive design with two little scrolls on either side of the top flange and base. Seen most often as a set of candlesticks although an occasional console set (with large centerpiece bowl) shows up.

Candlesticks, pair
Amberina   425 (1998)
Marigold   90–180
Red   250–400
Teal   200–350
Smoke   200–300
White   300–450

Console set (bowl and candlesticks)
Red   500–800

Console bowl
Smoke   55 (1998)

Double Star, Cambridge

The pattern derives its name from the two stars on the trunk of each shape; one large whirling star and a smaller hobstar. Some pieces in this pattern are marked "Nearcut," a Cambridge trade name. Most items are green but an occasional marigold or amethyst piece turns up.

Water set, 7 piece
Green   650–900

Pitcher, water
Amethyst   650 (1994)
Green   250–400
Marigold   500–700

An extraordinary rarity, this green Double Star spittoon whimsey, made from a tumbler, is from the collection of Floyd and Cecil Whitley.

Tumbler
Amethyst   175–250
Green   30–55   most common color
Marigold   275–350

Double Stem Rose, Dugan

Six roses with stems doubling down into a central rose. This pattern has a domed foot like many Dugan pieces. This deep ice cream-shaped bowl is typical of the pattern. While plates will be more than the usually required 2" off the table because of the dome foot, they must be flat and not cup up at the edge.

Bowl, about 8", ruffled, 3/1, or ice cream shape.
Amethyst/purple   60–100
Amethyst/purple   500 (1996)   electric iridescence
Aqua   40–70   scarce color
Blue   85–130
Celeste   450–750   not rare—but desirable
Marigold   25–40   most common color
Peach opal   55–80
Lavender   100 (1998)   3/1 edge
White   110–175

Plate
Amethyst, fiery   325 (1995)
Amethyst/purple   375 (1996)   electric iridescence
Marigold   50 (1995)
Peach opal   195 (1996)
White   125–200   most common color in plates

Dozen Roses

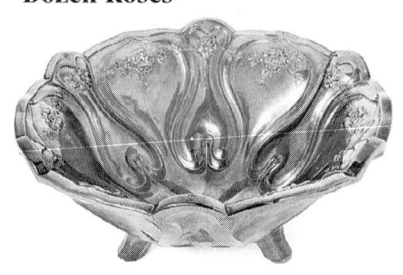

The pattern has 12 small roses within curved panels. The back has a modified wide panel design with three small feet—prompting some collectors to suspect Imperial as the maker. Found mostly in amethyst with two green bowls reported. An amethyst bowl, somewhat flatter than the one shown here, sold for $1,100 at a 1997 Jim Seeck auction. Another, in marigold with minor damage on the edge, brought $250 in 1997. An amethyst brought $550 in 1998.

Dragon and Lotus, Fenton

Fenton made several other patterns with a ring of two alternating designs: Dragon and Strawberry, Peacock and Dahlia, and Peacock and Grape.

Fortunately, Dragon and Lotus was made over a long period of time and thus is found in many colors and shapes—enough to satisfy even the most compulsive collector. Shown above are a marigold ice cream shape spatula-footed bowl; a ruffled green bowl with collar base; and a pastel marigold with opal three-in-one edge. They brought $65, $275, and $175 respec-

tively at a 1995 auction. Low ruffled and ice cream shapes are common in collar base bowls but scarce in spatula footed. Tall ruffled bowls are easy to find in spatula foot but aren't found in collar base.

Bowl, 8½–9", ruffled, 3/1, or ice cream shape
Amber	120–200	fairly common color
Amber opal		bowls had been selling in 300–500 range until 1998 when two sold for 1,000 and 2,800
Amberina	500–700	ice cream-shaped, rare
Amberina, rev.	1,150 (1998)	ice cream shape
Amethyst	85–150	common color
Amethyst opal	1,000–1,300	rare color
Aqua opal	2,100 (1993)	ruffled
Blue	100–200	most common color
Blue	250 (1995)	with enameled flowers
Green	100–200	spatula-footed bowls common
Lavender opal	900–1,400	ruffled
Lime green	125–200	
Lime green opal	350–600	
Marigold	35–75	common color
Mar/moonstone	450–700	ruffled or ice cream shape
Olive green	175 (1998)	
Peach opal	200–400	3/1 edge
Peach opal	750 (1998)	ruffled, collar base
Purple	225 (1995)	slag swirl in base
Red	1,300–2,500	readily found
Red	2,500–4,500	spectacular color
Red opal	2,000–4,000	ice cream-shaped
Smoke	200–315	ruffled, spatula-footed
Vaseline	200–300	ruffled or ice cream shape
Vaseline opal	600–1,000	rare color
Yellow opal	575 (1997)	8" collar base

Nut bowl shape, spatula-footed
Blue	425 (1995)

Plate (rare in any color)
Amethyst	250 (1993)	spatula-footed, spotty irid
Blue	1,200–2,300	
Marigold	2,500–3,300	

Dragon and Strawberry, Fenton

Another of Fenton's patterns with dual themes—this one alternating dragons and strawberries. The pattern was produced in much more limited colors and shapes than Dragon and Lotus. Some bowls are collar-based as above, some are spatula-footed. The only reported plates actually have no dragons and are referred to as the "Absentee Dragon and Berry."

Bowl, 9–9½", ruffled or ice cream shape
Amethyst	2,000–4,000	rare color
Blue	400–700	
Blue	1,500 (1998)	spectacular color
Green	1,000–2,000	scarce color
Marigold	400–700	most common color

Dragon's Tongue, Fenton

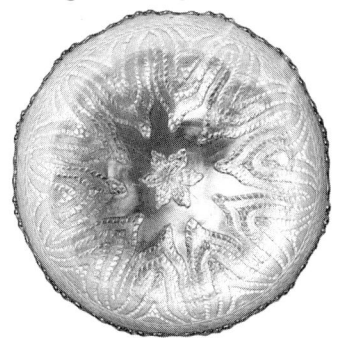

Aside from lamp shades, Dragon's Tongue is found only rarely—and then only in bowls. These 10½- to 11-inch bowls are found in marigold and will set you back $1,500 to $2,000 when you find one. The ice cream-shaped bowl above brought $2,000 in 1998.

Lamp shade
See Lamps and shades

Drapery, Northwood

The rosebowl and candy dish in Northwood's Drapery pattern are from different molds. The candy dish mold was used to make the vase (see Vases). Note that a contemporary Fenton rosebowl looks much like this one except that the Fenton version has three feet rather than a collar base. The toes on the candy dish are often damaged. Most rosebowls have a beaded (or sawtooth) edge, but a few white pieces have a plain edge. Aqua opal is the most frequently seen color in the rosebowl.

Candy or nut dish, usually tricorner
Blue	150–275	scarce color
Green	200–300	scarce color
Ice blue	125–200	most common color
Ice green	200–350	rare color
Marigold	70–120	scarce color
Purple	90–130	
White	100–150	scarce color

Rosebowl
Amethyst/purple	175–300	
Aqua opal	225–400	most common color
Blue	200–400	
Blue, electric	600–900	
Blue, Renninger	2,700 (1993)	one known
Ice blue	500–900	
Ice green	1,500 (1993)	flaws
Lavender	700 (1995)	
Marigold	220–350	scarce color
White	250–375	
White	500–800	plain edge

Vase
The candy dish was also pulled up into a vase. See Vases.

Drapery variant, Riihimäki

This is an entirely different pattern than Northwood's Drapery. Riihimäki is a Finnish glassmaker and this pattern is shown in a 1939 catalog—although it probably dates from an earlier period. This shot glass and pitcher are courtesy of Carl and Eunice Booker. Cups and saucers are also known.

Plate, 6"
Marigold   350–500

Shot glass, 2" tall
Marigold   100–200

Tumbler, small 2⅜" (may be wine glass)
Marigold   105 (1994)

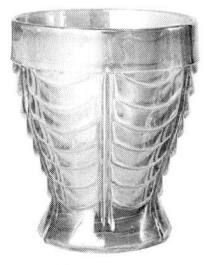

Tumbler
Marigold   100–185

Dreibus Parfait Sweets
See Lettered section

E.A. Hudson advertising
See Lettered section

Eagle Furniture advertising
See Lettered section

Eat Paradise Sodas
See Lettered section

Elegance

Very little is known about this pattern and only a few plates and shallow bowls have been reported. This plate, in ice blue, sold for $3,500 at a 1994 Tom Burns auction. It is also known in marigold.

Elektra, Riihimäki and Brockwitz

One of many pieces to find its way to the US from Europe. There were quite a few shapes in this line shown in both Riihimäki and Brockwitz catalogs, including bowls and vases. This 5" wide marigold compote has alternating many-rayed and whirling stars. It sold for $20 at a 1996 auction.

Elks items
See Lettered section

Embossed Scroll
See Scroll Embossed

Embroidered Mums, Northwood

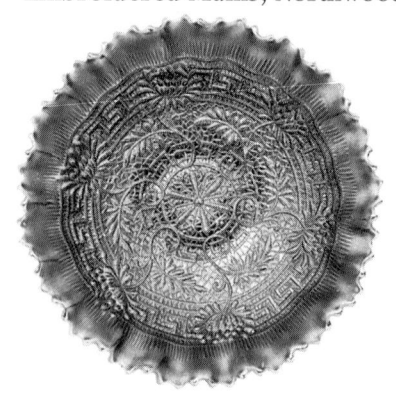

The above purple bowl, the only one known in this color with a pie crust edge, is courtesy of Fred Stone.

Bonbon (rare shape)
White   600–950

Bowl, ruffled
Aqua   2,000–2,500   rare color
Aqua opal   2,000–3,000   rare color
Blue   400–750   most common color
Ice blue   600–900   fairly common color
Ice blue opal   3,250 (1997)
Ice green   700–1,000   rare color
Lavender   450–675   scarce color
Lime green opal 3,000 (1993)
Marigold   400–750   scarce color
Purple   300–550   fairly common
Sapphire   1,200 (1998)
White   200 (1995)   very rare, worth more

Plate
Blue, one known
Ice green   1,000–2,000
White   1,000 (1993)   one known, light irid.

Enameled items
See Enameled section

Estate, Westmoreland

Westmoreland's Estate pattern, also called Capital, is seen mostly in small pieces such as the perfume bottle and small jar shown here.

Perfume
Smoke   200–300

E-F

Pin dish, covered, round
Smoke 80
Pin tray, 3 footed
Gray/smoke 45 80

This breakfast set in peach opal sold for $85 at a Mickey Reichel auction in 1995.

Breakfast creamer and sugar
Blue opal 150–250
Marigold 90 with souvenir lettering
Peach opal 50–80
Creamer
Blue opal 140–165
Peach opal 45–60 some with souvenir lettering
Sugar bowl
Amethyst 45 (1998)
Peach opal 45 (1994)
Mug
Marigold 25–60 some with souvenir lettering
Toothpick holder
Gold flash 45 (1994)
Marigold, pale 85 (1993)
Smoke 60–75 some with souvenir lettering
Vase/hatpin holder, about 5" tall
Smoke/gray 60–100

Fan, Dugan

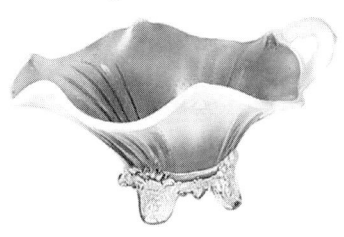

Mostly seen in a rather elaborately footed gravy boat (or sauce boat or occasional dish), made from a creamer shape, usually in peach opal.

Gravy Boat
Peach opal 75–125
Purple 80–150
Bowl, small, footed (sometimes called sugar bowl)
Peach opal 25–40

Fanciful, Dugan

A typically elaborate Dugan pattern characterized by abstract floral themes including heart-shaped leaves. Everything else being equal, ice cream-shaped or low ruffled bowls are more desirable than other shapes. Interestingly, marigold is quite scarce in Fanciful but still does not bring a premium price. Blue is very rare in bowls but fairly common in plates.

Bowl, 8½–9", ruffled, 3/1 edge, or ice cream shape
Amethyst/purple 150–300
Marigold 80–120 scarce color
Peach opal 160–275 common color
White 100–170 common color
Low ruffled
Amethyst/purple 200–400
Lavender 525 (1997)
Marigold 80–120 scarce color
Peach opal 200–300 common color
Purple, electric 900 (1997)
White 125–200
Plate, flat, about 9"
Amethyst/purple 250–400
Amethyst/purple, spectacular examples up to $900
Blue 500–800 quite obtainable
Blue, spectacular examples up to $1,700
Green 200 (1995) rare but silvery
Marigold 175–225 relatively scarce
Peach opal 250–400 fairly common
White 160–250 fairly common

Fancy Flowers, Imperial

This is a cut-style pattern known only in this low compote (or stemmed bowl), about 9" across. The pattern is on the exterior; the interior is plain. Worth between $100 and $200.

Fans, maker unknown

Also called Double Fans, this rare marigold tumbler sold at the 1995 Air Capital convention auction (Jim Seeck) for $215. The milk pitcher, also in marigold, is worth about $50.

Fantail, Fenton

Fantail has Fenton's Butterfly and Berry as an exterior pattern, which you can see through the interior of the above chop plate. This example is one of two known in marigold and sold for $5,500 at a Jim Seeck auction in 1994. Two blue chop plates also are known. All pieces were made from the ball-footed bowl shape. Some are ruffled, some are flared into an ice cream shape. Bowls reissued by Fenton in red, blue, and perhaps other colors.

Bowl, ruffled or berry shape
Blue   200–300
Marigold   100–150

Bowl, centerpiece (flared to ice cream shape)
Blue   300–500
Marigold   100–150

Farmyard, Dugan

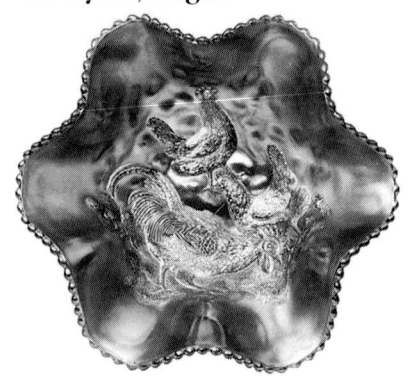

Dugan's Farmyard is one of the most desirable pieces in the carnival pantheon. It is mostly seen in purple with a ruffled edge like the example shown here. Green and peach opal colors are also known and there are square and square ruffled bowls and one round bowl—almost low enough to be a plate (see page 156). All have Dugan's Jewelled Heart exterior. The pattern has also been reproduced in bowls and chop plates in a number of modern colors.

Bowl, 6 ruffles
Purple   3,000–4,000
Purple   5,000 (1998)   blue iridescence
Purple   7,500 (1997)

Bowl, 8 ruffles
Purple   3,500–5,000
Purple   15,500 (1994)

Bowl, 3/1 edge
Purple   3,500–6,000

Bowl, square ruffled
Purple   3,000–5,000
Purple   8,000 (1997)

Fashion, Imperial

While Imperial's Fashion pattern is most often seen in water pitchers, tumblers, or punch sets, there are a few bowls around. Often they go unnoticed as they appear to be simply another of the many Imperial cut-style pieces. The pattern is only on the exterior, showing through in the photo above. A 9¼" ice cream shape in clambroth sold at a 1998 Mickey Reichel auction for $90. A 12" ruffled fruit bowl in amber sold at another 1998 Reichel auction for $100.

Complete breakfast sets are not often seen—but quite desirable. The set above, in green, sold at a 1997 Jim Seeck auction for $250. A purple set sold for $450 at the same auction.

Breakfast set (sugar and creamer)
Green   200–300
Marigold   50–90   msot common color
Purple   400–450
Smoke   100–180

Breakfast creamer
Marigold   40–60
Purple   160–200
Smoke   50–90

Breakfast sugar
Helios green   200 (1997)
Marigold   25–50

Compote
Smoke   475–550

Water set, 7 piece
Marigold   175–300
Smoke   1,150 (1994)

Pitcher, water
Marigold   85–130
Purple   450–700
Smoke   350–650

Tumbler
Marigold   30–50
Purple   200–300
Purple   800 (1998)
Smoke   60–100

Punch set, 8–10 piece (also found with round top)
Marigold   170–300

Punch cup
Lavender   40 (1996)
Marigold   5–10
Red   425 (1993)   525 (1997)
Smoke   50 (1996)   pale blue base glass

Rosebowl
Green   300–400
Marigold   100–200
Purple   1,500–2,200

Feather and Heart, Millersburg

The pattern is distinguished by the feather-like designs around the top. The above amethyst pitcher and four tumblers sold as a 5-piece water set at the 1995 Air Capital auction (Jim Seeck) for $1,000.

Water set
Amethyst   1,000 (1995)   5 piece
Marigold   650–800   7 piece

Pitcher, water
Amethyst   450 (1997)
Green   400–900
Marigold   350–500
Vaseline   14,000 (1994)   only one known

54 A Field Guide to Carnival Glass

Feather and Heart tumbler
Amethyst 80–140
Green 250 (1997)
Marigold 50–90
Whimsey from tumbler
Marigold 7,000 (1994) one known

Feather Stitch, Fenton

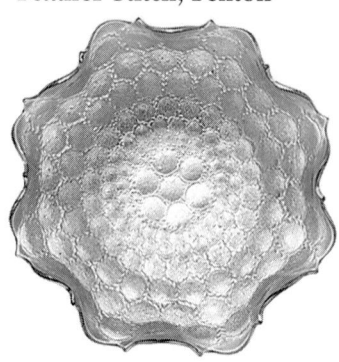

Alan Pickup first pointed out that quite possibly Fenton's Coin Dot mold was retooled to produce Feather Stitch. Whatever the provenance, there aren't many pieces around.

Bowl, about 8½", ruffled or ice cream shape
Amethyst, fiery 65 (1998) open bubble
Aqua 250 (1996) ice cream shape
Blue 95–140
Green 195 (1998)
Marigold 50–70
Plate, 9¼"
Marigold 500–850 very rare

Feathered Serpent, Fenton

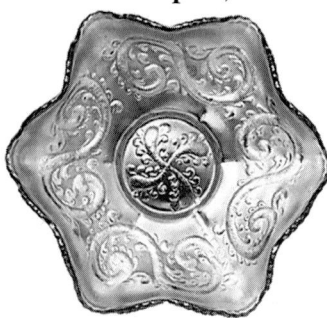

Another scarce Fenton pattern found only in large and small bowls with a variety of edge treatments—ruffled, ice cream shape, and three-in-one. One green cuspidor, whimsied from the small bowl, is in the collection of Floyd and Cecil Whitley.

Bowl, 9–10"
Amethyst 85–115 most common color
Amethyst 175 (1998) in metal bride's basket
Blue 150–250 usually ice cream shape
Green 65–100
Marigold 50–80
Sauce or small berry, 5"
Amethyst 15–25
Amethyst 135 (1997) tricorner
Green 25–35
Green 50 (1995) tricorner

Fenton's Flowers, Fenton

This pattern could be listed with Fenton's Orange Tree since that's the pattern on the exterior, but it has traditionally been called Fenton's Flowers. When purchasing these pieces, look carefully at the feet; they're very susceptible to damage. Fenton reissued the pattern in rosebowls and ruffled bowls with Lions as the interior pattern.

Nut bowl or candy dish shape
Amethyst 100–175
Blue 425 (1997)
Green 100–200
Marigold 25–45
White 125–200
Rosebowl
Amberina/red 3,500 (1997) foot flake
Amethyst 100–200
Blue 90–125
Blue 325 (1995) rare smooth top
Clambroth 80–140
Green 125–200
Ice green opal 375 (1997)
Marigold 40–75
Peach opal 1,400–1,600
Red 1,800 (1992)
Red 400–800 with damaged feet
Smoke 350–450
Vaseline 250 (1997)
White 130–200

Fentonia, Fenton

Fentonia has a basic diamonds design with alternating diamonds filled with a scale pattern or nine small hobs on a web background. The central hob is encircled with a stitched ring. A scarce pattern with pieces seldom up for sale. Berry set and table set pieces are footed.

Water pitcher
Blue   650 (1994)
Marigold   700–900
Tumbler
Blue   45–75
Marigold   30–50
Sauce or small bowl, 5"
Blue   25–40
Butter dish
Blue   350 (1996)
Creamer
Marigold   80 (1997)
Spooner
Blue   120 (1996)
Marigold   50 (1995)

Fentonia Fruit, Fenton

A very rare variation of Fentonia. Instead of the diamond panels with nine hobs, this one has fruit—hanging cherries. Only a handful are known. This blue one is from the collection of Floyd and Cecil Whitley, who also have a tumbler in marigold. Also found in rare berry sets.

Fern, Fenton

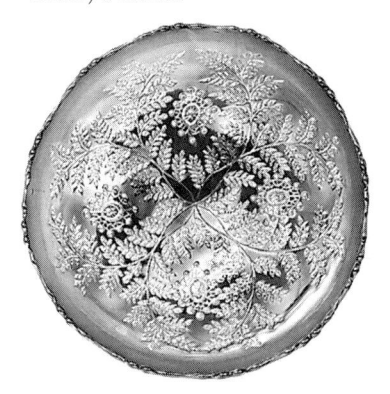

Among the mysteries of carnival glass is why only one piece in this pattern has ever been found. It's a blue three-footed bowl, flat but cupped up at the edges. It was at one time on loan to the Fenton Museum and is now in the collection of Floyd and Cecil Whitley.

Fern, Northwood

This compote is seen so seldom that it often gets lost in the shuffle. Easily confused with other compotes such as Northwood's Harvest Poppy or Fenton's Holly.

Compote
Amethyst/purple 70–125   most common color
Green   125–180   common color
Marigold   100–150

Fern Brand Chocolates
See Lettered section

Fern Panels, Fenton

Another of Fenton's hat shapes, this one with fern fronds radiating out from the center of the base. Usually ruffled, sometimes crimped or JIP. This red example is courtesy of Carl and Eunice Booker. Also known in amethyst and green.

Hat
Blue   25–35
Marigold   15–25
Red   150–225
White   70 (1997)

Fieldflower, Imperial

Fieldflower is one of Imperial's few water sets with a realistic floral theme. This one has three panels with a flower and foliage dominating each one. Reissued watersets are found in a variety of colors.

Water set, 7 piece
Marigold   175–250
Purple   625 (1994)

Pitcher, water
Amber   175–200
Marigold   165 (1998)
Purple   350–600
Smoke   750 (1995)
Teal   170–235

Tumbler
Blue violet   250–475
Green   50–65
Marigold   30–40
Purple   80–130
Red   1,400 (1992)
Violet   50 (1995)

Field Thistle, US Glass

Although made in crystal in a wide range of shapes, the iridized pieces are quite scarce. The six- and nine-inch plates are very desirable. Pitchers and tumblers are also rarely seen. These are from the collection of Carl and Ferne Schroeder. One celeste blue breakfast creamer is known.

Water set, 7 piece
Marigold   200–350

Pitcher, water
Marigold   125–200

Tumbler
Marigold   60 (1996)

Sauce or small bowl
Marigold   15–25
Ice blue   250 (1995)

Compote
Marigold   80–125

Creamer
Marigold   20 (1996)

Spooner
Marigold   40–75

The above 9" Field Thistle plate in marigold with extraordinary iridescence brought $425 at the 1996 Lincoln-Land club auction (Tom Burns).

Plate, 6"
Marigold   200–265
Plate, 9"
Marigold   200–350
Chop plate, about 10"
Marigold   550 (1998)
Vase whimsey
See Vases

File, Imperial

The File pattern is aptly named, with vertical sawtooth ribs. It was also used on the exterior of other patterns such as Scroll Embossed. Also known in a rare spittoon shape made from the chop plate mold. Mostly seen in marigold but an occasional purple piece shows up. Marigold is the only color in which table sets have been reported.

Bowl, 7½"
Purple   45 (1996)   plain interior
Chop plate
Marigold   35 (1994)
Butter dish
Marigold   55 (1995)
Spooner
Marigold   35 (1994)

Pitcher
Marigold   300–500
Tumbler
Marigold   75–140

Shown above are a vase whimsey and a spooner from the table set.
Vase whimsey
Marigold   200–400

File and Fan, Westmoreland

The pattern is seen only in this smallish (about six inches across) compote. The pattern is on the exterior, the iridescence on the inside. Most are ruffled. In addition to blue opal, the compote is occasionally found in blue opaque glass. This same mold is still being used to make miniature punch sets.

Compote
Blue opal   105–200   common color in pattern
Marigold   65 (1994)   scarce color
Mar/milk glass   90–160
Peach opal   50–80

Fine Cut Flower, Imperial

Usually found in marigold for $35 to $45. A green example sold at the 1998 Heart of America club auction (Seeck) for $60.

Fine Cut and Roses, Northwood

Most Fine Cut and Roses rosebowls and candy dishes were made from the same mold. There was another mold, though, which did not have the usual circular ring at the bottom of the bowl (right example above), referred to as the variant. There is also a rare rosebowl with a smooth band rather than ruffled top. The feet on all pieces are quite susceptible to damage.

Rosebowl, plain interior
Amethyst/purple	75–145	most common color
Custard/nutmeg	55–100	scarce color
Green	165–235	common color
Marigold	100–150	common color
White	150–250	scarce color

Rosebowl, Fancy interior
Amethyst/purple	100–175	scarce color
Aqua opal	1,400–2,300	scarce color
Custard	800 (1997)	pearlized
Horehound	525 (1997)	
Ice blue	225–400	most common color
Marigold	60–100	
White	250–400	scarce color

Rosebowl variant, no collar base (plain interior)
Amethyst/purple	150–275
Green	300–550
Lavender	245 (1995)

About one third of rosebowls and candy dishes have an interior pattern called Fancy—shown in this candy dish to excellent advantage.

Candy or nut dish, plain interior
Amethyst/purple	30–55	most common color
Blue, electric	250 (1996)	nick on toe
Green	50–80	common color
Marigold	25–40	scarce color
White	70–100	

Candy dish, Fancy interior
Amethyst/purple	50–85	
Aqua opal	300–500	common color
Ice blue	150–270	
Ice green	200–300	
White	80–110	

Fine Rib
See Vases

Fircone, Riihimäki (Finland)

Known in a pitcher as well as the tumbler. This light blue example is courtesy of Bob Smith. The pattern is unrelated to a vase of the same name.

Firefly, Riihimäki (Finland)

These candlesticks have an insect design on the top of the foot and are shown in a 1939 Riihimäki catalog (they probably date from somewhat earlier). A pair in marigold is worth $200 to $300.

Fisherman's Mug, Dugan

With this mug, only one side has the fish design; the other is blank. Some collectors speculate that this was a container for candy or food and that the label was applied to the blank side.

Mug
Amethyst, black	100–125	scarce color
Blue reported, very rare		
Horehound	170 (1995)	
Lavender	185 (1994)	
Marigold	150–250	common color
Peach opal	1,000 (1997)	
Purple	80–150	most common color
Purple	70 (1998)	Rose Presznick's Museum

Fishnet, Dugan

Some of these 8-inch tall epergnes have the elaborate ruffling shown here, while others do not. This one, in peach opal, sold for $475 at a Jim Seeck auction in 1995. Damage around the insertion point of the lily can affect the price of these pieces.

Epergne, 2 piece
Amethyst/purple	200–325
Peach opal	150–250

Fishscale and Beads, Dugan

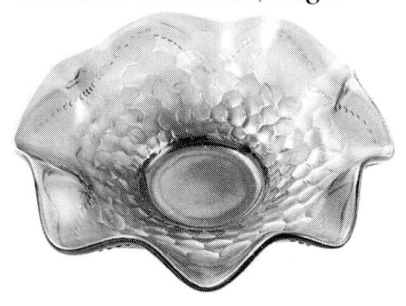

The pattern gets its name from the fishscale effect on the front while the back has a garland of beads. Sometimes called Fishscales, or misidentified as Scales (a similar Westmoreland pattern).

Bowl, 6–7", ruffled or candy ribbon edge
Amethyst/purple	70–110	
Amethyst/purple	95 (1994)	tricorner
Blue	100–150	rare color
Marigold	30–50	common color
Peach opal	45–70	common color

Bowl, banana boat shape, about 7"
Peach opal	110–135

Bowl, 2 punch cups (factory grouped item)
Marigold	25–50

Plate, 6–7"
Amethyst/purple	150–250	
Amethyst/purple	450 (1996)	souvenir of Sturgis, Mich.
Marigold	70–110	
Peach opal	65–95	scarce color in plates
White	85–140	

Five Hearts, Dugan

Similar to Starfish which is found only in bonbons and compotes. Five Hearts bowls are sometimes referred to as compotes because of the high foot.

Bowl, about 8"
Amethyst   250–300
Marigold   90–150

Rosebowl, whimsey, two known
Marigold   1,500 (1993) 900 (1996)

Flaming Cornucopia

A rare sugar bowl from the John and Lucile Britt collection.

Flashing Star, Riihimäki

One of the few known, this small, light blue tumbler is from the John and Lucile Britt collection.

Fleur de Lis, Imperial

In old Imperial catalogs this pattern was numbered 5½, although collectors refer to it as Fleur de Lis #5. While many shapes were shown, not all were made in carnival. The ruffled bowl above and the celery vase below (both in marigold) are two of the few known carnival shapes. The bowl is courtesy of Ingrid Spurrier, the celery courtesy of Bob Gallo.

Fleur de Lis, Millersburg

Fleur de Lis is a busy pattern made all the more difficult to see when the back pattern, Country Kitchen, shows through. Bowls are usually found with a dome foot that has the sawtooth edge seen on several other Millersburg patterns. Collar-based pieces are less often seen. One compote, in green, has been reported. Fleur de Lis is found on some Hobstar and Feather punch bowls

Bowl, 9–10", dome-footed, ruffled or ice cream
Amethyst   300–500
Amethyst   800 (1996)   oblong crimped, damage
Green   185–300
Marigold   160–300

Bowl, 9–10", dome-footed, tricorner
Amethyst   700 (1995)
Green   200–350
Marigold   325–450

Bowl, 9–10", collar base, ruffled or ice cream
Amethyst   400–625
Green   175–300
Marigold   135–250
Vaseline, one known

Rosebowl shape, collar base
Amethyst   3,250 (1997)   only one known

Rosebowl shape, dome-footed
Amethyst   2,250 (1994)   two known

Fleur de Lis, Josef Inwald

This chop plate, with the pattern only on the back, was made by Josef Inwald A.G. of Czechoslovakia. Their pattern was not named, but has come to be called Fleur de Lis because of that design element in the pattern. Inwald also made several other shapes in the pattern including vases (see Vases). This plate sold for $300 in 1994, another for $220 in 1998. A 6" plate in marigold sold for $185 in 1998.

Flora, Sowerby

This Sowerby (England) float bowl has a plain interior and is known only in blue. It sells in the $60 to $90 range.

Floral and Grape, Dugan, Fenton

Both Dugan and Fenton made very similar Floral and Grape water sets. On the Dugan pitcher the ribs in the bands lean to the left; on the Fenton pitchers they lean to the right. The Dugan tumblers have a thin raised cable on either side of the band of ribs; the Fenton tumblers do not have the cables. The Dugan pattern is Floral and Grape; the scarcer Fenton pattern is Floral and Grape variant. Yet another rare variant pitcher, Fenton bandless, has no bands at all.

Water set, 7 piece
Amethyst/purple   300–425
Blue   400–500
Green   800 (1996)
Marigold   125–165
White   800–1,000

Water pitcher
Amethyst/purple   190–300
Blue   250–350
Lime green   600 (1995)
Marigold   100–165
White   180–350

Tumbler

Amethyst/purple	20–40	common color
Blue	40–60	
Green	75–100	scarce color
Marigold	10–20	common color
White	30–50	scarce color

Hat, JIP whimsey from tumbler

Marigold	20–35

Floral and Optic, Imperial

A rather common pattern with a plain interior, pieces seldom bring much except in unusual colors. All pieces are made from the same mold—the plate flattened from the bowl, and the rosebowl cupped in from the bowl. The red bowl above, with stretch effect, brought $400 at the 1995 Great Lakes club auction (Tom Burns).

Bowl

Mar/milk glass	30–50	
Red	250–400	
Known in smoke		
Teal	125–150	
White	50 (1998)	stretchy iridescence

Plate, (sometimes listed as cake or chop plate)

Clambroth	10–20
Marigold	20–30
Red	350–500
Smoke	100–150
White	60–90

Rosebowl

Clambroth	25–40	
Marigold	18 (1993)	crimped edge
Mar/milk glass	80–150	
Smoke	75–105	
Teal	175 (1996)	

Floral and Wheat

Exterior pattern for Puzzle bonbon

Florentine, Fenton

Found only in candlesticks although items with similar panelled characteristics are sometimes identified as Florentine. This misnaming may be partly attributable to the green color sometimes referred to as florentine. Because of the finish, Florentine items may be referred to as stretch. Florentine candlesticks are known in two sizes, just over 10 inches tall and about 8 inches tall. Russet and sapphire items are probably a similar Northwood pattern.

Candlesticks, pair

Amethyst	60 (1996)	8"
Celeste	70–110	either size
Celeste	100–185	10", gold trim
Ice green	125 (1996)	10"
Marigold	40–50	8"
Marigold	70 (1995)	10"
Red	750–975	either size
Red	500 (1995)	decorated
Russet	100–165	10"
Sapphire blue	80–100	8"
Vaseline	75–125	either size
Violet	170 (1998)	8"
White	375 (1998)	10"

Flowering Dill, Fenton

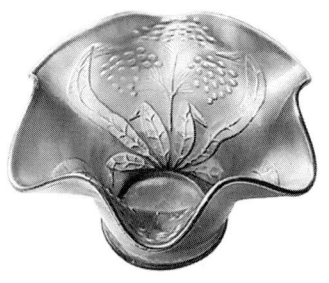

Yet another of Fenton's little hat shapes, this one not seen as often as the Open Edge or Holly. Some are ruffled, some jack-in-the-pulpit shaped, a few tri-corner.

Hat
Amethyst	25–40	
Blue	20–30	
Marigold	20–30	most common color
Mar./moonstone	100–150	

Flowering Vine, Millersburg

Very few examples of this nine-inch tall compote are known; two in amethyst and the one above in green. It sold to Don Doyle in the 1994 John and Lucile Britt auction (Jim Seeck) for $9,000. John had purchased it at Don's auction several years earlier. It has since passed on to another owner.

Flowers and Frames, Dugan

We tend to think of frames as being rectangular, but in this case they loop around the flowers. Note the small plumes between the ends of the loops.

Bowl, 9" dome-footed
Peach opal	70–150	ruffled
Peach opal	85–160	tricorner
Purple	225–400	ruffled
Purple	350–500	tricorner

Flowers and Spades, Dugan

This is an extremely rare Dugan pattern. This 9" peach opalescent example is the first that I've had the opportunity to photograph. It sold at a 1998 Mickey Reichel auction for $400. Small berry bowls have also been reported. The pattern is said to be found in deep amethyst as well as peach opal.

Fluffy Peacock, Fenton

Although the name would suggest that the peacock is a dominant part of the design, it's rather small on both the tumbler and pitcher.

Water set, 7 piece
Amethyst	700–1,000	most often seen
Green	900–1,300	
Marigold	300–550	

Water pitcher
Blue	400–600	
Green	500–800	most common color
Marigold	200–350	

Tumbler
Amethyst	60–90	most common color
Blue	55–80	scarce color
Green	70–130	common color
Marigold	30–50	fairly common color

Flute, Imperial

The Imperial breakfast set, consisting of a sugar and creamer, is typical of the Imperial version of Flute. Note the base flare and the shape of the handles.

Breakfast set, 2 piece
Purple   100–185

Breakfast creamer
Purple   80–100

Berry set, 7 piece, small bowls have handles
Purple   275–325

Bowl, 6"
Purple   20–30

Bowl, large berry
Purple   120 (1997)

Nappy
Amethyst   20   Flute #3

Punch set, 8–10 piece
Marigold	150–200	
Helios/green	200–400	
Purple	1,350 (1996)	1,900 (1997)

The above pitcher (#700) and six of these tumblers (all in purple) were sold at a 1995 auction for $1,150. While they may both be Imperial, there is another style of flute tumbler with a collar base and nine flutes (#3) that would have better matched this pitcher.

Pitcher
Marigold	300–500
Purple	750–1,000

Tumbler
Purple	80–110	
Red	275 (1992)	

Tumbler, variation #3 (collar base, 9 flutes)
Aqua	325 (1997)
Blue	325 (1997)
Marigold	20 (1998)

Salt dip or nut cup
Marigold   80–120   Iron Cross mark

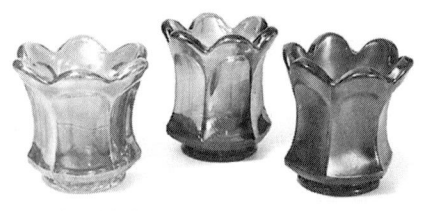

Toothpick holder
Blue	600–900	rare color
Green	45–75	
Helios	30 (1997)	
Lavender	70 (1996)	
Lime green	145 (1994)	
Marigold	40–65	
Purple	40–70	most common color
Vaseline	625 (1998)	marigold overlay

Wine glass
Marigold   145 (1998)   three known

Flute, Heisey

Toothpick holder
Marigold   95 (1994)   signed Heisey

Flute, Northwood

Flute pitchers come in a variety of styles. This one is attributed to Northwood. Courtesy of Steve Morrow.

Berry set, 6 piece
Marigold   70–110
Breakfast set (creamer and sugar)
Purple   100–150

Creamer and sugar
Green   30 (1994)   minor roughness, signed
Marigold   30 (1995)   signed
Table set, 4 piece
Marigold   150–200
Butter dish
Marigold   220 (1998)
Nut or salt set, 5-7 piece
Marigold   160–225
Sherbert
Green   15–25
Lavender   15 (1994)
Marigold   10–15
Tumbler
Green   100–150
Marigold   10–15
Water set, 6 piece
Marigold   250 (1996)
Purple   500–800

Flute and Cane, Imperial

Made only in marigold, Flute and Cane was manufactured in a number of shapes—although few ever come to market. These rare candlesticks are from the John and Lucile Britt collection. Tumblers in two sizes and a wine glass are also known.

Compote, large
Marigold   30–60
Cordial
Marigold   475 (1997)
Sherbert
Marigold   10–15
Goblet
Marigold   20–35
Pitcher, milk (several sizes known)
Marigold   90–150

Pitcher, water, 8½" tall
Marigold   75–125

Fluted Scroll, Dugan

Fluted Scroll was made in noniridized glass prior to the Carnival period. This amethyst spittoon shape is courtesy of Carl and Ferne Schroeder. A light marigold example sold in 1995 for $500.

Folding Fan, Dugan

Other than a purple example that sold in 1993 for $170, these compotes are invariably in peach opalescent. They range in price from $60 to about $100. Most are ruffled like that above but are occasionally seen with two sides up. One such banana boat shape in peach opal sold in 1998 for $165.

Footed Shell, Westmoreland
See Novelties/miniatures

Formal, Dugan

These 7-inch tall shapes are known in two top treatments—the vase-like shape shown is generally considered a hatpin holder, and a Jack-in-the-Pulpit vase (see Vases). The hatpin holders in purple vary between $500 and $750 with great examples occasionally selling up to $1,000 or so. Marigold with good color tends to be worth a bit more. A black amethyst example brought $1,250 at a 1998 Mickey Reichel auction.

Forty Niner

The Forty Niner pattern, which was probably made in Europe, has a series of sharply etched concave diamonds around the body of the piece. The set above, consisting of three glasses, a decanter, and a tray, was found by Bob Smith in Czechoslovakia in 1997. The pattern is so scarce that it seldom comes up for sale. A pitcher is also known.

This Forty Niner powder jar and ring tree are courtesy of Joyce Seale.

Four Flowers, Dugan

The pattern has four large flowers separated by overlapping crescent shapes. The Dugan version, above, usually has the Soda Gold exterior and has no spear-like shapes in the center of the overlapping crescents. It is sometimes called Pods and Posies.

Bowl, small, or sauce (about 6")
Peach opal   35–55
Purple   105 (1993)   electric blue iridescence

Bowl, about 8½"
Amethyst/purple   50 (1998)
Marigold   30–50

Bowl, large (about 10")
Peach opal   70–120
Purple   200–350

Bowl, large, tricorner
Peach opal   135–225

Bowl, banana boat shape
Peach opal   100–125
Purple   250–325

Chop plate
Peach opal   250–400   common color
Purple   3,300 (1997)   3,800 (1996)

Plate, small (6–7")
Peach opal   100–150   common shape and color
Purple   250–375

Rosebowl, Soda Gold exterior, scarce
Marigold   60–100

Four Flowers variant (unknown maker)

The variant is distinguished from the Dugan version by the spear-shaped objects between the overlapping crescents. The variant also has a scalloped edge and either a Thumbprints or a plain exterior.

Bowl, large (8–10")
Amethyst/purple   135–200   scarce color
Amethyst, black   200 (1996)
Olive green   30–45   scarce color
Teal   100–175   fairly common
Yellow amber   75 (1998)

Plate, 9–10"
Amber   400 (1998)
Amethyst/purple   250–400
Green   200–375
Green, emerald   400–600
Olive green   150–200

Chop plate, 10½"
Green   225 (1998)
Peach opal   100–190
Purple   900–1,800

Four Pillars
See Vases section

Four Seventy Four, Imperial

Four Seventy Four is one of Imperial's most endearing patterns, combining a typical cut-style pattern with an almost realistic daisy. The pattern is also found in vases (see Vase section). The name comes from the numerical designation in Imperial catalogs. Note that the water set has been reproduced.

Punch set, 8 piece
Marigold   175–300
Purple   4,500 (1997)   only set known in purple

Punch bowl and base
Marigold   150–200

Punch base only
Marigold   35–50
Purple   155 (1997)

Punch cup
Green   30–50
Green, emerald   125 (1998)
Marigold   10–15
Purple   40–60

Compote
Marigold   120 (1998)

Goblet
Marigold   30–55

Cordial
Marigold   450 (1998)   3" tall

Wine glass
Marigold   85–105

Sherbert, 4" tall
Marigold   60 (1998)

Pitcher, milk
Green   225–300   fairly common color
Helios   110–140
Lavender   550 (1992)
Marigold   125–200   most common color
Olive   250 (1995)   weak color, irid
Purple   1,800–2,200   few known

68 A Field Guide to Carnival Glass

Pitcher, water, large size
Marigold   110–180
Purple   5,250 (1995)   electric iridescence
Pitcher, water, mid-size
Purple   3,000–3,300
Water set, 7 piece
Marigold   200–350

Tumbler
Aqua   85 (1995)
Also known in helios
Marigold   35–55   most common color
Purple   65–120

French Knots, Fenton

Another of Fenton's hat-only shapes. This one comes with a design of leaves and French Knots—the embroidery stitch for which the pattern in named. Also check similar patterns Holly and Pepper Plant. A white example is known.

Hat, ruffled
Amethyst   40–60
Blue   25–40
Green   35 (1997)
Marigold   20–35

Frolicking Bears

An extremely rare pattern, Frolicking Bears is known only in the pitcher and tumbler, always a sort of olive green. Both show bears in various playful poses against a mountain backdrop. No pitchers or tumblers have sold publically in recent years, but there are club souvenirs using this theme. The pattern is believed to have been made by US Glass. This pitcher is from the collection of Carl and Ferne Schroeder. See page 182 for color photo of tumbler.

Frosted Block, Imperial

A unique and rather un-carnival like pattern. The squared panels would be more stunning in dark colors, but pieces are known only in marigold, clambroth, white, and occasional smoke. Collector Bruce Dooley reports having 19 shapes in clambroth alone, including a small round plate, a square plate, a single-handled nappy, a nut bowl, a two-handled pickle dish, and a large oval celery.

Bowl
Clambroth   20–35   square or ruffled
Plate, 9"
Clambroth   30–55
Marigold   60
Smoke   75 (1997)
Plate, 7–7½"
Marigold   30–50
Smoke   60–80
Compote
Clambroth   25–40
Creamer
Clambroth   20–35
Creamer and sugar
Clambroth   25–45
Marigold   30–50

Pitcher, milk
Clambroth   50–70
Rosebowl, large (some marked "Made in USA")
Clambroth   45–60
White   20–40

Rosebowl, small, 4½" opening (some marked "Made in USA")
Marigold   40–60
White   40–70
Vase
Clambroth   145 (1997)
Smoke   65 (1996)

Fruit Basket, Millersburg
The same exterior as Millersburg's Roses and Fruits but with fruit in the center of basketweave background. Very few examples known, all amethyst. The most recent of these footed bonbons to sell brought $1,150 in 1994.

Fruit Salad, Westmoreland

Fruit Salad, found only in punch set pieces, has a distinctive design with prominent ears around the edge of the bowl. This same unusual edge is also found in Westmoreland's Orange Peel that has a stippled pattern rather than fruit.

Punch set, 6 piece
Peach opal   1,500 (1993)
Punch set, 10–12 piece
Marigold   250–350
Punch set, 14 piece
Amethyst   525 (1992)
Punch bowl and base
Marigold   200 (1996)   500 (1998)
Peach opal   825 (1996)
Punch bowl only
Marigold   115 (1995)
Punch cup
Amethyst   10–15
Marigold   20–30

Fruits and Flowers, Northwood

Fruits and Flowers is similar to Northwood's Three Fruits that is seen only in plates and bowls. Both have the same three fruits arranged in the same way, but Fruits and Flowers lacks any pattern in the center (excepting the rare variant). You can confirm the pattern by finding the small flowers that curl in toward the center from the fruit spray.

The footed bonbon is the most frequently seen item in Fruits and Flowers. Because it is stemmed, it is sometimes identified as a two-handled compote. The exterior can be either plain or basketweave. The green example above sold for $135 at a 1995 Mickey Reichel auction. Repros are known in purple—see Reproductions sections.

70 A Field Guide to Carnival Glass

Fruits and Flowers Bonbon
Amethyst/purple	70–125	most common color
Aqua opal	450–600	fairly common color
Aqua opal	800 (1998)	more like sapphire opal
Blue	80–150	common color
Blue, electric	150–250	
Green	80–125	common color
Ginger ale	300 (1998)	
Ice blue	425–625	
Ice blue opal	875 (1996)	
Ice green	600–700	
Lavender	400–600	
Marigold	80–150	common color
Olive green	190 (1996)	
Sapphire	900–1,000	
White	225–350	

Bonbon, stippled
Blue	200–300
Blue, Renninger	900 (1998)
Marigold	110–140

Berry set, 7 piece
Amethyst/purple 240 (1998)

Bowl, 9–10"
Amethyst/purple	80–150
Green	80–150
Ice green	550–700
Marigold	40–60
Violet	310 (1996)

Bowl, about 7"
Amethyst/purple	50–90
Amethyst opal	425 (1996)
Aqua/teal	155–300
Blue	125–200
Green	50–80
Ice green	300–425
Sapphire	450

Bowl, stippled, about 7"
Green	135–210
Marigold	35–70

Sauce, 5–6"
Amethyst/purple	45–80
Green	45 (1998)

Plate, 7–7½"
Amethyst/purple	90–170
Green	250–350
Lav/amethyst	70–90
Marigold	70–120

Plate, 8–9"
Marigold	90–135
Purple	150–300

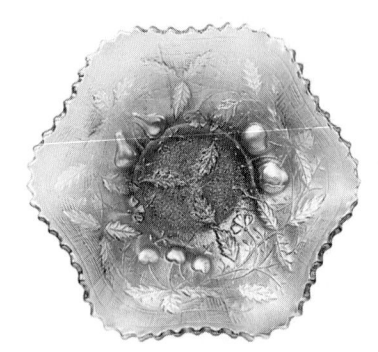

This is the variant Fruits and Flowers bowl. Note the three leaves pointing toward the center and the stippling around them. This green example sold at a 1998 Mickey Reichel auction for $175. Another in green and a marigold example have been reported.

Plate, handgrip
Amethyst/purple 95–175

Plate, banana dish or double handgrip
Amethyst/purple	60–110
Green	80–140

Fuchsia, Fenton

A rarely seen pattern, this bonbon sold at a Jim Seeck auction in 1993. At one time it had been on loan to the Fenton Museum. In blue, it brought $1,500. A marigold example with a hairline crack sold for $475, also in 1993.

Garden Mums, Fenton

A six-inch plate or bowl, Garden Mums, always in amethyst, was used as a basis for some of the patterns found in the Lettered section. The example above was enameled with hand lettering, often used for shorter production runs. Plates are in the $300 to $500 range. Bowls, although more scarce, bring about half what plates do. Handgrip plates fall somewhere in between.

Garden Path and variant, Dugan

Two of the more confusing patterns in carnival, the Garden Path and Garden Path variant are very similar. The variant (above) is the more elaborate, adding, as the early carnival glass writer and researcher Marion Hartung put it, "stylized palm trees" and "winged hearts" around the edge. Most have the Soda Gold pattern on the exterior. The purple 10-inch ice cream-shaped bowl above sold for $1,300 in 1996.

Bowl, small, or sauce, about 6"
Peach opal   70–120
White   60 (1998)

Bowl, 9–10½"
Marigold   40–75
Peach opal   400–550
Purple   1,300 (1996)
White   325–450

Plate, small, about 6"
Marigold   85–125
Peach opal   400–650
White   350–525

Chop plate, about 11"
Amethyst/purple   3,000–5,000
Amethyst/purple   13,500 (1998)   spectacular example

Rosebowl
Marigold   120–180

Garland, Fenton

Garland is a fairly common rosebowl, except in amethyst and green. The amethyst piece above sold at the 1993 Great Lakes club auction (Tom Burns) for $375.

Rosebowl
Blue   70–120   very common color
Blue, electric   245 (1996)
Marigold   40–60

Garland and Bows, Riihimäki

This unusual pattern was made by the Finnish company Riihimäki. This marigold compote is eight inches high and sold for $55 at a 1996 auction. Sugar, creamer, salver, and bowls are also known.

Gay Nineties, Millersburg

The rare Gay Nineties tumbler has vertical panels with shell designs. It is widely considered to be one of the top 10 or 15 tumbler rarities. The green pitcher listed below is thought to be the only one in that color, while three have been reported in amethyst.

Pitcher, water
Green   10,000 (1996)
Tumbler
Amethyst   550 (1995)
Marigold   450–650   very rare

Goddess of Harvest, Fenton

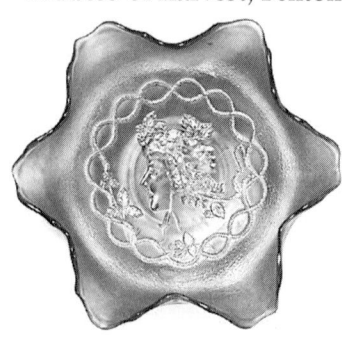

Goddess of Harvest is known in marigold, blue, and amethyst. Edges for bowls are ice cream shape, ruffled, three-in-one, and tightly crimped. Two plates have been reported. Pieces seldom come up for public sale. This example is courtesy of Tom and Sharon Mordini.

God and Home, Dugan

Once considered the epitome of carnival, God and Home has lost a bit of its lustre but still commands an excellent price. The tumblers are thought to have been given away as store premiums; the pitcher awarded when six tumblers had been acquired. With both pitchers and tumblers, one side is lettered with "In God We Trust," the other side "God Bless Our Home." The original set is known only in blue but has been reproduced in other colors.

Water set, 7 piece
Blue   2,750–3,500
Tumbler
Blue   125–200

Golden Grape, Dugan

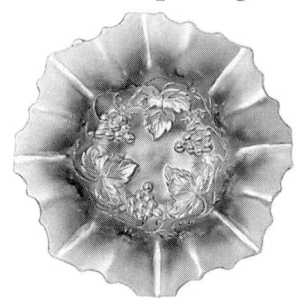

Found only in small bowls and an occasional rosebowl. Golden Grape has no exterior pattern and is known only in marigold. Bowls run around $25, rosebowls a bit more.

Golden Harvest, Dugan

Golden Harvest is found only in wine decanters and glasses. The distinguishing feature are sheaths of wheat that appear on two sides of the decanter separated by bunches of grapes—all against a basketweave pattern. The stopper has a grape pattern.

Wine set, 8 piece
Marigold 110–175
Wine decanter, with stopper
Marigold 40–55
Wine glass
Amethyst 10–20
Marigold 10–20

Golden Honeycomb

With a plain interior and hexagons on the exterior, this scarce marigold compote brought $50 at a 1998 Mickey Reichel auction.

Good Luck, Fenton

Fenton made its own version of the Good Luck, but used its Heart and Vine pattern. Rarely seen and very desirable, even though it is only found in marigold. Also called Heart and Horseshoe. They sell in the $1,500 to $2,500 range.

Good Luck, Northwood

A stroke of genius, the Northwood Good Luck pattern touches on a number of popular themes. These bowls and plates were desirable when first made and continue to be so. There is a wide range of colors as well as stippled and unstippled versions. Some variants have fewer berries and less foilage. While these variants have little additional monetary value, they make interesting comparisons. In both bowls and plates, some have the basketweave exterior, others a ribbed back. Good Luck bowls have been reproduced.

Bowl, ruffled
Amethyst/purple	225–325	most common color
Aqua/teal	1,300–1,600	scarce
Aqua opal	3,000–4,000	rare color
Blue	200–375	common color
Blue, electric	300–500	
Green	300–500	fairly common color
Green, emerald	1,700 (1998)	
Horehound	300–450	scarce color
Ice blue	3,000–4,000	very rare color
Ice blue opal	3,800 (1993)	
Ice green	4,500 (1998)	
Lavender	750 (1997)	
Lime green	350 (1995)	975 (1997)
Marigold	175–300	common color
Marigold	950 (1998)	spectacular iridescence
Sapphire blue	1,500–2,200	rare color

Bowl, pie crust edge
Amethyst/purple	250–400	common color
Blue	300–500	common color
Blue, electric	350–600	
Green	300–500	
Green, emerald	550 (1995)	
Ice blue	2,100 (1993)	
Lavender	460 (1998)	
Marigold	250–375	common color

74 A Field Guide to Carnival Glass

Bowl, stippled, ruffled
Blue	300–400	
Blue, electric	1,000 (1997)	
Blue, Renninger	1,200–2,000	rare color
Marigold	185–300	

Bowl, stippled, pie crust edge
Blue	400–625
Marigold	200–300

Plate, about 9"
Amethyst/purple	400–700	common color
Amethyst	1,000 (1994)	electric irid
Blue	1,500–2,500	
Blue, electric	3,000–4,500	rare color, very desirable
Emerald green	3,100 (1995)	
Green	550–800	
Green	2,250 (1996)	spectacular iridescence
Horehound	1,100 (1996) 550 (1997)	
Ice blue	10,000 (1998)	three known
Marigold	450–700	average color & iridescence
Marigold	1,600–2,400	pumpkin iridescence

Probably the most desirable and rarest shape is the stippled plate, found only in blue, marigold, and purple. The stippling goes to the edge of the pattern, not the edge of the piece itself.

Plate, stippled
Blue	1,200–2,000
Marigold	800–1,400
Purple	900–1,100

Gothic Arches
See Vase section

Graceful
See Vase section

Graceful
A tumbler by this name has been reported. The design is unrelated to the vase of the same name. The tumbler has four scroll-type designs around the body which pinches in slightly about half way up. The base diameter is two inches. The reported tumbler is blue.

Grand Thistle, Riihimäki (Finland)

One of the more angular and unusual designs in carnival. The diamond-shaped base is carried into the rest of the pitcher design and the tumbler. Also known as Wide Panelled Thistle.

Water set, 7 piece
Amber	500 (1995)

Pitcher
Amber	650 (1994)
Blue	450–625

Tumbler
Amber	300 (1994)
Blue	85–140

Grape, Imperial
See Imperial Grape

Grape Arbor, Dugan

While this has the same name as the Northwood pattern, it is by Dugan and found only in this large fruit bowl. The exterior pattern is Inverted Fan and Feather also seen on other Dugan bowls. Not easy to find.

Bowl, fruit
Amethyst/purple	200–300
Blue reported	
Marigold	90–140

Grape Arbor, Northwood

A dramatic use of the grape theme, the fruit on the pitcher is almost as large as the real thing. The grapes are combined with a lattice design around the base on both pitcher and tumblers.

Water set, 7 piece
Ice blue	2,000–3,400	
Marigold	300–500	
Purple	650–900	
White	800–1,000	

Pitcher, water
Amethyst/purple	500–600	
Ice blue	600–1,000	scarce color
Marigold	210–400	most common color
White	350–500	

Tumbler
Amethyst/purple	35–50	common color
Aqua	120 (1997)	
Blue	350–450	rare color
Iridized custard reported		
Clambroth	90 (1996)	
Ice blue	150–215	scarce color
Ice green reported		
Lavender	50–80	scarce color
Marigold	20–35	most common color
Marigold	23 (1994)	etched "SMS, 1914"
White	50–85	common color
White	40 (1994)	"W.M. Dobson 1914"

Enough of these ruffled hats were made from tumblers that they must have been a production item. They are found with several degrees of flaring.

Hat, from tumbler
Blue	140–200
Ice green	250–325
Marigold	60–80
White	80–110

Grape and Cable, Fenton

Fenton made only small bowls, plates, and large fruit or orange bowls in their Grape and Cable Pattern. The bowl pattern is much like the Northwood version with four groups of grapes. With the Fenton, however, the grapes are arranged very evenly with 14 grapes in each group. The edge pattern on the small bowls, like that above, is typical Fenton. As well as collar-based, Fenton Grape and Cable is found in ball- and spatula-footed bowls and plates.

Bowl, 7–8"
Amberina	375–525	rare color
Amethyst	40–60	scarce color
Aqua	55–80	scarce color
Blue	30–50	common color
Blue opal	1,500	one known
Blue, powder	140 (1998)	8", ball footed
Celeste	900–1,500	rare color
Green	40–65	common color
Lime	70–110	scarce color
Marigold	25–45	
Mar/moonstone	150–275	rare color
Peach opal reported		
Red	400–600	scarce color
Red	3,200 (1997)	spectacular color
Smoky Lavender	65 (1995)	
Vaseline	90–140	scarce color

Sauce, footed, Persian Medallion interior
Marigold	65–115

Bowl, fruit or orange, Persian Medallion interior
Amethyst	250–325	
Blue	210–375	
Green	400–700	
Marigold	100–170	
Marigold	600 (1998)	great color

76 A Field Guide to Carnival Glass

Bowl, fruit or orange, plain interior (used for Pacific Coast Mail Order bowl, see Lettered section)

Amethyst	185–250
Blue	120–215
Green	225–350

Plate, 9", spatula-footed

Amethyst/purple	65–100	
Blue	100–200	
Green	110–160	most common color
Marigold	70–100	

Grape and Cable, Northwood

Northwood's Grape and Cable was the most successful of all carnival patterns. Produced in more than 50 shapes plus several variations in design, it was widely copied by other manufacturers. Some, such as Fenton's version, are almost identical. The bowls are found in several sizes in both collar base and spatula-footed—although neither is more desirable than the other.

Bowl, small berry or sauce, 5–6"

Amethyst/purple	15–25	common color
Green	25–40	common color
Lavender	25–40	(light amethyst)
Marigold	20–30	common color

Bowl, 7–7½"

Amethyst	65–95	common color
Aqua opal	4,700 (1993)	
Green	30–50	scarce color
Ice blue	500–750	rare color
Marigold	25–40	common color

Bowl, 8–9", ruffled or round

Amethyst/purple	50–80	common color
Amethyst/purple	650 (1996)	electric iridescence
Aqua opal	2,600 (1996)	
Green	70–100	common color
Ice blue	500–650	
Ice green	375 (1998)	
Marigold	40–65	common color
Olive	50–70	

Bowls with pie crust edges are usually more desirable, assuming color and condition are equal.

Bowls, 8–9", pie crust edge

Amethyst/purple	60–100	common color
Emerald green	220 (1996)	
Green	65–110	most common color
Ice blue	1,100 (1994)	
Lavender	160 (1996)	
Marigold	60–110	common color

Bowl, large (10–11"), or large berry

Amethyst/purple	100–165	most common color
Blue	100–200	scarce color
Blue, electric	1,300 (1995)	
Custard, nutmeg	325 (1998)	pearlized
Green	120–185	scarce color
Ice green	1,150 (1996)	
Lime green	95 (1995)	
Marigold	60–100	common color

Bowl, stippled, 9–10"

Amethyst/purple	200–300	
Aqua	1,000 (1998)	ruffled
Aqua opal	1,800 (1995)	pie crust edge
Blue	225–450	
Blue, electric	1,700 (1998)	ruffled
Green	250–400	
Green	1,100 (1997)	
Ice blue	900–1,200	usually pie crust edge
Ice green	2,500 (1997)	
Marigold	135–225	

Also see Grape and Cable variant, page 84

Berry set, 5 piece

Amethyst/purple	120–220
Marigold	100–150

Berry set, 7 piece

Amethyst/purple	180–300
Green	200–300
Marigold	150–250

G 77

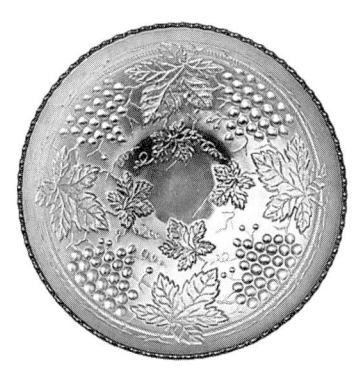

The large ice cream-shaped bowls are the most desirable of the collar-base bowls. To be considered ice cream shape, the edges must be perfectly round and scooped up—not with a straight flare.

Bowl, large ice cream shape, 10–11"
Amethyst/purple	250–350	most common color
Blue	700–1,200	rare color in this shape
Green	350–450	fairly common color
Ice blue	1,200 (1994)	
Ice green	1,100–2,000	
Lavender	325 (1997)	
Marigold	125–225	scarce color
White	225–350	fairly common color

Bowl, small ice cream shape
Blue	95–175
Ice green	175–325
White	70–120

Other than rosebowls, very few carnival glass pieces cup in as does the Grape and Cable centerpiece bowl. Some have the points straight up rather than cupping in—and are more rare—but don't seem to bring a premium price. A few examples have been flattened into chop plates.

Bowl, centerpiece
Amethyst/purple	300–500	most common color
Blue	275 (1995)	
Green	400–600	scarce color
Green	450 (1998)	points straight up
Ice blue	900–1,200	rare color
Ice green	550–950	fairly common color
Ice green	550–650	points straight up
Marigold	160–300	scarce color
Marigold	150 (1997)	points straight up
White	450–600	scarce color
White	375 (1995)	points straight up

This is the small fruit bowl and is found in most of the colors that the large fruit bowl, below, is found in. Such pieces are about 11 inches wide. This one, in amethyst/purple, brought $80 in 1994; a similar example in marigold sold for $200 in 1995.

The large fruit bowl or orange bowl is one of the most massive pieces of carnival, aside from punch bowls. Fenton made almost identical bowls, some of which have the Persian Medallion interior. There are also a few known with a blackberry interior, maker not yet positively identified.

Bowl, fruit or orange, large or small
Amethyst/purple	180–300	
Blue	350–550	
Green	370–600	
Ice green	650–900	
Marigold	110–190	
Olive green	200 (1998)	small
White	450–750	

The banded fruit bowl. Northwood made variations of some of its Grape and Cable pieces that had a wide band rather than the cable. Relatively few such pieces are seen. This example in electric blue sold for $425 in 1995.

There are several bowls that could be considered salad bowls. Usually they are large bowls with straight sides. This one, in marigold, with a pie crust edge, was sold as a salad bowl for $160 in 1995. A green example sold for $125, also in 1995.

The banana boat shape rests on four legs and is about 12½ inches long. They are fairly easy to find.

Banana boat

Amethyst/purple	185–275	common color
Blue	500–650	rare color
Custard/pearl	200–300	rare color
Green	210–350	
Ice blue	350–650	
Ice green	275–500	fairly common color
Marigold	125–200	common color
White	350–475	scarce color

Banana boat, banded

Aqua	575 (1995)
Blue	450–575
Blue, Renninger	500 (1996)
Green	375 (1995)
Marigold	155–275

This is the typical bonbon shape. With the card tray shape the non-handled sides are flattened out. Such pieces should be valued at the higher end of the range.

Bonbon or card tray shape

Amethyst/purple	40–70	common color
Aqua opal reported		
Blue	140–200	fairly common
Blue, electric	155–250	
Custard, pearl	175, 525 (both 1998)	
Green	85–135	common color
Marigold	60–100	common color
White	155–285	scarce color

Bonbon, stippled (all colors scarce or rare)

Amethyst/purple	60–85	
Amethyst, black	70–120	
Aqua	1,000 (1998)	
Blue	125–200	
Green	115–200	
Marigold	65–120	
Mar/moonstone	3,250 (1994)	only one known
Violet	425 (1997)	slag effect

The breakfast set is made up of two pieces, the open sugar and creamer—both smaller than those in the table set.

Breakfast set

Amethyst/purple	125–180
Green	130–160
Marigold	100–150

Breakfast creamer

Amethyst/purple	50–70
Lime	55 (1998)

Cup and saucer sets are rare in any pattern.

Cup and saucer

Amethyst/purple	115–165
Green	100–180
Marigold	120–150
White	150–225

The Grape and Cable bride's basket is very rare—only a few are known. The one above, in blue (with a 3" crack in the base), sold for $1,900 in 1998.

Candlesticks, pair
Amethyst/purple   300–400
Green   200–300
Marigold   200–300

The candle lamp is made from a candlestick with a metal bracket that holds the shade. Given that the base is simply a candlestick, it would appear that the metal holder and shade are the most expensive part of the set. Found in approximately equal numbers in amethyst/purple, green, and marigold, they sell for about $500 to $800 or so—depending on iridescence and condition.

The Grape and Cable dresser set. Old catalogs show the set with two cologne bottles, a powder jar, a hatpin holder, small pin tray and large dresser tray. Perfume bottles were not included.

Cologne bottle with stopper
Amethyst/purple   200–275
Green   205–300
Ice blue   575–600   rare color
Marigold   100–175
Marigold   250 (1997)   stippled and banded
Purple   375 (1996)   banded

Cologne bottle, missing or damaged stopper
Amethyst/purple   75–100
Marigold   75–100

Dresser tray
Amethyst/purple   190–300
Green   250–325
Ice blue   650–1,000
Marigold   180–225
Marigold   250 (1998)   stippled
Marigold   125–200   stippled and banded

Pin tray
Amethyst/purple   200–350
Custard   375 (1997)   pearlized
Green   225–385
Ice blue   500–800
Marigold   125–200

Pin tray, banded
Custard   250 (1995)   nutmeg stain
Marigold   275 (1995)   stippled
Purple   260 (1994)

Hatpin holder
Amethyst/purple   250–400
Amethyst, black   300–350   scarce color
Aqua opal   12,000 (1992)   one of two known
Aqua opal   10,000 (1993)   epoxied flake on bottom
Blue   900–1,500   rare color
Emerald green   750–1,000
Green   275–400
Ice blue   2,000–2,500   rare color
Ice green   1,000 (1993)
Lavender   600–650   scarce color
Lavender, smoky   700 (1995)
Lime green   2,100 (1997)
Marigold   225–350
White   2,200 (1993)

80 A Field Guide to Carnival Glass

Hatpin holder, banded (band rather than cable)
Amethyst/purple 250–400
Blue 1,200 (1997)
Marigold 200–350

Powder jar
Amethyst/purple 165–250
Aqua opal 2,150 (1992) base crack
Blue 625 (1993) small chips in rim
Green 265–350
Ice green 750–850 rare color
Lavender 500 (1997)
Marigold 85–120

Powder jar bottom only
Amethyst/purple 10–15
Horehound 60 (1995)
Ice blue 65–125
Ice green 75 (1993)

The spittoon whimsey on the left was made from the powder jar bottom by pinching in the neck and flaring the top. Known in marigold, purple, and one green, few of these exist and rarely come up for sale. This spittoon and powder jar are courtesy of Carl and Ferne Schroeder.

Perfume bottle (made by Dugan)
Amethyst/purple 425–750
Amethyst/purple 85–150 no stopper
Marigold 220–400

Lamp, miniature, made from perfume bottle
Purple 250–400

A curiosity. I first photographed the little ruffled spittoon on the left at the 1993 auction where it sold for $3,000. It was offered as having been made from a perfume but, as you can see from the perfume next to it, the details and base diameter are quite different. Several people have suggested other origins, but until we can find proof we'll just call it a curiosity.

While all these nappies were made from punch cups, not all flare as much as this one. This one is in ice blue and sold for $850 at the 1994 HOACGA convention auction. Sometimes called a pin dish.

Nappy, from punch cup
Amethyst/purple 40–60
Green 60–95
Ice blue 600–850 3 or 4 known
Marigold 35–50

Northwood made two covered stemmed pieces in the Grape and Cable pattern; the covered compote on the left, and the sweetmeat on the right. Note the difference in shapes and base styles.

Compote, covered
Amethyst/purple 250–400 most common color
Marigold 1,000–1,300

Sweetmeat
Amethyst/purple 175–275
Blue 500 (1993) base cracked
Horehound 400–750
Marigold 1,200–1,500 rare color
White 900 (1993) damage

Compote, open (giant or large)
Amethyst/purple 300–475
Green 1,100 (1996)
Marigold 350–425

The compote whimsey is the sweetmeat base flared out.
Compote whimsey
Amethyst/purple 95–170
Marigold 60–100

The tobacco humidor and cracker jar are about the same size. The humidor, shown here on the left, has a three-pronged holder for a sponge on the inside of the cover. The cookie jar has two handles. The humidor has been reproduced: see Contemporary section.

Humidor or tobacco jar
Amethyst/purple 325–525
Aqua opal two known, one damaged
Blue 525 (1994) nick on lid
Marigold 275–450

Humidor, stippled
Blue 675 minor nick under lid
Marigold 400–500

Cracker jar
Amethyst/purple 300–500
Ice green 700–1,000 rare, rim nicks
Marigold 250–425
Smoke 275 (1995) amethyst top
White 900–1,300

Cracker jar, stippled
Marigold 275–325

Whiskey set, decanter and 6 shot glasses
Marigold 650–1,000
Purple 900–1,100

Decanter, whiskey, with stopper
Marigold 250–400
Purple 400–650

Shot glass
Amethyst/purple 125–200
Marigold 100–175

Fernery
Custard, irid 500 (1994) heavy nutmeg coloring
Custard 700 (1998) with blue stain
Ice blue 1,600–2,100
Ice green 16,250 (1993)
Marigold 450–600
Purple 600–900
White 650–800

Note that the butter dish has been reproduced in ice blue and amber. The new butter has a scalloped edge on the base rather than the sawtooth as seen here. See Reproductions section.

Table set, 4 pieces
Amethyst/purple 350–500
Green 450 (1995)
Ice green reported, rare
Marigold 250–400

82 A Field Guide to Carnival Glass

Butter dish
Amethyst/purple 125–210
Green 185–260
Marigold 75–125

Butter dish, stippled, rare
Amethyst/purple 475 (1995)

Creamer
Amethyst/purple 70–115
Green 85–125
Marigold 40–65

Spooner
Amethyst/purple 85–140
Green 65–120
Marigold 60–95

Sugar, covered
Amethyst/purple 100–175
Green 75–125
Marigold 65–95

Northwood made water sets with two styles of pitchers—the table, or standard size, shown above, and the tankard style.

Pitcher, water, table size
Amethyst/purple 190–300 common color
Green 250–400 common color
Ice green 15,000 (1994) only three known
Marigold 185–350 common color
Smoke 500–800 rare color
Smoke opal 625 (1997) cracked

Water set, table-style pitcher, 7 piece
Amethyst/purple 350–450
Green 350–550
Marigold 250–400 most common color

This is a tankard-style water set. Note the differences in the proportions of the pitcher as well as the slight flaring to the rims of the tumblers. Tankard water sets are much more difficult to find than table-style. In recent years amethyst/purple and marigold seven-piece water sets have sold for $600 to $700.

Pitcher, tankard style
Amethyst/purple 500–750
Ice green 4,500–5,000 rare color
Marigold 400–700

These are the tumblers for the tankard-style water set (on the left) and the regular water set. The regular tumbler is four inches high, the tankard-style flares slightly and is one-eighth to one-quarter inch taller. White tumblers are reproductions.

Tumbler, for tankard water set
Amethyst/purple 40–75
Green known, very rare
Marigold 50–90

Tumbler, standard (for table-style water set)
Amethyst/purple 20–35 most common color
Green 30–70
Horehound 150 (1998)
Ice green 215 (1995) base chip
Lime green 400 (1995)
Marigold 20–35

Tumbler, stippled
Amethyst/purple 85–100
Marigold 65 (1997)

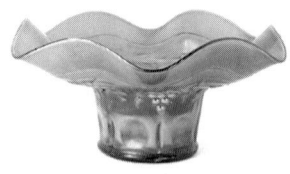

This widely flared and ruffled hat was made from a tumbler. Not all were given this extreme treatment and these wider versions often command a better price.

Hat, from tumbler
Amethyst/purple 45–75
Green 40–60
Marigold 20–35

Sherbert, stemmed
Amethyst/purple 30–50
Marigold 25–40

Plate, 6–6½"
Amethyst/purple 125–190

Plate, 7–8"

Amethyst/purple	110–160	most common color
Amethyst	350 (1997)	slag opal streaks
Amber	95 (1993)	
Green	125–200	
Marigold	900 (1996)	
Mar/custard	2,150 (1994)	

Plate, 8½–9" or unspecified size

Amethyst/purple	150–250
Green	165–250
Marigold	100–195

Grape and Cable plates are also found in the spatula-footed version with Meander back—used in several other Northwood patterns. This marigold example sold for $190 in 1994.

Plate, spatula-footed, Meander back, about 9"

Amethyst/purple	90–150
Green	100–185
Ice green	300–550
Marigold	80–125

Plate, with brass carrier

Marigold	70 (1993)

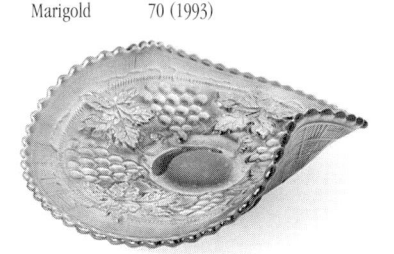

Plate, handgrip, 6–8"

Amethyst/purple	85–155
Green	120–185
Marigold	65–95

Plate, double handgrip, banana dish, card tray, or 2-sided

Amethyst	55–85
Green	80–125
Lavender smoky	110 (1998)
Marigold	40–75

Some Northwood Grape and Cable plates have a stippled background. Note that the above example is also the variant pattern with the tendrils sneaking into the center of the design. The green version of this plate sometimes carries the Old Rose Distillery advertising on the back. See Lettered section.

Plate, stippled, 9"

Amethyst/purple	350–500	
Blue	700–1,200	
Green	600–900	most common color
Green, emerald	1,800–2,700	
Marigold	400–650	scarce color
Sapphire	2,000–3,000	rare color

Northwood's Grape and Cable small punch set in aqua opal. It was the first uncovered in this color in 1996. Photo and glass courtesy of Don and Becky Hamlet. By the way, punch bowls and their bases count as two pieces when part of a set.

Punch set, small, 8 piece

Amethyst/purple	425–650	
Aqua opal	one known set	
Blue	800–1,000	stippled
Blue, electric	3,400 (1995)	stippled
Green	1,800 (1997)	
Ice blue known		
Ice green known		
Marigold	375–500	
Marigold	400 (1995)	straight sides
Marigold	500–900	stippled
White	5,000 (1997)	

84 A Field Guide to Carnival Glass

Punch set, mid (table) size, 8 piece
Amethyst/purple	650–1,000	
Blue	1,000–1,500	
Blue	5,000 (1996)	stippled cups
Blue	1,000 (1996)	stippled
Green	1,800 (1996)	
Green	1,050 (1998)	6-piece
Marigold	1,200–1,600	
Marigold	700 (1996)	stippled
White	4,750 (1996)	

Punch set, banquet or master, 12–14 piece
Amethyst/purple	1,500–2,500	
Blue	7,500 (1995)	2–3 known, 8 piece
Blue	11,000 (1996)	12 piece
Green	4,000–5,000	8–10 piece
Ice blue	25,000 (1994)	10 piece
Marigold	1,600–2,400	8–10 piece
Marigold	2,000–2,600	12–14 piece
White	5,000–8,000	

Punch bowl and base
Amethyst/purple	350–575	small size
Amethyst/purple	950 (1997)	mid-size
Blue	600–800	stippled
Green, emerald	1,250 (1996)	mid-size
Marigold	225–400	small size
Marigold	1,100–1,250	master size
Smoke	375	damage (missing flute)
Teal	4,600 (1996)	green base, mid-size

Punch base only
Amethyst/purple	30–50	small or mid-size
Amethyst/purple	40–80	large size
Green	65–100	
Ice blue	70–100	
Marigold	25–40	small or mid-size
Marigold	40–80	large size

Punch cup
Amethyst/purple	15–25	
Aqua opal	1,500 (1997)	
Blue	40–55	stippled
Green	40–60	
Green	30–40	stippled
Ice blue	75 (1998)	
Ice green	60 (1995)	
Lime green	65 (1995)	
Marigold	15–25	
White	20–40	

Grape & Cable variant, Northwood

Northwood made Grape and Cable plates and bowls from may different molds. One of the most frequently seen is the variant in which tendrils of the leaves around the center of the bowl creap into the middle. Another variation has a leaf in the center.

Variant bowl
Amethyst/purple	100–200	
Aqua opal	1,600 (1994)	
Aqua opal	2,300 (1996)	stippled
Aqua/teal	1,000 (1997)	
Blue	350–500	
Blue	150–250	stippled
Green	100–200	
Green	200–350	stippled
Green, electric	1,100 (1997)	
Ice blue	1,000 (1997)	pie crust edge
Lavender	80–135	
Marigold	50–80	
Smoke	105 (1997)	

Variant plate
Amethyst/purple	125–235	
Blue	500–900	stippled
Clambroth	350 (1996)	
Green	275–500	
Green	350–500	stippled
Green, emerald	2,800 (1996)	stippled
Marigold	100–200	
Marigold	200–400	stippled
Sapphire blue	3,400–3,750	stippled

Grape Delight, Dugan

Dugan used the same mold to make both the rosebowl and nut bowl, crimping in the rosebowl and flaring the nut bowl. While the grape design is similar to others, the six little feet are distinctive—and easily damaged. Blue, an otherwise scarce Dugan color, is fairly common in this pattern; peach opal is rare. The nut bowl has been reproduced.

Rosebowl

Amethyst/purple	45–85	most common color
Amethyst/purple	65 (1998)	scalloped, not ruffled
Blue	50–95	
Clambroth	65 (1995)	
Horehound	175–300	rare color
Marigold	45–80	
Peach opal	80 (1995)	
White	60–95	common color

Nut bowl

Amethyst/purple	40–75	most common color
Blue	50–85	fairly easy to find
Marigold	40–60	scarce color
Purple, elect	255–525	especially nice examples
White	55–95	rare in nut bowl

Grape and Cherry

Not too often seen. This is an intaglio design (the grapes and cherries are cut into the exterior, giving a raised look when viewed by from the top). Some attribute to Northwood, others to Sowerby. This marigold example is about eight inches wide. Such pieces sell for less than $30.

Grape and Gothic Arches, Northwood

A classy pattern, made in a wider range of shapes than most. The pattern predated carnival glass and is sometimes found without iridizing. This 8½" marigold bowl, in spite of its relative scarcity, sold for only $35 in 1997.

Berry set, 7 piece

| Blue | 150–200 |
| Marigold | 140–190 |

Bowl, large berry

| Blue, electric | 225 (1998) |
| Marigold | 30–50 |

Bowl, small berry or sauce

Aqua	225 (1995)
Blue	45 (1998)
Marigold	10–20
Green	40–50
Teal	55 (1998)

Table set, 4 pieces

Blue	250–450
Green is known, rare	
Marigold	300–400

Butter dish

Blue	115–150	
Custard	135 (1995)	pearlized
Marigold	90–125	

Creamer

Blue	50–70	
Custard	60 (1995)	pearlized, wear on gold
Green	85 (1995)	
Marigold	25–40	

Spooner

Blue	55–70	
Custard	60 (1995)	iridized, wear on gold
Green	50–85	
Marigold	15–25	

Sugar, covered

| Custard | 75 (1995) | pearlized, wear on gold |
| Green | 60–95 | |

Sugar and spooner

| Blue | 225 (1995) |

Water set, 7 piece

Blue	500–800
Green	775 (1994)
Marigold	350–500

Pitcher, water

Blue	300–500
Pearlized custard known	
Marigold	250–450

Tumbler

Blue	30–45	common color
Custard	60–100	pearlized
Green	50–85	
Marigold	20–35	

Grape Leaves, Northwood or Dugan

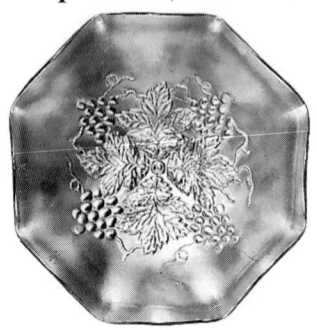

Another grape pattern, this one has the design crowded into the center of the bowl. Most bowls are ruffled but an occasional three-in-one edge, round or eight-sided (above) is seen. The typical Dugan three-in-one edge and eight-sided treatments cause some collectors to suspect that Dugan really made these pieces—in spite of the Northwood "N" mark.

Bowl, 8–9", ruffled, round, three-in-one or eight-sided

Amethyst/purple	70–100	common color
Amethyst, fiery	70 (1998)	
Amber	100 (1997)	ruffled
Green	45–85	most common color
Ice blue	1,600–2,000	rare color
Lavender	275 (1997)	
Marigold	25–45	common color

Grape Leaves, Millersburg

Millersburg's Grape Leaves pattern has the same wreath design as the Blackberry, Grape, and Strawberry Wreath patterns but has four leaves radiating out from the center grape bunch. Unlike the Wreath patterns, which have a panelled exterior, Grape Leaves has a cut-type pattern, Mayflower.

Bowl

Amethyst	750 (1994)	8", deep, round
Amethyst	800–900	3/1 edge, radium
Marigold scarce		
Green	3,750 (1996)	7¼" square, one known
Green	4,750 (1996)	tricorner, one known
Vaseline, one known		

Grape and Lotus
See Lotus and Grape

Grape Wreath, Millersburg

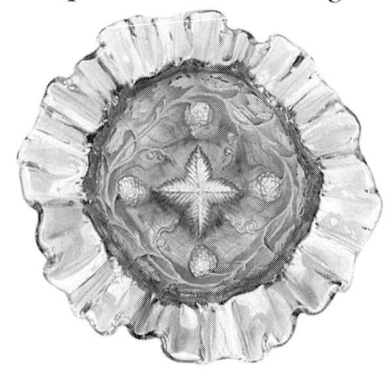

Millersburg used the same berry wreath motif in a number of patterns, changing only the center medallion. Grape Wreath bowls have one of four different designs in the center. The feathered leaf design, above, is the one drawn in Marion Hartung's book and is considered the standard. Shown below are two variants, the clover and feather and the eight-pointed star (or multistar) which is the most frequently seen. Yet another has a plume or propeller design over a four-pointed star. Shape, color, iridescence and other qualities affect the price more than the center design.

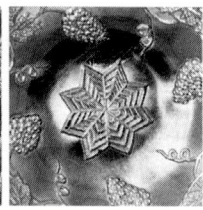

Small bowl (or sauce), 5–6"

Amethyst	90–135	most are ice cream-shaped
Green	65–120	
Green	140–180	tricorner
Marigold	100–165	

Bowl, 7–9", round, ice cream shape, ruffled or 3/1 edge

Amethyst	85–150
Green	90–175
Marigold	55–100

Bowl, 10"

Green	350 (1994)	round, crimped edge
Marigold	205 (1994)	tricorner
Marigold	300 (1995)	9½", square

The Grape Wreath whimsey spittoon is very rare, with only a couple of examples known. This amethyst example, with an eight-pointed star in the center, is from the collection of Carl and Ferne Schroeder.

Grapevine Lattice, Dugan

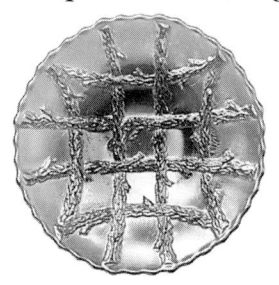

Plates and bowls in Grapevine Lattice can sometimes be confused with Dugan's Apple Blossom Twigs. This pattern, however, has just a lattice of vines, not the center blossom. Peach opalescent, so prominent in most Dugan patterns, is almost unknown here.

Bowl, 6–7"
Amethyst/purple 80–140
Marigold 25–40
Lavender 65 (1997)
White 50–85 most common color

Plate, 6–7"
Amethyst/purple 200–350
Amethyst 275–290 souv. lettering, Gettysburg PA 1863
Lavender/purple 325 (1997)
Marigold 60–100
Peach opal 300 (1994)
White 65–110 common color

Hat, from tumbler
Marigold 25–40

Pitchers and tumblers in the Grapevine Lattice patterns are sometimes confused with Fenton's Lattice and Grape. Tumblers have been reproduced.

Pitcher, water
Amethyst 475–550
Purple 1,300 (1995)

Tumbler
Amethyst/purple 40–70
Blue 15 (1995)
Marigold 20–30
White 185 (1995)

Water set, 7 pieces
Amethyst/purple 500–800
Blue 600–1,000
Marigold 300–400

Greek Key, Northwood

In addition to the well known plates, bowls and water sets with the Greek Key design, the pattern is used on Northwood Stippled Rays dome-footed bowls as an exterior motif (below).

88 A Field Guide to Carnival Glass

Nut bowl, dome-footed, stippled rays interior
Amethyst/purple 45–85
Green 45–55
Marigold 40–65

Bowl, about 9", basketweave exterior
Amethyst/purple	115–225	ruffled
Amethyst/purple	200–250	pie crust edge
Blue	450–700	ruffled
Blue, electric	2,000 (1995)	pie crust edge
Green	155–200	ruffled
Green	300–500	pie crust edge
Marigold	110–165	ruffled
Marigold	125–200	pie crust edge

Plate, 9", most with basketweave exterior
Amethyst/purple	450–750	
Blue	700–1,000	
Green	500–800	
Marigold	475–800	
Marigold	2,050 (1995) 5,750 (1993)	ribbed back

Note that during the manufacturing of the pitcher and tumblers some retained sharp detail, others lost it. Sometimes the difference is so extreme that auctioneers have thought them different patterns.

Water set, 7 piece
Amethyst/purple 1,000–1,500

Pitcher, water
Amethyst/purple 500–900
Green 800–1,000
Marigold 650 (1996)

Tumbler
Amethyst/purple	75–125	
Amethyst	55 (1994)	etched "Hazel Atlas"
Green	80–135	
Marigold	50–80	

Hanging Cherries, Millersburg

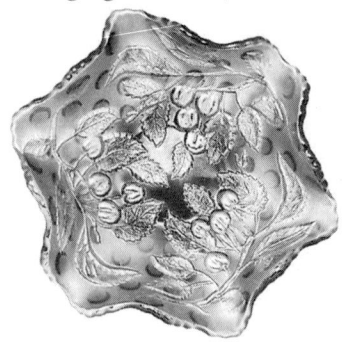

This pattern is sometimes called Millersburg Cherries. Above is one of quite a few rarities in the pattern, an amethyst sauce with hobnail exterior. It is owned by Harold and Dolores Wagner.

Berry set, 5 piece
Green	175 (1998)	chip on large bowl

Bowl, small berry or sauce, 5–6"
Amethyst	100–150	
Blue	1,100–1,700	3/1 edge, rare color
Green	70–110	
Marigold	60–100	

Bowl, 7", usually ice cream shape or round
Amethyst	100–200	
Blue	2,500 (1996)	7½", ruffled, satiny
Green	85–115	ice cream shape
Green	200–300	6 ruffles
Marigold	60–100	ice cream shape

Bowl, large, about 10"
Amethyst	250–325	ice cream shape
Amethyst	175–275	3/1 edge
Aqua	400–600	ice cream shape
Green	285–325	ice cream shape
Green	175–275	6 ruffles
Marigold	165–275	ice cream shape
Marigold	100–200	3/1 edge

Bowl, large, hobnail exterior
Amethyst 600–950
Marigold 1,000–1,500

G-H 89

Plates are very rare in Hanging Cherries and always fetch a good price. This one is the only known eight-inch plate in green and sold for $4,250 at a 1994 Jim Seeck auction.

Plate
Amethyst	2,100 (1994)	8", silvery
Green	4,250 (1994)	8", only one known
Marigold	1,900–2,600	6", radium

Chop plate, 11"
Amethyst	1,900 (1997)	silvery, only one known
Marigold	3,000 (1993)	only one known

Table set, 4 piece
Amethyst	450–650
Green	600–750
Marigold	350–500

Butter dish, covered
Amethyst	225–300
Green	400–500
Marigold	160–210

Creamer
Amethyst	60–100
Aqua	80–125
Green	75–135
Marigold	40–60

Spooner, 2 handles
Amethyst	130–225
Green	65–105
Marigold	100–175
Teal	125–200

Sugar, covered, 2 handles
Green	195 (1997)
Marigold	40–60

This is the typical flared compote shape but the compote is also found in a rare square shape.

Compote, round
Green	1,200–1,500

Compote, square, two known
Amethyst	3,000–3,500 (both 1996)

Pitcher, milk
Amethyst	850 (1997)	
Green	470–500	damage
Marigold	1,000–1,700	

Any Hanging Cherries water pitcher is hard to find. The regular one like that on the left is what you'll likely see when you do find one. If you find an example like that on the right, you've got a true rarity; there are only two known in this variation with the sides dropping straight down to the base. Courtesy of Don and Linda Grizzle.

Water set, 7 piece
Green	1,800 (1996)

Pitcher, water
Amethyst	550–800	
Green	2,300 (1995)	pinhead on rim
Marigold	600 (1995)	

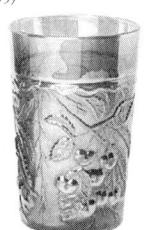

Tumblers are also found in a variant, which is the one on the right. They're known in amethyst, green, and marigold. Courtesy of Carl and Eunice Booker.

Tumbler
Amethyst	100–200	
Green	110–205	most common color
Marigold	55–100	
Marigold	250–300	variant

The powder jar is rarely seen. This green example, even with an epoxy repair to the base, brought $500 at a 1994 auction. None have sold publicly since.

Harvest Flower, Dugan

Harvest Flower has a design theme of wheat banded with a tie and a flower over that. Only tumblers and a rare pitcher are known. The tumbler shown is purple and courtesy of John and Lucile Britt.

Harvest Flower water set
Marigold 500 (1998) pitcher has line below handle
Pitcher
Marigold 2,700 (1995)
Tumbler
Lime 110 (1995) marigold overlay
Marigold 85–150

Harvest Poppy, Northwood

At first glance Harvest Poppy looks like other floral-interior compotes, but this design has the flowers extending out from the center. Blue is very rare.

Compote
Amethyst/purple 225–400
Blue 775 (1993)
Green 400 (1994)
Marigold 225–350 most common color

Hatpins
See Hatpins section

Hattie, Imperial

This pattern is most easily recognized by its arched lines and small floral elements. Busy yet distinctive. Supposedly the only carnival pattern in which the outside has the exact pattern as the inside.

Bowl, 8–9" ruffled or round
Amber 155 (1994)
Green 55 (1994)
Marigold 25–40 most common color
Purple 100–175
Smoke 45–60

Chop plate, 10¼"
Amber 3,000–5,000 fairly common color
Green 300–500
Helios 250–385
Marigold 1,300–1,600 rare in this shape
Purple 1,400–1,800 most common color

Rosebowl whimsey, rare
Known in amber
Marigold 400–700
Purple 2,500 (1995) only one known in purple

Headdress

Headdress is found as the interior pattern of some US Glass Cosmos and Cane bowls (above) and also Brockwitz (Germany) Curved Star bowls. Collectors tend to think one firm copied it from the other, but remain divided as to which. Marigold bowls sell in the $40 to $60 range.

Heart Band, McKee

Apparently popular as souvenir items, many pieces in this pattern are found with hand-lettered or etched names.

Creamer, miniature
Green flash	20–30	Souv. Columbus, OH
Marigold	20 (1998)	light color
Marigold	55 (1996)	Annie 1909
Marigold	50	etched, Toronto Exhibition 1909
Vaseline/teal	50 (1996)	base nicks

Mug, small
Green	165 (1994)	
Marigold	50–90	
Marigold	75 (1995)	Souv. Syracuse

Tumbler, small
Green	85 (1994)	Souv. Columbus, OH
Marigold	165 (1995)	decorated
Marigold	40	etched, Toronto Exhibition 1910

Heart and Horseshoe

See Good Luck, Fenton

Heart and Vine, Fenton

Heart and Vine is found in plates and bowls with three-in-one, ruffled, and crimped edges.

Bowl, 8–9", various edges
Amethyst	55–85	
Blue	60–95	most common color
Green	45–75	
Marigold	40–65	

Plate, 9"
Amethyst	400–600	
Blue	400–650	common color
Green	600 (1994)	rare color

Hearts and Flowers, Northwood

Characterized by the circular band of heart shapes, Hearts and Flowers is an extraordinarily popular pattern, available in a great array of colors. If you like the idea of collecting colors within a pattern, there are few better places to start. Note that Fenton has a similar contemporary pattern, but such pieces should be marked with their logo.

Bowl, 9", ruffled
Amethyst/purple	200–325	
Aqua opal	1,300–2,000	rare color
Aqua	1,000–1,500	rare color
Blue	375–550	scarce color
Blue, electric	1,050 (1996)	
Blue, Renninger	225–350	rare color
Green	1,700 1,950	rare color
Ice blue	300–450	relatively common color
Ice green	650–1,000	scarce color
Lavender	375 (1998)	

92 A Field Guide to Carnival Glass

Lime	650 (1998)	
Marigold	300–550	scarce color
White	225–350	common color

Bowl, 9", pie crust edge

Amethyst/purple	750–1,000	scarce to rare color
Blue	700–1,200	scarce color
Blue, electric	2,700–3,600	
Green	1,400 (1998)	
Ice blue	900–1,700	most common color
Ice green	1,400–2,000	rare color
Lime green	1,700–2,000	scarce color
Marigold	500–800	common color
Marigold	1,300–2,400	spectacular examples
White	800–1,000	scarce color

Plate, 9"

Amethyst/purple	1,500–2,500	fairly common color
Cobalt blue, rare		
Green	2,000–3,500	average availability
Ice blue	1,800–3,000	common color
Lime/ice green	3,400–5,500	rare color
Marigold	900–1,700	most common color
Sapphire, rare		
White	2,400–3,200	rare
Vaseline, rare		

Hearts and Flowers compotes are found with both plain and ribbed exterior. There is probably as great a variety of colors in this compote as any Northwood pattern.

Compote

Amethyst, black	750 (1994)	
Aqua opal	500–800	common color
Blue	350–500	fairly common color
Blue opal	3,700–4,250	rare color
Blue, Renninger	1,500–2,000	rare color
Cobalt opal	600 (1997)	some epoxy, little opal
Custard	4,000–6,000	pearlized
Green	1,400–2,000	scarce color
Ice blue	400–700	common color
Ice blue opal	1,800 (1996)	
Ice green	700–1,200	scarce color
Lavender	1,00–1,200	scarce color
Lime green	1,200–2,000	scarce color
Marigold	175–325	fairly common color
Powder bl opal	3,000–4,000	rare color
Purple	400–700	scarce color
Sapphire blue opal reported		
White	130–225	common color

Hearts and Trees, Fenton

At a glance this pattern would appear to be Butterfly and Berry—that's what the exterior pattern is. The interior, though, is the seldom seen Hearts and Trees pattern that has heart-shaped flowers on the bottom and trees along the vertical sides—almost like a forest glen. Except for one green ice cream shape, these bowls are known only in marigold and sell for $300 to $500.

Heavy Grape, Dugan

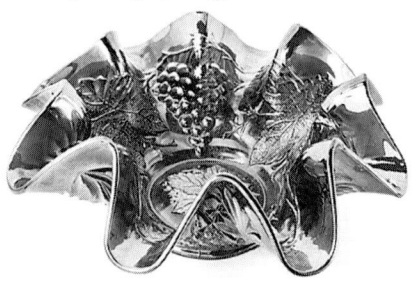

Both Dugan and Imperial made grape patterns that use the same name. The Dugan version has the grape design around the edge and a cut-style back pattern called Compass. Found mostly in the ruffled shape shown here but occasionally squared off and an ice cream shape has been reported—as have small bowls. Also known in blue and marigold.

Bowl, 10–11", ruffled or square

Peach opal	250–425	
Purple	400–650	most common color

Heavy Grape, Imperial

Imperial's Heavy Grape pattern is distinguished by a quilted diamond effect around the edge and has a simple fluted back. Shown here are a chop plate and an eight-inch plate—both highly desirable. The eight-inch plate is seen more frequently than any other shape. Reproductions are known.

Bowl, small (5–6"), scarce size
Green   20 (1994)
Lime   10 (1996)
Purple   50–80   most common color

Bowl, 7–8"
Amber   20 (1994)
Green/helios   20–30
Lime   35–50
Marigold   15–25
Purple   20–35   most common color
Smoke   150 (1998)
Vaseline   35–50

Bowl, large (10–11")
Amber   45–60
Amethyst/purple 100–200   most common color
Marigold   20–35
Smoke   40–50   scarce color

Plate, 6¼", from small bowl
Marigold   850 (1993)

Plate, 8"
Amber   145–265   fairly common color
Green   50–75   fairly common color
Helios green   40–60
Lime   225 (1996)
Marigold   50–95   common color
Purple   60–100   common color
Smoke   425 (1996)
Teal   150 (1997)   glows in black light

Chop plate, 10–11¼"
Amber   100–200   fairly common color
Green   150–225
Helios green   155–300
Marigold   90–170   common color
Purple   275–450   most common color
Smoke   2,500 (1993)
White   295–550   rare color

Nappy, single handle
Helios green   25–40
Marigold   10–20
Purple   40–60

Punch bowl and base
Amethyst/purple 1,100 (1997)   questionable base sliver
Marigold   275–400

Punch bowl, base and one cup
Green   200 (1995)   chipped

Punch set, 5 piece
Helios green   400 (1995)

Punch set, 10 piece
Green   750 (1995)

Punch cup
Marigold   90–150

Heavy Iris, Dugan

A heavily sculpted design that looks like it had been dipped in flowers—and is about ready to bloom. In addition to colors listed, tumblers have been found in ice blue. Pitchers and tumblers were reproduced in 1978 by Westmoreland for L.G. Wright, who owned some Dugan molds. Beware of pieces iridized on the bottom. The neck on the newer pitchers is taller than the old and has no pattern.

Water set, 7 piece
Amethyst/purple 1,000–1,500
Marigold   400–600

Pitcher, water
Amethyst/purple 1,000–1,200
Amethyst/purple 2,600 (1998)   spectacular example

Heavy Iris water pitcher, continued
Marigold   225–400
Peach opal reported
White   1,000–1,300
White   1,200 (1995)   straight top, not ruffled
Tumbler (see page 181)
Amethyst/purple 65–100   most common color
Amber   85 (1993)   souvenir writing
Horehound   65–100   scarce color
Lavender   100 (1995)
Marigold   65–100
White   190–255   scarce color
Hat, JIP, whimsey from tumbler
Marigold   400–425
White   475 (1997)

Heavy Pineapple, Fenton

A rare pattern found on the exterior of large footed orange bowls. Marigold, blue and white are known. Marigold bowls are worth $1,000 to $1,500.

Heavy Prisms

These marigold celery vases are quite rare; they sell so infrequently that determining value is difficult. The most recent sale I know of was for $35 in 1993. The value should be at least $100 today.

Heavy Vine

An unusual design with the vine incised around the middle. Maker not known but thought to be one of the European manufacturers. This is the cologne. Also known in a DeVilbiss atomizer and covered powder jar.

Heavy Vine cologne, with stopper
Marigold   80–140
Perfume, with stopper
Marigold   50–80
Pin tray, oblong, 4¼"
Marigold   80–150
Ring tree
Marigold   80–150
Covered bowl, 3½"
Marigold   30 (1998)
Rosebowl, miniature
Marigold   130 (1998)
Shot glass
Marigold   100–200
Tumbler, 4¼ or 3⅞"
Marigold   150–200

Heavy Web, Dugan

A large, curious design with a distinct web as the interior theme. Bowls are seen with a variety of edge treatments.
Bowl
Peach opal   800–1,200   flared
Peach opal   2,200 (1997)   deep round
Peach opal   550 (1994)   square
Chop plate
Peach opal   3,100 (1993)

Heisey
Breakfast set
Marigold   30 (1995)
Candlesticks, pair, panelled
Marigold   95 (1993)
Candy dish, covered
Marigold   30 (1995)
Creamer with underplate or sugar tray
Blue, smoky 195 (1993)
Ice green   100 (1996)   dated 6/20/16
Marigold   70 (1995)   signed
Creamer and sugar
Marigold   375 (1996)

H 95

Cuspidor or spittoon
Marigold   165–300
Old Williamsburg candlestick with prisms
Marigold   350 (1995)

Hen on Nest
See Covered Hen

Heron Mug, Dugan

Similar to another Dugan mug, Stork and Rushes, but in this case, the single bird faces to the left. With the Stork and Rushes, there are four birds. Be aware of the difference—this one is much more valuable.

Mug
Amethyst, black   225 (1997)
Marigold   3,100 (1993)
Purple   190–325

Herringbone and Beaded Ovals, Imperial

Sometimes called Herringbone and Beads (and perhaps several similar names), these marigold compotes are worth between $50 and $80.

Hobnail, Millersburg

A very desirable, but seldom seen pattern, Millersburg's Hobnail is known in water sets, table sets pieces, rosebowls, and spittoons. Other companies also made hobnail-style patterns, so finding a hobnail piece doesn't necessarily mean it's Millersburg—or old.

Pitcher
Amethyst   800 (1992)
Green known
Blue   4,000 (1996)
Marigold   3,500 (1995)

Tumbler
Amethyst   750 (1997)
Blue   800–1,350
Green known
Marigold known

Rosebowl
Amethyst   250–400
Green   1,600 (1994)
Marigold   150–250

The rosebowl and spittoon (shown above) were made from the same mold.

Spittoon or cuspidor
Amethyst   700–900
Green   1,700 (1996)   rare color
Marigold   600–900

Table set, 3 piece (no spooner)
Blue   2,900 (1992)   amethyst butter bottom
Also known in amethyst, green and marigold, all rare

Butter dish
Amethyst   250 (1997)   Springtime bottom

Sugar, covered
Amethyst   300 (1997)   few known

Hobnail Swirl, Millersburg
See Swirled Hobnail

Hobnail, Soda Gold, Imperial
Spittoon
Marigold   20–35

Hobstar, Cambridge
Napkin ring
Marigold   200 (1994)

Hobstar, Imperial

The biscuit or cracker jar is probably the most frequently seen piece in this pattern, but many of them are reproductions, usually in green. Repros should have the IG logo on the bottom but it's relatively easy to grind off—so beware. By the way, the pattern is sometimes called Carnival Hobstar or Imperial Hobstar.

Biscuit, cookie or cracker jar
Marigold   35–65
Pickle caster in silverplate bracket
Marigold   400–600

This marigold Hobstar 11-inch bowl sold for $40 at a 1997 Mickey Reichel auction.

Table set, 4 piece
Marigold   115–200
Also known in green and purple
Butter, covered
Marigold   90–130
Purple   120–200

Creamer
Marigold   30–55
Purple   85–135
Spooner
Marigold   15–25
Green   100 (1997)
Purple   135 (1998)
Sugar
Green   100 (1997)

Hobstar Band

The pattern takes its name from the band of hobstars around the trunk of the pieces. The pitcher and tumbler above are actually the variant; the regular version of the pitcher has straight sides (not the pedestal foot); the tumbler flares slightly at the top. The maker is unknown, but some suggest Imperial. The pieces above are part of a seven-piece marigold water set that sold at the 1996 International Carnival Glass Association auction for $200.

Tumbler, regular (flared top)
Marigold   30–50
Tumbler, variant (straight top)
Marigold   40–70
Water set, 7 piece
Marigold   150–250

This marigold Hobstar Band compote sold at a 1998 Mickey Reichel auction for $40.
Bowl
Marigold   25–40

Above is the Hobstar Band celery vase in marigold, courtesy of Carl and Ferne Schroeder. A green celery with light iridescence sold in 1993 for $35. Good examples in either marigold or green would probably be worth several times that.

Hobstar and Cut Triangles

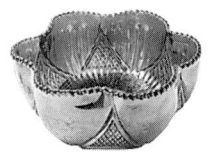

This curiously shaped six-inch bowl in amethyst has sold for $35 to $50. Marigold is probably worth somewhat less. Rosebowls in amethyst and marigold are known in three sizes: 5", 6" and 7".

Hobstar and Feather, Millersburg

Millersburg made a lot of this pattern in crystal, including quite a few shapes that don't exist in carnival. The sauce above is one of the few pieces of Hobstar and Feather known in white Carnival. Courtesy of Winnie Brim.

Bridge set piece (diamond)
Marigold   300 (1993)

Punch set, 16 piece
Marigold   2,600 (1993)   tiny base nicks
Punch set, 10 piece
Marigold   1,300–1,500   Fleur de Lis interior
Punch cup
Amethyst/purple   20–35
Green   70–100
Marigold   20–30
Rosebowl, giant (shown below)
Amethyst/purple 2,800–2,400
Green   1,800–3,000

Spittoon-shaped whimsey from rosebowl
Purple   4,000 (1995)   epoxy spot
Sauce
Amethyst   375 (1993)   5" round
Spooner (7 or 8 table set pieces known in total)
Green   825 (1994)   handled, elect iridescence

Hobstar Flower, Imperial

According to Glen and Stephen Thistlewood in their journal *Network*, Hobstar Flower is Imperial's #302, which is also found in a decanter or cruet identified sometimes as the Imperial pattern Crabclaw.

98 A Field Guide to Carnival Glass

Hobstar Flower compote, ruffled
Green	95–150	rare color
Green, emerald	550 (1998)	
Lavender, smoky	90–105	scarce color
Marigold	35–55	common color
Purple	95–150	common color

Hobstar and Fruit, Westmoreland

These small two-sides-up bowls are fairly scarce and, in some colors, bring a good price. Blue opal has also been reported, as well as a 10-inch bowl.

Banana dish or card tray shape, about 5"
Blue opal	200–300
Marigold	60–85
Marigold/milk	350 (1995) 775 (1998)
Peach opal	100–130

Bowl or sauce, 5", ruffled
Blue opal	190–250
Marigold	35–60
Peach opal	40–75

Hobstar Reversed

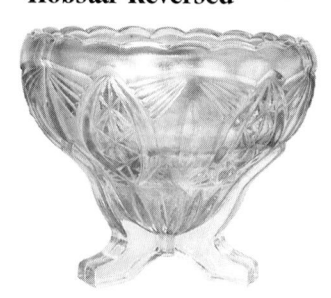

Quite an obscure pattern, this marigold rosebowl is one of the few pieces around. It sold for $60 at a 1998 Mickey Reichel auction. Note the peculiar slab-sided legs and feet on this piece. Also known in a celery vase.

Hobstar and Shield

I've not been able to determine who made this pitcher and tumbler. These marigold examples (the only color reported) were photographed at the time they sold at the 1994 John and Lucile Britt auction. The pitcher fetched $175, the tumbler $90. Another pitcher sold for $65 in 1996, tumblers have brought generally $65 to $85 but one sold for $375 in 1996.

Hobstar and Waffle Block, Imperial

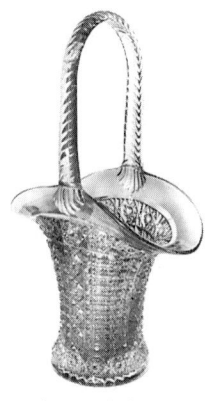

Aptly named, this pattern almost appears to be the better known Imperial Waffle Block pattern on which small hobstars have been applied.

Basket, giant, handled
Ice green	250 (1996)
Marigold	150–250
Smoke	225 (1993)
Teal	220 (1997)

Hoffman House

This red Hoffman House goblet with blue iridescence on the bowl brought $375 at the 1998 Heart of America club auction (Jim Seeck).

Holiday, Northwood

An atypical Northwood design, found only in the large tray and only in marigold. This one sold for $25 at the 1995 Lincoln-Land club auction.

Holly, Fenton

Another of those very popular patterns available in a variety of colors, if not many shapes. A good place to start a collection. The pattern is sometimes referred to as Carnival Holly. The above ruffled bowl, in marigold on moonstone, brought $1,100 at a 1995 John Woody auction. Fenton has also issued reproductions of this pattern.

Bowl, about 9", ruffled or three-in-one edge
Amber	115–175	scarce color
Amethyst	70–110	fairly common color
Amethyst, black	300 (1994)	
Amberina	350–450	rare color
Aqua	165–275	rare
Aqua opal, one ruffled known		
Blue	50–80	common color
Blue, powder	80–150	scarce color
Blue opal	1,500–2,500	or cobalt opal, rare color
Green	125–200	common color
Green	650 (1996)	exceptional iridescence
Ice green, one ruffled known		
Lavender	95 (1995)	
Lime	100–200	scarce color
Marigold	40–75	common color
Marigold	225 (1998)	flat, 3/1 edge
Mar/moonstone	650–1,000	rare color
Peach opal	2,150 (1995)	
Purple known, rare		
Red	700–1,300	relatively easy to find
Teal	100–200	scarce color
Vaseline	100–175	fairly common color
White	95–160	fairly common color

Bowl, ice cream shape or round
Amethyst	95–170	
Amethyst, black	95 (1995)	deep, round
Aqua	350 (1996)	
Blue	80–140	most common color
Celeste	2,200–3,000	rare color
Green	120 (1994)	
Ice blue	2,700 (1993)	
Ice green	2,150 (1995)	one known
Lime	140–170	scarce
Marigold	35–55	common color
Marigold/moonstone known, rare		
Vaseline	150–285	scarce color
White	495 (1997)	exceptional iridescence

Rosebowl, from bowl
Blue	150–225	
Marigold	85–120	
Vaseline known		

Plate, 9-10"
Amethyst	600–900	relatively common
Amethyst, black	1,000–1,800	rare color
Aqua opal, one known		
Blue	250–400	common color
Celeste known, rare		
Clambroth	140–250	scarce color
Green	600–800	relatively common
Marigold	150–250	most common color

Holly plates, continued
Red known, rare
Teal   1,000 (1996)
White   180–300   relatively common

Holly compotes are found with a variety of top treatments. The dark one at the back is considered the goblet shape. These are courtesy of Carl and Eunice Booker.

Compote
Amber	100–175	scarce color
Amethyst	50–80	scarce color
Amethyst, black	160 (1995)	ruffled
Aqua/teal	110–185	scarce color
Blue	45–90	common color
Green	110–200	scarce color
Lavender	80–150	scarce color
Lime	75–115	rare color
Lime opal	550–600	goblet shape
Marigold	35–60	most common color
Marigold	95 (1998)	candy ribbon edge
Pink	60–95	scarce color
Red	700–1,000	usually amberina base
Red opal	1,200–1,600	rare color
Vaseline	75–125	
Violet	175 (1996)	2 sides up
Yellow/green	115 (1994)	ruffled

In the Fenton Holly hat, the combination of red base glass and a crimped jack-in-the-pulpit edge treatment is fairly easily found. This one sold for $350 at the 1995 Texas club auction (Jim Seeck). A variation of the Holly hat shape is called Pepper Plant with the primary difference being a hexagonal base rather than round.

Hat, ruffled or crimped
Amber	50–70	scarce color
Amberina	225–300	rare color
Amethyst opal	310 (1997)	
Aqua	55–95	scarce color
Aqua opal	1,200 (1995)	
Blue	25–40	common color
Blue, smoky	65 (1996)	flattened out
Lavender opal	125 (1995)	
Marigold	15–25	
Moonstone	140 (1995)	
Red	275–450	common color
Vaseline	50–75	scarce color

Hat, two sides up
Aqua	45–70
Lime	65 (1997)
Marigold	90–125
Red	400–475
Vaseline	60 (1998)

Hat, jack-in-the-pulpit shape
Amber	50–80	
Amberina	275–325	
Aqua	200 (1994)	
Blue	40–65	fairly common color
Marigold	25–40	
Red	300–400	common color
Vaseline	65–125	
Violet	55 (1994)	

Hat, square or four-sided
Aqua	60–80
Blue	20–30
Marigold	25–40

Holly and Berry, Dugan

Sometimes called Dugan's Holly. The pattern has holly leaves around the outer edges and in the center. The single-handled nappy (above) is called a gravy boat if it has a well-defined spout.

Bowl, 7–8", ruffled
Amethyst/purple	80–150
Peach opal	45–75

Nappy, ruffled or tricorner
Amethyst/purple	60–90
Amethyst, black	50–80
Peach opal	45–75

Gravy boat (has spout)
Amethyst	70–105
Peach opal	40–75

Holly, Millersburg

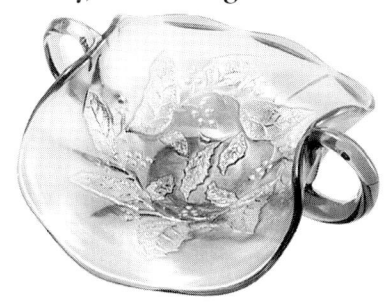

At one time collectors called this pattern Holly Sprig or Holly Whirl, depending on the size of the pattern. As the design is very much the same regardless of size, collectors now simply call it all Millersburg Holly. The pattern sometimes covers the center (but that's not enough to consider it a separate pattern). Bowls are usually more desirable than the more easily found bonbons or nappies. A rare rosebowl whimsey is known in marigold.

Bonbon
Amethyst   75–95
Green   60–85
Lavender   60–100
Marigold   25–45

Bonbon, card tray shape
Amethyst   65–115
Green   60–100   some with olive tint
Marigold   50–90

Card tray, Isaac Benesch advertising on back
Marigold   75–110

Compote, short-stemmed, crimped
Amethyst   1,300 (1998)

Sauce or small bowl, about 6"
Amethyst   210 (1994)   deep, round
Amethyst   125–190   tricorner
Green   100–180   tricorner
Green   85–150   crimped
Green   375 (1994)   square crimped, rare shape
Marigold   300–400   crimped

Bowl, 7–8"
Amethyst   90–170
Green   85–125   ruffled
Marigold   45–75   ruffled
Marigold   425 (1996)   deep round
Marigold var   100–180   8-point star center, ruffled

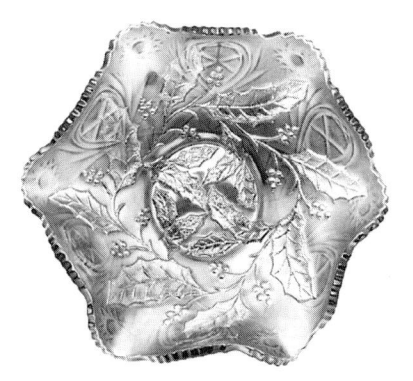

Large bowls are usually seen in this ruffled shape.

Bowl, large, 9–10"
Amethyst   170–270
Amethyst   280 (1996)   ice cream shape
Green   85–120
Green   120 (1997)   tight crimp
Marigold   90–150

The nappy is usually seen in this tricorner shape.

Nappy
Amethyst   75–125
Green   75–110
Marigold   60–95
Vaseline   1,600 (1998)

Holly and Poinsettia

Whether it's a ruffled bowl or a dome-footed compote, it's a very unusual piece. I originally photographed it at the 1993 American convention; Titus Hartley had found it at a nearby shop. John Britt, in writing about it later, named it for the floral elements around the exterior. Nobody knows who the maker might have been, but a guess is Dugan as it has the dome foot and a general Dugan "feel." It also looks a little like the Christmas Compote, although smaller.

Homestead, Imperial

These spectacular chop plates are sometimes signed with a NUART mark at the lower edge. Beware of reproductions. The exterior on the old plates is ribbed.

Chop plate, about 10½"

Amber	2,000–3,000	NUART
Blue	4,500–7,000	NUART
Emerald green	3,700–5,100	NUART
Green	2,700 (1996)	NUART
Green	2,500–3,900	
Green, forest	4,000 (1996)	NUART
Helios	475 (1995)	light iridescence
Helios	2,500 (1996)	not signed
Marigold	400–600	
Purple	1,200–1,500	NUART
Purple	1,000–1,800	not signed
Smoke	1,200–1,800	not signed
White	525 (1993)	NUART

Honeycomb, Dugan

This rosebowl was probably a package for honey in its original form. It is known only in peach opal and currently sells for $125 to $200.

Honeycomb

See also Golden Honeycomb

Honeycomb and Beads, Dugan

This pattern appears to be closely related to Dugan's Fishscale and Beads. This one has a more honeycomb-like pattern on the front and the addition of flowers along with the beads on the reverse. The example here, in amethyst, sold at a 1997 Mickey Reichel auction for $70. Plates in peach opal and purple sold at another 1997 Mickey Reichel auction for $105 and $130, respectively. Mickey also sold a ruffled peach opal bowl for $70 in 1998.

Honeycomb and Clover, Fenton

Honeycomb and Clover is seen on the backs of bonbons and plates; the interior is plain. A spooner is also known in marigold. The pattern was also used as the exterior for Fenton's Feathered Serpent and Pebbles patterns. It has been reported in compotes, but I suspect these may be the honeycomb exterior compotes called Golden Honeycomb. Green bonbons bring $20 to $40.

Horse Medallion, Fenton

The horse design on this pattern was based on the famous painting, Pharaoh's Horses, by John Frederick Herring. The pattern is also called

Horsehead Medallion. Shown are a typical plate and nut dish, which is a little more drawn up than the plain bowls and always round. Bowls are found in both collar base and footed versions.

Bowl, 7–8", ruffled, round, or ice cream shape
Amber	900–1,500	collar base
Amethyst	625 (1995)	collar base, ruffled
Blue	140–225	common color
Celeste blue	2,500 (1996)	ruffled
Green	200–350	common color
Marigold	60–100	most common color
Red	1,000–1,500	collar base
Vaseline	300 (1997)	round

Horse Medallion is one of the few patterns in which bowls are found in the jack-in-the-pulpit shape.

Bowl, jack-in-the-pulpit shape, footed
Amber	200–300	
Amethyst	140 (1994)	
Blue	125–200	common color
Green	350 (1998)	
Marigold	80–145	most common color
Vaseline	200–325	scarce color

Nut bowl, round
Amber	185 (1996)	
Blue	150–250	fairly common
Marigold	75–110	most common color
Red slag	1,100–1,600	fairly common
Red	1,900 (1998)	
Smoke	700 (1995)	
Vaseline	300–400	common color

Plate, 7–8"
Amethyst	4,000 (1994)	two known
Blue	900–1,600	
Blue, smoky	1,900 (1997)	
Green, two reported		
Marigold	200–350	most common color

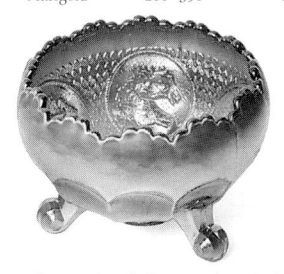

The rosebowl above is in red, the first one found—in 1995. It sold for $8,000. Shortly thereafter, another one came to light and sold for $9,000. One of these sold for $5,500 in 1998.

Rosebowl
Aqua	2,200 (1996)	
Blue	225–350	
Green, one known		
Marigold	125–175	most common color
Red	5,000–7,000	2 known
Vaseline	300–550	

Hudson, E.A., Furniture
See Lettered section

Illinois Daisy

In spite of its midwestern-sounding name, this covered jar is European in origin. They are marigold and usually sell in the $20 to $40 range.

Illusion, Fenton

Similar to several other Fenton bonbons except that the center design looks like a maze. Card tray-shaped bonbons are more scarce but not necessarily more valuable. Found in about equal numbers of marigold and blue.

Bonbon
Blue	55–85
Marigold	45–70

Imperial Daisy, Imperial
See Daisy, Imperial

Imperial Flute
See Flute, Imperial

Imperial Grape, Imperial

This was Imperial's response to Northwood's Grape and Cable and the line includes most of the common shapes found in carnival. There is no cable in this pattern, and there is one large grouping of grapes and leaves in the center of plates and bowls. The nine-inch low-ruffled bowl above is in electric blue (a very scarce color) and sold for $2,200 in 1994 and again in 1997 for $5,000.

Basket, handled, about 10" tall
Marigold	30–40
Smoke	40–70

Berry set, 5 piece
Purple	65–100

Berry set, 7 piece
Green	95–135

Bowl, small berry or sauce, 5–6"
Amber	20–35
Marigold	10–15
Purple	15–25

Bowl, small, 7"
Marigold	15–25
Purple	35–50

The nut bowl shape is seldom seen. This one is in Helios and is courtesy of Dennis and Denise Harp.

Bowl, 8–9"
Amber	35–60	
Blue, electric	2,200 (1994) 5,000 (1997)	low ruffled
Blue, pastel	75 (1997)	round
Clambroth	30–50	ruffled
Green	40–60	
Helios	15–30	
Lavender	85–100	ruffled
Marigold	20–35	common color
Olive	20–30	
Purple	55–90	most common color
Purple	300 (1996)	low ruffled
Smoke	20–35	

Bowl, large, 10–11"
Aqua/teal	100–170
Blue	250 (1993)
Marigold	20–35
Purple	90–170
Smoke	50–90

Plate, small, 6"
Amber	325 (1994)	
Blue, three or four known		
Green	50–90	
Helios	55–90	
Lavender	200–300	
Lime green	90–145	
Marigold	45–80	most common color
Olive	90 (1994)	
Purple	150–250	

Plate, 9"
Amber	600–1,000
Aqua	400 (1997)
Clambroth	50–80
Green	45–70
Lavender	170 (1994)
Marigold	50–80
Purple	1,700–3,000
Vaseline/lime	110 (1998)

Sandwich server or cookie tray
Marigold	15–25
Smoke	20–35

Although commonly known as a water carafe, this unstoppered piece, according to old ads, was really intended for use as a vase.

Carafe, water
Amber known, rare		
Amethyst/purple	125–200	most common color
Green	80–100	
Helios	85–105	
Marigold	55–70	
Smoke	600 (1997)	

Goblet, water
Amber	25–40
Green	10–20
Marigold	15–25
Purple	30–50

The compote has a threaded base and stem, much like the wine goblets.

Compote
Amber	30–50	
Aqua	160 (1996)	
Green	70–125	
Helios	45–70	
Lavender	85 (1998)	
Marigold	15–25	
Olive	60–90	
Purple	50–90	
Purple	235 (1998)	spectacular example
Smoke	50–90	

Cup and Saucer
Clambroth	20–35	
Green	40–60	
Helios	30–50	common color
Marigold	45–60	most common color

Punch bowl and base
Amber	525 (1993)	
Marigold	95–150	
Purple	2,000 (1997)	round

Punch base only
Marigold	30–45

Punch cup
Green	35–50
Marigold	10–15
Purple	20–35

Punch set, 8 or 9 pieces
Green	200–300
Marigold	160–220
Purple	1,200–2,000

Rosebowl
Amber   425 (1998)
Green and marigold also known, rare

There are a handful of these six-inch wide spittoons known, mostly in marigold, that were made from a bowl. The above example is green and is from the collection of Carl and Ferne Schroeder.

Water sets, along with several shapes, were reproduced by Imperial.

Water set, 7 piece
Green	250–350	
Marigold	140–220	most common color
Purple	400–600	
Smoke	450–500	

Pitcher, water
Amber	650 (1996)	
Aqua	400 (1996)	some buffing on base
Marigold	45–75	common color
Purple	200–350	common color
Purple	550 (1998)	blue iridescence
Smoke	225–350	scarce color
Violet	200–275	rare color

Tumbler
Amber known, rare
Aqua	50–90	rare color
Green	110–190	rare color
Helios	30–45	scarce color
Marigold	15–25	common color
Purple	45–60	most common color
Smoke	50–90	scarce color

106 A Field Guide to Carnival Glass

Wine sets are often found with an odd number of glasses. Base your purchasing decisions accordingly.

Imperial Grape wine set, 7 piece
Helios	175–225	
Green	165–225	
Marigold	125–175	most common color
Purple	250–350	

Decanter, wine, with stopper (unless indicated)
Green	70–100	
Marigold	50–80	common color
Marigold	20–30	no stopper
Purple	150–250	common color
Purple	35–50	no/cracked stopper
Smoke	150–250	rare color

Wine glasses
Clambroth	10–15	scarce color
Green	20–35	scarce color
Green, emerald	90–160	rare color
Helios	20–30	scarce color
Lavender	25 (1996)	
Lime	20–25	scarce color
Marigold	15–20	common color
Olive	25–35	scarce color
Purple	20–30	most common color

Imperial Jewels, Imperial

Imperial Jewels is more of a stretch glass than true carnival. Still, it often is found for sale at carnival venues so it's good to be aware of it. The creamer and sugar above (in red), courtesy of Carl and Eunice Booker, are typical of the line. Red sets, such as these, sold for $750 and $825 in 1998.

Bowl, 6¾" round
Amethyst	100 (1998)	Iron Cross mark

Candlesticks
Red	100–200

Plate
Amberina	45 (1994)

Rosebowl
Marigold	75 (1995)	square, Iron Cross mark
Purple	95 (1993)	pinched in

Hair receiver
Amethyst	75 (1996)

Vase
Amethyst/purple	45–75
Marigold	50–60

Imperial Rose, Imperial

You'll note that we've grouped Lustre Rose and Open Rose under this one name, Imperial Rose. While I'm normally opposed to changing the name conventions, I think it's warranted here as both Lustre and Open are essentially the same pattern and, as Carl O. Burns pointed out in his 1996 book on Imperial carnival, were shown with the same product numbers in old Imperial catalogs. I do, however, within these listings, include their conventional names

Berry set, 5–7 piece, collar base (Open Rose)
Green	40–70
Marigold	35–60

Bowl, small berry or sauce (Open Rose)
Blue	50–75
Blue violet	425 (1998)
Marigold	10–15
Smoke	20–35

Bowl, 7–9", collar base (Open Rose)
Amber	25–45
Blue	60–90
Clambroth	15–20
Lime	115 (1997)
Marigold	20–30
Purple	80–150
Smoke	40–75

Bowl, 9–10", footed (Lustre Rose)
Amber 25–40
Clambroth 20–35
Green 25–50
Lime 35–50
Marigold 20–40
Purple 45–80
Purple 140 (1998) electric iridescence

Note that the footed fruit bowls like that above were reproduced and should have the IG mark.

Bowl, fruit, 11–12", footed (Lustre Rose)
Aqua 190–250 rare color
Clambroth 20–45
Green 40–70
Marigold 30–55 most common color
Olive 90 (1996)
Purple 220 (1997) 1,800 (1998)
Red 1,500–2,500
Smoke reported

Plate, 9", collar base (Open Rose)
Amber 190–350 common color
Green 85–150 fairly common
Helios 95 (1998)
Lime green 180–200 scarce color
Marigold 70–125 most common color
Purple 1,500–2,000 rare color
Purple 2,000–3,000 outstanding examples

Fernery, footed (Lustre Rose)
Aqua 125–150
Clambroth 40 (1998)
Blue 75–125 relatively common color

Marigold 35–50 most common color
Olive/russet 40–60
Smoke 95 (1998)
Violet 235 (1996)

Centerpiece bowl (opened from fernery)
Amber 140–225
Purple 220 (1997)
Also known in marigold, helios, and smoke

Rosebowl (Open Rose)
Amber 35–55 most common color
Olive 135 (1996)
Purple 600 (1998)

Table set, 4 piece (Lustre Rose)
Marigold 115–200
Green 200–300
Purple 1,300–1,500

Butter dish
Amber 100–200
Marigold 50–75

Creamer
Marigold 30–45
Purple 75–140

Spooner
Purple 70–120

Sugar
Marigold 30–45

Water sets have been reproduced in several colors.

Water set, 5 piece (Lustre Rose)
Marigold 150–200
Purple 900–1,200

Water set, 7 piece
Green 130–150
Marigold 110–160

Pitcher, water
Amber 200 (1997)
Purple 950 (1998) electric blue iridescence

This flared whimsey, made from an amber tumbler, sold for $500 at the 1995 Lincoln-Land auction.

Tumbler
Amber   160 (1993)
Green   35 (1994)
Marigold   10–15
Olive   15 (1998)   base damage
Purple   55–85   most common color

Intaglio Daisy

This pattern, with incised flowers around the exterior, is also known in bowls.

Rosebowl
Marigold   60–100

Intaglio Flower, Westmoreland

This miniature flared plate was sold at a 1993 Tom Burns auction for $500. It is peach opal and just over four inches in diameter. The intaglio floral design is on the back, the interior is plain.

Almond cup, stemmed
Marigold   350 (1996)
Basket, 4-sided, wire handle
Peach opal 80–110
Bowl, 3", 4 ruffles
Peach opal 250 (1995)

Interior Poinsettia, Northwood

The poinsettia pattern is only on the inside. No carnival pitchers have been reported.

Tumbler
Marigold   150–250

Interior Swirl, Northwood
See Swirl

Inverted Coin Dot, Fenton

This pattern is often identified as regular Coin Dot or as Westmoreland's Pearly Dots. In bowls and plates, stippled dots mean it's Fenton. If the dots are smooth, it's Westmoreland. The inverted Coin Dot pattern, with smooth dots, however, is usually credited to Fenton. A small ruffled compote with smooth dots, sometimes identified as Inverted Coin Dot, is most likely from Westmoreland.

Water set, 5 piece
Marigold   375 (1997)
Pitcher, water
Aqua   500 (1995)   vary rare color
Marigold   40–60

Tumbler
Marigold   25–40

Inverted Feather, Cambridge

Most of these cracker jars are green but purple has also been reported. In addition to the shapes listed below, there is one known marigold milk pitcher, one marigold water pitcher, and table sets in amethyst/purple and marigold. Tumblers and cordials are also known. Some pieces marked Near Cut.

Cracker jar
Green   140–225

Above is a whimsey bonbon made from a green spooner. It was discovered by Owen Loudon in 1993 and sold at a 1996 Tom Burns auction for $2,750. Thought to be the only one.

Creamer
Amethyst   160–275
Marigold   55–70
Spooner
Amethyst   300–450

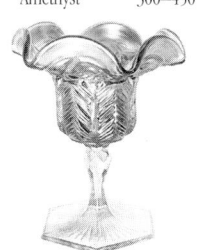

Parfait or compote (most available shape in pattern)
Marigold   45–60
Wine glass
Marigold   450 (1995)
Powder jar
Green   205 (1997)   rim roughness
Marigold   275 (1997)

Cordial
Marigold   500 (1998)

Punch set, 8 piece
Known in green
Marigold   1,500–2,500
Punch cup
Marigold   30–45

Inverted Feather and Fan, Dugan

This is an exterior pattern used on the Butterfly and Tulip and Grape Arbor bowls. Toothpicks and other shapes with this pattern are probably contemporary.

Inverted Honeycomb, US Glass

A strange piece with an unusual handle. This milk pitcher with a very washed out marigold iridescence got little attention at its 1993 auction. Consequently, it brought only $5.

Inverted Strawberry, Cambridge

Inverted Strawberry was one of Cambridge's most popular carnival patterns and was made in a wide range of shapes and—for Cambridge—colors. Many pieces are marked with Cambridge's trademark, Near Cut.

110 A Field Guide to Carnival Glass

Berry set, 7 pieces
Amethyst   200–250
Also known in green and marigold

Bowl, about 7"
Blue   250 (1993)
Green   40–70

Bowl, 10½", signed Near Cut
Amethyst/purple   225 (1998)
Green   145 (1998)   ruffled

Some collectors consider this a large rosebowl, others just a turned-in centerpiece bowl. Regardless of how it's described, this amethyst example sold for $200 at a 1995 auction. Another sold for $700 at the 1997 Lincoln-Land club auction. The pieces are about 8½ inches wide with a 7-inch opening and were probably made from the 10½" bowl.

Breakfast set, pedestalled
Amethyst   750 (1995)
Known in blue

Inverted Strawberry candlesticks are very desirable. This marigold pair is courtesy of Bruce Hill.

Candlesticks, pair
Green   1,000–1,500
Marigold   300–400

Candlestick, single
Green   325–500
Marigold   90–125

Celery vase
Blue   850 (1994)
Green   750–950
Purple   350 (1998)

All compotes in Inverted Strawberry are hard to find, and the smaller example above, in blue, is one of two known in that color. The larger is amethyst. There is also a tall compote, 6" high and 5" wide.

Compote
Amethyst   375 (1993)   large, manufacturing flaw
Blue   2,700 (1993)   small, 4" diameter
Marigold   275–350   large, most common color
Marigold   450 (1998)   small
Purple   195 (1996)   large

Rare and highly prized, the spittoon was probably made from a small bowl. They measure about five inches wide. Such pieces are not true whimsies as they were made in considerable quantities.

Spittoon or cuspidor
Known in amethyst
Green   800–1,500
Marigold   700–1,000

There are very few of these large spittoon-shaped whimsey bowls made from the large berry. This amethyst example sold at the 1997 Lincoln-Land convention auction for $700.

Like many pieces in the Inverted Strawberry pattern, the eight-inch milk pitcher is very rare. There are few examples known, all purple.

Milk pitcher
Purple   5,750 (1996)

Water set, 7 piece
Amethyst   3,600 (1995)

Water pitcher (has been reproduced)
Green   1,600 (1993)
Purple   1,900 (1996)

Tumbler (has been reproduced)
Amethyst/purple 100–180
Green   110–200
Marigold   90–150

Powder jar
Green   200–350
Marigold   150–275

Table set, 4 piece
Known in blue
Green   800–1,000
Marigold   1,050 (1995)
Purple   2,800 (1995)   wrong butter bottom

Butter dish
Marigold   500–900

Creamer
Amethyst   180 (1997)
Green   400 (1996)
Marigold   350–450

Spooner, 2-handled
Amethyst/purple 120–180
Marigold   60–100

Bonbon, whimsey from spooner
Green   1,600 (1998)

Inverted Thistle, Cambridge

This pattern is not seen as often as Cambridge's companion pattern, Inverted Strawberry, with about one-quarter the number of items selling over the last five years as that of Inverted Strawberry.

Bowl, large berry
Amethyst   90–140
Known in green

Small berry
Known in amethyst and green

Chop plate, 11"
Known in amethyst

Water pitcher
Known in marigold, rare
Purple   1,300–2,000

Water set
Purple   1,200 (1996)

Tumbler (see page 183 for photo)
Amethyst/purple 150–250

Milk pitcher
Known in green, rare

Compote, 8" tall
Known in green

Table sets, 4 piece
Known in amethyst, green and marigold

Creamer
Amethyst   65 (1997)   225 (1995)

Spooner, 2 handles
Amethyst   225–300
Green   100–200

112 A Field Guide to Carnival Glass

Sugar, covered
Amethyst   205–325
Green   85 (1993)
Sugar and spooner
Purple   500 (1995)

Iris, Fenton

The Iris buttermilk goblet has the flower inside the bowl of the goblet. It was cupped up from a shape that was somewhat flatter so it could be gotten out of the mold. The same shape was also used to make the ruffled compote, below.

Buttermilk goblet
Amethyst   40–75
Green   55–85
Marigold   35–50   most common color

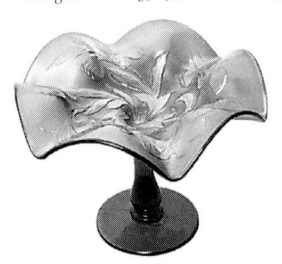

The compote, always ruffled, is found in about equal amounts of amethyst, blue, green and marigold.

Compote
Amethyst   75–100
Blue   90–160
Green   75–100
Marigold   35–70
White   300–500   rare color

Jacobean Ranger, Inwald

Jacobean Ranger is thought to have been made by the Josef Inwald Company of Czechoslovakia according to Glen and Stephen Thistlewood in their journal, *Network*. There were apparently dozens of shapes available. The oblong pitcher above is one of two that have sold in recent years; one bringing $600 in 1994, the other $275 in 1996. This pattern is often confused with a similar one from Australia called Blocks and Arches.

Tumbler
Marigold   55 (1997)
Juice glass
Marigold   60–100
Shot glass
Marigold   100–150
Creamer
Marigold   15–20

This grouping of Ranger pieces includes a tumbleup (leftmost), cologne bottle, ring dish, perfume, pin tray and covered jars. Courtesy of Joyce Seale.

Cologne bottle
Marigold   60–75
Covered jar
Marigold   90–110
Perfume bottle
Marigold   145–225
Pin tray
Marigold   60–100

Jacob's Ladder, US Glass

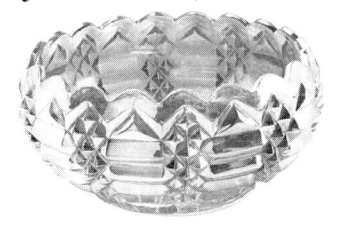

The design is comprised of alternating sections of small diamonds and horizontal prisms. They're pretty rare and always in marigold. This one sold in 1994 for $375, another brought $220 in 1998.

Jewelled Heart, Dugan

Jewelled Heart is an old pattern, predating Carnival. It was originally called Victor. All pieces in the pattern are rare, with the tumbler perhaps being seen most often. It is the exterior pattern found on many Dugan bowls.

Basket, handled, whimsey, applied handle
Peach opal   625–725   crimped, rib interior
Bowl, 6"
Peach opal   35–50   ruffled
Peach opal   50 (1995)   tricorner, candy ribbon edge
Bowl, large, about 11"
Peach opal   85–145   ruffled, rayed interior
Plate, 6", pattern on exterior only
Amethyst/purple   100–150
Peach opal   125–160

Pitcher, water
Marigold   425 (1994)
Water set, 5 piece
Marigold   950 (1993)
Tumbler (see page 181)
Marigold   75–110
White, rare

Jockey Club
See Lettered section

Kings Crown, Westmoreland

Found in a wide range of shapes in crystal, ruby-stained and amber-stained glass, but few known in carnival. This 3½" tall marigold cordial, is from the John and Lucile Britt collection.

Goblet
Marigold   10–25
Wine glass
Marigold   35–60

Kittens, Fenton

Although there is no shortage of Kittens pieces, they continue to be highly popular and very desirable. Above are most of the shapes seen in the pattern. Shown are a cup and saucer, a cereal bowl, a banana dish (or card tray), a toothpick holder, a six-ruffled bowl, and a flat plate. Amethyst is a rare color for Kittens, blue difficult to find. Most pieces have four sets of kittens; some just two sets.

Banana dish, card tray, or two-sides up dish
Amethyst   600 (1997)
Blue   300–475   scarce color
Blue, powder   250–400   very scarce color
Marigold   125–200   most common color
Vaseline   175 (1996)
Bowl, six ruffles, about 4½"
Blue   200–350   scarce color
Marigold   100–175   most common color
Bowl, four ruffles or sides
Amethyst   175–325   rare color
Aqua   425 (1994)
Blue   250–450   scarce color
Marigold   100–150   most common color
Vaseline   225 (1997)
Bowl, cereal, round, about 3½"
Amethyst, light   105 (1994)   heat check, base
Blue   300–500   scarce color
Marigold   125–200   most common color

114 A Field Guide to Carnival Glass

Cup and saucer
Amethyst opal   500 (1998)   not iridized
Blue   1,000–1,500 rare color
Marigold   125–225

Cup only
Blue   425–550
Marigold 85–150

Saucer only
Marigold 125–205

Plate, about 4½", round
Amethyst   400–700
Blue, powder   200–350
Marigold   150–250
Marigold, dark 600 (1995)   very flat

Toothpick holder, 2–2½" tall (fairly common)
Blue   250–400
Marigold 125–200

Vase, about 3" tall
Blue   225–400
Marigold 145–255

Three Kittens spittoon whimsies are known. These purple and marigold examples are from the Rinehart collection.

Knotted Beads
See Vase section

Kokomo

This unusual example of the Kokomo rosebowl came complete with a flower form that fits perfectly into the top. Courtesy of Bill and Sharon Mizell.

Marigold rosebowls without the frog sell in the $40 to $60 range.

Lacy Dewdrop, Phoenix

The rare Lacy Dewdrop pattern is only found in pearlized milk glass. This compote, shown upside down, is courtesy of Lee Markley.

Bowl, covered, large
Pearlized milk   165 (1993)

Cake plate
Pearlized milk   150–200

Compote, covered
Pearlized milk   150–250

Creamer
Pearlized milk   225–375

Sugar, covered
Pearlized milk   200–325

Water set, 7 piece
Pearlized milk   1,250 (1995)

Lamps
See Lamps and shades section

Lattice and Daisy, Dugan

Another lattice water set, this one with daisies and with the design in relatively low relief.

Water pitcher, tankard style
Amethyst   1,000–1,200
Marigold   125–175

K-L 115

Water set, 7 piece
Also known in amethyst and blue
Marigold   175–300
Tumbler (see page 181 for photo)
Amethyst   65 (1997)
Blue   40–70
Marigold   10–15

Lattice and Grape, Fenton

Sometimes confused with Dugan's Grapevine Lattice because of the similar name and design.

Water pitcher, tankard style
Blue   300–525
Marigold   125–200
White   350 (1994)

Water set, 5 or 6 pieces
Blue   300–500
Marigold   120–225

Water set, 7 piece
Blue   500–700
Marigold   150–250

Tumbler (see page 181 for photo)
Blue   35–60
Marigold   20–35
White   180–225

The Lattice and Grape whimsey, above, was made from a marigold tumbler and is the only one known. It is in the Rinehart collection.

Lattice Heart, Dugan

Because the design is only on the exterior there is generally little interest in this pattern—in spite of its rarity. This is the only example I have seen; it is purple and sold in 1993 for $70. One sold in a 1994 auction for $150; another in 1998 for $140.

Lattice and Poinsettia
See Poinsettia and Lattice

Lattice and Points, Dugan

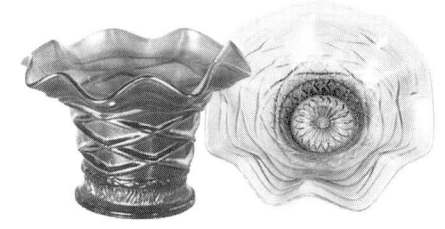

Lattice and Points is found in a variety of small bowls and hat shapes as well as vases—all made from the same mold. Some have a daisy in the interior bottom. This pattern is sometimes called Vining Twigs. There are a few plates.

Bowl, from hat mold
Marigold   10–20
Purple   30–50
White   35–50

Hat
Marigold   25–40
Peach opal   30–45
Purple   290 (1998)   7" diameter, low ruffled
White   45–85

Vase
Blue   80–100   scarce color
Marigold   25–45   common color
Purple   100–150   scarce color
White   70–90   scarce color

Laurel Band

Probably made in the Depression era or later. Tumblers appear to be aqua when the base is viewed from the side. The maker is unknown.

Water set, 7 piece
Marigold 110–130
Water pitcher
Marigold 40 (1998)
Tumbler
Marigold 50–85

Lea, Sowerby

Typical of European sets, the sugar is substantially larger than the creamer. Either piece is valued between $15 and $25; a set $35 or so. The Lea pattern was an extensive line of tableware.

Leaf and Beads, Northwood

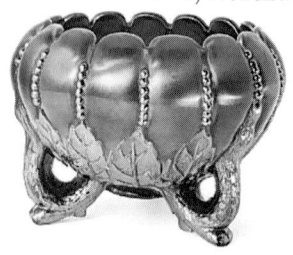

This rosebowl is the typical configuration of the Leaf and Beads pattern. Most have a plain or rayed interior, some a sunflower design—which is slightly more desirable. A few are found with a sawtooth edge rather than the scalloped edge. Even more rare are those with a smooth top. Aqua opal is a common color in the rosebowl, rare in the nut bowl shape.

Rosebowl, plain or rayed interior
Amethyst/purple	95–150	
Aqua	275 (1997)	
Aqua opal	225–350	butterscotch iridescence
Aqua opal	300–500	pastel iridescence
Blue	140–200	common color
Blue, electric	300–450	
Blue, Renninger	575 (1997)	
Blue, sapphire	350–425	rare color
Green	115–165	
Ice blue	1,000–1,600	rare color
Ice blue opal	1,400 (1993)	
Ice green	900–1,200	rare color
Ice green opal	2,800–3,000	rare color
Lavender	600–900	scarce color
Marigold	75–100	common color
Sapphire	275 (1998)	
White	300–500	

Rosebowl, sunflower interior
Amethyst/purple	100–200
Aqua/teal	1,200 (1997)
Blue, sapphire	1,500 (1996)
Green	100–175
Marigold	60–90

Rosebowl, smooth edge
Amethyst/purple	200–250	
Custard	300–400	pearlized
Lavender	185 (1997)	
Marigold	150–200	

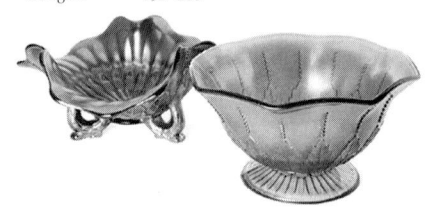

Northwood opened the rosebowl to make a candy dish. The one shown on the left is also a tricorner and extremely ruffled. The nut dish on the right has an unusual dome foot.

Candy dish or nut bowl (some tricorner)
Amethyst/purple	80–150	
Aqua opal	800 (1998)	
Blue	450 (1998)	
Green	35–55	plain or rayed interior
Green	60–100	Sunflower interior
Marigold	25–40	plain or rayed interior
Marigold	50–80	Sunflower interior
White	300–400	

Plate, flattened from nut bowl
Green 115 (1998)

Leaf Chain, Fenton

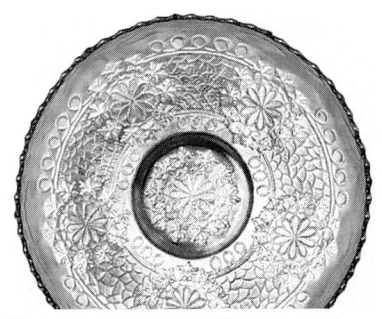

This is the same chain motif as Fenton's Cherry Chain, but if it doesn't have cherries, it's the Leaf Chain. The rarest color in the pattern is an aqua opal plate. Red bowls are fairly common but still desirable. Small plates and bowls have the Berry and Leaf Circle back; the large bowls and plates the Bearded Berry back.

Bowl, about 7", ruffled, round, or ice cream shape
Amethyst	100–150	scarce color
Aqua	75–130	relatively common
Blue	60–90	common color
Clambroth	40 (1998)	
Green	75–110	scarce color
Lavender	50–100	scarce color
Marigold	20–35	most common color
Red	600–1,000	fairly common color
Vaseline	100–200	scarce color
White	70–110	fairly common color

Bowl, about 9", ruffled or ice cream shape (scarce size)
Amethyst known		
Amberina	1,300 (1995)	chipped
Aqua opal known		
Blue	50–90	
Green	40–65	
Ice green	2,500–3,500	rare color
Marigold	40–60	
Red known		
White	70–90	

Plate, small, about 7"
Blue	85–145	
Marigold	90–175	most common color

Plate, 9"
Amethyst	6,000 (1994)	two known
Blue	600–900	
Clambroth	150–250	common color
Green	200–350	common color
Green, emerald	300–500	scarce color variant
Marigold	400–700	most common color
Marigold	950 (1998)	spectacular iridescence
White	150–250	relatively common color

Leaf Columns
See Vases

Leaf and Little Flowers, Millersburg

The Leaf and Little Flowers compote is quite small, only about three inches high and four inches wide. Most are ruffled as shown; others a sherbert shape.
Compote
Amethyst	350–450
Green	350–450
Marigold	250–350

Leaf Rays, Dugan

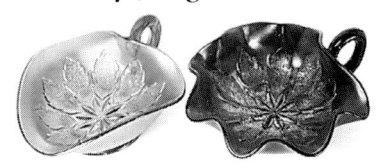

One of the most common patterns, yet often attractive. Usually found in the tricorner or spade shape; the other shapes are more desirable.
Nappy
Amethyst/purple	40–70	
Amethyst, black	60–80	
Lavender	45–60	
Lavender	170 (1998)	7 ruffles
Marigold	15–25	
Peach opal	25–40	
White	30–60	

Leaf Swirl, Westmoreland

Known only in a smallish compote with the pattern on the exterior.
Compote
Amber	40–60
Amber, yellowish	50–90
Amethyst	45–60
Aqua/teal	90–140

Leaf Tiers, Fenton

A satisfying design with an overall pattern of vertical leaves. Too bad Fenton didn't make it in more shapes and colors. There are two pitchers known in blue, one with a foot glued on. A rarity in this pattern is a spittoon whimsey made from a tumbler. There's one known, in marigold, and is in the collection of Floyd and Cecil Whitley. All shapes are rare with the exception of the marigold tumbler. The pattern was also used on lamp shades (see Lamps and Shades section).

Pitcher, water
Marigold   600 (1994)
Tumbler
Blue   500–600
Marigold   70–110   most common
Berry set
Marigold known
Table set, 4 piece
Marigold   580 (1995)
Butter dish
Marigold   150 (1994)

Lightning Flower, Northwood

Until a couple of years ago this was considered a very rare and desirable piece. Recently, however, several nappies have come on the market and have brought steadily declining prices. There is also a ruffled bowl known in marigold with a pattern only on the exterior. All known nappies are marigold and currently sell in the $100 to $150 range.

Lily of the Valley, Fenton

Another rare pattern, found only in blue pitchers and tumblers. There are about a dozen reported pitchers in blue; the only reported marigold pitcher was destroyed in a California earthquake.

Pitcher, water
Blue   6,000 (1995)

Lily of the Valley tumblers are very similar to Fenton's Strawberry Scroll tumblers and have the same band around the middle.

Tumbler
Blue   200–300
Marigold   325 (1998)

Lined Lattice
See Vases section

Lions, Fenton

Like Fenton's Panther pattern, Lions pieces display prowling cats. These, however, are clearly lions and there are four rather than two among the foliage. Blue and marigold are the only colors known. The exterior pattern is Berry and Leaf Circle. The pattern has been reproduced by Fenton in a bowl with the Fenton's Flowers exterior.

Bowl, 6–7", ruffled, round or ice cream shape
Blue   250–350
Blue, powder   115–170
Marigold   70–125

Plate, 7–8"
Marigold   600–1,000

Little Barrel
See Novelties/miniatures

Little Beads, Westmoreland

These compotes are rather small, measuring about 5½" across. A single line of beads circles the 8-fluted underside while the interior is plain. Sometimes confused with Beaded Panels, but that is an entirely different pattern. Amber and teal sell in the $15 to $25 range. A rare whimsey plate in amethyst sold in 1994 for $55.

Little Bo Peep
See Bo Peep

Little Daisies, Fenton

Little Daisies is a rather rare Fenton pattern with a circle of daisies surrounding a beaded center. The daisies look almost like fireworks against the sky. Marigold bowls have sold for $900 to $1,100 lately; no blue bowls have sold in recent years.

Little Fishes, Fenton

This pattern is reminiscent of another Fenton design, Coral. In this case, however, it is a band of fishes that circles between the decorative borders. Most pieces have three ball-shaped feet but some sauces are found with a collar base. There is one reported 11" chop plate in marigold with electric blue iridescence—supposedly one of the most spectacular pieces of carnival known.

Bowl, 9-10", ruffled or ice cream shape
Blue   350–500
Ice green   7,500 (1995)   only one known
Marigold   135–200

Sauce, 5–6"
Amethyst   100–150
Aqua   190–260
Blue   125–200
Marigold   50–90

Little Flowers, Fenton

The pattern is rather hard to remember, but if you visualize the little flowers nestled among the trees it may help. Found only in two sizes of bowls and plates made from the bowl molds.

Berry set, 7 piece
Amethyst   205 (1998)

Bowl, large, about 10", ruffled, three-in-one edge, or ice cream shape
Amethyst   75–130
Amberina   900–1,200

120 A Field Guide to Carnival Glass

Little Flowers large bowls, continued
Aqua   70 (1997)
Blue   85–150
Green   80–130
Marigold   40–65
Red   3,000–4,500

Bowl, small berry or sauce, 5–6"
Amethyst   25–40
Amethyst   150 (1996)   tricorner
Aqua   75–125
Blue   35–60
Marigold   20–30

Chop plate, 10¼"
Marigold   500   1,550 (1995)   2,800 (1997)

Plate, 6–7"
Blue, powder   230 (1996)   marigold iridescence
Marigold   110–145   whimsey—4 sides up
Marigold   150–250

Little Stars, Millersburg

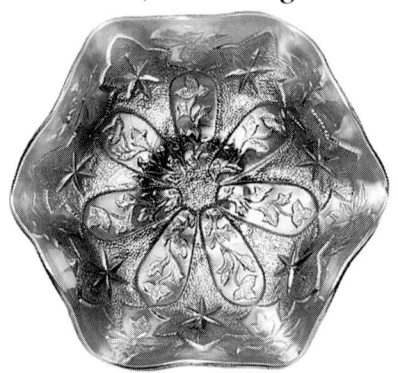

Not to be confused with another Millersburg pattern, Many Stars. The stars here are very slender six-pointed ones outside a seven-petal design radiating from the center. Mostly found in ruffled seven-inch bowls but also in two larger sizes and a rare sauce.

Sauce
Amethyst   600–800
Blue and green known

Bowl, 7–8"
Amethyst   200–300
Blue   3,000 (1995)   nick on base, ruffled
Green   150–250   ruffled
Green   300–450   ice cream shape
Marigold   100–175   ruffled
Marigold   500 (1996)   3/1 edge

Bowl, about 9"
Green known
Marigold   250–400   ice cream shape
Marigold   375–450   ruffled
Marigold   650 (1998) ice cream shape, exceptional

Bowl, 10"
Blue, green and marigold known

Loganberry
See Vases section

Long Hobstar, Imperial

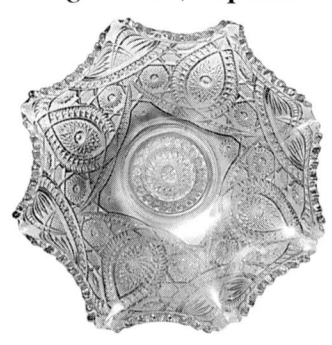

The name is derived from hobstars in pointed oval shapes. Not to be confused with Imperial's similar Diamond Rings which do not have hobstars but have larger diamonds at intersection of the pointed oval.

Fruit bowl, 11", ruffled
Marigold   30–45
Purple   250 (1992)   rare color

Long Thumbprint, Dugan

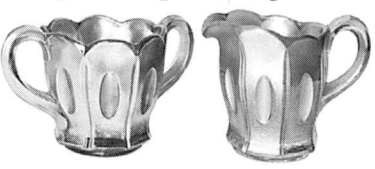

Breakfast set (sugar and creamer)
Marigold   15–25

Long Thumbprint, Fenton
See Vases section

Loop
See O'Hara

Lotus and Grape, Fenton

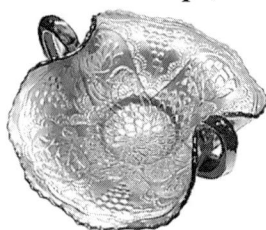

Lotus and Grape is another of Fenton's panelled designs with dual themes. The name is very appropriate as there are both lotus blossoms and grape bunches. The rarity in this pattern is a ruffled bowl lacking the grapes. It has not sold at auction in recent years although one with enameled flowers rather than the grapes has (see photo, next column).

Bonbon or 2-handled card tray shape
Amethyst	80–125	scarce color
Aqua	300–400	rare color
Blue	65–95	most common color
Green	85–145	common color
Marigold	20–35	common color
Red	350–600	fairly common
Red slag	650–900	fairly common
Teal	175–225	rare color
Vaseline	125–200	scarce color

Bowl, small, 5–6", footed
Amethyst	50–70	scarce color
Blue	35–50	
Green	150–200	scarce color
Marigold	20–30	most common
Vaseline	300–500	

Bowl, 7–8", some footed, some collar based
Amethyst	45–65	
Blue	75–140	
Blue, Persian	450–700	ice cream shape, rare
Green	120–180	
Marigold	35–50	
Marigold	125 (1998)	3/1 edge (rare shape)
Teal	375 (1996)	
Vaseline	70–125	

Bowl, about 9"
Blue	100–140
Green	125–200
Marigold	60–80

Lotus and Grape plates in any color are highly prized. The example above, in green, sold for $1,500 at a 1994 auction.

Plate, 9"
Amethyst	2,300–3,000
Blue	1,300–2,000
Green	1,800–2,500

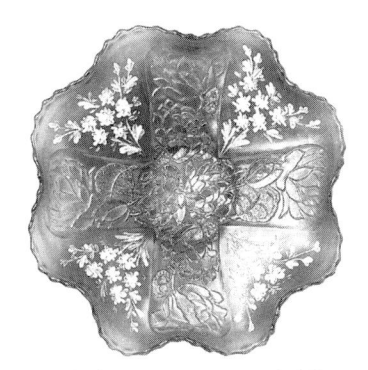

Bowl, absentee grape, enameled flowers instead, two known
Blue   1,450 (1993)

The rosebowl whimsey is very rare. This marigold example sold for $400 in 1998.

Lotus and Poinsettia
See Water Lily

Lotus Land, Northwood

The Lotus Land pattern is very rare and found only in bonbons. The only known marigold example changed hands for $1,400 at the 1992 Heart of America club auction. An amethyst example brought $850 at a 1998 Tom Burns auction. This amethyst bonbon above is from the collection of Floyd and Cecil Whitley.

Lotus and Thistle, Fenton

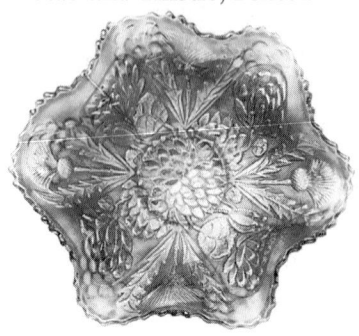

Despite their rarity, pieces in this pattern don't get much attention when they come up for sale. Marigold bowls, either ruffled or ice cream shape, bring $70 to $100 as a rule.

Louisa, Westmoreland

The rosebowl is the most frequently seen shape in the Louisa pattern. The low relief of the design relegates the pattern to the lower part of the pecking order. Still, unusual colors can bring good prices and in 1997 the first known example in marigold on milk glass sold for $450. Reproduced by Jeanette in 1950s (Floragold) but not in these shapes.

Rosebowl, three ball feet
Amber	70–90	
Amethyst	25–45	
Blue	80 (1993)	
Green	35–60	most common color
Horehound	95 (1996)	
Lavender	100–135	scarce color
Mar/milk glass	450 (1997)	first one reported
Teal	65–80	common color
Vaseline	100 (1996)	

Bowl, about 9", footed
Aqua/teal   25–40

Nut bowl (opened out rosebowl)
Amethyst   25–45
Green   40–60
Teal   210 (1998)

Plate, footed
Marigold   20–40
Teal   30–50

These charming little sauces have the pattern on the interior—in contrast to the better known rosebowl.

Sauce, footed, oval
Amethyst   35–50
Aqua/teal   40–70

Lovely, Northwood

Most of these rare bowls are flared like the one above, but a few are ruffled into a tricorner shape.

Bowl, Leaf and Beads exterior, flared
Green	700–1,000	
Purple	550 (1994)	flared
Purple	1,000–1,200	tricorner

Lucile

This pattern was named for Lucile Britt. US Glass offered a very similar pattern but collectors think the carnival examples were made by Brockwitz of Germany.

Water set, 7 piece
Blue   900 (1996)

Pitcher
Blue   400–500

Tumbler
Blue   175–235

Lustre and Clear, Imperial

This little creamer and sugar show the usual shapes seen in Lustre and Clear. They are shown in old Imperial catalogs along with other shapes.

Breakfast set (creamer and sugar)
Marigold   10–15
Candlesticks, pair, bell-shaped
Red   150–250
Plate
Clambroth   10 (1997)   9"
Marigold   25 (1997)   7"
Relish dish
Amethyst, black 80 (1998)
Marigold   3 (1997)

Lustre Flute, Northwood

An early Northwood pattern, produced extensively in crystal and opalescent. A limited number of shapes were made in Northwood's early carnival colors — marigold, purple and green with Alaskan iridescence.

Breakfast set (sugar and creamer)
Green   25–40
Punch cup
Purple   10–15
Hat
Amethyst/purple 10–15
Amethyst   60 (1995)   with silverplate carrier
Green   15–25

Lustre Rose
See Imperial Rose

Majestic, McKee

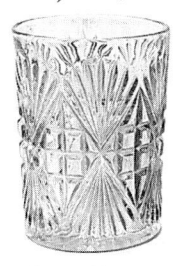

This tumbler pattern has a double-fan design separated by quartered blocks. There is a 24-point star in the base. Extremely rare. This marigold example sold in 1994 for $250—in 1998 for $375.

Malaga, Dugan

Dugan's Malaga pattern is quite hard to find. The pattern has a large group of grapes and leaves in the center with the outer part and edges plain. The rosebowl above, from the collection of Carl and Eunice Booker, is extremely rare. A deep, round bowl in amethyst sold in 1996 for $90 and a six-ruffled marigold bowl at a 1998 auction for $30.

Many Fruits, Dugan

Many Fruits, found only in punch set pieces, uses grapes and peaches on the exterior of the punch bowl with cherries on the inside. Some bowls are ruffled, as are some bases. Bases have the cherry part of the pattern; cups just the grapes and leaves.

Punch set, 7 piece
Blue   950 (1995)
Punch set, 8 piece
Marigold   300–450
Purple   600–900
White   2,400 (1997)
Punch bowl and base
Purple   375–500
White   925 (1995)
Punch cup
Marigold   40–60
Purple   25–40

Many Stars, Millersburg

The Many Stars pattern is found with either a five-pointed or six-pointed star in the center. Ruffled amethyst bowls with the six-pointed star are the most frequently seen combination. Marigold is surprisingly scarce in any shape; vaseline is rare. Trefoil Fine Cut is the exterior pattern. Many Stars was used as the basis for the Bernheimer Bros. advertising bowl. See Lettered section.

Bowl, 9–10"

Amethyst	450–700	ruffled
Amethyst	700–1,000	3/1 edge
Amethyst	1,000–1,500	ice cream shape
Amethyst	2,700 (1996)	tricorner
Amethyst	1,400 (1996)	7⅞", deep, round
Blue	2,700 (1994)	ruffled
Green	450–600	ruffled
Green	900–1,200	ice cream shape
Green	625 (1993)	3/1 edge
Marigold	325–500	ruffled
Marigold	350–500	3/1 edge

This rare, square-crimped six-pointed star version in amethyst sold for $6,500 at the 1994 John and Lucile Britt auction (Jim Seeck).

Chop plate (only one known)
Marigold   4,750 (1996)   2⅛ inch high

Maple Leaf, Dugan

Maple Leaf has a background pattern similar to Soda Gold. Note that on the bowls the leaves form the stem, rather than embellish the sides. Some bowls have a peacock tail-style interior.

Berry set, 7 piece
Amethyst/purple   80–105
Marigold   50–90

Bowl, large berry
Amethyst/purple   60–90
Marigold   40–70

Bowl, small berry
Amethyst/purple   15–25
Marigold   10–15

Table set, 4 piece
Amethyst/purple   300–425
Blue   190 (1998)   nicks, amethyst sugar lid
Marigold   165–225

Butter dish
Blue   150–250

Creamer
Amethyst/purple   35–50
Amethyst, black   60 (1998)
Blue   50–80   scarce color
Marigold   25–40

Spooner
Amethyst/purple   40–75
Blue   60–100   scarce color
Marigold   25–45

Sugar
Amethyst/purple   40–70
Blue   60–90   scarce color
Marigold   25–40

Water set, 7 piece
Amethyst/purple   225–350
Marigold   200–250

Pitcher, water
Amethyst/purple   200–300
Marigold   70–100

Tumbler (see page 181 for color photo)
Amethyst/purple 30–45
Blue 50–75 scarce color
Marigold 10–15

Marilyn, Millersburg

Not a widely known pattern, except among Millersburg collectors, probably because there are so few examples.

Pitcher
Amethyst 500–650 most common color
Green 1,000 (1997)
Marigold 500–600
Purple 375–475

Tumbler (see page 183)
Amethyst 100–185 most common color
Green 250–300
Marigold 125–200 scarce color

Mary Ann, Dugan

Found in two versions. The one referred to as a loving cup has three handles (shown above) and is quite rare. The other is similar but has only two handles and is called a vase.

Loving cup, 3 handles
Marigold 400–700

Vase, 2 handles
Amethyst 200–300
Marigold 60–95

Massachusetts, US Glass

A rare tumbler, seldom coming up for sale. This one is from the collection of John and Lucile Britt. The pattern is found in an extensive line of crystal glass; a mug and vase are also known in carnival.

Mayan, Millersburg

An abstract leaf design, found mostly in eight-inch ice cream-shaped bowls in green. There are a few rare examples in aqua, olive and marigold. Average green bowls sell for about $70; better examples for $100 or so.

May Basket, Brockwitz (Germany)

These six-inch baskets with the oddly attached handle are usually marigold and sell $20 to $30.

Meander, Northwood

Meander is a back pattern seen in combination with spatula feet. The pattern was obtained from the old Jefferson company by Northwood and was used on some Grape and Cable, Three Fruits, and Rays as well as all the examples of Sunflower.

Melon Rib

This spittoon is marked with the Heisey logo. It is light marigold and sold at the 1997 Lincoln-Land auction (Tom Burns) for $105. A light blue example sold at a Burns auction in 1994 for $125. The vertical segment effect is typical of the pattern.

Salt and pepper
Marigold   25–40
Decanter, wine
Marigold   45 (1996)
Wine or brandy glass, 3" tall
Marigold   15–25

Memphis, Northwood

Although it has many characteristics of other cut-style patterns, Memphis is distinguished by its panel of raised square hobs. A point of constant confusion, however, is the difference between the punch bowl and the fruit bowl (both sometimes come with punch cups). The punch bowl has a small collar base that fits *into* the stand, as shown above. The fruit bowl has a large octagonal collar base that fits *over* the top of the stand (shown in the set following). The punch bowl and stand above, in ice green, sold for $15,000 at a 1996 auction.

Bowl, large berry
Marigold   100–160
Purple   350–450
Berry set, 7 piece
Marigold   200 (1997)

Even though this is called the fruit bowl, it is known to come with punch cups and some collectors remember their family having such sets for many years. This eight-piece set, in green, sold for $1,050 in 1996 and again in 1998 for $1,700.

Fruit bowl and stand
Amethyst   250–300
Green   600–900
Ice blue   3,750 (1994)
Marigold   250–300
Fruit bowl set, 8 piece (six cups)
Amethyst/purple 500–800
Green   1,000–1,500
Ice blue   4,000–4,500
Ice green   11,000 (1997)
Marigold   300–500
White   3,000 (1996)
Punch bowl and stand
Ice green   15,000 (1996)
Lime/ice green   2,300 (1997)   U-shaped crack in bowl
Punch set, 8 piece
Amethyst/purple 500–700
Green   2,800 (1995)
Marigold   400–650
White   3,500 (1995)

Punch set, 14 piece
Marigold 450–700
Punch base only (for both fruit and punch bowls)
Blue 185–200
Green 70–100
Marigold 30–50
Ice green 70–100
Purple 60–80
Punch cup (for both fruit and punch sets)
Amethyst/purple 20–30 most common color
Green 20–35 common color
Ice blue 75–110
Ice green 125–200 rare color
Lime 25 (1998)
Marigold 10–15 common color
White 15–25

Mikado, Fenton

These large compotes are the only shape in which the pattern is seen. The exterior design is similar to Fenton's Cherry Circles and Cherry Chain. There is some variation in the shaping of the top, with ruffling the most common, but some are flared or ice cream shaped (as above). Reported in white.

Compote, large
Amethyst/purple 700–1,000 scarce color
Blue 500–900 common color
Blue 1,200 (1998) flat, ice cream shape
Blue, powder 400 (1996) marigold overlay
Green 1,200–1,500 rare color
Marigold 175–250 common color

Milady, Fenton

According to John Britt, these are Bachelor Button-type flowers. They cover the background panels rather handsomely. Predominantly seen in blue, there are a few marigold pitchers and tumblers. It's difficult to establish a price for pitchers as the iridescence varies so much. Poor examples sell for less than $500, great ones for well over $1,000.

Water set, 7 piece
Blue 1,500–2,000
Pitcher, water
Blue 500–900
Marigold 550–700
Tumbler (see page 181 for color photo)
Amethyst 85 (1998)
Blue 50–95
Marigold 45–80

Mirrored Lotus, Fenton

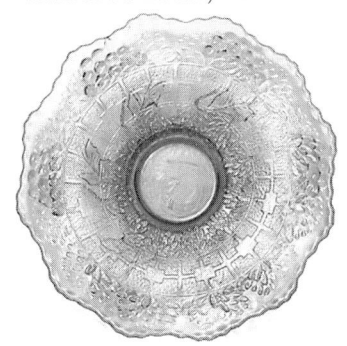

Circling the bowl are a series of rectangles, with the title flowers mirrored on either side of this ring. The exterior pattern of Horse Chestnut can be seen through the pattern. Shown above is a small plate in celeste blue, of which two are known.

Plate, 7"
Celeste blue 5,500 (1996)
Bowl, about 7"
Blue 70–110 common color and shape
Ice green 2,400 (1997) ruffled, one known

Mirrored Lotus Rosebowl
Marigold   250–400
White   550–625

Mitered Ovals
See Vases section

Moonprint, Brockwitz (Germany)

Like many European patterns, Moonprint was made in a large number of shapes. Shown above are the midsize pitcher and butter dish. Below is a fruit bowl. The stand, as with some US patterns, does extra duty as a compote and open sugar.

Fruit bowl (or punch bowl) and base
Marigold   80–150
Bonbonierre (covered dish)
Marigold   290 (1995)   small lid chip
Bowl
Marigold   35–60
Butter dish
Marigold   70–90
Open sugar (also base of fruit bowl)
Marigold   40–60
Cordial set (decanter, 6 cordials and tray)
Marigold   450 (1998)

Pitcher
Marigold   250–400
Wine
Marigold   30–50

Morning Glory, Imperial
See Vases section.

Morning Glory, Millersburg

An extremely rare pattern, known only in pitchers and tumblers. The pitcher is a very tall, slender tankard-style with a morning glory around the middle. About ten are known in approximately equal quantities of amethyst, green and marigold. An amethyst pitcher sold at a 1996 Tom Burns auction for $10,000; an amethyst tumbler for $1,100. The green tankard shown here is courtesy of Bill and Carole Richards.

Multi-Fruits and Flowers, Millersburg

Millersburg's Multi-Fruits and Flowers pattern is pretty much embodied in the name. The flowers—grapes, apples and pears—are in high relief. Some collectors shorten the name to Multi-Fruits, but it is the same pattern. Don't confuse it with Dugan's

M-N

Many Fruits. The punch bowl above is unusual with its cupped-in top, referred to as tulip-shaped. Bowl, base, and cups courtesy of Pat Davis. One set known in blue; 8 pieces with the tulip top. There is one known variant that has a pattern called Scroll and Grapes on the interior of the bowl. This amethyst piece last sold at a 1996 Mickey Reichel auction for $1,100.

Punch set, 8 piece
Amethyst   1,000–1,600
Amethyst   3,900 (1997)   tulip-shaped bowl
Green known
Marigold   1,000–1,600
Marigold   2,800 (1993)   tulip-shaped bowl

Punch set, 11 piece
Marigold   2,000 (1998)

Punch cup
Amethyst   40–50
Green   40 (1997)
Marigold   10–20

The pitcher above has appeared in many collections over the years; it is amethyst and has painted fruit. It most recently sold at a 1994 Jim Seeck auction for $3,000 (with a heat check).

Pitcher, water
Amethyst   3,000   painted fruit, heat check in base
Amethyst   900 (1993)   base crack

Tumbler
Marigold   650 (1994)

Sherbert (or compote)
Amethyst   850 (1993)
Green   325–550

Nautilus, Northwood/Dugan

The Nautilus pattern predated the carnival era and has been called Argonaut Shell. Northwood produced an extensive line in custard and opalescent—some molds contain the early "Northwood" in script. The molds were transferred to Dugan who produced the few limited shapes in carnival. The piece above is the shape called a sugar bowl, although some are stretched out and have the ends curled up and in. Others have one end curled over and are considered creamers.

There were at least two different size molds, the larger of which was used to make the rare marigold banana boat shown above; courtesy of Larry and Mary Yung.

Creamer (whimsied spout and handle)
Peach opal   100–175
Purple   135–225

Sugar
Peach opal   90–160
Purple   165–275

Bowl whimsey, 7½"
Peach opal   175 (shown above)
Purple   260

Nautilus vase whimsey
Marigold   150–275
Purple   250–350

Near Cut Souvenir, Cambridge

Cambridge's Near Cut design is found in only a few shapes; a very rare decanter, small souvenir mugs, and the creamer above. The creamer, in light marigold, sold for $275 at a 1997 Mickey Reichel auction. On the mugs, the pattern is the same as the creamer with souvenir lettering invariably stenciled on the top part. The tumblers flare at both top and base and have no collar base.

Mug
Marigold   70–100   souvenir lettering
Tumbler
Marigold   200 (1997)   souvenir lettering

Nesting Swan, Millersburg

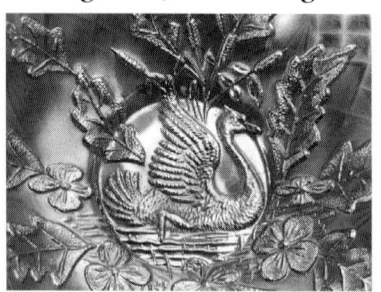

Millersburg's swan pattern is found only in bowls in the usual Millersburg colors, although rare blue, vaseline, and honey amber are known. Diamond and Fan is the exterior pattern.

Bowl, about 10"
Amethyst   225–400   ruffled
Green   225–400   ruffled
Green   900–1200   square
Green   1,600–2,100 square or diamond crimped
Marigold   150–250   ruffled
Marigold   425 (1993)   8½", deep, tight crimp
Marigold   365 (1997)   ruffled, blue iridescence

While the pattern is a little difficult to see in the photo, this marigold Nesting Swan rosebowl is the only one known in any color.

Night Stars, Millersburg

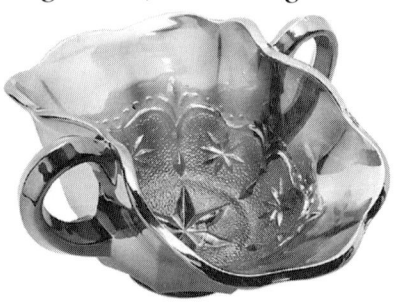

In any shape, Night Stars is in demand among Millersburg collectors. The green that these pieces are often found in are a sort of smoky color called olive that is more common than marigold. This unusual cupped-up bonbon is courtesy of Carl and Eunice Booker.

Bonbon
Amethyst known
Marigold   700–850
Olive green   1,000–1,700

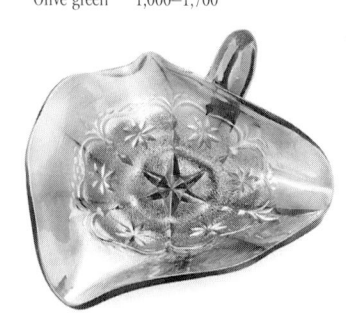

A rare version of Night Stars in a tricorner nappy shape. This one is olive green and courtesy of Charles and Eleanor Mochel.

Nine Sixteen
See Vases section

Nippon, Northwood

Don't mistake Northwood's Nippon for Fenton's Peacock Tail. Nippon has a circular design in the center (the Imperial Crest of the Empress of Japan); on the Peacock Tail pattern the design continues into the center. Bowls and plates in Nippon are found with either the basketweave back or the ribbed back; a few with plain back have been reported. Pie crust edge bowls are more desirable than the ruffled although there appear to be more of those than the ruffled. The bowl shown above is blue, one of the few known in this color.

Bowl, ruffled
Amethyst/purple	160–225	scarce color
Green	250–450	common color
Ice blue	300–450	common color
Ice green	400–575	
Marigold	100–175	common color
White	150–250	scarce color

Bowl, pie crust edge
Amethyst/purple	250–500	scarce color
Amethyst, fiery	475 (1998)	
Aqua opal, one known		
Aqua/teal	1,600–1,900	rare color
Green	400 (1996)	
Ice blue	250–400	most common color
Ice green	600–850	scarce color
Lime green	650–900	scarce color
Marigold	200–350	scarce color
White	150–250	fairly common color

Plate, 9" (scarce)
Amethyst/purple	900–1,100	scarce color
Aqua opal, one known		
Green	550–750	common color
Ice blue	9,000 (1997)	only one known in color
Marigold	500–800	scarce for plates
White	1,350 (1993)	few known

Nola, Inwald (Czechoslovakia)

This pitcher is owned by Nola Schmoker and named in her honor. The pitcher, which is about 7½ inches high, is one of a number of shapes found, if rarely, in the pattern created by the Czechoslovakian glass manufacturer, Josef Inwald. The dresser set pieces and tumbleup (at rear) shown below are courtesy of Galen and Kathi Johnson.

Northern Lights

This small blue rosebowl, four inches in diameter, sold at a 1994 auction for $150. A larger example is also known, as well as an epergne and probably other shapes. It is thought to be a product of either Brockwitz or Eda.

Nugget or Nugate

See Contemporary glass

Northern Star, Fenton

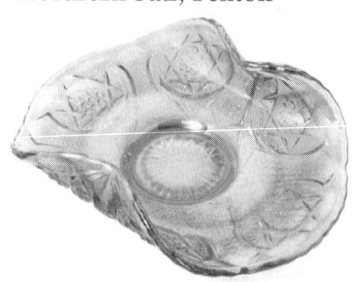

This is an early carnival glass pattern found only in marigold. The pattern is on the exterior. Despite its rarity, it doesn't draw much attention. Seen mostly in this card tray shape selling for $15 to $20.

Northwood basket
See Bushel Basket

Octagon, Imperial

Found in a wide range of shapes, Octagon was one of Imperial's most enduring patterns. Shown here are a tumbler, water pitcher, toothpick holder and goblet. There are two sizes of water pitchers as well as a smaller milk pitcher (and a creamer). In addition to the shapes listed here, there are also punch cup and small berry bowls. The toothpick holder, wine goblets, and vase have been reproduced. Purple is rare and very desirable.

Bowl, about 9"
Marigold   15–25

Compote (either large or small size)
Marigold   45–80
Purple   150–225

Cordial
Marigold   175–300

Goblet, water
Marigold   15–25

Salt and pepper shakers
Purple   500 (1994)

Salt shaker
Marigold   90 (1996)
Purple   400 (1998)

Table set, 4 piece
Marigold   130–200

Butter dish
Marigold   180–225
Marigold   275 (1998)   base only
Purple   475 (1994)

Creamer (from table set)
Purple   190–210

Sugar base only
Amethyst   65 (1997)

Sugar and creamer set
Marigold   115 (1998)

Sherbert
Marigold   30–50

Toothpick holder
Marigold   100–185
Purple   305 (1994)   chipped base

Toothpick holder (new), marked IG
Various colors 10–20

Water set, 7 piece
Marigold   150–250   large size pitcher
Marigold   100–150   small size pitcher(8")

Pitcher, large water, two tumblers
Purple   600 (1995)

Pitcher, water
Marigold   85–140   large size
Marigold   45–80   small size (8")
Purple   400–550   large
Purple   1,800 (1997)   small, super example

Pitcher, milk
Marigold   60–85

Tumbler
Marigold   20–35
Purple   85–160

Vase, 8"
Marigold   65–100

Wine set, 7 or 8 piece
Marigold   125–200

Wine decanter
Marigold   40–80
Marigold   35–65   stopper damage
Purple   700 (1998)

Wine glass
Marigold   15–25

Octet, Northwood

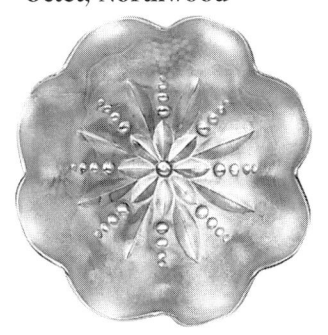

A simple pattern with an 8-petalled flower in the center and hobnails extending out from that. Found only in dome-footed bowls. Scarce pattern.

Bowl, 8"
Amethyst/purple   125–200
Green   85–150
Marigold   100 (1994)

O'Hara or Loop, McKee

This is McKee's version of the Colonial pattern. These had a light marigold iridescence and sold at a 1994 auction. The pitcher brought $100, the goblet $25.

Ohio Star, Millersburg

Aside from the better-known vases, this clear-stemmed compote is one of the few shapes in the pattern in Carnival, although Millersburg made quite a few shapes in crystal. See also Vases section.

Compote, 8" tall
Marigold   1,000–1,500

This unusual Ohio Star whimsied tricorner sauce in marigold is is the only known piece in this shape.

Oklahoma, Cristales de Mexico

This is the only carnival tumbler pattern known in which the mouth is narrower than the base. It is marked with a C-M trademark that stands for the Mexican glass maker. This marigold example is courtesy of Carl and Eunice Booker. A similar piece sold in 1998 for $335 and a wine decanter in the pattern sold for $600 in 1993.

Old Rose Distilling
See Lettered section

Olympic, Millersburg

These small compotes are made from the same exterior form used for the Millersburg Leaf and Little Flowers compote, which is a scant three inches tall. The Olympic has a garland design around the inside of the bowl and a star in the center. There are two known; one each in amethyst and green. The amethyst sold for $4,600 at a 1994 Jim Seeck auction. It had sold for $2,850 in 1990.

Olympus, Northwood

This unusual piece appears to be a lamp shade that did not have the center cut out for the mounting hole. It is a deep cobalt with rich purple iridescence and is seven inches wide. The Northwood logo is in the bottom.

Omnibus, Brockwitz

A cut-style pattern known only in a few marigold and blue tumblers and a couple of pitchers in both colors. This pattern is known to have been made in crystal by US Glass. The carnival examples—blue and marigold—are believed to be made by Brockwitz of Germany. The marigold pitcher above sold for $425 at a 1998 Mickey Reichel auction. Tumblers, in marigold, sell for between $150 and $250. See page 183 for color photo of tumbler. In 1997, a marigold seven-piece water set sold at a David Ayers auction for $1,000.

Open Edge, Fenton

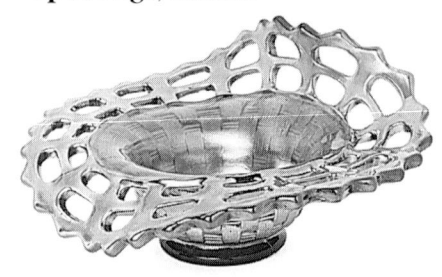

Fenton made a similar pattern with a blackberry design in the center (see Blackberry open edge). There are versions with two rows of openings and with three rows—which are hard to find. The smallest basket, with a 1⅞" base, is the most frequently seen. The larger baskets, with a 2½" base, are fairly scarce. The small basket above, in green with jack-in-the-pulpit shaping, sold for $180 at a 1998 Mickey Reichel auction. The pattern has been reissued by Fenton.

Basket or hat, small 2 row, *ruffled*
Amethyst	50–80	scarce color
Amethyst, black	90–160	scarce color
Aqua	70–110	fairly common color
Blue or cobalt	40–50	scarce color
Celeste	200–300	scarce color
Green	60–100	scarce color
Ice blue	275–500	scarce color
Ice green	125–225	scarce color
Lavender	65–100	scarce color
Lime	100–175	rare color
Marigold	25–45	common color
Red	200–350	most common color
Vaseline	50–80	scarce color
White	100–150	scarce color

Basket or hat, small 2 row, *two sides up*
Amberina	300–450	rare color
Amberina opal	350–600	rare color, reverse amberina
Amethyst, black	90–160	fairly available
Aqua	70–130	scarce color
Blue or cobalt	40–75	common color in this shape
Green	200–300	scarce color
Ice blue	400–550	rare color
Ice green	300–400	rare color
Lime	100–150	rare color
Marigold	20–30	common color
Red	325–450	fairly common color
Smoke	550 (1994)	
Vaseline	65–100	scarce color in this shape
White	260 (1994)	

Basket or hat, small 2 row, *four sides up (square)*
Aqua	60–90	scarce color
Celeste	375 (1998)	
Blue/cobalt	25–40	
Green	225 (1993)	
Ice green	125 (1998)	
Marigold	40–70	common color

Red	300–500	common color
White reported		

Basket or hat, small 2 row, *jack-in-the-pulpit shape*

Amber	125–200	scarce color
Amethyst	240 (1994)	
Aqua	125–225	
Blue	45–70	fairly common color
Celeste	275 (1998)	
Green	150–275	scarce color
Green, forest	425 (1993)	opal swirl base
Marigold	30–50	common color
Red	250–400	most common color
Red slag	500 (1994)	
Vaseline	85–135	scarce color

Basket or hat, large 2 row

Blue	40 (1998)	2 sides up
Celeste	225 (1997)	square
Celeste	400 (1998)	ice cream shape
Ice blue	525 (1996)	2 sides up
Ice blue	225 (1995)	square
Ice green	200–300	
Marigold	40–60	
White	235 (1998)	2 sides up
White	220 (1994)	ruffled

Bowl, 2 row, (5–7"), ice cream, jack-in-the-pulpit, or ruffled

Celeste	275–450	
Ice blue	375 (1996)	ice cream shape
Ice blue	375 (1998)	2 sides up
Ice green	175–300	
Marigold	40–70	
Red	275–375	
White	100–175	

Plate, 8"

Red	1,750 (1993)	only one known
Ice green opal	550 (1994)	marigold overlay
Vaseline opal	450 (1993)	marigold overlay

John H. Brand or Miller Furniture Open Edge
See Lettered section

Basket or hat, 3 row

Ice blue	200–300	
Ice green	130–200	
White	125 (1997)	square

Bowl, 3 row, 8-9"

Celeste	200–300	
Ice blue	200–300	
Ice green	200–300	
White	80–150	

Open Ovals
See Beaded Panels

Open Rose
See Imperial Rose

Optic and Buttons, Imperial

While similar to other patterns with fine flutes, this one has a single row of cane-type buttons circling the piece. The above rosebowl is probably the most often seen shape. Reproduced rosebowls have been reported. Quite a few pieces are marked with Imperial's Iron Cross mark.

Rosebowl
Marigold 25–35

Bowl, small berry
Marigold 18–25   Iron Cross mark

Bowl, with underplate
Marigold 25–35

Chop plate, 11"
Clambroth 30

Creamer, pedestalled
Clear/white 45

Cup and saucer
Marigold 350 (1995)

Punch cup
Marigold 50 (1998)   Iron Cross mark

Wine glass
Marigold 10 (1998)   Iron Cross mark

Plate, 7¼"
Marigold 40 (1996)

Optic and Buttons, continued

Salt dip, pedestalled, 2 handles
Marigold   600–700   Iron Cross mark

Pitcher, water
Marigold   400–550   Iron Cross mark

Orange Peel, Westmoreland

The name says it all; pieces appear to have thin overlays of orange peel (complete with stippling) extending from bottom to top. Shown are custard cups; punch cups do not have the extended lip.

Punch set, 8 piece
Marigold   125–200

Punch cup
Amethyst   40 (1998)
Marigold   10–15

Sherbert, footed
Amethyst   50–65
Peach opal   25–40

Orange Tree, Fenton

Orange Tree and Butterfly and Berry were probably Fenton's most popular patterns. Orange Tree, however, has shapes not found in Butterfly and Berry: plates, loving cups, mugs, a powder jar and a punch set. Plates and bowls are found with a variant center where part of the trunk of the tree extends into the center (see plate above and circled part of closeup below). Some of the Orange Tree shapes have squared feet, providing a distinctive and charming ambiance to those shapes.

Plate, 9"
Aqua opal   15,000 (1995)   two known
Blue   275–500   most common color
Blue, electric 500–700
Blue   1,500 (1998)   stretchy iridescence
Clambroth   180–275   common color
Ice green   7,000 (1995)   edge flaw, three known
Marigold   300–500   very common color
White   150–250   common color

Plate, 9", with trunk center
Amethyst	4,500 (1996)	
Blue	275–450	most common color
Clambroth	150–250	
Green	4,000–5,000	extremely rare
Ice green	16,000 (1994)	three known
Marigold	150–275	scarce color
White	200–270	common color

Bowl, 8–9", collar base
Amber	125–175	scarce color
Amberina	1,200 (1996)	ruffled
Amethyst	100–200	scarce color, ICS or ruffled
Blue	90–170	common color
Celeste	1,500–2,000	rare color
Clambroth	35–55	scarce color
Green	220–350	scarce color
Green, electric	550 (1993)	ruffled
Marigold	55–80	most common color
Mar/moonstone	500–800	ice cream shape
Red	2,000–3,500	fairly common color
Sapphire	200 (1998)	
White	80–150	fairly common color
Vaseline	200–300	scarce color
White	65–100	scarce color

Bowl, with trunk, collar base, ruffled (more scarce than plates with trunk)
Blue	125–200
Green	100–200
Marigold	40–70

Note that the berry bowls are quite different from the regular bowls and have four feet—which, of course, are quite susceptible to damage.

Berry set
Blue	45 (1995)	7 piece, repairs on feet
Blue	110 (1995)	6 piece, some chips
White	145 (1996)	5 pc, usual feet roughness

Bowl, large berry
Marigold	50–70	ruffled
White	75 (1998)	gold trim around edge

Bowl, fruit or orange, about 10", scroll feet
Blue	150–235
Marigold	80–140

Centerpiece whimsey bowl from large fruit
Amethyst	4,500 (1996)	one known

Breakfast set (small sugar and creamer)
Amethyst	80–150
Blue	70–125
Marigold	70–100
White	100–150

Table set, 4 piece (all are footed)
Blue	400–600
Marigold	250 (1996)

Butter dish, covered
Marigold	150–250	
White	155 (1996)	foot chips

Creamer
Blue	145 (1994)	
Marigold	25–35	
White	200 (1997)	gold trim

Spooner
Marigold	60–80

Sugar, covered
Marigold	100–150

Compote
Aqua	165 (1997)	
Blue	70–100	ruffled
Marigold	30–50	ruffled
Purple	170 (1997)	swirl
Teal	450 (1994)	

Goblet, water (also check wine glass)
Aqua	65 (1995)	
Blue	40–75	
Marigold	15–25	
Marigold	50 (1997)	Souv. Grand Rapids, WI
Vaseline	90 (1993)	

Sherbert
Blue	10–15

Marigold	5–10	
White	150 (1994)	

Hatpin holder

Amethyst	700 (1993)	chip, only one known
Blue	200–350	most common color
Green	350–500	rare color
Marigold	200–350	
Marigold	220 (1997)	factory painted
White	800–900	foot damage

Powder jar

Amethyst	150–275	scarce color
Blue	75–125	common color
Green	700 (1994)	
Marigold	65–100	common color

Loving cup

Amethyst	500–750	scarce color
Aqua opal, one known		
Blue	200–325	common color
Green	350–550	
Ice blue, one reported		
Marigold	175–275	common color
Peach opal, one known		
White	500–900	rare color

Orange Tree mugs were made in substantial quantities and a wide range of colors. There are two sizes; the larger (above left) is referred to as the shaving mug, the smaller is the standard size mug. The standard size is found both flared as above and with straight sides. Several molds were used as there are standard mugs with slight variations in the patterns.

Mug, standard (2½" base), flared or straight

Amber	35–60	scarce color
Amberina	250–350	rare color
Amethyst/purple	55–90	average availability
Aqua	70–130	scarce color
Blue	35–55	most common color
Blue, powder	45 (1996)	marigold overlay
Green	325–500	scarce
Marigold	15–25	common color
Red	300–450	relatively common color
Red slag	400 (1997)	
Sapphire	250–350	rare color
Vaseline	120–200	fairly common color
Teal	120–200	

Mug, shaving or large size (3" base)

Amber	70 (1997)	
Amethyst	90 (1996)	some inside wear
Aqua	200–270	
Blue	45–75	common color
Blue, electric	100–175	
Green	900 (1996)	
Lime	575 (1993)	
Marigold	25–40	common color
Red	400–650	fairly common color
Vaseline	200–375	scarce color

Punch set, 8 piece

Blue	400–550	most common color
Marigold	250–350	
White	600–800	

This is the flared version of the punch bowl. It is more desirable than the ruffled although prices may not always reflect that.

Punch bowl and base

Blue	200–350	most common color
Blue	1,100 (1997)	whimsey, 3/1 edge
Green	7,000 (1996)	flared top, two known
Marigold	90–140	

Punch cup

Blue	15–25	
Marigold	15–25	
White	50–85	

Creamer whimsey from punch cup

White	105 (1998)

Orange Tree water sets are much more rare in marigold than in blue. These sets are often referred to as Footed Orange Tree.

Water set, 7 piece
Blue   700–900

Pitcher, water, footed
Blue   600–800

Tumbler, footed (see page 181 for color photo)
Blue   45–80
Marigold   45–70
White   55–130

Wine glass (also check goblet)
Blue   55–90
Blue   100 (1995)   top rolled down
Green   250–300
Marigold   15–20
Marigold   100 (1998)   Souv. Sheridan, WY
Vaseline   85 (1994)

Orange Tree Orchard, Fenton

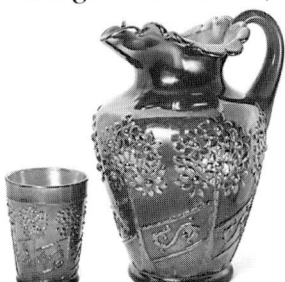

The Orange Tree Orchard has a pattern of orange trees connected by a scrolled fence; thus it can be confused with Orange Tree Scroll. The design, as well as the shape, is quite different than the Orange Tree Scroll. The above pitcher and tumbler, both in blue, sold for $600 and $90, respectively, at the 1994 John and Lucile Britt auction (Jim Seeck).

Water set, 7 piece
Blue   500–700
Marigold   300–500

Pitcher, water
Blue   500–600
Marigold   275–450
White   250–350

Tumbler
Blue   75–125
Marigold   30–45
White   80–140

Orange Tree Scroll, Fenton

The dominant pattern on the Orange Tree Scroll is the orange trees circling the center of the tankard. It is named for the scroll design around the neck area and also referred to as Orange Tree variant.

Pitcher, water
Blue   850–1,000

Tumbler
Blue   50–85
Marigold   40–70

Oregon/Beaded Loop

We've been unable to confirm anything about this 3½" tall vase or spittoon. It is in light marigold and sold for $200 at a 1994 auction.

Oriental Poppy, Northwood

A pattern similar to Northwood's Dandelion tankard, Oriental Poppy displays a large poppy wrapping around either side of the pitcher.

Water set, 7 piece
Amethyst/purple 950–1,500
Green 1,000–1,750
Ice blue 2,500–4,000
Marigold 400–600
White 1,600–2,200

Water pitcher
Amethyst/purple 500–800
Blue 600 (1997) cracked
Green 900–1,500
Ice blue 2,400–3,600
Ice green 4,000 (1997)
Marigold 325–450
White 800–1,200

Tumbler
Amethyst/purple 40–65 most common color
Blue 325 (1994)
Blue 165 (1997) Etched 1914
Green 35–65
Ice blue 150–250 rare color
Ice green 120–200 rare color
Lime green 250 (1995)
Marigold 35–55 common color
White 75–115 fairly common color

Oval and Round, Imperial

This pattern has large ovals separated by vertical creases and a horizontal crease. The pattern is said to have been the inspiration for the later Moonprint.

Bowl, about 9"
Marigold 20–35
Smoke 70 (1997)

Bowl in metal bride's basket
Marigold 100 (1998)

Chop plate, 11"
Marigold 60–90

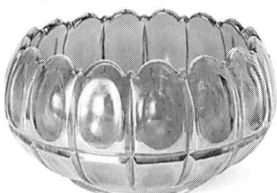

Rosebowl, about 6½"
Marigold 40–70

Oval Star

This 2¼" tall marigold child's tumbler sold for $145 at the 1998 International club auction (Jim Seeck).

Oxbow

This marigold mug sold at a 1995 Mickey Reichel auction for $25.

Palm Beach, US Glass

Palm Beach was the US Glass grape pattern. It is distinctive for the prominent vine that starts at the base and curves up to the top overlapping the adjoining

O-P 141

vine. Above is the large berry bowl. In addition to the many whimsey shapes in the pattern, pieces are often decorated with gold or silver trim. Some also have interior amethyst flashing. Honey amber is a color unique to US Glass and, while similar to marigold, has a lustrous brown effect that looks like honey.

Berry set, 5 piece
Honey amber 385 (1993)

Bowl, small berry or sauce, 4–5", usually with berry interior (Gooseberry)
Honey amber 45–80
White 25–45

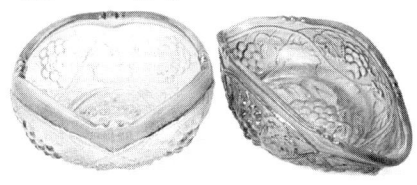

US Glass craftsmen frequently turned common bowls or sauces into unusual shapes. Here are a rosebowl in white with silver trim (the interior is Gooseberry) and a small banana boat in honey amber.

Rosebowl
Honey amber 275 (1996)
Lime green 115 (1995) marigold overlay
Marigold 150–250
White 175–250 Gooseberry interior, common

Bowl whimsey, from small berry or sauce
Amethyst, light 250 (1998) banana boat shape
Honey amber 145–200 banana boat shape
Honey amber 175 (1998) tricorner
Marigold 45–75 banana boat shape
Marigold 70–130 square ruffled
Marigold 110 (1996) 7½", gold trim, banana boat
Marigold 200 (1995) tricorner

Hair receiver
Marigold 100 (1998)

Plate, 7", gold trim
Marigold 300 (1998)

While there are a few known complete four-piece table sets (mostly in white) none have found their way to public sale in recent years. The above covered sugar is typical of these pieces.

Butter dish
White 120–200

Creamer
Marigold 70–110
White 90–125

Butter, sugar, and spooner
White 400 (1995)

Spooner
White 100–175

Sugar, covered
Honey amber 55–90

Pitcher, water
Honey amber 300–500
White 400–600

Tumbler
Honey amber 50–75
Marigold 125–175
White 90–120
White 250 (1995) silver trim

These unusually shaped pieces, probably made from a large bowl, often have gold trim. Some call this treatment Goofus glass but I prefer the "gold trim" nomenclature. They're also referred to as jardinieres (sometimes described as spittoon-shaped) so we've included them here—although we prefer to call them vases. Several Palm Beach shapes were made into vases. See Vases section.

Jardiniere
Marigold 450–600 or honey amber
White 550–725

Palm Leaf and Fan

An odd little piece that didn't quite make it to full card tray shape. When this marigold 5½-inch handgrip plate sold at his 1994 auction for $210, John Britt pointed out that it was the only one he had seen.

Panelled Cherries, Dugan
See Cherries, panelled

Panelled Daisy and Cane

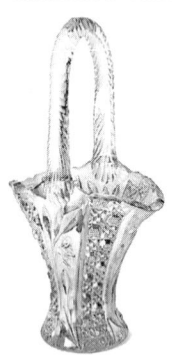

This 11-inch tall marigold basket is very rare. In fact, this example, which sold at the John and Lucile Britt auction in 1994 (Jim Seeck), is the only one John had ever seen although it is noted in Rose Presznick's book 4. It brought $155. The pattern is similar to the Cane and Daisy Cut vase and may have been made by the same manufacturer.

Panelled Dandelion, Fenton

With its six panels dominated by individual flowers, Panelled Dandelion is easy to spot. Most of the pitchers have the handle applied on one of the panels. A rare variation (right) has the handle attached at the seam. A vase made from the pitcher without handle and the top ruffled is also known.

Water set, 7 piece
Amethyst	500–800	
Blue	500–800	
Green	500–850	
Marigold	400–500	

Pitcher, water (tankard style)
Amethyst	400–700	
Blue	450–600	
Green	500–700	most common color
Green	950 (1994)	handle applied on seam
Marigold	250–350	

Tumbler (usually with factory-ground base)
Amethyst	40–70	scarce color
Blue	35–60	scarce color
Green	50–85	most common color
Marigold	25–40	common color

Panelled Diamond and Bows
See Vases section

Panelled Holly, Northwood

This is the only iridized pitcher known in the Panelled Holly pattern. It is purple and resides in Wisconsin.

On the left is an unusual spooner in the Panelled Holly pattern—rarely seen. The more commonly seen bonbon is on the right. The spooner, in green, brought $300 at the 1998 Lincoln-Land auction (Tom Burns).

Bonbon or handled candy dish
Amethyst reported		
Green	35–65	most common color
Marigold	30–45	

Pansy, Imperial

Pansy is a straightforward design with limited shapes available. The ruffled plate above, in smoke, has brilliant multi-color iridescence. It sold for $200 at the 1994 Air Capital convention auction (Jim Seeck). The plates, by the way, are invariably ruffled. Purists among carnival collectors will say these are really bowls, as plates are not ruffled but flat or slightly flared. Amber is quite common in most shapes in this pattern. Note that plates marked with the Northwood "N" are fakes. The nappy and pickle dish have been reproduced.

Plate or low ruffled bowl, about 9"
Lavender   100–170   (light amethyst)
Smoke   200 (1994)
Purple   85–140   most common color

Bowl, 9", ruffled
Amber   60–90
Green   45–65
Lavender   70–110   (light amethyst)
Marigold   25–45   fairly common
Purple   70–130   most common color
Smoke   135–200   scarce color

Breakfast set (creamer and sugar)
Amber   25–40   most common color
Green   35–45
Marigold   40–60
Purple   50–90

The often seen Pansy nappy is also found in a very rare blue, as in this example owned by Elvis Randell.

Nappy, single handle
Amber   15–20
Amethyst/purple 35–60
Green reported
Marigold   15–20

Pickle dish or relish tray, oval (don't confuse with Northwood's similar Poppy)
Amber   35–65   common color
Clambroth   25–40
Green   15–25
Marigold   25–40   common color
Purple   40–70   fairly common color
Purple   700 (1998)   flat, spectacular iridescence

Panther, Fenton

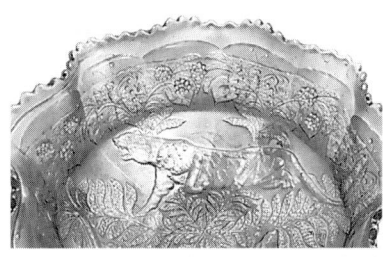

This pattern is named for its interior motif—the exterior pattern is Butterfly and Berry. There are two panthers, stalking among jungle-like foliage. Shown above is a large berry bowl. All pieces have ball feet.

Berry set, 7 piece, ruffled
Marigold   150–250

Bowl, large berry
Aqua   450 (1996)
Blue   250–400   fairly common color
Green   400–500   scarce color
Marigold   95–170   most common color
Marigold   525 (1995)   spectacular color
One bowl known in unusual Nile green
Olive green   250–350

Bowl, centerpiece, ice cream from large berry
Marigold   400–600

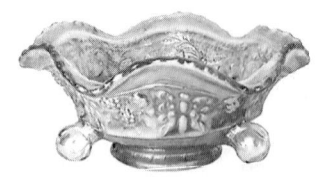

The piece above, which some call a sauce, others a small berry, has been whimsied so that the feet do not rest on the table. It is marigold and courtesy of Carl and Ferne Schroeder. A similar blue whimsey sold for $170 at the 1996 American Carnival Glass Association auction (Tom Burns).

Bowl, small berry or sauce (5–6")
Amberina	600 (1997)	
Amberina, rev.	1,000 (1996)	
Amethyst	150–225	scarce color
Aqua	195–225	
Blue	60–90	common color
Clambroth	35–50	
Green	175–250	
Ginger Ale	145 (1994)	
Lavender	195 (1997)	
Marigold	25–40	most common color
Red	600–1,000	

Parlor Panels
See Vases section

Pastel Panels, Fenton

These slightly flared tumblers are about 4½ inches tall and are found in pastel shades of blue and green. There are eighteen panels around the tumbler. The last recorded sale for such a tumbler was for an ice green example that sold in 1993 for $30. In 1998, Mickey Reichel sold a covered pitcher and six tumblers for $275.

Pastel Swan
See novelties/miniatures, Swan salt

Peach, Northwood

Understated but elegant, Northwood's Peach design is rarely seen in marigold—the most common carnival color. Most of the white examples have gold trim (fired on before iridizing). No pieces in this pattern are common, but all are highly collectible.

Water set, 7 piece
Blue, average	800–1,100	
Blue, electric	1,200–1,600	

Pitcher, water
Blue, average	600–900	
Blue, electric	900–1,500	
White	1,000 (1995)	gold trim

Tumbler
Blue, average	45–80	
Blue, electric	100–200	
White	80–150	gold trim

Table set, 4 piece
White	700 (1997)	gold trim

Butter dish
White	890 (1996, yes, $890)	gold trim

Creamer
White	200–300	gold trim

Spooner
White	150–250	gold trim

Sugar
White	125–225	gold trim

Berry set, 7 piece
White	300–350	gold trim

Bowl, large berry
White	125 (1997)	gold trim

Bowl, small berry
Sapphire blue	175–250	
White	20 (1997)	gold trim

Peach and Pear, Dugan

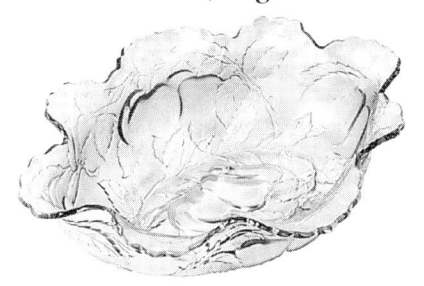

Very similar in size and shape to the large bowls in Dugan's Wreathed Cherries pattern. This pattern has the design mainly on the exterior while the interior has fruit on the bottom. Sometimes called Apple and Pear—the peaches could just as well be apples.

Banana boat
Amethyst   100–150
Marigold   45–75

Brides Basket (bowl with silverplate holder)
Amethyst   250 (1996)

Peacock Lamp/base
See Lamps, shades

Peacock patterns

The peacock was a popular design theme at the turn of the last century. That, coupled with the bird's natural iridescence, made it irresistible for carnival glass designers. The presence of so many peacock patterns can be confusing. The most confusing, however, are the Peacock and Urn designs made by Fenton, Millersburg and Northwood. To complicate matters further, a slight variation in the Millersburg pattern (without the bee) is often referred to as Millersburg Peacock or just Peacock. There are also additional Millersburg variations. Note that I have departed somewhat from strict alphabetical order in this section so that I may present the peacock patterns more logically.

Peacock and Dahlia, Fenton

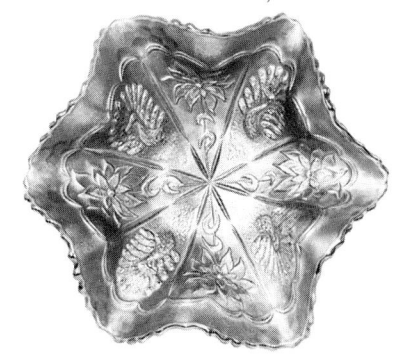

One of Fenton's dual theme patterns. Peacock and Dahlia is similar to Peacock and Grape but much more scarce. Only known in bowls and plates. The ruffled bowl above, in blue, sold at the 1995 Texas club convention auction (Jim Seeck) for $115.

Bowl, about 7"
Aqua   120–200   fairly common, most ruffled
Blue   55–125   ruffled, round or ICS
Marigold   40–75
Vaseline   250–300

Plate, about 7"
Marigold   400–550

Peacock and Grape, Fenton

One of Fenton's most collectible patterns, Peacock and Grape is found in many colors. The ruffled bowl above, for example, is in peach opal, an unusual color for Fenton. It sold at the 1994 Heart of American convention auction for $900. Bowls and plates are found with both the spatula feet and collar base, as shown on the next page.

146 A Field Guide to Carnival Glass

Bowl, 8-9", ruffled, ice cream shape, or 3/1 edge

Amber	100–160	ice cream shape
Amberina	700–1,000	ice cream shape
Amethyst	60–90	spatula footed, common
Amethyst	175–250	collar base, scarce
Amethyst/red	175 (1998)	amethyst base, red sides
Amethyst, black	105 (1998)	
Blue	75–125	common color
Green	100–200	
Lime green	150–250	
Lime green opal	250–400	scarce
Marigold	40–75	most common color
Mar/moonstone	300–425	scarce
Peach opal	150–250	scarce
Red	700–1,000	relatively available
Red slag	700–1,000	scarce
Vaseline opal	400–700	scarce

Nut bowl shape (deep, ruffled or ice cream shape)

Blue	75–100	
Marigold	40–60	collar base

Plate, 9"

Blue	400–600	spatula footed
Blue, electric	2,000–3,000	collar base
Green	350–600	
Marigold	250–400	
Marigold	700–1,000	great iridescence
Marigold	1,150 (1998)	scalloped whimsey

Peacocks (Peacocks on the Fence), Northwood

Northwood's Peacocks pattern has two birds sitting on a fence—thus the alternate name. This bowl has the pie crust edge—which is generally more desirable than the ruffled version. Virtually all pieces have Northwood's ribbed back, although a few are known with basketweave or a plain back. That distinction makes little difference in the price although another variation does; pieces with a stippled background are valued more highly. Some pieces have a slightly thinner collar base than others. The extreme rarities in the pattern are two ruffled bowls in powder blue slag. By the way, if you should miss out on a piece at an auction, never fear. A similar piece is bound to come up again before too long: between one and two percent of carnival pieces are Northwood's Peacock pattern. It should be noted that bowls have been reproduced although the quality should not fool the savvy collector (see contemporary glass).

Bowl, 8–9", ruffled

Amethyst/purple	400–700	common color
Amethyst/purple	700–1,000	outstanding examples
Aqua opal	1,000–1,700	average pieces
Aqua opal	1,700–3,000	outstanding examples
Aqua	750–1,000	rare color
Blue	350–550	common color
Blue, powd. opal	7,000–9,000	(powder blue opal)
Blue slag, two known		
Pearlized custard known		
Green	750–1,000	common color
Horehound	1,150 (1994)	
Ice blue	1,000–1,500	scarce color
Ice blue opal	1,350–1,500	rare color
Ice green	850–1,000	scarce color
Lavender	425 (1997)	
Lime green opal known		
Marigold	225–375	common color
Smoke	1,200–2,000	
White	600–1,000	

Bowl, 8–9", pie crust edge

Amethyst/purple	300–550	most common color
Aqua opal known		
Blue	425–650	common color
Blue	850 (1995)	thin collar base
Blue, electric	600–1,000	scarce
Blue, Renninger	700–1,200	rare color
Green	700–1,000	common color
Green, emerald	1,600–2,300	rare color
Ice blue	1,200–1,600	scarce color
Ice green	1,400–1,900	rare color
Lime green known		
Lavender	700–850	
Marigold	200–300	common color
Smoke known		
White	600–900	relatively common

Bowl, stippled, about 9"

Amethyst, black	1,100 (1994)	pie crust edge
Aqua opal, one known		
Blue	450–700	ruffled
Blue	600–900	pie crust edge
Blue, Renninger	850–1,200	pie crust edge
Marigold	225–375	ruffled
Marigold	250–450	pie crust edge

Plate, 9"

Amethyst/purple	500–900	average availability
Blue	525–800	all rib back, common color

Blue	1,400 (1996)	thin collar base
Blue, Renninger	2,000 (1997)	rib back
Green	750–1,300	plain back
Green	1,300 (1998)	basketweave back
Green	1,400–2,300	rib back
Horehound	1,800 (1998)	rib back
Ice blue	1,600–2,300	scarce color, rib back
Ice green	350–600	common color
Lavender	600–900	scarce color
Lime ice green	650–900	scarce color
Marigold	350–600	common color
Sapphire, one known		
Smoke	1,900 (1998)	pastel iridescence
Smoky/lavender	2,000 (1998)	
White	375–500	common color

Plate, stippled, 9"
Blue	650–1,000	common color
Blue, Renninger	1,200–2,200	rare color
Marigold	375–650	common color
Marigold	1,500–2,600	outstanding examples

Peacock at the Fountain, Northwood

In this Northwood pattern, the single peacock faces left toward a fountain. Above are small and large berry bowls, which have a plain interior. The small berries do not show the peacocks.

Berry set, 7 piece
Amethyst/purple	250–400
Blue	475 (1995)
Marigold	200–300
White	400–600

Bowl, large berry
Blue	195 (1993)
Green	250–350
Ice blue	425–525
Marigold	100–175

Bowl, small berry
Amethyst/purple	30–50
Blue	15–25
Green	40–75
Ice blue	50–65
Marigold	30–50
White	95 (1996)

Bowl, large fruit or orange, 3 feet
Amethyst/purple	500–850	common color
Aqua opal, two known (see color photo, page 177)		
Blue	800–1,200	common color
Blue, electric	1,900 (1996)	
Green	2,700–3,100	rare color
Horehound	1,300 (1995)	
Marigold	220–350	common color
Purple	1,300 (1996)	straight sided—no ruffles
Purple	5,200 (1993)	top turns in

Unlike other shapes in Peacock at the Fountain, the birds on the compote face to the right.

Compote
Amethyst	800 (1993)	
Aqua opal	3,700–4,200	rare color
Blue	950–1,200	scarce color
Blue, electric	1,000–1,500	
Ice blue	800–1,200	fairly common color
Ice green	1,400–1,700	scarce color
Marigold	600–900	scarce color
Purple	600–850	scarce color
White	400–500	scarce color

148 A Field Guide to Carnival Glass

A few punch sets are known to exist in aqua opal, although none in that color have sold in recent years.

Punch set, 8 piece
Amethyst/purple 1,000–1,500
Blue 1,200–2,000
Ice blue 6,500–9,000
Ice green 7,000 (1996)
Marigold 600–900
White 4,500–7,500

Punch bowl and base
Ice/lime green 6,500 (1995)
Marigold 400–500
Purple 650–900

Punch bowl only
Blue, Renninger 600 (1995)

Punch base only
Marigold 30–40
Purple 40–65

Punch cup
Amethyst 25–35
Blue 60–90
Ice blue 65–100
Ice green 400 (1995)
Marigold 25–45
Purple 50–95
White 50–90

The table set above is in ice blue, a very rare color. It is courtesy of Chuck Kremer. Northwood used the same mold to make the butter base for this pattern and that of Singing Birds.

Table set, 4 pieces
Amethyst 350 (1996)
Blue, rare
Ice blue 2,700 (1993)
Marigold 325–450 most common color
Purple 650–800

Butter dish
Amethyst/purple 220–350
Blue 300 (1996) small chip on base rim
Green 300 (1993)
Ice blue 1,000–1,300

Creamer
Amethyst/purple 60–100
Ice blue 250–300
Marigold 60–90

Spooner
Amethyst/purple 100–150
Green 275 (1997)
Ice blue 175–225
Marigold 35–75

Sugar, covered
Amethyst/purple 150–225
Green 250–350
Ice blue 400–550
Marigold 45–85

Pitchers and tumblers were made by both Dugan and Northwood and there are subtle differences in the pattern. Most Dugan examples are blue.

Pitcher, water
Amethyst/purple 350–450 scarce color
Blue 450–650 most common, some Dugan
Blue, electric 500–700
Green 2,500–4,000 rare color
Ice blue 2,600–3,500 rare color
Marigold 300–400 scarce color
White 650–900 some with gold decor.

Water set, 7 piece
Amethyst/purple 600–800
Blue 525–675
Blue, electric 1,300–1,700
Blue 600 (1994) Dugan top edge rough
Ice blue 1,250 (1993)
Marigold 450–600
White 1,300 (1993) 5 pieces

Both Northwood and Dugan made tumblers in this pattern. The Northwood tumbler is on the left and has less detail and is usually marked with the logo; Dugan tumblers have no mark. Note the slight difference in sizes and the greater flare to the Northwood. Unless indicated, prices below are for Northwood.

Tumbler
Amethyst/purple	40–60	
Amethyst	235 (1997)	
Blue	50–80	most common color
Blue, electric	60–80	
Blue	40–55	Dugan
Blue, electric	45–65	Dugan
Green	225–300	rare color
Ice blue	100–175	fairly common color
Lavender	70 (1998)	
Lavender slag	180 (1995)	
Marigold	30–45	common color
White	150–250	

This Peacock at the Fountain spittoon whimsey in green, made from the bottom of a sugar bowl, is one of two known. The other, in amethyst, sold for $15,000 at a 1996 auction.

Peacock and Urn, Fenton

Fenton's version of Peacock and Urn is perhaps easiest to distinguish; it has a sawtooth edge and Fenton's pattern called Bearded Berry on the back. You'll also get to recognize the straight, stiff neck of the bird.

Bowl, 8–9", ruffled or ice cream shape
Amethyst	175–300	fairly common color
Aqua	250 (1994)	mfg. check on mold line
Blue	150–250	very common color
Blue, Persian	1,000–1,600	rare color
Green	225–350	on scarce side
Marigold	80–150	most common color
Mar/moonstone	2,000 (1993)	
Olive green	275 (1995)	
Purple	250–350	ice cream shape, scarce
Red	7,500 (1998)	few known
Vaseline	450–525	scarce color
White	125–185	moderately common

Bowl, three-in-one edge (more scarce than other shapes)
Amethyst	150–250
Green	250–325
Marigold	90–165

Plate, 9"
Blue	450–800	common color
Blue	4,250 (1998)	outstanding example
Marigold	350–600	most common color
Marigold	1,300 (1995)	outstanding example
White	300–500	scarce color

Fenton's Peacock and Urn compote is quite different and much smaller than the Millersburg piece of the same name. The goblet-shaped example above, in blue, has not been flared or ruffled as most are. Courtesy of Carl and Eunice Booker.

Compote
Amethyst	225 (1993)	
Aqua	110–190	fairly common color
Blue	80–150	common color
Blue, light	245 (1995)	goblet shape
Green	150–200	rare color
Lime green	125–175	rare color
Marigold	25–40	most common color
Red	575–900	rare color
Vaseline	100–190	fairly common color
White	130–225	fairly common color

Peacock, Millersburg

Millersburg's Peacock pattern is easy to confuse with Millersburg's Peacock and Urn — as well as Fenton's and Northwood's Peacock and Urn. Millersburg's Peacock, shown here, has no bee; Peacock and Urn does.

Note that neither of these berry bowls has bees or beads on the urn—they're Millersburg Peacock. These amethyst pieces sold at a 1995 auction. The larger berry brought $450; the smaller, $100.

Berry set, 7 piece
Amethyst	800–1,000

Bowl, large berry, 9–10", flared or ruffled
Amethyst	325–450	most common color
Green	325–450	
Green	525 (1997)	3/1 edge, rare shape
Green	650 (1995)	crimped edge
Marigold	200–350	
Marigold	375–475	flattened out, scarce shape

Bowl, small berry or sauce, about 6"
Amethyst	100–180	most common color
Amethyst	1,500 (1994)	3/1 edge
Blue	2,400 (1996)	exceptional example
Blue	350 (1995)	3/1 edge, poor iridescence
Green	200–300	
Marigold	125–225	

Large ice cream shaped bowls are generally the most desirable in the Millersburg Peacock pattern.

Bowl, large ice cream-shape, 9–10"
Amethyst	1,100–2,200	
Amethyst	4,200 (1998)	outstanding example
Green	1,400–2,500	

Marigold very rare but valued less than amethyst or green

Bowl, small ice cream shape, about 6"
Amethyst	100–200
Green	300–475
Marigold	425 (1995)

Plate, small (about 6"), very rare
Amethyst	1,200–1,600

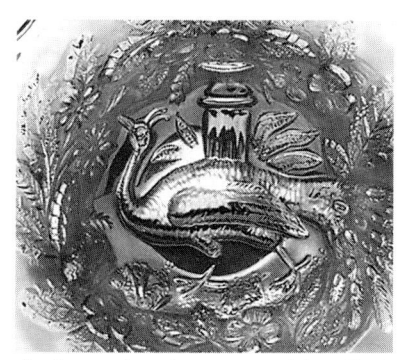

Peacock and Urn, Millersburg

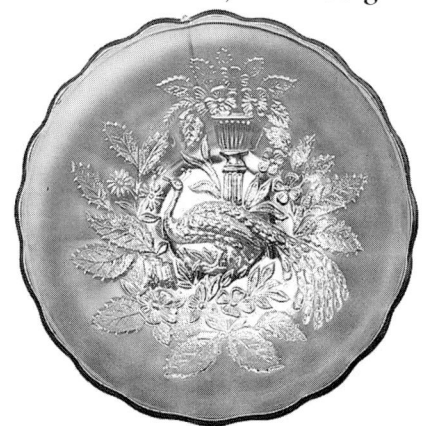

The distinguishing characteristic of the Millersburg Peacock proof above (sometimes called the "whimsey proof") is the missing part of the forward leg—the foot appears to be unconnected to the leg. Also missing is the urn—just the urn stand and column are present.

Proof, 5" sauce
Amethyst   135–200
Marigold   200–310

Above is the only known Millersburg Peacock bowl whimsied into an oval. It is in vaseline and owned by Charles and Eleanor Mochel.

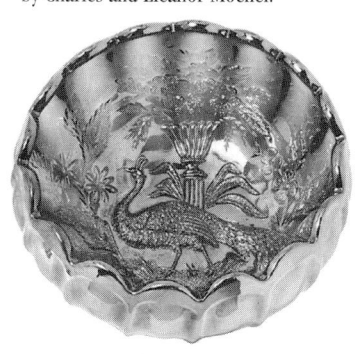

A very rare Millersburg Peacock rosebowl in amethyst made from a large ice cream bowl.

Millersburg's Peacock and Urn, like that of Fenton and Northwood, has a bee just beyond the bird's beak. But it has neither the sawtooth edge of the Fenton nor the stippling under the bird of the Northwood. A rayed star in the base is the easiest way to determine if it is Millersburg. The wide panel exterior is otherwise similar to Northwood's.

Bowl, 10", large ice cream shape
Amethyst   350–600   most common color
Green   450–750
Marigold   250–350   scarce color

Bowl, 10", ruffled or 3/1
Amethyst   275–450   ruffled
Amethyst   550–1,000   3/1 edge
Green   250–425   ruffled
Green   200–350   3/1 edge
Marigold   150–250   ruffled
Olive green   250–300   ruffled

Bowl, large, round
Amethyst   275 (1997)
Marigold   150–250

Bowl, 5–6", small berry or sauce, ruffled
Amethyst   70–115
Blue   550 (1995)   3/1 edge, silvery
Blue   2,400 (1996)   ruffled

Bowl, small ice cream shape
Amethyst   150–250
Horehound   300 (1998)

152   A Field Guide to Carnival Glass

This is the Millersburg Peacock and Urn 11¼-inch chop plate (Northwood also made such a shape). It was formed from the same mold as the large bowls. This one, in amethyst, is the only amethyst to sell at auction in recent years—it brought $9,500 at a Tom Burns auction in 1993.

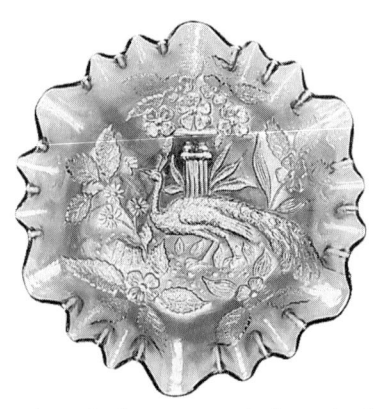

This is the shotgun variant that has no bowl on top of the urn.

Shotgun bowl, 7½", 3/1 edge
Amethyst	600–700
Green	400–650
Marigold known	

The Peacock and Urn mystery bowl, shown above, is so named because its attribution was a mystery for a long time. It has beads only on the top of the bowl and top of the column. It can be distinguished from the other Millersburg Peacock and Urn patterns by the small leaf that overlaps the front right side of the urn (Fenton's pattern has a leaf overhanging on the *left* side). One plate has been reported in the pattern.

Millersburg's Peacock and Urn variant has three rows of beads and four rows of tail feathers. It is only found in amethyst and is the only sauce-size Millersburg piece with a bee. Only six or eight are known—all six-inch ice cream-shaped sauces.

Mystery bowl, 9", 3/1 edge
Amethyst	275–400	common color
Blue	4,250 (1996) 850 (1998), sliver	
Green	300–450	
Marigold	135–225	scarce color

Mystery bowl, 9", ruffled
Amethyst	225–350	common color
Amethyst	475–525	ice cream shape
Blue	1,700–2,900	rare
Green	275–400	common color

Compote, giant (much larger than Fenton's)
Amethyst	1,500–2,000
Green	1,500–2,000

Listings continue on page 185

Learning about carnival glass 153

The essence of carnival glass

Carnival glass is distinguished by three characteristics: it is colorful, it has an iridescent surface, and much of it was hand finished.

The pieces here exemplify these qualities. The ruffled bowl is Dugan's Cherries in deep amethyst. It has the spectacular color and iridescence for which collectors search.

The Northwood Corn vases show a range of colors, mostly of the pastel base glass. While marigold is common in most patterns, it is rare here.

How carnival glass was made

Carnival glass is pressed glass that has been sprayed with a coating of liquid metallic salts to give the surface an iridescent luster. Not all iridized glass is carnival, of course. Art glass or Tiffany-style glass is made from glass with the iridescence throughout the glass, not just on the surface. Tiffany-style glass is not fabricated in a mold, but blown.

Carnival was intended to be affordable for the average homemaker of the early 1900s. The only way to make glass so affordable was to turn it out on a production line and the use of a pressed glass mold was ideal for this.

Molds for pressed glass are heavy objects, made out of cast iron. They are made by metalworkers who carefully cut the pattern of the desired piece in reverse into the mold.

Molds are designed so that the finished glass will be easy to remove. The molds are made in several pieces, with the parts that form the sides hinged so they can be opened and closed. On some pieces there are only two side parts, plus a base, a ring cap, and a plunger that forms the inner pattern of the piece. On more complex pieces, there may be as many as four hinged side pieces—making it a four-part mold.

To make a piece of glass, the mold is closed and locked, molten glass is poured in, and the plunger is pushed in on top of the hot glass. Pressure is applied to the plunger to force the glass into the nooks and crannies. That's how pressed glass got its name.

The piece is removed from the mold, sometimes reheated for shaping, then sprayed with the chemical mixture that produces iridescence. This mixture varies according to the surface color desired and pieces are sometimes sprayed several times to create a richer effect.

This is a typical two-part pressed glass mold. The top photo shows the mold open revealing the finished piece. In the rear is the plunger, sitting upside down. In the front are the ring cap and locking handle. The lower left photo shows the ring cap about to be positioned on the closed mold. On the right is a closeup of the cavity showing the shape of the piece to be made.

This mold is shown through the courtesy of the Fenton Art Glass Company.

The makers of carnival glass

As the twentieth century dawned, families everywhere were becoming prosperous enough to purchase household goods that were more than simply utilitarian. Housewives could now afford the pretty glass that their Victorian mothers could only wish for.

To cater to this burgeoning public, glass manufacturers sought techniques that would differentiate their wares from those of the competition. Fenton, which had started business as a glass decorating company, was the first to introduce commercial production of iridescent glass, in 1907, using existing molds. With success apparent, Fenton began making molds that were largely used just for iridescent ware.

Northwood and Dugan/Diamond soon entered the market and in 1909 and 1910, so did Millersburg and Imperial. Other players, Westmoreland, Cambridge, and US Glass, although mostly makers of other styles of glass, also introduced modest lines of iridescent ware to stay in competition. Heisey, Fostoria, and McKee iridized some of their glass but, for the most part, used only patterns that were readily available in noniridized glass. European and Australian makers began production in the 1920s. Iridescent glass has been made continually; even today there are many manufacturers of this glass.

As the homemaker's interest in iridescent ware waned in the early 1920s, the glassmakers found that they could still manufacture the glass cheaply enough that they could offer it as premiums for use in retail store promotions or prizes at carnivals and fairs. It is said that this is how carnival glass got its name.

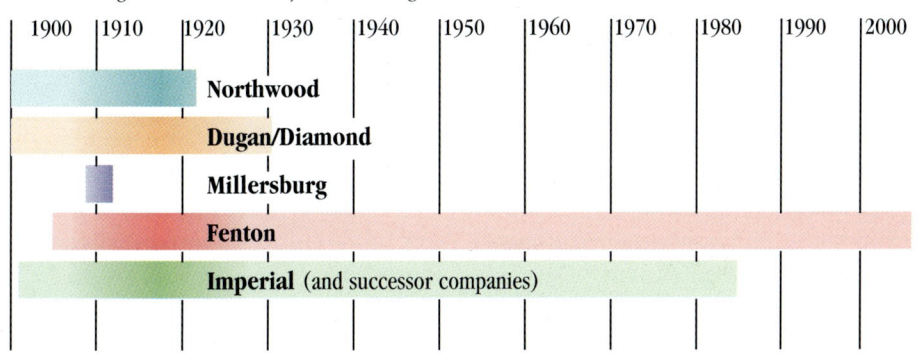

A carnival glass timeline for major iridescent glass manufacturers

- Northwood
- Dugan/Diamond
- Millersburg
- Fenton
- Imperial (and successor companies)

Classic era of carnival   1950s: reproductions and reissues begin

Shaping carnival glass

Because pressed glass remains malleable until it cools to a certain degree, it could be shaped in many ways using simple tools. It is this individual shaping that sets carnival glass aside from other mass-produced glass.

A bowl shape, for instance, could be flattened into a plate. Or it might have been curled up into a deep nut bowl or the edge curved in to form a rosebowl. In extreme examples, there were vases made from bowl shapes—although in most cases vases were made from tumbler shaped molds that were then swung to make them long and slender.

Even when left as a bowl, a piece could be given different edge treatments while still hot. Each manufacturer had its unique edge treatments although all used a ruffled effect. Northwood, for example, used a ruffling called pie crust that looked exactly like the crimping on a pie. This is often more desirable than other edging. Dugan specialized in a deep three-in-one edge. Northwood did not make a three-in-one edge, but Fenton and Millersburg did use such an edge, though usually less precise than that of Dugan. Fenton sometimes used an edge called candy ribbon edge (CRE) that is so heavily crimped that it looks exactly like the ribbon candy we knew as children.

The pieces shown here are in the famous Farmyard pattern by Dugan. These examples provide a good idea of the variety of shapes (and colors) their glassmakers gave them—though few patterns were made in such variety.

The eight-ruffle purple bowl (1) is the most commonly found shape. The green three-in-one-edged bowl (2) is very rare. The six-ruffle bowl in peach opal (3) is the only one known. There are a handful of the purple square bowls (4), and they are only known in that color. The round purple bowl (5) is very low, barely more than two inches off the table, and is the only one known. The square ruffled bowl in green (6) is very rare.

Exploring the shapes of carnival glass

Along with pattern, glass color, and quality of iridescence, the shape of a piece of carnival determines the value.

There are two aspects of shape: the way edges are treated (usually on bowls and compotes) and the general configuration of a piece—water pitcher, mug, vase, bonbon, and so on. Most shapes are fairly obvious, but watch for subtle differences.

One of the things that makes carnival collecting so interesting is that some collectors may call one shape by one name, while others may call it by another name. If you're buying a piece, make sure you understand exactly the shape—as well as the quality and condition.

Pie crust edge and round
The bowl in front is the famous Northwood pie crust edge (often referred to a PCE). No other maker is known to have used this treatment. The other is a round bowl, a term used to designate a bowl just as it came out of the mold—with no additional shaping. Both of these bowls are Grape and Cable in green by Northwood. Note the differences in the bases; one has a collar base, the other is spatula footed.

Ruffled, ice cream, and three-in-one
These are three of the most frequently found edge shapes—seen here in Fenton Dragon and Lotus bowls. The ruffled on the left is green (although it looks purple); in back is an ice cream shape in marigold (scoop shaped with edges curving up smoothly); and a three-in-one in peach opal (an unusual color for Fenton, by the way).

Candy ribbon edge
Sometimes referred to as "tight crimp," the candy ribbon edge looks just like that ruffled Christmas candy. May be known simply as CRE. Both of these bowls were made from the same mold, which probably was a standard round shape, slightly cupped up. Such radical change to glass shape is easily made while the glass is hot. What's the shape in the back? No, it's not a rosebowl, as the curved-in top would suggest. In this Fenton Vintage pattern it's known as a fernery or fern dish. Both are in amethyst.

Three-in-one edge

Dugan used this edge extensively, often in the extreme versions shown here. Fenton and Millersburg used a less exaggerated version. I know of no Imperial three-in-one examples. Northwood did not use this edge style. These are an Apple Blossoms Twigs bowl in amethyst and a peach opal Fishnet epergne.

Candy and nut bowls

Generally taller and deeper than regular bowls, these shapes were made from bowl shapes that have been stretched up or rosebowl shapes that were opened out—such as the purple Fine Cut and Roses by Northwood on the left. At the right is Westmoreland's Louisa pattern in teal. Note that it is iridized only on the inside.

Bowl sizes and sets

Bowls were often made in several sizes. The most frequently seen bowl is eight or nine inches across while small bowls are in the five to six inch range, although there were many other sizes made. Sometimes the bowls were sold as a set, usually referred to as a berry or ice cream set, depending on shape. A set usually consists of six small bowls plus a larger one. These are Northwood's Peacock at the Fountain in green.

Fruit bowls

Fruit bowls are usually thought of as large open bowls with feet and are sometimes called orange bowls. A typical example is this marigold Northwood Grape and Cable—found also in a lower version. There are some two-piece fruit bowls such as the Dugan Persian Garden shown here. In this pattern, bowls with the round, rather than ruffled, top are called punch bowls. That characteristic does not always define punch bowls, however, as there are many ruffled punch sets.

Rosebowls

These small bowls are distinguished by their cupped-in tops, often with additional crimping. The pattern may or may not have feet, and the bowls are fairly small. There are a few large rosebowls, usually rather scarce. These rosebowls are a red Fenton's Flowers, a Northwood

Centerpiece and banana bowls

While they are sometimes found in other patterns, the best known of the centerpiece bowls is this cupped-in version of Northwood's Grape and Cable (in ice green). Banana boats, presumably intended to hold bananas, are always oblong. These bowls are fairly large. The amethyst bowl on the right is Fenton's Thistle.

Learning about carnival glass

Plates

Plates were usually made from the same molds as the accompanying bowls, but flattened after molding. What makes a plate a plate, rather than a low bowl? The rule of thumb is that if a piece is two inches or less off the table, it is a plate. It must not be cupped up significantly nor ruffled (although those with crimping are accepted as plates by some collectors if the other factors are present). Unless otherwise designated, plates are in the nine-inch range. Plates in the six- to seven-inch range are referred to as small plates. Chop plates must be at least 10 inches in diameter. Shown here are a Dugan Wishbone and Spades chop plate and a six-inch plate. Interestingly, there are no known nine-inch plates in this pattern.

Bonbons

Bonbons always have two handles (although there are other shapes that also have two handles such as some sugar bowls and cracker jars). Most bonbons rest on a small collar base like the green Fenton Birds and Cherries on the left. With the ends flat as in this one, it is called a card tray. A few are found with a short stem like the blue Fenton Fuchsia on the right (a rare pattern, by the way). Occasionally these stemmed bonbons will be referred to as handled compotes, but I prefer the former description.

Nappies

Nappies always have one handle and the shape may vary considerably. Shown here are Dugan's Leaf Rays nappies in amethyst and purple. In marigold, the tricorner example is probably the most common nappy seen, and one of the most common pieces of carnival. The ruffled purple is unusual.

Compotes

Compotes are a very popular carnival shape. Some are part of a pattern line, others have no other associated shapes. All are stemmed; most are ruffled as with the aqua Imperial Grape above. The other is an Australian Butterfly Bush (Crown Crystal) in the dark purple so often seen in Australian carnival. The wide flat shape with the edges turned up is referred to as a salver shape—common in Australian carnival but rare in American glass.

Baskets

Baskets may or may not have handles. In fact, some may be made from bowls or hat shapes and have handles attached. The Dugan Beaded Basket, on the left, is in amethyst. In the center is a teal basket in Imperial's Waffle Block pattern. It is part of a family that includes many other shapes. Finally, a Fenton Open Edge basket with jack-in-the-pulpit shaping. Those also are found in several other styles of ruffling.

Breakfast sets

These sets consist of a small sugar and creamer. They were not part of the four-piece table sets (below), for which the pieces are somewhat larger. These are Imperial's Fashion in purple.

Table sets

Table sets consist of a spooner (that held warm water for serving spoons), creamer, covered butter dish, and sugar (usually covered). This is Northwood's Springtime in green.

Dresser sets

We know that this is how the original dresser sets in the Northwood Grape and Cable pattern were sold, since these are the pieces shown in old ads. There are a small pin tray, a large dresser tray, two cologne bottles, a powder or puff jar, and a hatpin holder. The perfume bottles (below) were not part of the set. They were made by Dugan.

Water sets

The pitchers found with water sets can be seen in the style shown here or a tall slender shape called a tankard. In some patterns, there are several sizes of pitchers as well as smaller milk pitchers. This water set is Northwood's Greek Key in purple.

Punch sets

Collectors who appreciate truly massive pieces of glass put water sets at the top of their lists. When sets are sold, they are usually specified by the number of pieces—counting the bowl and base as two pieces. This is Imperial's Four Seventy Four in amethyst, as an eight-piece set.

Wine and liquor sets

There were a number of patterns that incorporated wine or cordial sets. Sometimes they had wine glasses as in this marigold Imperial Octagon set; other times sets included cordial glasses or even small tumblers.

Learning about carnival glass **161**

The effect of iridescence on glass

The iridescent spray is what gives carnival glass much of its character. Everything else being equal, the richness of the iridescence is what sets one piece apart from another. How much of the appearance of glass can be attributed to the iridescence? The two photos directly below demonstrate how much of the look of the glass is contributed by iridescence. The left photo shows a Millersburg Mayan bowl as it was photographed. In the second photo, I've removed much of the iridescence through the use of the computer. While an uniridized bowl might be attractive, it pales in comparison with the iridized version. Which would you want?

How does the quality of iridescence affect glass in the real world? The photos below are of two different Imperial Heavy Grape chop plates in purple. They sold at the same 1997 auction for choice— the winning bidder got to choose which he or she wanted at that price. The multicolor version on the left sold for $250. The silverish example on the right then brought $90 in subsequent bidding.

The colors of carnival glass

Description of carnival glass colors is stated in terms of the base glass color, not that of the iridescent coating—with a couple of major exceptions. In other words, if you look through a part of a piece of carnival glass that has no iridescence and see green, then that piece is green, regardless of whether there is blue, gold, or orange iridescence on the glass.

One of the challenges of identification comes up when the base glass color does not match our expectations of a color. Blues, for example, are found in a wide range of tints (lights and darks) and hues (greenish blues to blue violets). There was a time when collectors identified colors in more basic terms. There was blue and there was ice blue. That's all. Now, with more folks collecting and becoming more sophisticated about the available choices and with auctioneers trying to find descriptions that might trigger buying interest, we have names such as cobalt, teal, sapphire, celeste, Renninger, and so on.

Unfortunately, there is not always agreement about what each of the color descriptions represents. One person's teal is another's aqua. Color is very subjective and there is currently no way to provide a standard method of describing glass color, other than by the traditional method of referencing colors we hope others view the same as we do. There is substantial confusion.

What does this mean for you? If you're an experienced collector, you have no doubt formed your own thoughts about color descriptions. If you're new to collecting, I've attempted to provide, on the following pages, a visual and verbal description of many of the most frequently seen colors. Bear in mind that what you are looking at here are not pieces of glass, or even photos of pieces of glass, but printed reproductions. That's pretty far removed from the real glass and can be misleading.

To become familiar with the actual glass colors, you need to view a lot of glass. Auctions and conventions are a good way.

These Imperial Ripple vases exhibit a good range of the colors found in carnival glass. The vase on the left is in the aqua range. The large vase to the right is purple. In front of that is a vase with a very pale iridescence on clear glass that some call clambroth—although it is light enough to also pass for white. The tall vase behind is helios green, a light golden iridescence that allows the base color to show through. In front is a small marigold. Behind that is smoke—a grayish or brownish color—on clear glass. Finally, amber; in which the glass color may be yellow to brown.

Identifying carnival glass colors

Marigold

Marigold carnival glass is the color seen most often. In fact, many patterns are found only in this color. There are, however, a few patterns where it is quite rare and a few more where it is unknown.

Marigold is an exception to the general rule that carnival colors are determined by the color of the base glass. To be called marigold, the base glass must be clear. Granted, marigold iridescence is often found on colored base glass, but in these instances it is identified by the glass color. A good example of this is aqua opal glass, which was sometimes sprayed with the orange color we call marigold, and sometimes an iridescence with little color called pastel. Marigold iridescence on aqua opal is often referred to by collectors as butterscotch—that's what it looks like. Pastel iridescence allows the color of the glass to show (see page 176). Neither is considered better than the other although some collectors prefer one to the other.

This soft satin-like finish is called pastel marigold. How does it affect the value? This Hearts and Flowers plate sold for $1,000 in 1993, a very respectable price.

Not all marigold was created equal. Sometimes it is very pale, other times a darker color sprayed on heavily. The range in marigold can be dramatic and can affect the value.

Pastel marigold

Pastel marigold has a satin surface and reflects subtle pinks and blues. It's not a washed out marigold—but very soft and leaning toward yellow. It's easy to pass up pastel colors because they don't jump out. But watch for them as subtlety can be just as important in collecting as the more flashy characteristics.

Here is a very dark marigold that some refer to as pumpkin. Pieces with this rich coloring tend to be valued higher than ordinary marigold. This Northwood Peacocks bowl sold for $425 at a 1998 auction—at the high end.

More marigold

Because so much of carnival glass is this orange color, it pays to watch for the unusual as well as to avoid the less desirable. Watch for iridescence that has multiple colors reflecting from the basic marigold coloration. Always check the base glass color as the marigold can hide an interesting or unusual base glass.

Is it red? No, but it looks that way. This Fenton Captive Rose plate simply has an iridescent overlay with a reddish tint and is very desirable even though not red.

Which would you want? It shouldn't be much of a surprise that most folks would choose the Northwood Lightning Flower nappy on the left. It sold for $70 while the lighter one brought just $45—both at the same auction.

Honey amber and amber

Be careful not to confuse these two colors. Honey amber, mostly seen in US Glass products, is a brownish marigold iridescence on clear glass. The name describes the effect well.

Amber carnival is based on amber-colored glass and can vary from an almost yellow to brown—just as real amber does. Northwood also made a grayish amber called Horehound.

Most of the honey amber you'll see will be in the Cosmos and Cane pattern (above) or Palm Beach, both by US Glass. Honey amber is on clear glass with a soft brownish marigold iridescence.

True amber is a yellow-brown base glass and may have multicolor iridescence as in this Imperial Homestead chop plate. Imperial made most of the amber glass. It is said that Fenton amber was unintentional.

Learning about carnival glass

Clambroth

Clambroth is another of those special cases where the glass is clear and the color is determined by the iridescence. In this case it's a very pale ginger ale color. It has a very transparent quality.

There are collectors who view this color as simply a weak marigold, but most accept clambroth as a separate and distinct color or use the term to describe pale marigold that they find attractive. It should be noted that some collectors feel the base glass must have a faint tint to be called clambroth. As might be expected, this is a very hard color to photograph and reproduce. Your best chance of learning more about the subtleties of clambroth will be to look at actual examples.

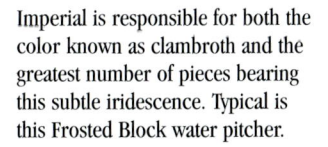

Imperial is responsible for both the color known as clambroth and the greatest number of pieces bearing this subtle iridescence. Typical is this Frosted Block water pitcher.

Northwood produced fewer pieces of clambroth than did Imperial. This Peacock and Urn large ice cream shaped bowl is typical of Northwood's efforts. The color is almost smoky but with frequently strong multicolor iridescence. In some Northwood clambroth there may be a slight tint to the base glass.

These two Imperial bowls demonstrate that there are differences in the appearance of clambroth depending on the nature of the pattern and the vagaries of application of the iridescent spray. As the items were hand sprayed, it was inevitable that there was sometimes wide variation. The bowl on the left is the Fashion pattern, found on the exterior of bowl. On the right is Windmill.

166 A Field Guide to Carnival Glass

Smoke

As with clambroth, smoke was a production color for Imperial. I'm convinced that the color we call smoke was originally two or more colors; there is just too much variation. In one old catalog, Imperial (who made most of the smoke color) listed two colors that could be smoke. One was Peacock and described as "Every color of the rainbow is represented, a golden yellow predominating. Many color variations." The other was Saphire (their spelling) that was "A dark blue-gray iridescent color on crystal glass."

As can be seen below, there are some smoke colors that are dark gray with overtones of blue and purple, others with brownish or amber tints, and still more with greenish casts—as well as others.

The two Imperial Gothic Arches vases in front demonstrate two of the colors called smoke. Both are on clear glass; the one on the left is what I think was called "saphire;" the one on the right is "peacock." Behind is a marigold vase.

This example of an Imperial Shell pattern (it is also found with a stippled background named Shell and Sand) is what is called smoke—but with definite overtones of green and highlights of blue and yellow. Certainly not saphire or peacock.

Yet another version of Imperial's smoke, this one a Fashion water pitcher with brown iridescence and red/gold and blue highlights.

Here's a Northwood piece in smoke—a ruffled Peacocks bowl. Northwood usually does have a slight gray tint to the glass. This example has pastel iridescence with blue tones and gold highlights.

Learning about carnival glass

White

At first flush, one would think white carnival should have a milky appearance, but it really consists of pastel iridescence on clear glass. In addition, the surface has been treated to give it a frosty look, which may seem to be a bit opaque.

White carnival is very subtle. It is best viewed, and displayed, against a dark background to enhance the highlights. Bear in mind that some patterns came in clear glass both with and without iridescence. Occasionally it can be hard to tell the difference.

There is also clear carnival, which will have a shiny, or radium, quality—without the frostiness usually associated with most white carnival.

Dugan made a great deal of the white carnival. This is their Roundup pattern in an unusual three-in-one edge. This example has particularly nice multicolor iridescence dominated by turquoise and pinks.

Northwood's white was as good as Dugan's and oftentimes better. Northwood and Dugan sometimes decorated their white with gold or silver trim. Dugan would sometimes paint fruit or flowers in red, blue, or gold. Shown is Northwood's Peacock at the Fountain.

This Fenton Leaf Chain plate in white demonstrates another aspect of white: transparency. Here, the back pattern (Berry and Leaf Circle) shows through, creating a rich juxtaposition of designs.

Millersburg made virtually no carnival in white although they did make quite a bit of crystal. This tricorner sauce in the Hobstar and Feather pattern is one of two known pieces—the other an Ohio Star vase.

Amethyst/purple/lavender

This color range can be particularly difficult to get a handle on as the difference between purple and amethyst carnival is quite subjective. While amethyst and purple are essentially the same glass color, with amethyst a midrange color and purple darker, it is the point where amethyst becomes purple that causes the most confusion. The consensus among experienced collectors is that the color is purple when it reaches the shade of grape juice.

Lavender is usually considered to be a lighter version of amethyst or purple and has pastel iridescence.

This is Dugan's Dogwood Sprays in a typical amethyst glass. It's a good piece on which to view the glass color as the iridescence is pastel and interferes little with the glass color.

This Fenton Peacock Tail is also amethyst, and the base glass is much like that of the Dogwood Sprays bowl at the left. The difference? The strong marigold overlay completely masks the glass color.

This rare pedestal footed Fleur de Lis rosebowl shows a pretty much standard Millersburg amethyst. There is a quite nice blue component in the iridescence that enhances the natural beauty of the glass.

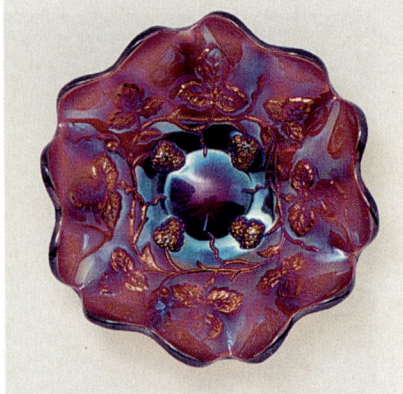

Millersburg made little glass that could be truly classified as purple. This Strawberry Wreath ruffled sauce is one example. It also has an extremely vibrant blue iridescence.

Learning about carnival glass 169

Talk about color! Scroll Embossed plates in amethyst/purple often have this spectacular multicolor iridescence that looks as though the iridescence was selectively applied.

Dugan also produced some spectacular color on amethyst. Here, however, is something a little different—green and red iridescence on an amethyst Apple Blossom Twigs plate.

Lavender is usually a lighter version of amethyst/purple and can be seen here in the color of the base on this Imperial Grape ruffled compote.

Northwood's lavender was pretty much like the other companies'—although there seems to have been quite a bit of variation between batches. This is a Singing Birds mug with blue iridescence.

Fiery amethyst is a deep amethyst bordering on red. The color is only visible when viewed through an uniridized area. This is Northwood's Good Luck bowl with rich iridescence.

Black amethyst is virtually opaque, with perhaps a hint of deep amethyst seen when the glass is viewed through a strong light. Much of this color is found in Australian pieces such as this large ruffled Swan bowl.

Blue

No color range is as broad and varied as is blue. From a very pale blue to deep cobalt and aqua to violet, there are many colors and variations.

Interestingly, blue is not frequently found among three of the major players in the classic carnival era—Millersburg, Imperial and Dugan. While Fenton made prodigious amounts of the color, its range of blues is not nearly as extensive as Northwood's. Northwood could be called the king of blues.

Cobalt blue in this Hearts and Flowers bowl with pie crust edge shows Northwood at its best. With red and blue iridescence flashed with gold highlights, this color is called electric blue.

A medium blue color with pastel iridescence on this Peacocks stippled plate. Unlike many colors in the blue range, this one has not acquired a specific name.

Ice blue is a very pale color, sometimes even lighter than seen here. Shown is Northwood's Daisy and Drape vase.

Fenton's Apple Tree water pitcher is shown here in a typical cobalt blue with both blue and gold iridescence.

Although Dugan made very little blue, the God and Home water set was made only in that color. It's a rich cobalt similar to that of the other companies. This is a multicolor iridescence.

Imperial made very little blue—most of that in the medium blue shown in this Lustre Rose fernery with a silverish iridescence. Millersburg also made few pieces in blue, and much of that for special orders like the Bernheimer Brothers advertising item at right.

Learning about carnival glass 171

Celeste, sapphire and Renninger

These three colors are in the middle of the blue range; neither as dark as cobalt nor as light as ice blue. Celeste and sapphire have the same base glass color; sapphire has marigold iridescence while celeste has pastel—often with a stretch finish. Northwood made most of the sapphire, Fenton and Dugan the celeste.

Renninger is similar to sapphire but a bit darker and sort of grayed. The hue also shifts slightly toward cobalt blue or purple but is still quite transparent.

This is Northwood's sapphire blue, shown in a round Bushel Basket.

Here is Fenton's celeste in a Horse Medallion ruffled bowl. Dugan made a similar color.

Northwood's Renninger color can best be seen in this Drapery rosebowl by looking at the color that shows through the back of the piece just above the opening. It has about the same intensity as sapphire, but with more purple or blue and is a bit more muted.

Aqua and teal

Aqua is blue glass with a touch of green in it. It could also be described as a lighter version of sapphire. Teal is green glass with a touch of blue.

In aqua, this Northwood Leaf and Beads rosebowl best shows the color on its twig-like feet.

The teal glass color can be seen around the outside edge of the Imperial Rose (Open Rose) large collar-base bowl.

Green

All classic era carnival manufacturers made green glass. While Dugan did make some green carnival, it seems to have been limited to just a few patterns, namely Vintage footed bowls and Farmyard pieces.

I've included vaseline here as it is often associated with ice green glass color. Real vaseline glass will glow when illuminated with a black (UV) light.

This Northwood Peacock at the Fountain pitcher shows off the green glass color well, although the iridescence masks it around the trunk.

Fenton's typical green is fairly intense and is quite consistent among the company's many patterns. It is shown here on a Ragged Robin three-in-one edged bowl.

Emerald green is recognized among carnival collectors as vivid green glass with predominantly blue iridescence that may be overshot with pink and gold highlights. This plate is Northwood's Rose Show.

Millersburg's green is often a thin, very transparent glass color as in this unusual crimped diamond shape Nesting Swan bowl. Millersburg also made a deeper green glass as well as an olive hue.

Learning about carnival glass 173

Imperial could also do emerald green. In this scarce Hobstar and Flower compote, note the transparency in the base that shows the pattern on the bottom.

Helios was Imperial's original name for this unique color—a pale golden iridescence on green glass. This is Imperial's Grape in the rare nut bowl shape.

With a few notable exceptions, most of Cambridge's carnival output was green. The Inverted Feather cracker jar is found only in this deep, rich green.

Northwood's Memphis punch bowl and base in ice green. Ice green, along with ice blue and white, were introduced by Northwood in 1912.

Northwood Raspberry milk pitcher. Northwood's lime green is an ice lime—with pastel iridescence. Other companies' lime green has marigold iridescence.

Vaseline glass was created when a small amount of uranium oxide was mixed into the glass batch. The color is a light greenish yellow, seen most easily here in the base of this Millersburg Strawberry Wreath compote. Note the unstippled leaf in the bowl.

Red and Amberina

In itself, red is the most desirable color—though for some patterns other colors may rival it. Curiously, only Fenton made any amount of red, while Imperial made red pieces in a few patterns.

Red glass is created by putting selenium into the molten mix. The color appears when it is reheated. Amberina is a yellowish glass color that occurs when red glass is partially reheated. Amberina is usually found as a blend of yellowish color to red. This is often seen in bowls where the base is yellow and the edge is red. When the opposite happens—red base and yellowish rim, it's called reverse amberina.

The iridescence can have a strong effect on red. The most desirable is a red iridescence, giving the piece a "cherry" look. At the other end of the scale is a red that is so dark and brownish that it's called brick red.

Northwood and Millersburg made no red.

A bright cherry red is considered the top quality of red carnival. This Fenton Orange Tree bowl with three-in-one edge is very rare and may be the only one with this shaping in existence.

On the left is a red Orange Tree mug. On the right is one in amberina. To the uninitiated, these can seem to be a mistake—with yellow at the base blending up into a strong red. Such color is far more valuable than more common colors and may sell for as much as some red.

While all red is considered rare and valuable, this Fenton Peacock and Urn ruffled bowl is among the rarest and most desirable.

Here is one of the few Imperial patterns to appear in red, Imperial Rose (Lustre Rose) in the large footed fruit bowl. It is generally a somewhat darker red than that of the average Fenton red.

Learning about carnival glass

Opalescent colors

Opalescent glass was created by putting bone ash in the glass mix and reheating the piece after allowing it to cool slightly. Certain parts then turned milky, giving the glass its unique appearance.

Most of the opalescent glass seen is peach opal—white opalescent glass with a marigold iridescence. It could have been called marigold opalescent, but the name peach opal sticks.

The next most frequently seen opal color is aqua opal—the most desirable of the opal colors and, according to some collectors, more desirable than red. Certainly the most expensive piece of carnival glass recently sold was aqua opal—a Northwood Grape and Cable small size punch set.

Far and away, the most prolific producer of peach opal carnival was Dugan. This is the Fan gravy boat or occasional dish. The marigold iridescence was usually applied to just one side of a piece; the front of bowls and plates and the exterior of water sets, for example.

The only other company to make significant quantities of peach opal was Westmoreland, typified by this File and Fan compote. Actually, Westmoreland is better known for its blue opal and marigold on milk glass than peach opal.

Northwood made only a few pieces of carnival peach opal, and nobody is quite sure why. There are two of these Beaded Cable rosebowls and a couple of Strawberry plates, but that's about it.

Fenton also had quite limited output of peach opal. This Peacock and Grape ruffled bowl is quite rare; less so are Dragon and Lotus bowls. At least one each of Acorn bowls, Pond Lily bonbon, and Fenton Flowers rosebowl are known.

Aqua opal

Aqua opal has a special place in the pantheon of carnival glass colors. Given a choice, most collectors would pick aqua opal over any other color—not just because of its rarity but because most examples are quite handsome. Nonetheless, a few patterns are found quite often in this color—Beaded Cable rosebowls coming to mind. Even so, such pieces are valued more highly than other colors that may be more scarce.

Aqua opal was a production-line color only for Northwood; the few Fenton pieces were experimental or unintentional.

Both of these pieces are considered aqua opal. The difference? The base glass is the same, an opalescent version of aqua glass, but the iridescence gives the pieces a different look. The example on the left is called butterscotch iridescence.

It is really marigold that, when applied to the aqua color, provides the rich effect that looks like butterscotch. The iridescence on the example directly above is called pastel. It is a more subtle iridescence that may be obvious only when rotated in the light.

The top photo is Northwood's ruffled Wishbone in aqua opal—very rare. Immediately above is their Good Luck bowl with pie crust edge. It is much rarer than the regular ruffled version in aqua opal.

These two Fenton ruffled bowls are thought to be the only ones known in these patterns in aqua opal. The top photo is Holly, immediately above is Leaf Chain. Fenton aqua opal is sometimes toward the blue side.

Learning about carnival glass 177

Here is the extremely rare and very desirable Northwood Peacock and Urn large ice cream with light iridescence between pastel and butterscotch.

Also Northwood, this is the cracker jar in the Grape and Cable pattern. A beautiful balance between opal and iridescence. Two examples are known.

This is the extraordinary Peacock at the Fountain fruit bowl. Two of these are known in aqua opal.

Northwood Grape and Cable hatpin holder.

Fenton's Orange Tree Loving Cup. This is the only one known in aqua opal.

Just 6 or 8 examples are known of this Northwood midsize Tree Trunk vase.

There are only a few of these Northwood Thin Rib midsize vases in aqua opal.

This MiniRib vase is 7½ inches tall and is the only one known.

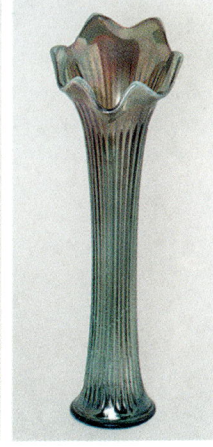

There are only a few known of Fenton's Fine Rib in aqua opal.

Other opalescent colors

While peach opal and aqua opal represent the majority of opalescent colors seen in carnival, a few odd ones pop up now and then. There is some question as to how they came about as there are so few examples (aside from the Westmoreland blue opal) to suggest production line colors. The consensus seems to be that they were either experiments or mistakes on the way to something else.

This is the Scales pattern in blue opal with pastel iridescence. Westmoreland frequently used this iridescence on their blue opal pieces.

Here is the only known Fenton Grape and Cable bowl in blue opal. It is deep blue base glass with dark multicolor iridescence.

Dugan's Double Stem Rose in cobalt opal. I've not seen or heard of another such Dugan piece.

Northwood's Hearts and Flower compote in powder blue opal. Note the amount of opal.

Fenton's Boggy Bayou vase in lime green opal.

Fenton's Blackberry Spray ruffled hat in red opal.

Millersburg's Ohio Star in green opal.

Learning about carnival glass

Rare and unusual colors

As one would expect in a craft where so much of the work is done manually, there are bound to be experiments, mistakes, and variations that fall outside the normal production run. That applies to some of these unusual glass colors. Others, however, were obviously short production runs as the glass was used over a range of products.

Powder blue slag is found in only a few pieces; the Northwood midsize Tree Trunk vase is the only one known in this color; the Peacocks bowl is one of two currently known.

Some colors are a result of variations in the glass-making process. This Fenton Waterlily ruffled sauce can best be described as amberina slag. Note the red streaks—possibly caused by imperfect glass mix.

This Northwood Grape and Cable centerpiece bowl is in iridized custard glass. It is additionally enhanced by gold applied to the rim.

Persian blue is slightly translucent with a cloudy appearance. It is seen occasionally in Northwood and a few Fenton items such as this Lotus and Grape.

Blue milk glass, like white milk glass, is completely opaque. This is Fenton's Pond Lily.

This is a Northwood Grape and Cable bonbon in marigold on moonstone. Moonstone has slight translucency.

Starting a collection of carnival glass

With about two thousand patterns, numerous colors, and a huge variety of shapes available, it's difficult for the new collector to limit his or her choices. Some prefer to collect a certain color, a particular pattern or shape, or to pursue a theme such as flowers, peacocks, or pieces with spectacular iridescence and color.

I submit, though, that a good place to begin is with tumblers. There are a number of reasons: you can learn a lot about patterns; a group of the same shape makes an attractive display (and take little space); they are widely available; and the cost can be minimal. Not all tumbler patterns have accompanying pitchers, but many do, so you can extend your collection that way.

Here, then, are a few tumblers you might consider when starting a collection. Tumblers on these two pages are available for less than $100; those on the following two pages are some of the more rare.

If you want to do more research into tumblers, you may want to acquire the Heart of America Carnival Glass Association's *Educational Series II* that lists and describes more than 180 tumblers.

Northwood Acorn Burrs in green

Fenton Apple Tree in blue

Dugan Beaded Shell in amethyst

Fenton Butterfly and Berry in marigold

Fenton Butterfly and Fern in amethyst

Imperial Diamond Lace in purple

Millersburg Diamonds in amethyst

Imperial File in marigold

Learning about carnival glass 181

Northwood Grape Arbor in purple

Dugan Heavy Iris in purple

Fenton Inverted Coin Dot in marigold

Dugan Jewelled Heart in marigold

Dugan Lattice and Daisy in blue

Fenton Lattice and Grape in blue

Dugan Maple Leaf in purple

Fenton Milady in blue with purple iridescence

Fenton Orange Tree in blue

Northwood Oriental Poppy in purple

Dugan Peacock at the Fountain in blue

Dugan Rambler Rose in blue

Fenton Ten Mums in blue

Fenton Waterlily and Cattails in marigold

Imperial Windmill in purple

Dugan Wreathed Cherry in marigold

182   A Field Guide to Carnival Glass

Australian Banded Diamonds in marigold

Beaded Spears in marigold by Jain of India

Big Butterfly in marigold

Fenton Bouquet in blue

Imperial Cape Cod in smoky amethyst

Fostoria Chain and Star in marigold

Imperial Chatelaine in purple

Dugan Circle Scroll in marigold

Imperial Cone and Tie in purple

US Glass Cosmos and Cane in honey amber

Cut Cosmos in marigold, maker unknown

Dugan Dahlia in white with gold flowers

Northwood Dandelion in smoky lavender

Fans in marigold, probably European

US Glass Frolicking Bears in green

Millersburg Gay Nineties in amethyst

Learning about carnival glass   183

Dugan God and Home in blue

Millersburg Hanging Cherries in green

Dugan Harvest Flower in lime green, marigold iridescence

Millersburg Hobnail in amethyst

Hobstar Shield, maker unknown

Cambridge Inverted Thistle in amethyst

Fenton Lily of the Valley in blue

Lucile in blue, possibly Brockwitz of Germany

Millersburg Marilyn in amethyst

Oklahoma in marigold by Crystales de Mexico

US Glass Omnibus in marigold

Millersburg Perfection in amethyst

Northwood Plums and Cherries in blue

Dugan Quill in amethyst

Rising Sun in blue, maker uncertain

White Oak in marigold, maker unknown

Sorting out Peacock and Urn patterns

One of the most confusing aspects of identifying carnival glass is determining the difference between the Fenton, Millersburg and Northwood versions of Peacock and Urn. All are very similar, but each has unique characteristics that make the job easier.

Fenton This is the easiest to identify. It's the only one with a sawtooth edge and berries on the back. As with others, there is always a bee just beyond the bird's beak.

Northwood The fastest way to determine whether a Peacock and Urn piece is Northwood is to check the base. None have a rayed base. There is always stippling under the bird. Has a bee.

Millersburg These will always have the rayed star in the base. A "mystery" variant has beads on the top of the bowl and top of the column. There is always a bee.

Millersburg Peacock This is the variant that has no bee. As such, it is referred to as a Millersburg Peacock rather than Peacock and Urn. There are additional Peacock and Urn variations as well.

Listings, continued from page 152

Peacock and Urn, Northwood

Northwood's Peacock and Urn can be distinguished from Millersburg's by the smooth base; if it has a many-rayed star in the base, it is Millersburg. In the large mold, shown here, the bee is next to a cigar-shaped leaf—unlike any other peacock pattern. A fair number of pieces in the Northwood pattern have stippling almost out to the rim, and are listed separately as "stippled."

Ice cream set, 5 piece (1 large, 4 small bowls)
Ice blue   1,900

Ice cream set, 7 piece (1 large, 6 small bowls)
Blue, electric   900–1,600
Purple   700–900
White   900 (1998)

Bowl, large ice cream, 9–10" (nonstippled)
Amethyst/purple	400–700	most common color
Aqua opal	31,000 (1993)	
Blue	800–1,400	somewhat scarce
Blue, electric	1,000–1,500	scarce
Blue, Renninger	3,000–4,000	rare color
Clambroth	750 (1993)	
Green	1,200–1,800	average availability
Green	2,500–4,500	exceptional examples
Honey amber	1,500 (1995)	
Horehound	330 (1994)	
Ice blue	800–1,100	fairly common color
Ice green	900–1,400	fairly common color
Lime green	2,400 (1994)	
Marigold	350–550	common color
Marigold, dark	500–800	
Marigold, pastel	1,000–1,300	
Sapphire blue	13,000–18,000	rare color
White	325–550	fairly common color

Bowl, large ice cream, stippled
Blue	1,200–2,000	scarce in stippled
Blue	1,200 (1993)	swirl effect
Blue, Renninger	3,000–3,500	rare color
Honey amber	1,400–1,600	rare color
Horehound	1,000–1,400	rare color
Ice blue	850 (1995)	
Marigold	375–600	most common color
Marigold	1,000–1,400	pumpkin orange
Sapphire	8,500 (1996)	
Smoke	1,600 (1994)	

This is Northwood's Peacock at the Urn small ice cream bowl. Note the stippling just under the bird. You'll also see an anomaly in this particular piece—there is no bee. Only a couple of these rarities are known. Courtesy of Tom and Sharon Mordini.

Bowl, small ice cream or sauce, 5–6"
Amethyst/purple	60–100	common color
Aqua opal	2,000–2,500	rare color
Blue	60–100	common color
Green	650–800	scarce color
Ice blue	170–275	fairly common color
Ice green	300–450	scarce color
Marigold	60–100	fairly common color
White	110–200	fairly common color

Bowl, small ice cream or sauce, stippled
Blue	90–160	
Blue, Renninger	1,500 (1994)	
Marigold	900 (1994)	chipped

Plate, chop, 10½–11", from large bowl mold
Amethyst/purple   600–900
Ice green, marigold, and white reported

Peacock Tail, Fenton

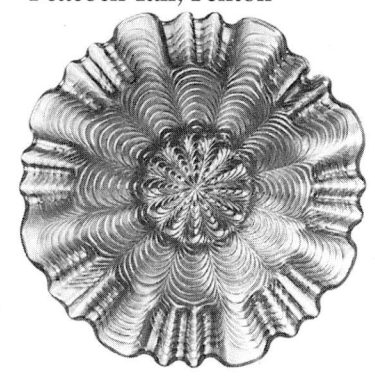

This especially nice green 3/1 edge large bowl sold for $325 at the 1994 John and Lucile Britt auction (Jim Seeck). What's surprising is the relative avail-

186 A Field Guide to Carnival Glass

ability of green and amethyst in this pattern—with blue rather scarce in some shapes. Most pieces carry the Wide Panel back.

Bowl, large, round, ruffled or candy ribbon edge
Amethyst	60–100	most common color
Amethyst	1,200 (1997)	low, 16 ruffles
Green	30–50	
Green	70–130	3/1 edge
Green	425 (1998)	square crimped
Marigold	90–105	tight candy ribbon edge
Marigold	55–70	3/1 edge
Marigold	100 (1998)	ice cream shape

Bowl, 7", round, ruffled or candy ribbon edge
Amethyst	25–40	common color
Blue	100–175	scarce color
Green	20–35	
Marigold	80–110	scarce color
Peach opal, rare		
Red	2,000–3,000	

Bowl, 7" with Horlacher advertising on back
Amethyst	75–100	
Green	80 (1998)	

The small Peacock Tail bowl is sometimes found in a tricorner shape like the one above. This small example, in green with a bit of opal at the edges, is courtesy of Galen and Kathi Johnson.

Bowl, small, tricorner
Amethyst	45–60	
Green	50–70	

Bowl, small, 6", ruffled, round or 3/1 edge
Amethyst	40–75	
Blue	50–85	
Green	20–30	most common color
Vaseline	195 (1995)	marigold overlay, damage

Bonbon, 2 handles, stemmed
Amethyst	30–50	
Blue	40–70	scarce color
Green	35–50	most common color
Marigold	15–25	

Compote, ruffled
Amethyst	20–35	common color
Blue	30–50	
Blue, electric	140 (1997)	
Green	25–45	common color
Marigold	20–35	

Hat, ruffled
Fenton also used the green hat shape to make advertising pieces for various companies. See Lettered section.
Blue	40–60	most common color
Green	25–40	

Plate, 6–7" (all rare)
Blue	800–1,000	
Green	295 (1995)	
Marigold	300–400	average iridescence
Marigold	700 (1998)	

Plate, 9", rare
Marigold	1,300 (1993)	

Peacock Tail variant, Millersburg

Found only in a compote, the Peacock Tail variant pattern is more of a medallion in the center—around which radiate feather-shaped rays. While traditionally credited to Millersburg, some collectors are now questioning this attribution. However, no one seems to be able to suggest a likely alternative.

Compote, ruffled
Amethyst	100–160	common color
Green	80–150	common color
Marigold	50–85	common color
Purple	175–275	scarce color

Peacock Tail and Daisy, Westmoreland

This pattern has six peacock's tails angling out from the center with a central medallion of a daisy-like flower. Known in ruffled bowls in amethyst, marigold, and iridized blue milk glass—all rare.

Pearly Dots, Westmoreland

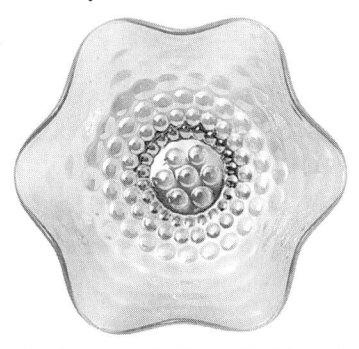

Pearly Dots can be distinguished from Fenton's Coin Dot by the lack of stippling on the dots. Blue opal is a common color.

Bowl
Amethyst	15–25
Blue, light	30–45
Blue opal	50–90

Compote
Amethyst opal	120–200
Blue opal	225–375
Peach opal	30–55

Plate, 9"
Amethyst	25–45

This Pearly Dots rosebowl whimsey, in aqua, sold for $275 at a 1996 Tom Burns auction.

Pebbles, Fenton

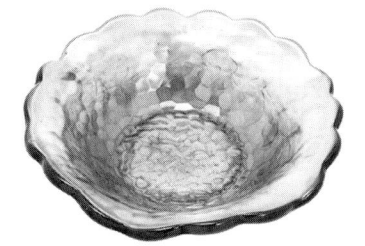

Much less often seen than the similar Imperial Cobblestones in which the dots are separate and distinct. Here the pebbles merge, forming small hexagons. You can confirm the pattern by noting the back. Pebbles has Honeycomb and Clover, a pattern used on other Fenton pieces. This sauce, in green (the most common color), sold at a 1997 auction for $10.

Pepper Plant, Fenton

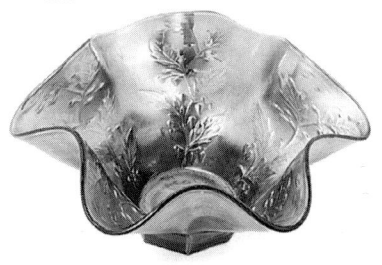

Some collectors feel that this is nothing more than a Holly hat in which the berry elements have become elongated during the forming and that the hexagonal base was simply an alternative Fenton exterior pattern. In any event, there is no reason for these to sell for significantly different prices than the Holly, everything else being equal.

Hat, ruffled
Amethyst	75 (1997)	
Blue	50–65	
Green	75 (1995)	
Marigold	30 (1996)	
Vaseline	85 (1997)	jack-in-the-pulpit shape

188 A Field Guide to Carnival Glass

Perfection, Millersburg

A highly prized pattern, Perfection pitchers are found with both ruffled and flared tops. The ruffled example above is in marigold (and cracked) and sold for $2,900 at the 1993 American Carnival Glass Club auction. The flared top in purple sold for $3,500 at the 1993 International Carnival Glass Club auction. With this pattern amethyst is quite dark and sometimes described as purple.

Water pitcher
Amethyst	2,700–3,500	most common color
Green	4,500–5,500	
Marigold	2,900 (1993)	ruffled, cracked

Tumbler (see photo on page 183)
Amethyst/purple	275–500	
Green	200–325	very rare color
Marigold, rare		

Persian Garden, Dugan

Overlapping crescents distinguish this pleasing pattern—it's almost more of a texture when seen from a distance. There seem to have been two molds; the larger one used for large bowls, chop plates, and punch bowl; the smaller for small bowls and plates.

Bowl, large ice cream, 11–12"
Amethyst/purple	450–600	common color
Peach opal	300–500	common color
White	200–300	very common color

Bowl, small ice cream or ruffled sauce, 6–7"
Peach opal	35 (1996)	
White	55–80	most common color

Berry set, 7 piece, ruffled
Amethyst/purple	400–550
White	395 (1998)

Bowl, large ruffled (more rare than ice cream)
Green, one known
Purple	450 (1998)	
Peach opal	300–450	

Chop plate, 13", from large bowl
Amethyst/purple	3,000–4,500	
Amethyst	11,000 (1993)	blue highlights
Lavender	8,000 (1998)	
Peach opal	7,000 (1993)	
White	1,800–2,400	

These small plates are very popular. The rare blue examples are probably worth $600 to $1,000. Most have a basketweave exterior—some white examples have the Pool of Pearls exterior.

Plate, small, 6"
Amethyst/purple	450–700	
Aqua	225 (1998)	
Lavender	200 (1995)	
Marigold	55–80	most common color
Peach opal	125–220	
White	80–150	very common color

Plate, 7½"
White	750 (1997)

The stand for the fruit bowls is made from a Big Basketweave vase mold that has been ruffled. Bowls are also occasionally found with a round top.

Fruit bowl, 2 piece
Amethyst/purple	450–700	ruffled top
Amethyst	325 (1995)	round top
Marigold	100–200	ruffled top
Marigold	675 (1996)	round top
Lavender	500 (1998)	ruffled, smoke iridescence

Peach opal	275–350	ruffled top
White	400–600	ruffled top
White	200 (1995)	round top

Fruit bowl base only
Amethyst 60–80

Persian Medallion, Fenton

Persian Medallion, with its ring of embroidered medallions, displays a definite Moorish influence. Several shapes in this pattern have been reproduced (See Contemporary glass).

Bonbon or card tray shape
Amber, rare		
Amberina	350–400	rare color
Amethyst	70–130	scarce color
Aqua	150–250	fairly common color
Blue	50–80	common color
Blue, pastel	105 (1995)	
Celeste	1,000–1,600	rare color
Green	150–225	scarce color
Marigold	40–70	common color
Moonstone, rare		
Red	650–900	fairly common color
Vaseline	100–200	fairly common color

Bowl, small (or sauce), 6–7"
Amberina	550 (1997)	
Amethyst	35–60	
Aqua	65–100	
Blue	35–50	common color
Green	40–60	
Green	225 (1996)	CRE, one known
Marigold	65–115	footed, Grape & Cable exterior
Vaseline	85–100	ice cream shape
White	40–60	

Bowl, midsize, about 8–9"
Amethyst	95 (1996)	
Aqua	140 (1997)	
Blue	90–150	
Green	50–70	
Marigold	75–110	
Red	2,500–3,500	rare

Bowl, large, about 10", ruffled, round, 3/1 edge
Amethyst	175–275	common color
Blue	200–350	
Blue, electric	300 (1997)	
Green	110–200	common color
Green	550 (1997)	super blue iridescence
Lavender	300 (1993)	
White	300 (1995)	

Fenton made two styles of Persian Medallion compotes. One is slightly larger than the other and has the medallion pattern on the exterior and foot as well as inside. The smaller compote has the Wide Panel exterior. Persian Medallion is also found on the exterior of Stream of Hearts compotes.

Compote, large
Amethyst/purple	250–350	scarce color
Blue	80–150	most common color
Green	115–200	common color
Marigold	70–125	common color
White	500–800	

Compote, small (scarce shape)
Amethyst	150–200	
Blue	60–100	common color
Green	60–100	
Marigold	50–80	common color
White	170 (1993)	

These Persian Medallion bowls with the Grape and Cable exterior are found in two sizes. The most frequently seen bowl is about 10" wide and $5^{1}/_{8}$" tall. The larger and much rarer bowl, measures 11" wide and $6^{3}/_{4}$" tall. They are reported in amethyst, green, and marigold. The small footed sauces with Grape and Cable exterior are said to have been made to match this piece.

Fruit bowl, footed, Grape and Cable exterior (regular size unless noted)
Amethyst	225–350	
Blue	150–275	common color
Green	350–550	
Green	1,000–1,800	large size
Ice green known		
Marigold	125–200	common color

190 A Field Guide to Carnival Glass

Punch sets
Persian Medallion was also used as the interior pattern for some of the Fenton Wreath of Roses punch sets. See that listing.

The hair receiver is simply a rosebowl with a square opening. Persian Medallion is the only such carnival pattern where the hair receiver was a production shape.

Hair receiver, square opening
Blue	165–250	
Marigold	70–100	most common color
White	160 (1997)	

Rosebowl, round opening
Amethyst	175–350	scarce color
Blue	125–200	most common color
Marigold	60–80	somewhat scarce color
White	90–170	

As with most patterns, plates rank near the top in desirability. This one has been whimsied into a tri-corner shape. It is blue, and courtesy of Betty Cloud. Small marigold plates are also known to have been whimsied into four-sides up shapes.

Plate, 6–7"
Amethyst	100–150	
Amethyst	800 (1997)	super example
Amethyst, black	175–300	
Blue	85–150	common color
Blue	130–200	Orange Tree exterior
Clambroth	125 (1996)	
Green	350–500	
Marigold	30–55	most common color
Vaseline	310 (1998)	

Plate, about 9" (rare size)
Amethyst known		
Blue	350–600	most common color
Blue, electric	1,300–1,500	
Green	3,000–4,000	3 or 4 known
Marigold	400–550	
Marigold	1,800–3,000	spectacular color
White	2,500–3,000	rare color

Chop plate, about 10" (blue is only known color)
Blue	500–850	
Blue	1,200 (1994)	super example

Petal and Fan, Dugan

These bowls, usually ruffled, have Dugan's Jewelled Heart exterior—the same as used on Farmyard and their version of Heavy Grape. Dugan used a similar petal theme in several patterns but the fan shapes around the outer edge distinguish this one.

Berry set, 7 piece
Peach opal	250–400

Bowl, large, 9–11", ruffled or ice cream shape
Marigold	130–200	scarce color
Purple	250–400	common color
Purple	550–925	electric iridescence
Peach opal	95–155	most common color
White	150–250	fairly common color

Small bowl or sauce, 5–6"
Amethyst/purple	60–100	
Peach opal	25–45	most common color
White	50–90	scarce color

Plate, 6", most with crimped edge
Amethyst/purple	300–500	common color
Peach opal	200–350	scarce color

Rosebowl (rare)
Purple	235 (1998)

Petals, Northwood

Not often seen, Petals seems to be attracting more attention lately as a few nice examples come out.

Compote
Amethyst/purple	45–65	most common color

Blue, rare		
Green	85–150	
Ice blue	800–950	few known
Marigold	35–50	pastel iridescence

Peter Rabbit, Fenton

The Peter Rabbit pattern has much the same overall design as Fenton's Coral and Little Fishes, but in this case rabbits are tucked among trees. Many of these have been found in England, leading to speculation that they were produced basically for export.

Bowl, about 8"
Blue	1,500–2,500	ice cream shape
Green	1,700 (1995)	ice cream shape
Green	1,600 (1994)	ruffled
Marigold	1,100–1,500	ruffled

Plate, about 9"
Blue	3,600 (1993)
Green	3,500–6,000
Marigold	6,000 (1996)

Pillar and Drape
See Lamps and Shades section

Pillar Flute, Imperial

Known in quite a few shapes but seldom seen in other than the rosebowl. Distinctive orange-section design with scalloped top edges. Shapes also include the bowl, compote, water pitcher and tumbler, among others.

Rosebowl
Clambroth	20–35	Iron Cross mark
Marigold	20–35	Iron Cross mark

Pickle dish or relish tray
Marigold	20–35	Iron Cross mark

Plate, 7"
Clambroth	20–35

Pillow and Sunburst, Westmoreland

These bowls were fashioned from the sugar bowl mold—the lid ledge can still be seen around the rim. The Westmoreland name for the pattern was Elite. This example (exterior shown), in blue opal, is courtesy of Carl and Ferne Schroeder.

Bowl
Aqua/teal	45–80
Blue opal	200 (1997)
Peach opal	50–95

Plate, about 9"
Amethyst	30 (1995)
Marigold	215 (1993)

Pinched Swirl, Dugan

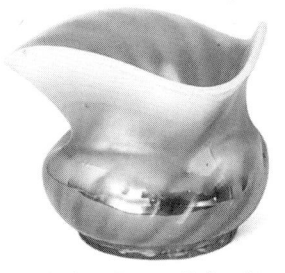

Pinched Swirl is usually found in a pinched-in rosebowl or vase. Above is the seldom-seen spittoon shape with tricorner top, courtesy of Carl and Ferne Schroeder.

Rosebowl
Peach opal	45–80

Tricorner spittoon shape
Peach opal	65–100

Vase, 6½" tall
Peach opal	45–85

Pineapple, Sowerby (England)

Apparently quite popular in its native setting of England, Pineapple is not often seen in the US and never commands much of a price. Above is the three-piece table set. The pattern on the butter is on the interior—the exterior is smooth. There is also a stemmed sugar, sometimes mistaken for a compote.

Table set, 3 piece
Marigold   50 (1997)   large chip on butter lid
Butter dish
Marigold   75 (1994)
Creamer
Amethyst   35–45
Marigold   15–25
Bowl, 6–8" (exterior pattern, probably flat sugar)
Marigold   15–25
Stemmed sugar, ruffled or round
Marigold   30–45

Pineapple rosebowl
Amethyst   85 (1994)   rare in this color
Marigold   85–120

Pineapple and Fan

Rare pattern. This cordial set and tumble-up (guest set), both marigold, are courtesy of John and Lucile Britt. A 7-piece marigold cordial set sold for $600 at a 1993 Tom Burns auction. A marigold wine set sold for $145 at the 1998 ICGA auction.

Pinecone, Fenton

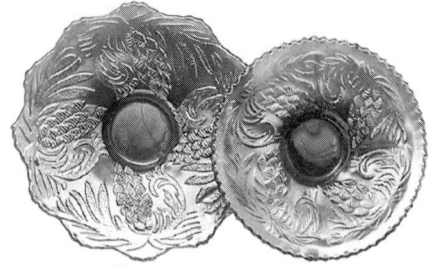

Fenton made this pattern in two sizes in both bowls and plates. Pieces made from the larger mold often have a scalloped edge that is sometimes called 12-sided. The smaller may also have the scalloped edge or as shown here with a sawtooth edge and narrow plain band. Interestingly, the smaller plates are seen more often than bowls, and bring a better price as a rule.

Bowl, small berry or sauce, 5–6", mostly ruffled
Amethyst   45 (1996)   ice cream shape
Blue   40–70   most common color
Blue, electric 330 (1996)
Green   50–75
Marigold   20–35
Sapphire   160 (1997)
Bowl, 7–8"
Blue   35–60   most common color
Green   30–50
Green   415 (1996)   ice cream, emerald irid.
Lavender   75 (1996)
Marigold   15–25
Plate, 6–6½"
Amethyst   200–300   scarce color
Blue   85–160   most common color
Green   125–225   common color
Marigold   80–140   common color
Marigold   300–400   exceptional examples
Plate, 7–8"
Amethyst   200–350
Amethyst   700 (1998)   exceptional example
Amber   600–900
Blue   175–300
Marigold   600 (1995)

Pipe humidor, Millersburg

One of the more fabled patterns, only a handful of examples are known each in marigold, amethyst and green. A green humidor sold for $6,500 in 1992. More recently, in 1998, a marigold example brought $12,000 and an amethyst $9,000.

Plaid, Fenton

A curious pattern, unlike anything else in Carnival. Many pieces in this pattern have been found in the northwestern US, leading to speculation that they may have been a special order for a glass distributor selling in that area.

Bowl, about 9"

Amethyst/purple	300–500	ice cream, scarce color
Blue	150–250	ruffled, common color
Blue	200–300	ice cream shape
Blue	350–450	squarish shape
Green	350–500	ruffled or ice cream
Marigold	200–400	most common color
Red	2,500–3,000	ruffled
Red	1,800–2,400	ice cream shape

Plate
Marigold 200 (1996)
Also known in blue and amethyst

Plain Jane, Imperial

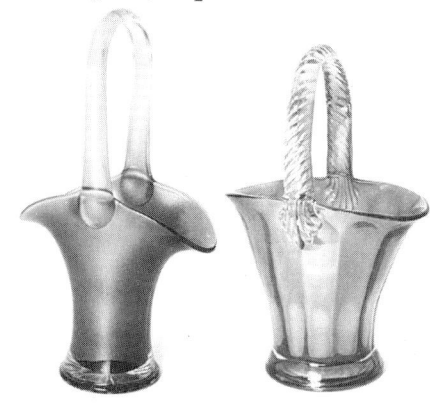

There seem to be two basket configurations that are considered Plain Jane, both of which I think are Imperial. Actually, any plain basket, bowl, or compote is subject to being labeled as "Plain Jane," so some confusion is inevitable.

Basket

Aqua/teal	45–70
Marigold	25–45
Purple	60–95
Smoke	40–65
White	45–60

Plums and Cherries, Northwood

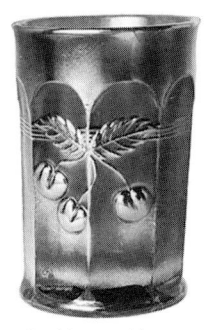

This blue tumbler is considered to be the only carnival tumbler known in this pattern. One lidless sugar in amethyst is also known. Northwood produced an extensive line in this pattern prior to carnival. The opposite side shows the plums. Courtesy of Cecil Whitley. See page 183 for color photo.

Plume Panels
See Vases

Pods and Posies
See Four Flowers

Poinsettia, Imperial

Only known shape is the milk pitcher. The marigold pitchers are easily found while the purple is rare and green scarce. The purple example above, even with a base crack, brought $350.

Milk pitcher
Green	300–550	
Marigold	50–90	
Purple	2,100 (1996)	
Smoke	150–225	

Poinsettia and Lattice, Northwood

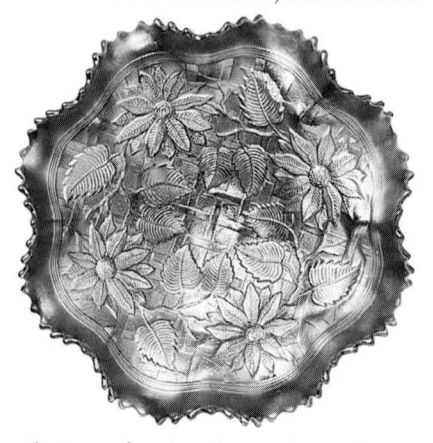

This is one of Northwood's most pleasing designs—an attractive combination of flowers, latticework and stippling. Seen only in ruffled footed bowls. Several aqua opal pieces are known, and green and white have been reported. The pattern is sometimes referred to as Lattice and Poinsettia or simply Poinsettia.

Bowl, about 9", footed
Amethyst/purple	400–700	most common color
Blue	375–600	
Blue, electric	550–800	
Horehound	950–1,250	scarce color
Ice blue	1,700–2,700	
Marigold	400–650	fairly common color

Pond Lily, Fenton

Pond Lily is one of Fenton's less frequently seen patterns. It has a wreath of pond lilies around the center. A ring of Fenton's scale band pattern circles the edge. This example, in an unusual blue milk glass, is courtesy of Mike and Linda Cain. See page 179 for color photo.

Bonbon or card tray (2 sides up)
Amethyst	40–65	scarce color
Blue	55–85	common color
Green	50–80	scarce color
Ice green	200 (1997)	lacks iridescence
Marigold	40–75	scarce color
Peach opal	900 (1997)	only one known
White	80–125	fairly common color

Pony, Dugan

Normally found in amethyst/purple or marigold, Dugan's Pony is occasionally seen in pastel colors. A couple of plates have been reported. Most bowls are ruffled. The above ice cream-shaped bowl in marigold is very rare. Courtesy of Dennis and Denise Harp. The pattern has been reproduced—with no trademarks.

Bowl, about 9", usually ruffled
Amethyst/purple	125–200	
Amethyst/purple	200–350	spectacular examples
Lavender	200–300	
Ice green	1,000–1,600	
Lime	650–800	
Marigold	50–80	most common color

Poppy, Millersburg

With the back pattern (Potpourri) showing through, it is difficult to see the poppies—of which there are four. Known only in the compote shape with several edge treatments and in the more rare salver shape which is a spread-out compote (below right).

Compote
Amethyst   500–800
Green   550–900
Marigold   450–600

Compote, flattened (salver shape)
Amethyst   1,500–2,500
Green   1,600–2,300
Marigold, rare

Poppy, Northwood

It's curious that Northwood made only this ruffled oval pickle dish in this pattern. It is found in a fair range of colors so it must have been more than an afterthought. Can be confused with Imperial's Pansy pickle dish which is of similar proportions.

Pickle dish or relish tray
Amethyst/purple 159–200   scarce color
Aqua   475 (1995)
Aqua opal   850–1,000   rare color
Blue   100–200   most common color
Green   125–200   fairly common color
Ice blue   200–500   scarce color
Lavender   225–275   scarce color
Marigold   80–150   common color
White   250–400   scarce color

Poppy Show, Imperial
See Vases

Poppy Show, Northwood

According to research by Bill Heacock, the Poppy Show and Rose Show molds may have been owned by George Mortimer, who possibly contracted with several manufacturers for production. From the colors, it's obvious that Northwood produced many examples. It is a highly desirable pattern for which pieces always fetch good prices. Because of the elaborate pattern, damage is sometimes difficult to see.

Bowl, about 9"
Aqua opal known
Blue   600–1,000   fairly common color
Blue, electric   1,500–1,700
Clambroth   425 (1993)
Green   1,500–2,100   scarce color
Ice blue   1,000–1,500   fairly common color
Ice green   1,000–1,600   scarce color
Lime green   700–900   rare color
Marigold   400–650   fairly common color
Purple   475–800   fairly common color
White   400–550   fairly common color

Plate, 9–9½"
Amethyst   900–1,400   scarce color
Aqua opal known
Blue   1,000–1,500   fairly common color
Blue, electric   2,100–3,300
Green   3,000–5,000   rare color
Ice blue   1,100–1,800   scarce color
Ice green   2,000–3,500   rare color
Marigold   800–1,500   most common color
Marigold, dark   1,500–2,500   scarce color
Purple   1,200–1,600   scarce color
White   400–700   common color

Portland, US Glass

Shown here are tumblers in the Portland pattern, the regular on the left and variant on the right. The regular is courtesy of Cecil Whitley, the variant courtesy of Robert Smith. None have sold in recent years but a marigold wine glass sold in 1995 for $165. One marigold water pitcher is reported. The pattern was produced in crystal in a wide range of shapes.

Potpourri, Millersburg

A very rare pattern, only three or four milk pitchers are known, all marigold. This one sold for $2,600 at the 1994 John and Lucile Britt auction (Jim Seeck). Another sold for $2,450 in 1993, and a third brought $2,090 in 1997. The pattern is also found on the exterior of the Millersburg Poppy compote.

Prayer Rug, Fenton

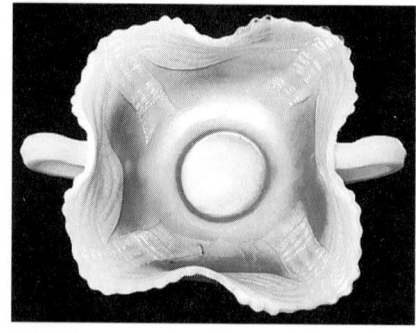

Prayer Rug was produced in custard glass—few iridized examples are known. The pattern has a ring of fabric-like texture around the edges and four scarf-like shapes pointing toward the plain center. Pieces often have weak iridescence. I've seen plates that had so little iridescence that they brought less than $200. This bonbon, in marigold on custard, is courtesy of Richard Jarnig.

Bonbon
Mar/custard   525–950

Plate, about 7"
Mar/custard   7,300 (1993)   only one known

Premium, Imperial

Carl O. Burns, in his 1996 book on Imperial Carnival Glass, says that Premium candlesticks sometimes came with a bowl to make a console set and that they are known in purple, helios, amber, clambroth and celeste blue—as well as the marigold and smoke listed here.

Candlestick, single
Marigold   30–40   plain base
Marigold   30–40   swirled base

Candlesticks, pair
Ice green   140 (1998)
Marigold   35–50
Smoke   80–125
Smoke   50–60   swirled base

Primrose, Millersburg

Primrose has eight of the flowers radiating out from the center of the bowl—the only known shape. As can be seen here, the back pattern (Fine Cut Heart) often shows through, making the front pattern hard to see. The above example, in blue with a 3/1 edge, is the only such combination known and sold for $4,000 at the 1996 HOACGA convention (Jim Seeck).

Bowl, about 10", ruffled
Amethyst	100–200	common color
Amethyst	175 (1998)	tricorner
Blue	4,000	3/1 edge, only one known
Green	100–200	common color
Marigold	80–120	common color
Vaseline	3,500–4,000	9", oval, tight crimp

Prism Panels

Little is known about this rather plain pattern. The 9¼ inch marigold example above sold at a 1997 auction for $15.

Prisms, Westmoreland

This is a squat, wide compote with two circle-like handles and an exterior pattern of vertical prisms. It's quite small, only about 5 inches across.

Compote
Amethyst	20–35
Marigold	15–20
Teal	40–75

Propeller, Imperial

An early Imperial pattern, Propeller was made in many shapes in crystal but only a few shapes have been found in carnival. There are two different sized compotes, the smaller ruffled one shown above with a 2½" base and is about 5" across; and a larger one in a bowl shape that is 8 or 9 inches across—and quite rare.

Compote, small
Green	45–60
Marigold	15–25

Vase
Marigold	40–60

Pulled Loop
See Vases

Puritan, McKee

This is the only carnival piece in the Puritan pattern we have seen. It's a marigold six-inch plate, signed

198 A Field Guide to Carnival Glass

Prescut, and brought $325 at a 1994 auction. It sold again at a 1998 auction in which it brought only $105. John Britt reported a cobalt sauce in Puritan. McKee made very little Carnival. Other McKee patterns in which carnival is known are Aztec, Martec, Majestic, Sunbeam and O'Hara.

Puzzle, Dugan

The elements for which the pattern is named are the little double-fishhook designs on the interior. The exterior pattern is called Floral and Wheat. Some pieces are ruffled or have been pulled into a banana boat shape. Because it is stemmed, some collectors refer to this shape as a handled compote.

Bonbon or compote
Amethyst/purple	50–90	common color
Blue	95–135	common color
Lavender	100 (1994)	
Marigold	30–45	
Peach opal	40–70	common color
White	75–115	common color

Quartered Block

This marigold creamer sold in 1995 for $13.

Queen's Jewels

A rare pattern, this pale marigold rosebowl was described as the only one known when it sold at a Jim Seeck auction in 1993 for $250.

Question Marks, Dugan

Closely related to Dugan's Puzzle, this pattern is found in two-handled footed bonbons, compotes, and plates spread from the compote. Some examples have a plain exterior and foot, others a peach pattern called Georgia Belle on the exterior and the Puzzle (double-fishhook) pattern on the foot. The piece shown is the plate with the two exterior patterns.

Bonbon
Amethyst/purple	25–40	most common color
Blue, cobalt	250–350	rare color
Lavender	70 (1998)	
Marigold	15–25	
Peach opal	35–60	common color
Vaseline	90 (1996)	
White	25–45	

Compote
Amethyst	40–60	most common color
Amethyst, black	55–70	
Marigold	35–50	
Peach opal	60–90	all crimped, common color
White	75 (1997)	

Plate, from compote
Amethyst/purple	100–200	fairly common color
Marigold	155–225	scarce color
Peach opal	115–200	scarce color
White	160–300	fairly common color

Quill, Dugan

A few water sets and pitchers are known, but the tumbler most often comes up for sale. Known only in marigold and purple.

P-Q-R   199

Water set, 7 piece
Purple   1,550 (1998)
Pitcher
Marigold   1,000–1,200
Purple   2,800 (1995)
Tumbler (see page 183 for color photo)
Marigold   140–225
Purple   150–250

Ragged Robin, Fenton

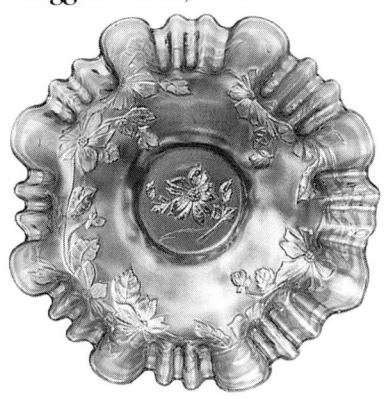

Named for the flower circling the outer part of the pattern and in the center. Notice how the flowers around the edge are unevenly placed—an apparent quirk as most pattern designers attempted to keep things neatly arranged.

Bowl, 8", all 3/1 edge
Amethyst   150–250   scarce color
Blue   125–200
Green   150–250
Marigold   125–200   most common color

Rainbow, Northwood

Few collectors pay much attention to these as there is really no pattern except for the basketweave design on the back. The name comes from the color spectrum displayed on the plain interior of bowls or compotes. The purple pie crust-edged bowl above went for $55 at a 1997 Jim Seeck auction.

Bowl, pie crust edge
Marigold   20–35
Purple   35–55
Plate, basketweave exterior
Purple   30 (1998)

Compote
Amethyst/purple 25–45   most common color
Green   30–50
Marigold   10–20

Raindrops, Dugan

Not frequently seen, "raindrops" describes these dome-footed Dugan bowls perfectly. Usually seen in peach opal, dark colors are especially hard to find and are quite dramatic. The exterior pattern on these pieces is known as Keyhole. The purple example above is courtesy of Betty Cloud.

Bowl, ruffled or 3/1 edge
Peach opal   65–115
Purple   175 (1998)   crimped, 2 sides up
Purple   500 (1996)

Rambler Rose, Dugan

A nice overall pattern without being too busy. Pitchers have a sort of diamond-block band around the neck and are particularly hard to find. L. G. Wright produced water sets in amethyst from 1977.

Water set
Blue	450 (1994)	7 piece
Marigold	230 (1994)	6 piece

Water pitcher
Amethyst	300–500
Blue	175–300

Tumbler (see color photo, page 181)
Amethyst	40–80	
Blue	40–70	most common color
Marigold	25–40	

Ranger
See Jacobean Ranger

Raspberry, Northwood

Northwood's Raspberry underwent production over many years and is found in water sets, milk pitchers, the compote (sometimes called Blackberry) and the gravy boat (or occasional piece). The milk pitcher, above left (7 3/8" high), is lime green and the water pitcher (9" high) is blue. The milk pitcher sold for $2,000 at the 1998 Lincoln-Land auction (Burns).

Water set, 7 piece
Amethyst/purple	400–650	most common color
Green	500–800	

Ice blue	3,200 (1992)	factory flaw, top edge
Marigold	250–450	

Milk pitcher
Amethyst/purple	200–300	most common color
Green	300–450	common color
Ice blue	2,200 (1993)	
Lime green	3,000–3,700	rare color
Marigold	125–225	scarce color
White	800–1,200	scarce color

Water pitcher
Amethyst/purple	175–275	most common color
Blue, very rare		
Green	225–350	fairly common color
Ice blue	1,000–1,500	rare color
Ice green	4,000–6,000	rare color
Marigold	175–300	fairly common color
White	750–1,000	rare color

Tumbler
Amethyst/purple	40–75	most common color
Blue, very rare		
Green	40–75	scarce color
Green, emerald	205 (1994)	
Horehound	50 (1993)	
Ice blue	165–300	rare color
Ice green	300–475	rare color
Marigold	20–35	very common color
White	700 (1994)	rarer than white pitcher

This is the compote that is variously called Blackberry or Raspberry. The blossoms and leaves are in groups of three and it has a basketweave exterior. The pattern is also found in some Daisy and Plume candy dishes and rosebowls.

Compote
Amethyst/purple	75–150	most common color
Amethyst/purple	950 (1998)	spectacular example
Green	75–150	scarce color
Marigold	30–50	scarce color

Gravy boat, sauce boat, or occasional
Amethyst/purple	100–150	most common color
Green	100–160	
Marigold	80–115	

Rays

Name sometimes given to Smooth Rays and other rayed patterns.

Rays and Ribbons, Millersburg

Named for the rays extending from the center and the ribbon-like band around the edge. Known only in bowls except for this single chop plate, 10" across and purple. Marie McGee reports bowls in both vaseline and blue. Bowls are 9"–10" in diameter. The exterior pattern is called Cactus.

Bowl, ruffled, crimped, or 3/1 edge
Amethyst   90–175
Green   85–160
Marigold   85–160

Bowl, ice cream shape or round
Amethyst   200–300   ice cream shape
Green   115–145   round
Marigold   55–95   ice cream shape

Bowl, 8" square (rare shape)
Amethyst   1,050 (1995)
Green known
Marigold   300–500

Rex

Identified as either Rex or Fine Ribbed variant in Richard Owens' tumbler book, there is virtually no pattern except for a subtle vertical paneling.

Pitcher
Marigold   25–30

Water set, 7 piece
Marigold   40–55

Rib and Panel

There has been some confusion over this pattern as it was identified as a variation of Imperial's Colonial Lady vase in a recent book. Rib and Panel is a blow molded piece (not press molded like Colonial Lady) and was made in at least two sizes. It is seen mostly in vases and only in marigold. The pattern is shown as both vase and spittoon in Sherman Hand's 1972 book on carnival glass. Hand gave it this name. This spittoon example is courtesy of Carl and Ferne Schroeder.

Ribbed, Fenton

This stemmed rosebowl is marigold and 3½" high. Courtesy of Carl and Eunice Booker.

Ribbed Band and Scales

Found in Argentina, this 3½" tall marigold tumbler has the initials N.C.P. molded into the base. It is from the John and Lucile Britt collection.

Ribbed Swirl

See Swirl, Northwood

Ribbon and Leaves, Sowerby

A small bowl (5 inches in diameter) sold by Sowerby as a flat open sugar. This marigold piece is courtesy of Carl and Ferne Schroeder.

Ribbon Tie, Fenton

Occasionally called Comet, Ribbon Tie has a unique pattern of whirling rays. Known in plates and bowls in a limited range of colors with ruffled or 3/1 edge, or in an ice cream shape. While purists say plates cannot be ruffled, the above piece does meet the requirement that plates be less than 2" high—although it is ruffled, common with the Ribbon Tie pattern. This example in electric blue sold for $325 in 1994.

Bowl, 8–9"
Amethyst	60–100	most common color
Blue	100–175	common color
Blue, smoky	300 (1993)	
Green	65–100	scarce color
Marigold	50–85	

Plate, 9–10" (or low ruffled bowl)
Amethyst	70–115	
Amethyst, black	65 (1993)	chips
Blue	150–250	most common color

Ripple
See Vases

Rising Sun, US Glass

While generally attributed to US Glass (it is found in old US Glass catalogs under the name "Sunshine"), some collectors also think these carnival examples were made at a European glass factory. As shown above, there are two pitchers: the large pedestaled water pitcher and the smaller dome-footed piece called a juice pitcher. The tumbler shown with the juice pitcher is smaller (3½") than the regular tumbler and is referred to as a juice glass.

Water pitcher, pedestaled
Blue   1,100 (1996)
Marigold   300–400

Tumbler
Marigold   80–135
Blue   305 (1998)

Juice pitcher (dome-footed)
Marigold   250–300

Juice glass
Marigold   80–150

Juice set, 7 piece (juice pitcher, 6 small tumblers)
Marigold   1,100 (1997)

The small (4 inch) bowls or round sauces sold for $30 each.

Butter dish, covered
Marigold   350 (1995)

Sugar, covered
Marigold   150 (1995)

Robin, Imperial

One of Imperial's realistic patterns, Robin is seen almost exclusively in marigold (rare tumblers also in smoke) but was reproduced in other colors. Reproduction tumblers have the IG mark on the inside base.

Water set, 7 piece
Marigold   325–450
Pitcher, water
Marigold   125–200
Tumbler
Marigold   20–30
Smoke   350 (1993)

Mug
Marigold   35–60
Smoke, rare

Rococco, Imperial

The shapes in this pattern include a seldom seen large berry bowl, a compote or nut dish, and a vase. The smaller pieces appear to have been made from the same mold and modified to suit various purposes. Above are a typical compote or nut dish shape and a vase. Note though, the difference in the dome feet. The vase has the correct foot. I suspect that the compote base has been ground off.

Berry bowl, large (few known)
Marigold   35–50
Candy dish, nut dish, small bowl or compote
Marigold   25–40   most common color
Smoke   50–75
Vaseline   55–80   rare color
Vase, 4–5" tall
Lavender   200–300   rare color
Marigold   90–175   common color
Smoke   100–200   common color

Roll or Roll-type

Roll-type patterns look like stacked donuts and were made by several manufacturers. These examples of a tumbler, salt shaker, and perfume are typical of the design. Courtesy of Carl and Eunice Booker.

Cordial, miniature
Marigold   125
Shot glass
Marigold   25–40
Tumbleup
Blue, smoky   50 (1997)
Marigold   35–75
Pitcher
Marigold   25–40
Tumbler
Marigold   18–25
Water set, 5 piece
Marigold, pale   145 (1993)

Rosalind, Millersburg

Rosalind is comprised of radiating arcs that are reminiscent of peacock tail designs. It is a scarce pattern found in several sizes of bowls, a rare plate, two sizes of stemmed compotes, and was also used as the interior pattern on Millersburg's Dolphins compote.

Large bowl (about 10–10½")
Amethyst   200–325   ruffled or 3/1 edge
Amethyst   300–400   ice cream shape
Aqua   450–575   ruffled
Green   175–250   ruffled
Green   150–200   ice cream shape
Marigold   125–175   ruffled
Marigold   1,650 (1997)   ice cream shape

Medium sized bowl, about 9" (rare size)
Amethyst   300–400
Green   225–300   ice cream shape

Small bowl or sauce
Marigold   1,300 (1994)   only marigold known

Plate, 9"
Amethyst   1,700 (1996)
Green   2,000–2,800

Small compote, 6" tall
Amethyst   600–750
Green   700 (1998)

These are the Rosalind jelly compotes. On the left is a green example that sold for $4,500 at the 1996 Heart of America auction (Jim Seeck). The compote on the right is amethyst and sold for $4,250 at the same auction.

Jelly compote, 8½" tall
Amethyst   4,250 (1996)
Green   4,000–4,500

Rosalind variant compote. Although there are similarities to the Peacock Tail variant compote, this one appears to be a separate pattern. It has a round base, while the Peacock Tail variant an octagonal base. This pattern is attributed to Millersburg but some collectors doubt the company made it.

Compote, variant
Amethyst   575–900
Green   475 (1996)

Rose Band, Brockwitz

A rare pattern, this tumbler and shot glass are from private collections. Brockwitz was a German company and their name for the pattern was Ariadne.

Pitcher
Marigold   110 (1994)

Juice glass
Marigold   185 (1995)

Rose Columns, Millersburg
See Vases section

Rose Bouquet, Fenton

This two-handled bonbon has a spray of roses around the edge and one in the center. An example in white (the only color known) sold for $255 in 1996.

Roses and Fruits, Millersburg

The design, found only in a stemmed bonbon, has a band of large rosebuds around the edge and four smaller ones leading down toward the center. The center has a pear, grapes and other fruit. The lower part of the handles ends in a leaf design. Known in amethyst, green, marigold and one or two examples in blue. The marigold example above is courtesy of Carl and Eunice Booker.

Bonbon
Amethyst   750 (1997)
Blue   2,500 (1998)
Green   800–1,100
Marigold   650–900

Rose Garden, Brockwitz (Germany)

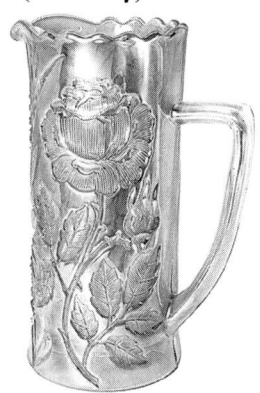

This is an intaglio pattern and unusually realistic for a European pattern—most tended to be geometric. While the pattern was made in a number of shapes, few pieces are seen and usually command a premium. While shown in Brockwitz catalogs, some shapes may have been made by Eda of Sweden. Made in several vase variations—see Vases.

Milk pitcher
Marigold   550 (1994)

Communion pitcher
Marigold   350 (1993)

Rosebowl, small
Blue   250 (1996)
Marigold   350 (1998)

Rosebowl, large
Marigold   1,950 (1995)

Rose Pinwheel

A mysterious pattern that few collectors ever see. The pattern of this 9" bowl has five roses around the edge with swirled ribs reaching into the center. This example is marigold. Amethyst and green reported.

Rose Show, Northwood

Without a doubt, Rose Show and the similar Poppy Show are patterns most collectors would die for. Fortunately, there are enough so that the only sacrifice may be a little cash. Although neither pattern has ever been found with a Northwood mark, most collectors accept them as Northwood if for no other reason than the color range. While Rose Show has not been reproduced, it is occasionally found in uniridized blue opal.

Bowl, about 9", ruffled

Amethyst	300–550	scarce color
Aqua	700–1,000	rare color
Aqua opal	800–1,500	fairly common color
Aqua opal	2,900 (1998)	spectacular example
Blue	500–800	fairly common color
Blue, electric	800–1,000	
Blue, powder, opal		
Custard	14,000 (1995)	two known
Green	1,600–2,400	scarce color
Green, emerald	3,500–6,000	rare color
Horehound	2,750–4,000	rare color
Ice blue	900–1,400	fairly common color
Ice blue opal	1,000–2,000	rare color
Ice green	700–1,200	fairly common color
Ice green opal	3,900–4,400	very rare color
Lime green	1,800–3,000	rare color
Marigold	400–550	common color
Purple	500–650	common color
Sapphire	2,300–3,500	rare color
White	250–400	fairly common color

Rose Show Variant, Northwood

The Rose Show Variant is most quickly distinguished from the regular by its sawtooth edge. The variant also has a ribbed back and a smooth base (the base of the regular pattern is indented, following the shape of the front pattern). Renninger blue is seen only in the variant.

Bowl, variant

Blue	900–1,400
Blue, Renninger	800–1,200
Marigold	550–675

Plate, 9"

Amethyst	800–1,100	scarce color
Blue	900–1,500	common color
Blue, electric	1,100–1,800	
Custard	16,500 (1995)	dark, pumpkin overlay
Green	2,500–4,000	rare color
Green	6,000 (1998)	electric iridescence
Green, emerald	4,000–6,500	rare color
Ice blue	1,800–3,000	fairly common color
Ice green	2,000–3,500	rare color
Ice green opal	10,700 (1995)	
Lavender	3,100 (1997)	
Lavender	950 (1998)	light amethyst
Lime green	3,000–4,000	rare color
Marigold	900–1,500	common color
Purple	1,000–1,800	scarce color
White	450–750	common color

Plate

Blue	1,500–2,500
Blue, Renninger	3,000–4,000
Marigold	1,300–2,200

Roses and Greek Key

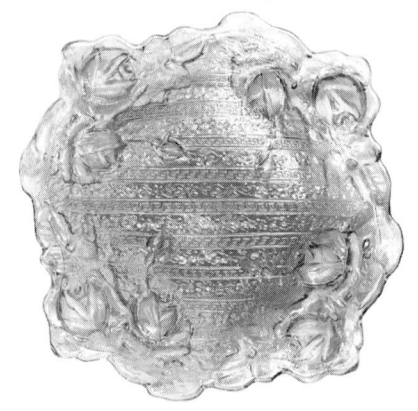

This is an exotic squarish plate, about 10¼" from tip to tip, of which there are only two confirmed examples. The pattern has four groups of heavily sculpted roses covering the outer portions of the front. The center is plain except for bands of the greek key theme interspersed with bands of small flowers. These bands are repeated on the reverse. This marigold plate is owned by Nola Schmoker. One other is known with a smoky amberish iridescence. The maker is unknown.

Rose Spray, Fenton

Fenton's Rose Spray has a subtle ring of roses on the interior that almost disappears when stretched from the goblet shape to a ruffled compote. Known only in pastel colors and marigold, although non-iridized examples are found in darker colors.

Compote

Celeste	180–200	jack-in-pulpit shape
Ice blue	80–110	jack-in-pulpit shape
Ice green	100–175	jack-in-pulpit shape
Marigold	20–35	round (goblet-shaped)
Marigold	35–50	6 ruffles
White	145–225	jack-in-pulpit shape

Rose Tree, Fenton

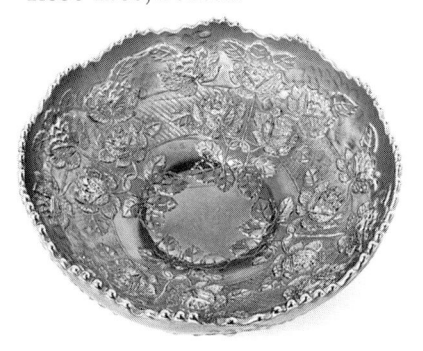

Rose Tree has a veritable garden of roses against a subtle band of diagonal lines. The exterior pattern is Orange Tree. Not many of these bowls are around.

Bowl

Blue	1,800 (1993)	ice cream shape
Blue	3,150 (1996)	ruffled

Rose Window

Notice that the design in this pattern resembles church windows. The pitcher is very rare, while tumblers turn up occasionally. The tumbler has six panels with the same church window effect and is said to be 4¼" high. This pitcher, in pale marigold, is from the John and Lucile Britt collection.

Rose Wreath

See Wreath of Roses

Rosette, Northwood

Rosette almost seems to be an orphan. It is not related to any other patterns (aside from the Ruffles and Rings that appears on the exterior) and is only found in bowls, invariably ruffled. A band of small rosettes circles a larger medallion of rays. Deeper versions of the bowl are sometimes referred to as nut dishes.

Bowl, or nut dish, about 8"

Amethyst/purple	40–70	most common color
Green	80–130	rare color
Marigold	25–40	hard to find

Roundup, Dugan

The squiggly lines on the inner ring resemble the brands used during a cattle roundup—thus the name. Like the similar Fanciful, Roundup is found only in bowls and plates in a limited color range.

Bowl, about 9"

Amethyst/purple	200–300	ruffled or 3/1 edge
Amethyst/purple	300–550	low ruffled
Amethyst/purple	500–800	low ice cream
Blue	180–325	ruffled, scarce color
Lavender	575 (1995)	low ice cream shape
Marigold	70–125	ruffled, ice cream, or 3/1
Peach opal	175–300	ruffled, ice cream, or 3/1
White	120–200	ruffled, ice cream, or 3/1

208 A Field Guide to Carnival Glass

Roundup plate, 9"

Amethyst/purple	300–450	scarce color
Blue	270–500	most common color
Marigold	250–400	rare color
Peach opal	550–800	fairly common color
White	175–300	scarce color

Royalty, Imperial

Royalty has a group of small elements arranged in a crown design. In fact, as Glen Thistlewood discovered, it is found in the 1909 Imperial catalog under the name Imperial Crown Design. While the pattern was made in many shapes in crystal, it is known in carnival only in punch sets and large fruit bowls. Thanks also to Kathi and Galen Johnson for their photo and help on this one.

Ruffled Rib, Dugan

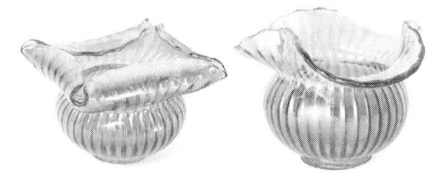

This is a very curious little marigold spittoon. I've seen four of these and heard of others. All are marigold and each seems to have a different ruffling. An eight-ruffled example sold in 1997 for $110. A two-sides up piece sold in 1998 for $275.

Ruffles and Rings, Northwood

Not often seen without the Wishbone or Rosette interior. This example, with a plain interior, is the only one to sell in recent years. It is peach opal with 1" of opal around the edge and brought $500 at a 1995 Jim Seeck auction.

Rustic, Fenton

See Vases section

Sailboats, Fenton

In addition to the small sailboats, this pattern is distinguished by the stippled, curved frames around the lake scene—divided by a smaller segment with a small windmill. The pattern is found in a curious range of small bowls and plates made from the same mold, wine glasses, and a goblet shape which is sometimes ruffled into a compote. Note the Orange Tree pattern on the exterior.

Bowl, small, or sauce, about 6"

Amberina	100–200	scarce color
Amethyst	55–90	scarce color
Aqua	85–150	ruffled
Blue	40–70	fairly common color
Green	70–100	common color
Lavender	45–80	or light amethyst, scarce color
Marigold	15–30	most common color
Red	450–600	scarce color
Vaseline	150 (1995)	

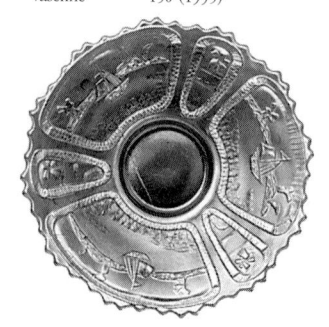

Plate, 6–6½"

Blue	500–900	
Blue	1,400 (1995)	exceptional color
Marigold	375–600	

R-S 209

These are the Sailboats compote and wine glasses. The swirled and stippled stem is distinctive. The goblets are somewhat larger, with a deeper bowl than the wines. Goblets are also known in green.

Compote
Blue   100–150   scarce color
Marigold   35–75   most common color
Wine glass
Blue   65–90   scarce color
Marigold   15–25   most common color
Goblet, water
Marigold   45–60

Scale Band, Fenton

Scale Band is most frequently seen on the back of small bowls and plates but is the primary pattern on the rarely seen pitcher and tumbler.

Bowl, about 6"
Marigold   10–15
Red   300–350
Plate, 6–7"
Marigold   15–25

Water set, 7 piece
Blue   500–750
Marigold   150–200

Pitcher
Vaseline   250 (1998)   only one reported
Tumbler
Blue and green scarce
Marigold   15–25

Scales, Westmoreland

Easy to confuse with Dugan's Fishscale and Beads, this pattern has convex-type (domed) scales rather than the indented or concave-type scales of the Dugan pattern. The 9" plate above, in marigold on milkglass, is very unusual—most plates in this pattern are 6" in diameter.

Scales plate, 8–9"
Mar/milk glass   120–155
Peach opal   80–125
Plate, 6"
Amethyst/purple   25–45   most common color
Lavender   25–45
Marigold   20–35
Mar/milk glass   120–200
Teal   50–70
Bowl, 8–9", round, ruffled, or ice cream shape
Blue opal   100–200
Mar/milk glass   60–100
Peach opal   30–55

Bowl (5") with underplate
Amethyst   35 (1995)
Banana dish (small plate with 2 sides up)
Peach opal   60–100

Scotch Thistle, Fenton

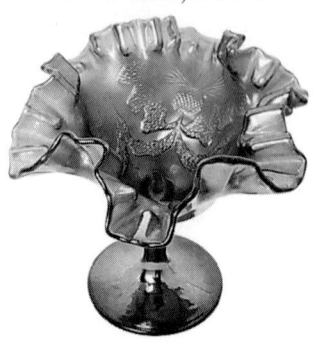

A not-too-frequently seen pattern, Scotch Thistle has thistles and foliage on the interior; the exterior is plain. One wonders if this compote wasn't intended to be part of Fenton's other Thistle line—for which only bowls and plates are known.

Compote, ruffled and crimped
Amethyst/purple	80–120	scarce color
Blue	60–95	common color
Green	55–85	most common color
Marigold	50–75	fairly common color

Scroll Embossed, Imperial

Certainly one of the most dramatic patterns in carnival. On purple the crescent shapes are often seen with differing colors of iridescence, appearing to be individually painted. Note the stretch effect around the edges—also quite common with the plate. Bowls and compotes have back patterns that vary between File, Hobstar and Tassel, Eastern Star (sometimes incorrectly identified as Curved Star), or plain. The pattern was copied by Sowerby and used as an interior pattern on their Diving Dolphins pieces, some small sauces, as well as an ashtray. Bowls were reproduced and marked LIG.

Plate, 9–9½", plain back
Aqua	195 (1994)	
Green	85–150	common color
Helios green	60–90	common color
Lavender	210 (1996)	
Marigold	75–130	common color
Purple	300–500	most common color
Vaseline reported		

Bowl, 7–9"
Green	35–55	
Helios green	10–20	
Marigold	15–30	common color
Purple	55–85	most common color
Smoke	35–50	File exterior
Vaseline reported		

Bowl, small berry or sauce, usually File exterior
Marigold	10–15	
Purple	50–80	most common color
Smoke	20–35	

Berry set, 6 piece, File exterior
Purple	175 (1996)

Compote, small
Green	80–120
Purple	100–180

Compote, miniature, round or ruffled
Lavender	175–300
Purple	150–275

This is the exterior of a large Scroll Embossed compote showing the Eastern Star pattern—one of several used with this pattern—along with File, Hobstar and Tassel, and plain.

Compote, large
Marigold	45–65	
Vaseline	130–160	
Purple	120–200	most common color

Scroll Embossed, Sowerby
See Novelties/miniatures

Scroll and Flower Panels, Imperial
See Vases

Seacoast, Millersburg

How many of these have been passed by or discarded simply because they look like cheap souvenirs? Yet the Seacoast pintray, with its fish and lighthouse, is always in demand today, even with the usual minor damage on the base. Amethyst, green and marigold are found in approximately equal quantities.

Pin tray
Amethyst	500–800	average iridescence
Amethyst	1,500 (1996) 1,800 (1998)	great pieces
Green	500–850	
Marigold	600–900	

Seagulls, Dugan

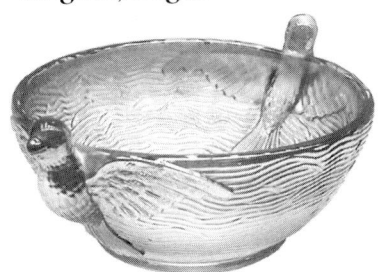

There's not much else like this pattern in Carnival. The birds, in full dimension, seem to emerge from the sides of the bowl while their wings rest gracefully against it. The bowl itself is reminiscent of waves. Completely charming. Marigold is the only color seen and finding one with good color is a challenge. They sell for $150 to $200.

Sea Thistle, Sowerby

Also known as Cane and Scroll. These marigold creamers sell in the $25 to $35 range. Rosebowls and flat sugar bowls are known in marigold.

Seaweed, Millersburg

A rather elaborate pattern dominated by question mark shapes swirling around the center. Found in several sizes of bowls and a very rare plate. The 10" amethyst ice cream-shaped bowl above sold for $1,600 in 1994. Five-inch sauces in amethyst, blue, green and marigold have also been reported.

Bowl, 8¼"
Marigold	180–300	ice cream shape

Bowl, 9"
Amethyst	400–500	
Green	350–400	3/1 edge
Green	1,500–1,800	ice cream shape
Marigold	150–250	ice cream shape
Purple	650 (1995)	

Bowl, large, about 10" (most plentiful size)
Amethyst	425–650	3/1 edge, most common
Amethyst	1,600 (1994)	ice cream shape, very rare
Aqua	400–725	ice cream shape, rare
Blue ice cream shape, rare		
Green ice cream shape, rare		
Green	200 925 (both 1998)	3/1 edge
Marigold	250–450	

Plate, 9"
Amethyst	2,200 (1993)	low, very rare
Green	1,650 (1995)	slight ice cream shape
Marigold, rare		

Serpentine Rose

This marigold creamer sold at a 1998 Mickey Reichel auction for $75.

Shell, Imperial

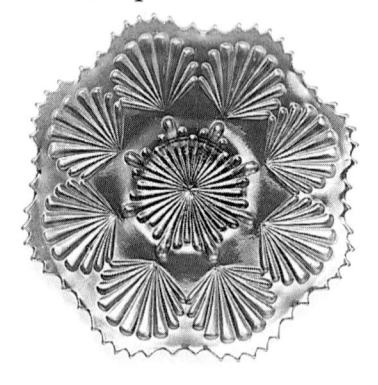

Same pattern as Shell and Sand but without the stippling that provides the "sand" effect. Seen less often than the Shell and Sand pieces. The above plate in smoke (with a greenish cast) sold at a 1998 Mickey Reichel auction for $725. See color photo on page 166.

Bowl, 7"
Amethyst   155 (1997)

Plate, about 9"
Marigold   700–1,200
Smoke   600–900

Shell and Fern

This salt shaker, in marigold on moonstone, sold at a 1994 auction for $250. The pattern has a shell design plus fern-type foliage around the top.

Shell and Jewel, Westmoreland

Part of an early Westmoreland line called Victor, only the sugar and creamer have been found iridized. In green, this sugar and creamer set sold in 1997 for only $15—no doubt because they are missing the lids that both pieces originally had.

Creamer and Sugar
Green   40–60
Marigold   25–40

Shell and Sand, Imperial

Imperial's Shell and Sand has an attractive but simple arrangement of abstract shells with stippling between the shells. Some pieces lack the stippling and are simply called Shell. Marigold is quite rare in either the bowl or plate.

Plate, about 9"
Green   550–800
Helios green   375–500
Marigold   475 (1994)
Purple   800–1,200
Smoke   750 (1993)   most common color

Bowl, 7–8"
Green   35–50   scarce color
Marigold   20–35   scarce color
Purple   70–125   average examples
Purple   150–275   spectacular electric examples

Shriner champagne glasses
See Novelties/miniatures

Silver Queen
See Decorated section

Singing Birds, Northwood

Singing Birds differs from Imperial's Robin in that the birds here are framed by panels. Northwood's own Springtime pattern was made in many of the same shapes as Singing Birds and has the same panels. If it has a butterfly and basketweave around the bottom, it's Springtime. Note that reproduced tumblers have been found in aqua opal.

Water set, 7 piece
Amethyst/purple 550–850   common color
Green   600–900   most common color
Green, emerald   1,700 (1994)
Marigold   500–650   scarce color

Water pitcher
Amethyst/purple 350–600   most common color
Green   400–550
Olive known
Marigold   300–500

Tumbler
Amber, scarce
Amethyst/purple 45–70   common color
Green   50–85   most common color
Marigold   45–70   scarce color
Smoke, scarce
Olive green   45–75   scarce color

Singing Birds mugs are found in two versions, plain and stippled. Stippled mugs, like that on the right, are much less often seen. This mug can also be confused with Imperial's Robin mug, but the Singing Birds displays the birds on panels.

Mug, unstippled
Amber   300 (1995)
Amethyst/purple 80–150   most common color
Amethyst   275 (1995)   swirl effect
Aqua opal   900–1,200   scarce color
Blue   75–140   common color
Blue, electric   140–215
Green   80–150   common color
Green, emerald   350 (1997)
Horehound   150–250   scarce color
Ice blue   350–550   fairly common color
Lavender   125–250   fairly common color
Marigold   60–110   common color
Purple   150–200   Amazon Hotel advertising
Smoke, rare
White   600–800   rare color

Mug, stippled
Amethyst, rare
Blue   600–800   scarce color
Blue, Renninger   1,500 (1997)
Green   450–600   scarce color
Marigold   95–175   most common color

Table set, 4 piece
Amethyst and green known
Marigold   400–650

Butter dish
The correct base to the butter will have a scalloped edge and topside with a fruit-floral design.
Marigold   100–190
Purple   250–350

Creamer
Purple   100–140

Creamer and sugar
Marigold   245 (1997)
Purple   240 (1993)

Spooner
Purple   150–250

Sugar, covered
Green   40   bottom rough
Purple   75 (1996)

Sherbert, known in marigold, rare

This marigold Singing Birds bowl is thought to be the only one in that color. It is 10¾" across and 3½" deep. The pattern is on the exterior.

Bowl, large berry
Green   200–240
Purple   270–300

Bowl, small berry or sauce
Blue   85–150
Green   40–70

Single Flower, Dugan

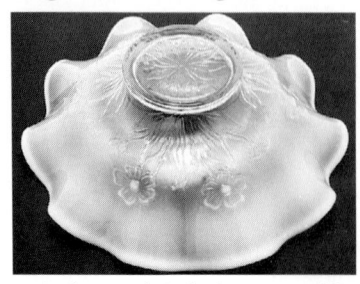

Single Flower and Single Flower Framed have small flowers on the exterior and a petal design on the interior center. These patterns are similar to Daisy Dear and Triplets which bring about the same prices. This peach opal bowl sold for $45 in 1997.

Bowl, 8–9" various edges
Peach opal   35–65
Basket, applied handle
Peach opal   150–250
Plate, handgrip, about 7"
Peach opal   50–90

Single Flower Framed, Dugan
Bowl, 7–9"
Peach opal	25–45	ruffled or CRE
Peach opal	45–65	tricorner
Purple	60–80	tricorner

Plate, 7"
Peach opal	95 (1996)	tight crimp
Peach opal	40–60	

Six Petals, Dugan

The easiest way to remember this pattern is to look for the six petals in the very center of the design, and a wreath of leaves and blossoms around that.

Bowl, tricorner
Peach opal	35–60	most common color
Purple	60–100	common color
Purple	125–200	electric iridescence

Bowl, 7–8", crimped or ruffled
Peach opal	45–85	most common color
Purple	80–125	common color
Purple	135 (1998)	3/1 edge
White	65–100	scarce color

Six-Sided, Imperial

Six-Sided candlesticks are easy to spot. Their unique feature is the bulbous segment two-thirds of the way up that contains six hexagonal hobstar medallions. Reported in smoke in addition to the colors below.

Candlesticks, pair
Marigold   300–450
Purple   900–1,200
Candlestick, single
Amber   300 (1995)
Helios   105 (1995)
Marigold   150–200

Ski Star, Dugan

A unique pattern and easily remembered. Overlapping crescents (I'm not sure they should be called skis) form large and small stars. The arcs are heavily stippled. Occasionally found in blue.

Bowl, small berry or sauce 5–6"
Peach opal   25–40
Purple   65–120
Bowl, large, 10–11", ruffled or crimped
Peach opal   65–100
Purple   250–400
Bowl, tricorner, crimped, about 8"
Peach opal   120–200

Bowl, banana dish shape, 8–9"
Amethyst 150 (1996)
Peach opal 70–130
Peach opal 525 (1998) pumpkin color
Plate, 6–7", usually crimped
Peach opal 90–175
Plate or bowl, handgrip
Peach opal 95–150
Peach opal 300 (1997) great color
Basket, applied handle (whimsey)
Peach opal 200–300
Bride's basket, silverplate holder
Peach opal 150–200

Smooth Panels, Imperial

Imperial's Smooth Panels is frequently seen but seldom correctly identified. There were at least six different sized molds from which several styles of bowls and plates were made, as well as vases in several base sizes and the more commonly recognized rosebowl. Colors are the usual Imperial set. Because of the generic look of Smooth Panels, the value is low. Also, see Vases.

Rosebowl
Clambroth 20–30
Marigold 25–45
Smoke 35–50

Smooth Rays; Fenton, Imperial, Northwood or Westmoreland

Almost every company that manufactured iridized glass had some form of smooth rays pattern, mostly on bowls and plates. The following listing reflects the maker when known.

Bowl
Amethyst/purple 20–40
Amethyst opal 155 (1993) ruffled, extremely rare
Amethyst, fiery 38 (1998) 8"
Blue 90 (1998) 9½", 3/1 edge
Blue opal 125–175 Westmoreland
Green 20–35
Ice green 65 (1996) 5", round
Lime 25–40 ruffled or 3/1 edge
Lime green opal 40 (1998) 5½", dome footed, ice cream
Marigold 10–15
Mar/milk glass 20–30 9", probably Westmoreland
Olive 15–25
Peach opal 25–45 Westmoreland
Plate, 6–9"
Amethyst 20 (1997) some wear
Marigold 20–40
Peach opal 65 (1998) 6", Dugan
Purple 90–110 6½", Dugan
Smoke 25 (1996) 8½", flat
Compote
Amber 75 (1998) stemmed, pinched in
Blue opal 60–100 Westmoreland
Green 20–35 Northwood

Snow Fancy, Imperial

Large circular medallions of hobs are separated by a smaller hobstar. The sawtooth half-circles under each circular medallion are unusual. Snow Fancy is shown in Imperial catalogs (pattern #455) in table sets and berry sets. At one point the spooner and creamer were offered as a tea set. That's possibly why this spooner was sold as a marigold open sugar. It brought $8 in 1997. Another sold for $25 in 1998.

Soda Gold, Imperial

Soda Gold is certainly distinctive although it doesn't attract much attention. Still, the console sets, water sets, and items in smoke bring fair prices. Sometimes called Spider Web or Tree of Life. Also confused with Crackle. This unusually shaped marigold centerpiece bowl is 7½" in diameter and sold at a 1997 Jim Seeck auction for $40.

Console bowl
Marigold 20–40
Smoke 40 (1998)

Console set, bowl and candlesticks
Marigold   75–100

Candlesticks, short
Marigold   25–30
Smoke   35–65

Chop plate, 12"
Marigold   40–70

Berry set, 7 piece
Marigold   15–25

Water pitcher
Marigold   45–85
Smoke   110–185

Tumbler
Marigold   15–25
Smoke   45–65

Water set, 5 piece
Smoke   215–275

Water set, 7 piece
Marigold   125–200
Smoke   300–450

I consider this pattern to be Crackle, but most such salt and pepper shakers are called Soda Gold and often come up for sale by that name.

Salt and pepper shakers
Aqua/marigold   125–250
Blue, light   90 (1998)
Marigold   75–100
Smoke   80–115

Soldiers and Sailors Home
See Lettered patterns

Soutache, Dugan

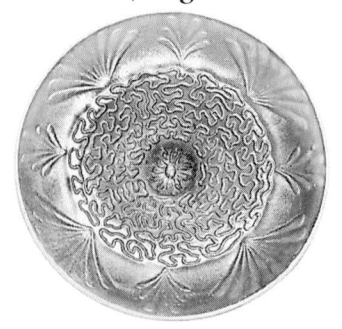

An unusual pattern with a distinctive meandering line and plumes or fans around the edge. Soutache was a type of trimming braid. I've not heard of the pattern in anything other than peach opal.

Bowl, dome-footed
Peach opal   85–140   crimped, ruffled

Plate, dome-footed
Peach opal   170–250

The edge has been oddly whimsied in this unusual Soutache piece. Courtesy of Larry Yung. A similar piece sold in 1998 for $425.

Spiralex, Dugan
See Swung vases section.

Split Diamond

At first glance this marigold fruit bowl appears to be the Split Diamond pattern—and that's the way it was listed in the 1995 auction where it brought $75. We think it iss another, similar, pattern however we've been unable to track it down. Glen Thistlewood points out that the feet and scroll band are identical to the US Glass pattern Colorado.

Butter dish
Marigold   35–50

Creamer
Marigold   15–25

Sugar (shaped like compote), 5½" wide
Marigold   50 (1998)

Springtime, Northwood

In general, a scarce pattern and never found in the pastel colors (the pattern apparently went out of production prior to Northwood's introduction of pastel colors about 1912). Springtime has butterflies and foliage on panels like that of Singing Birds—but no birds. This also has a basketweave design around the lower trunk, similar to Northwood's Raspberry.

Water set, 7 piece
Amethyst/purple   800–1,100
Green   1,300–2,000
Marigold   700–1,000

Water pitcher
Green   800–1,000
Marigold   350–425

Tumbler
Amethyst/purple   75–140
Green   65–110   common color
Marigold   55–90   common color

These are small and large berry bowls from a seven-piece marigold berry set that sold in 1996 for $200.

Bowl, small berry
Green   35–45
Purple   30–45

The table set has a spooner, creamer, covered butter and covered sugar. It is generally accepted that the butter bottom is shared among this pattern, Peacock at the Fountain, and Singing Birds.

Table set, 4 piece
Amethyst/purple   1,100 (1995)
Green   2,000–3,500
Marigold   500–700

Butter dish
Amethyst/purple   300 (1995)
Green   350–600
Marigold   250–350

Creamer
Marigold   65–85

Spooner
Green   325 (1995)
Marigold   55–100

Sugar, covered
Marigold   145–175

S-Repeat, Dugan

Dugan's S-Repeat pattern was also made prior to the Carnival era and was called National. The 10-piece punch set shown here is rare and is from a private

218 A Field Guide to Carnival Glass

collection. It changed homes recently for $6,000. Beware of toothpick holders in this pattern as all are thought to be new.

Punch set, 8 piece
Purple   6,500 (1996)

Punch base only
Purple   200 (1997)

Creamer, whimsey from punch cup
Amethyst/purple 45–75   not especially rare

Punch cup
Amethyst/purple 20–35

Stag and Holly, Fenton

With its romantic combination of animals and plants, it is little wonder that Stag and Holly is popular among collectors. Two molds were used for this pattern; the larger (with ball feet) for large bowls, chop plates, and giant rosebowls; the smaller (with spatula feet) for eight-inch bowls, nine-inch plates, and an occasional rosebowl. Bowls have been reproduced (see Contemporary section).

Bowl, large, 10–11", ice cream shape
Amber	150–225	scarce color
Amberina	650 (1997)	red streaks
Amethyst	250–425	scarce color
Amethyst, black	500–900	rare color
Aqua	500–700	rare color
Blue	300–500	common color
Blue, electric	700–900	
Blue, powder	250–425	
Green known		
Lavender	300–450	scarce color
Marigold	90–160	most common color
Mar/moonstone	4,250 (1998)	only one known
Vaseline	800 (1997)	

Bowl, large, 10–11", ruffled
Amber	110–200	scarce color
Amberina	3,100 (1996)	few known
Amethyst	200–400	scarce color
Amethyst, black	225 (1996)	
Aqua	400–600	rare color
Blue	175–300	common color
Blue, powder	250 (1996)	
Blue, smoky	300–425	rare color
Green	500–900	rare color
Lime	200 (1996)	
Marigold	100–200	common color

Chop plate, about 12"
Marigold   600–1,000

The giant rosebowl is made from the same mold as the large bowl and chop plate. This blue one brought $3,500 at a 1998 Mickey Reichel auction.

Rosebowl, giant
Blue	3,000–4,000	three or four known
Marigold	175–300	

Nut bowl shape, large ball-footed, 7½"
Marigold   200 (1996)

This is a typical shape for the smaller, spatula-footed bowl. This mold was also flattened into the regular plate and cupped into the very rare rosebowl.

Bowl, small, 7–8", ruffled or ice cream shape
Amethyst	125–200	fairly common color
Aqua	150 (1997)	open bubble on foot
Blue	110–200	common color
Blue, electric	350 (1993)	ice cream shape
Green	120–200	common color
Green	395 (1998)	great example
Lavender	300 (1997)	ice cream shape
Marigold	75–125	fairly common color
Red	1,500–2,500	scarce color
Smoke	150–250	rare color
Vaseline reported		

Plate, 8½–9"
Amethyst	2,000–3,000	rare
Blue, rare		
Marigold	650–1,000	common color
Smoke	550 (1996)	

Rosebowl, small spatula-footed
Blue   1,000   may be only one known

Starburst, Riihimäki

This pattern is characterized by two dominant star patterns—an eight-pointed and a whirling star. Riihimäki is a Finnish firm and this pattern is found in a 1939 catalog of their glasswares in a wide range of shapes. Also known in vases (see Vase section).

Creamer
Marigold   50–70
Perfume
Marigold   105 (1998)
Plate, 5½"
Blue   90–150

Rosebowl
Marigold   65–100

This amber Starburst spittoon looks like many American spittoon whimsies. It was, however, a production item. This example (with small chips) sold at the 1996 Lincoln-Land auction (Tom Burns) for $1,900.

Star of David, Imperial

Not hard to identify, but still occasionally confused with Northwood's Star of David and Bows. This one has Imperial's Arcs pattern on the reverse, which can be seen showing through this ruffled bowl. Known only in bowls. Also reported in marigold and smoke.

Bowl
Green   90–150   scarce color
Purple   150–250   common color

Star of David and Bows, Northwood

Northwood's version of the Star of David design incorporates bows as well, softening the total effect. Found only in dome-footed bowls.

Bowl
Amethyst/purple 60–100   common color
Green   100–150   rare color
Nut bowl (deep)
Amethyst/purple 65 (1997)

Star and Fan, European

The star in this pattern is four-pointed and found in bands around the base of the decanter and near the top of the cordials. This cordial or wine set appears to be the only shape in Star and Fan. Curved Star vases are occasionally identified as Star and Fan.

Wine set (decanter, tray, six cordials)
Marigold   600–1,100

Wine set (decanter, six cordials)
Marigold   350–500

Wine decanter or cordial bottle
Marigold   150–275

Cordial
Marigold   100–125

Star and File, Imperial

An eight-sided star within a hexagon flanked by vertical bands with a file texture. This rosebowl is typical of the pattern and such pieces sell for $30 to $50 in marigold. Carl O. Burns reports that the rosebowl is found, although rarely, in purple, helios, amber and ice green, in addition to marigold. One lime green has been reported. Found in many shapes with the water set drawing the most interest. The compote and wine set were reproduced.

Bonbon, large round
Marigold   10–20

Celery vase, handled (common shape)
Clambroth   20–30
Marigold   25–45

Nut bowl
Marigold   40–70

In almost any other pattern this square bowl would fetch serious money. At the 1994 auction where it sold, however, it brought just $25. I've seen many at flea markets in this range.

Bowl, 6–9"
Marigold   20–35
Marigold   25–50   6" square

Nut bowl (or deep bowl)
Marigold   10–20

Plate, 6–6½" (pattern on exterior only)
Marigold   60–110

Compote
Marigold   40–50

Cordial
Marigold   225–275

Sherbert
Marigold   5–10

Custard cup
Marigold, scarce

Creamer
Marigold   15–20

Creamer and sugar
Marigold   30–50

Spooner
Smoke   65 (1998)

Decanter, with stopper
Marigold   65–100

Goblet
Marigold   20–30

Wine glass
Marigold   20–30

Milk pitcher
Marigold   25–40

Water set, 7 piece
Marigold   400–600

Water pitcher
Marigold   100–175

Tumbler
Marigold   20–35

Iced tea tumbler, rare

Juice glass, footed
Marigold   175 (1993)   very rare

Relish or pickle dish
Marigold 20–30
Vase, footed
Marigold 30 (1997)

Starfish, Dugan

Similar to Dugan's Five Hearts but in this case the pattern is simpler and the heart shapes are more pronounced. Rare and very desirable in purple, this compote sold for $275 at the 1994 John and Lucile Britt auction (Jim Seeck).

Bonbon, stemmed
Amethyst/purple 100–175
Peach opal 80–130
Compote
Amethyst/purple 250–400
Peach opal 75–110

Starflower, Fenton

No tumblers that match this pattern have ever been found, although some collectors speculate that the Milady tumblers might have also been intended for use with this pitcher. Known only in blue that sell in the $1,500 to $2,000 range. Also known in a scarce marigold and rare white.

Star Medallion, Imperial

Star Medallion is aptly named with a large multi-point star on an octagonal medallion resting against a cane background. Lots of shapes seen in this pattern. Shown here are a tumbler, celery vase and milk pitcher. Some shapes have been reproduced.

Bowl
Clambroth 10–20
Marigold 10–20
Plate, 9½–10"
Clambroth 25–40
Marigold 25–40
Celery vase
Marigold 30–50
Smoke 40–70
Compote
Marigold 15–20
Goblet, water
Marigold 15–20
Smoke 20–30
Nut bowl
Marigold 15–20
Milk pitcher
Clambroth 25–35
Marigold 40–65
Smoke 50–90
Punch cup (or custard cup)
Marigold 10–20
Tumbler
Marigold 20–35 lemonade size (taller)
Marigold 15–25 regular size

Starspray, Imperial

Most interesting when found in a metal holder making it a bride's basket. Usually found in a 6¼" bowl with a spray of flowers on a stippled background around the exterior.

Bowl
Marigold 10–15
Smoke 20–30

Starspray bowl in metal holder
Marigold   30–50
Smoke   60–100

States, US Glass

According to John Britt, writing in the Heart of America Carnival Glass Association bulletin, States was the final pattern in a series that was named for each of the states—only a few of which can be found in carnival glass. This marigold butter dish is 7¼" across and has an unusual rayed star on the bottom of the base. It was found in Argentina along with an oblong bowl in the same pattern and color. This piece sold at the 1998 International Association auction for $375.

Stippled Daisy, Northwood

This marigold bowl sold at a 1997 auction for $10. The inside center has a stippled daisy with the Northwood mark in the center (visible through the base). The exterior pattern, shown here, is Poppy.

Stippled Diamonds, Millersburg

An extremely rare pattern, this piece was uncovered by Millersburg collector Steve Maag. It is green and consists of small diamonds radiating out from the center against a stippled background (the diamonds themselves aren't stippled). The spade shape is identical to that of several other Millersburg rarities, including the Night Stars Nappy.

Stippled Flower, Dugan

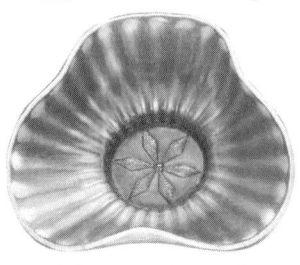

Stippled Flower is distinguished by its stippled six-petal design in the center. Usually seen in these tri-corner peach opal bowls selling for $30 to $45.

Stippled Petals, Dugan

The large stippled petals extend from the center of the piece. There is no other pattern. All pieces have the typical Dugan domed base. Most desirable with heavily ruffled edges and with two sides up as shown. The bowl is occasionally found with an applied handle making it a basket. A few bowls have been enameled.

Banana dish shape (2 sides up)
Peach opal 65–85 ruffled
Purple 200–350
Bowl, ruffled or crimped edge
Peach opal 55–95
Purple 75–125
Bowl, tricorner, 8"
Peach opal 35–50
Bowl, enameled, about 8"
Peach opal 70–120

Stippled Rambler Rose, Dugan

A seldom seen pattern found only in the nut bowl.
Nut bowl
Marigold 40–65

Stippled Rays, Fenton

Fenton's Stippled Rays pattern is often seen in small plates and bowls with a Scale Band exterior. Note the typical Fenton edge above. Red or amberina pieces will invariably be Fenton as will most in celeste and aqua.
Bonbon
Amethyst 25–35
Green 40–60
Bowl or sauce
Aqua 55–80 scarce
Blue 30–50 common color
Blue 125 (1998) 10" ice cream shape
Green 25–50
Marigold 5–10 common color
Red 300–500 common color
Red slag 450 (1996) ruffled, 9½" swirl base
Bowl, large, square
White 250 (1997)

Compote
Celeste 325–500 ice cream shape
Olive 15–25 ruffled
Vaseline 145 (1996) ice cream shape
Plate, usually with Scale Band back
Marigold 30–50
Red 1,000–1,500
Sugar, stemmed
Amber 20–30
Vaseline 110 (1997)

Stippled Rays, Northwood

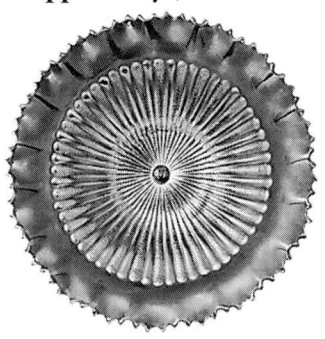

This is a typical Northwood Stippled Rays bowl, although the pie crust edge and dark color give it a bit of additional charm—and value.
Bowl, pie crust edge
Amethyst/purple 45–80
Green 25–40
Lavender 50 (1997)
Marigold 40–70
Bowl, ruffled
Amethyst 30–55
Blue, electric 280 (1993)
Green 60–100
Marigold 20–30
Purple 35–55

This is the Northwood Stippled Rays bowl with Greek Key exterior. In addition to the Greek Key theme on the exterior, it carries a texture of feathers or scales in the area from the foot up to the Greek Key. It is dome footed and found in amethyst, green, or marigold. Any of these is worth $40 to $65.

Stippled Strawberry, US Glass

Stippled Strawberry is a Depression glass pattern. It has a subtle design of strawberries but the most distinctive feature is the band near the top. There is a similar pattern with a cherry motif. This marigold example is courtesy of Carl and Eunice Booker. One sold in 1997 for $25.

Stork ABC

This pattern is seen in several forms and in a plate variant that has palm trees in the base.

Bowl, cereal
Marigold   45–80
Bowl, children's cereal
Marigold   35–60
Plate
Marigold   55–100
Plate, child's
Marigold, pale   235 (1993)   palm trees, minor nicks

Stork and Rushes, Dugan

The fairly large range of shapes found in Dugan's Stork and Rushes is typified by the water set. The standard pitcher and tumbler, shown here, have beaded bands encircling the neck and bottom of each piece. Compare these to the Stork and Rushes with Lattice Band seen on the following page. Unfortunately, several shapes have been reproduced in Stork and Rushes, reducing collectors' confidence in the pattern in general.

Water set, 5 piece
Amethyst   375 (1996)
Water set, 7 piece
Blue   400–700
Marigold   300–500
Water
Amethyst   200 (1994)   blue iridization
Blue   350–550
Marigold   165 (1998)
Tumbler
Amethyst   95 (1996)
Blue   30–55   most common color
Marigold   20–30
Berry bowl, small
Marigold   10–15

The stand for the punch set is questioned by some because it is so tall and tippy looking. It is actually the Summer Gardens vase turned upside down. And in this orientation, the flowers on the vase are upside down. Furthermore, the design is unlike that of the bowl and cups. However, every punch set I've seen has this base.

Punch set, 8 piece
Marigold   200–300
Punch base (Summer Gardens vase)
Amethyst/purple   50–80
Marigold   35–50
Punch cup
Amethyst   15–25
Marigold   10–15

The very rare four-piece table set includes a covered sugar, at one time thought not to have existed. Complete table sets are quite rare in any color and none have been available for public sale for the past several years. This marigold set is courtesy of Chuck Kremer.
Spooner
Marigold   50 (1994)

Stork and Rushes with Lattice Band, Dugan

All pieces in the Lattice Band variation of Stork and Rushes are scarce, if not rare. Very few of the above water pitchers are known. This one, in purple, is courtesy of Bill and Sharon Mizell.
Water pitcher
Blue   550 (1996)
Tumbler
Blue   65–90
Marigold   20–40

Mug
Amethyst   95–150
Blue   1,000–1,200
Marigold   15–25

Not all Stork and Rushes baskets are identified as the lattice band version, but most probably are.
Basket, handled, from tumbler
Amethyst   75 (1997)
Marigold   70–100
Hat or violet vase from tumbler (2 sides up)
Amethyst/purple 40–75
Marigold   30–45

Strawberry, Dugan

An unusual design, combining a strawberry interior bowl and a lily that has an abstract pattern of quilted diamonds and hobbed panels. As with other epergnes, this one is subject to damage around the hole where the lily fits—or to the end of the lily.
Epergne, single lily
Purple   700–1,000

Strawberry, Fenton

The pattern has two sprigs of strawberries. Some pieces have an additional berry in the bottom center and are slightly more valuable.
Bonbon or card tray shape
Amber   60–100   relatively common color
Amberina   200–350   or reverse amberina
Blue   55–90   most common color
Blue   70–100   berry in bottom

Fenton Strawberry, continued

Green, rare		
Lime green opal	300–400	scarce color
Marigold	20–30	scarce color
Marigold	60–115	berry in bottom
Red	400–500	rare color
Vaseline	60–115	scarce color
Vaseline opal	250–300	rare color

Strawberry, Northwood

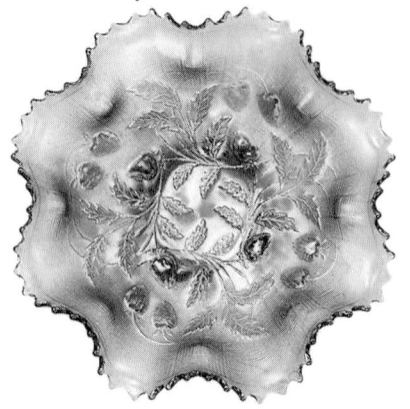

Only seen in bowls and plates, Northwood's Strawberry has a sprig of strawberries and leaves circling the surface. A similar design, Wild Strawberry, adds some small blossoms toward the outside edge of the pattern. Strawberry is found with plain, basketweave, or an occasional ribbed exterior.

Bowl, about 9", ruffled

Amethyst/purple	85–140	common color
Amethyst/purple	375 (1996)	outstanding iridescence
Green	85–150	average irid., common color
Green	200–350	exceptional iridescence
Horehound	750 (1993)	
Ice green	800–1,200	rare color
Lime green	725 (1997)	
Marigold	60–100	common color
Smoke	900 (1996)	

Bowl, about 9", pie crust edge

Amethyst/purple	120–200	common color
Amethyst, fiery	145 (1998)	
Green	90–180	common color
Green, emerald	850 (1998)	
Lilac	180 (1998)	
Marigold	65–115	common color
Smoke	700–900	rare color

Bowl, stippled, ruffled

Amethyst/purple	275–350	fairly common color
Aqua opal known		
Blue	350–500	common color
Blue, Renninger	750–1,100	rare color
Horehound	500–900	rare color
Ice green	600–1,000	rare color
Lavender	325	rare color
Lime green	600–1,000	scarce color
Marigold	120–160	common color

Bowl, stippled, pie crust edge (all scarce to rare)

Amethyst/purple	375–500	
Blue	400–700	
Green	1,000–1,400	ribbed exterior
Horehound	550–700	
Marigold	300–500	

Plate, about 9", most with basketweave backs, some with plain backs or ribbed backs

Amethyst/purple	150–250	most common color
Ame., smoky	395 (1995)	
Green	150–250	common color
Lavender	275–500	light amethyst, rare color
Marigold	140–225	common color
Peach opal	600–1,000	three known

Plate, stippled, about 9", ribbed exterior only

Amethyst/purple	350–600	common color
Green	1,400–2,400	scarce color
Green	800 (1995)	etched "To Mother from May"
Ice blue	23,000 (1995)	only one known
Marigold	1,600–2,000	rare color in stippled

Plate, handgrip, 6–7"

Amethyst/purple	175–300	
Green	90 (1996)	pulled point
Marigold	115–200	

Strawberry, unknown maker

These small bowls, part of a miniature berry set, sold at a Seeck auction in March 1994 for $250. The larger bowl is about five inches across. The strawberry design is in the bottom of the bowls.

Strawberry Intaglio, Northwood

Like Northwood's two other similar intaglio patterns, Strawberry has the design cut into the outside of the bowl—which is very thick glass. The iridescence is also on the outside, not the inside. Rarely sells at auction but like the others, is valued between $70 and $100.

Strawberry Scroll, Fenton

Strawberry Scroll has a pinched-in waist and a scroll design around the chest. The few pitchers available always sell at good prices. Even tumblers are hard to find and often pricey.

Water set, 7 piece
Blue   3,200 (1994)

Water pitcher
Blue   1,500–2,000
Marigold   2,900–4,000

Tumbler
Blue   85–155
Marigold   90–185

Strawberry Wreath (or Millersburg Strawberry), Millersburg

While the tricorner shape of this bowl is unusual, the pattern is typical. This is similar to Blackberry Wreath and Grape Wreath, but lacks any design in the center except for a small dot. This amethyst example is courtesy of Floyd and Cecil Whitley.

Bowl, 3/1 edge, ruffled, or ice cream shape
Amethyst	275 (1995)	10", 3/1 edge
Amethyst	110 (1993)	7", 3/1 edge
Amethyst	280 (1995)	10", deep, ruffled
Amethyst	150–300	8", crimped edge
Green	150–300	large, ruffled or crimped
Green	750 (1998)	9½", ice cream shape
Marigold	150–300	9–10", CRE or ruffled
Marigold	250 (1995)	3/1 edge
Marigold	110 (1996)	ice cream shape
Marigold	40–60	7", 3/1 edge, radium
Olive known		
Vaseline	700–800	10", ruffled

Bowl, tricorner
Amethyst	450–800	large, crimped
Green	300–400	large

Bowl, square
Amethyst	250–450	10"
Amethyst	150–250	8"
Green	450 (1997)	10"
Marigold	650 (1995)	10"

Bowl, small berry or sauce, about 6"
Amethyst	75–140	ice cream shape
Green	175 (1994)	ruffled
Marigold	45–60	
Purple sauce known		

Possibly a one-of-a-kind, this vaseline Strawberry Wreath bowl has been whimsied into a gravy boat shape. Courtesy of Carl and Eunice Booker.

This unusual vaseline compote is missing the stippling in one of the leaves (center). It sold for $2,100 at a Jim Seeck auction in 1994. See color photo, page 173.

Compote
Amethyst	300–425	most common color
Green	250–400	
Marigold	450–700	square, crimped
Marigold	150–250	

Strawberry Wreath, continued
Compote, blank leaf
Amethyst known
Marigold	1,050 (1998)	
Olive green	825 (1992)	sherbert shape
Vaseline	2,100 (1994)	

Stream of Hearts, Fenton

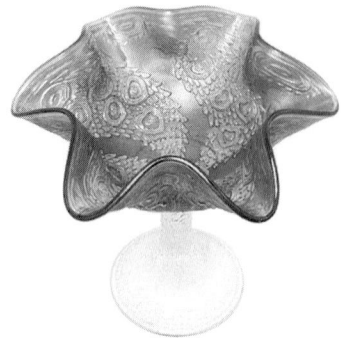

Stream of Hearts (sometimes called Streaming Hearts) is closely related to Fenton's Heart and Vine, and Hearts and Trees. All have the same type of heart-shaped leaf design. The compote, found only in marigold, has Fenton's Persian Medallion on the exterior. There are two reported goblets. The current price range for compotes is $80 to $140.

Stretch glass

Stretch glass was produced at about the same time as, or a little later than, classic carnival glass. It is usually considered a close relative of carnival as it has an iridized surface—though there is generally no pattern. Because stretch often finds its way into sales of carnival glass, I include it here. This is a representative list of typical examples.

Ashtray with matchbox
Celeste	50
Vaseline	50

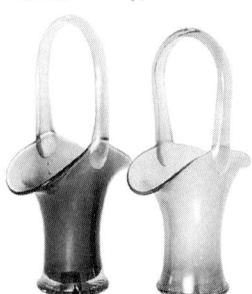

Basket, plain jane style, about 10" to handle top
Ice blue	100–150
Smoke	30–40
Teal	50–70
White	60–75

Basket, miniature
Amethyst/purple 65–100

Bowl, 7–10"
Amber	15 (1997)	
Blue opaque	55	9½", deep round
Celeste	40–60	
Red	50–90	
Red	105 (1998)	ruffled
White	110 (1998)	Floral & Optic, flared

Fruit bowl
Ice blue 135 (1997)

Plate
Celeste	10	footed
Ice blue	5	8"
Ice green	10	9"
Red	105	8¾", not panelled
Red	50–80	7–8", Wide Panel
Teal	75	
Vaseline	25	8½"
Vaseline	60	with silverplate bracket
Vaseline	35	stemmed, Tree of Life base

Chop plate
Celeste	120	gold trim
Red	200	11½"
White	65	14", Imperial Jewels

Candlestick (single)
Celeste	30–50	
Marigold	75	9¾" high, black base
Marigold	110	Fenton #352, black base
Vaseline	35	8¼", Northwood #657

Candlesticks (pair)
Blue opaque	55	9", gold trim
Celeste	60–90	
Celeste	130	hexagonal base
Celeste	300	8", black base
Ice green	25	3"
Olive	65	7"
Purple	550	white bases
Purple	200	bell shaped
Red/amberina	300	9", six-panelled
Russet	100	8½", Northwood Florentine
Tangerine	90	3", glows in black light
Vaseline	60	9", hexagonal base
Vaseline	75	6½", Northwood #868
White	80	hexagonal base

Console or centerpiece bowl
Blue opaque	30–60	
Ice blue	50	11", deep ribs
Marigold	25	12"
Red	155–175	
Tangerine	90	10¼"
White	30	16"

Console set (bowl and two candlesticks)
Celeste	25	
Red	250	10" bowl, bell-shaped candlesticks
Olive	80	

This covered candy dish is typical of those made by several manufacturers. It is in vaseline and sold for $25. The compote is celeste and sold for $30. Both sold at a 1997 Jim Seeck auction.

Covered candy dish
Celeste	10–20	
Ice green	65	Dolphins
Lavender	105	Fenton #634
Red	450	Cathedral-shaped
Tangerine	60	Wide Panel, cone-shaped
Vaseline	25	

Compote
Blue opaque	35	9"
Celeste	20–30	
Ice blue	80	jack-in-the-pulpit
Ice green	35–55	ruffled
Ice green	130 (1998)	7", Stippled Rays
Ice green	135	dolphins
Red	270	
Tangerine	160 (1997)	panelled, ruffled
Tangerine	1,000	8" across, Fenton Dolphins
Vaseline	25–50	

Dresser bottle, Fenton
Celeste	260	
Marigold	100	pair, decorated
Pink	550	pair, decorated

Goblet
Celeste	20–40

Guest set, 2 piece, Fenton
Ice green	270	cobalt handle
Marigold	230	cobalt handle
Vaseline	400	cobalt handle
Velva	205	pink handle
White	325	cobalt handle

Lemonade set, 15 pieces
Celeste	400	coasters, cobalt handles

Mug, footed
Celeste	75	Pastel Panels

Nut cup
Celeste	20–60	
Ice green	23	
Marigold	25	
Vaseline	25–38	

Pitcher, juice
Pink	150

Pitcher, water, covered
Vaseline	145–240	cobalt handles

Punch bowl and base
Red	3,800 (1998)	ruffled top

Punch bowl top only
Celeste	625 (1998)

Rosebowl
Amber	85	Imperial Iron Cross Mark
Celeste	30–40	
Marigold	20	square
Red	30–75	
Red	75	with stand
Smoke	30	

Salt dip
Ice green	55	individual, flared
Pink	205	flared, scarce color
Vaseline	45	individual, flared

Salt set
Marigold	300	7 piece, Wide Panel
Vaseline	475	6 piece, Wide Panel

Shade, lamp
Marigold	60

Snack tray, 6–7"
Vaseline	45

Spittoon, Imperial
Amethyst	70	Iron Cross Mark

Sugar
Vaseline	20	blue handle

Toothpick
Purple	25–30

Vase
Amber	50–95	5–6"
Blue	20	6"
Celeste	50–60	6–8"
Celeste	155	15", horizontal bands
Ice green	125	11"
Ice green	30–55	6 or 7"
Ice green	250 (1998)	15", Interior Ripple
Marigold	8	
Red	85–170	8–9"
Red	210	6", ruffled
White	30–50	
White	95	11"
Wisteria	95–145	

Vase, fan shape
Blue	15	6"
Vaseline	20–55	

Vase, trumpet shape
Red	200–250	9", amberina base
Red	275	9", crimped top, gold decor.
Vaseline	75	

Strutting Peacock, Westmoreland

Strutting Peacock is found only in this breakfast set of a small covered creamer and sugar. For some reason the lids are never iridized. Westmoreland reproduced these in the 1970s, with iridized lids. Known only in amethyst, prices range from $40 to more than $100, with most selling for $70 or $80.

Studs, Jeanette

Depression glass pattern made in the 1940s and found in a wide range of shapes seen mostly in juice sets and milk pitcher (above). Six- or eight-piece marigold juice sets sell for $60 to $100, milk pitchers $15. Juice sets bring a little more if they have a tray.

Sunflower, Northwood

A simple yet effective design with a huge sunflower in the middle of the bowl. Found only in spatula-footed bowls with the Meander pattern on the back.

Bowl
Amethyst/purple	100–200	most common color
Blue	400–600	scarce color
Blue, electric	600–1,000	scarce color
Blue, Renninger	600–1,000	scarce color
Green	80–150	common color
Green, emerald	575 (1998)	superior iridescence
Ice blue	1,500–2,000	scarce color
Marigold	50–75	common color

Sunflower, Millersburg

These little pin trays are among Millersburg's most cherished patterns. Bear in mind, though, that a newer design by Fenton is very similar.

Pin tray
Amethyst	550–700
Green	500–650
Marigold	950 (1997)

Sunflower and Diamond
See Vases

Sunken Daisies, Riihimäki

A seldom seen pattern, Sunken Daisies has an intaglio (cut into the surface) design. This blue rosebowl is 4⅞" wide and sold at the 1998 International Association auction for $475. A blue bowl sold in 1996 for $350.

Swan on Nest
See Covered Swan

Swan, pastel
See Novelties/miniatures

Sweetheart, Cambridge

Sweetheart is a very scarce pattern known only in this cracker jar in green and marigold and a handful of marigold tumblers. No items have changed hands publicly in recent years. This green cracker jar is courtesy of Bob and Geneva Leonard.

Swirl, Northwood

Northwood's Swirl is sometimes called Interior Swirl. There are several variations on this pattern, but all are rather similar to that above. This example is green with marigold iridescence on the top third only—a treatment Northwood called "Alaskan." This pitcher and tumbler sold for $220 and $105, respectively, at a 1996 Mickey Reichel auction.

Water set, 7 piece
Marigold   90 (1998)
Pitcher
Green   200–350
Marigold   50–80
Tumbler
Green   70–105
Marigold   30–45

Swirled Hobnail, Millersburg

The rosebowl and spittoon, as well as the vase, were all made from the same molds. Millersburg also made both rosebowl and spittoon in the non-swirl version (see Hobnail). So far, green has only been reported in the form of two spittoons—both damaged. This pattern is sometimes known as Hobnail Swirl.

Rosebowl
Amethyst/purple 250–450
Marigold   200–350
Spittoon
Amethyst/purple 500–800   most common color
Green   7,000 (1996) 1,700 (1998) same piece
Green   3,000 (1996)   cracked and bruised
Marigold   600–900
Vase (also see Vase section)
Amethyst   200–350   most common color
Green   200–300
Marigold   150–250

Sword and Circle

A very rare tumbler with vertical creases (swords) and thumbprint-like indentations (circles). This one in light marigold sold at a 1993 auction for $125. A juice glass brought $100 at a 1995 auction. The maker is unknown.

Sydney, Fostoria

The Sydney pattern is rare in any shape. Only the regular tumblers and a smaller tumbler called a champagne glass were known until Galen and Kathi Johnson found this marigold pitcher. No items in this pattern have sold publicly in recent years.

Target, Dugan
See Vases.

Tartan, Brockwitz (Germany)

The Tartan pattern is sometimes referred to as Daisy and Cane or Daisy and Button. Tumblers, vases, epergnes, carafes and a celery have been reported.

Compote
Marigold   25–40

Ten Mums, Fenton

Not to be confused with Northwood's Embroidered Mums—there are, in fact, ten chrysanthemums on the Ten Mums bowl—although the pitcher and tumbler sport twelve mums.

Bowl, 9–9½", collar base, ruffled or 3/1 edge
Amethyst	200–350	common color
Blue	150–500	common color
Blue, electric	275–475	
Green	160–300	common color
Marigold	175–300	
Marigold	525 (1997)	crimped, deep
Marigold	200–325	scarce footed version

Water set, 7 piece
Blue	1,200–2,000
Marigold	800–1,200

Water pitcher
Blue	550–800
Marigold	450–600
White, rare	

Tumbler (see page 181 for color photo)
Blue	55–90	most common color
Marigold	40–70	
White, rare		

Texas Shot Glass, Brockwitz

Dubbed the "Texas Shot Glass," these six-inch tall celeries are quite likely Northern Lights, according to research by Glen and Stephen Thistlewood. This blue example sold at the 1998 Heart of America auction for $450.

Thin Rib, Northwood
See Vases

Thin Rib and Drape
See Vases

Thistle, Fenton

Fenton made two completely different thistle patterns: the banana boat shown above, with a Waterlily and Cattails exterior, and the bowl (from which the plate was also made) shown in the next column.

Banana boat
Amethyst	200–250	scarce color
Blue	200–350	most common color
Blue, electric	300–500	
Green	300–450	scarce color
Marigold	100–175	common color

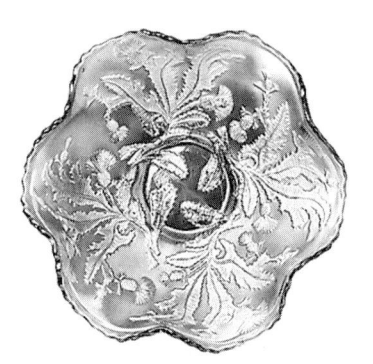

Bowl, 8–9", crimped, ruffled or 3/1 edge
Amber	165 (1996)	
Amethyst	70–100	common color
Amethyst	180 (1994)	fabulous iridescence
Aqua	250–325	rare color
Blue	95–165	common color
Green	60–90	common color
Marigold	40–70	fairly common color
Root beer	175 (1998)	
Vaseline	275–350	rare color

Bowl, Horlacher advertising on base
Amethyst	100–170
Green	120–180

Plate, 9"
Amethyst	3,500–4,500	
Green	3,000–4,500	
Marigold	6,700 (1994)	two known

Thistle and Lotus
See Lotus and Thistle, Fenton

Thistle and Thorn

This is a pretty pattern found in marigold and in ordinary shapes. The pattern is only on the exterior of the bowls and gets to be quite distorted when the bowl is flared widely. The sugar bowl that goes with the above creamer is quite large (and has four feet) so is often thought to be a nut bowl. Any of the pieces would be worth $15 to $25.

Threaded Butterfly, US Glass

This one-of-a-kind 8⅝" plate has a wreath of four butterflies and plumes and another butterfly in the center. There are three small spade-like feet in the Colorado pattern which prompts the attribution to US Glass. The color is green with a pastel iridescence. Thanks to Tom Burns and Maxine Burkhardt.

Three Fruits, Fenton

The Fenton version of Three Fruits has a distinctive edge with 12 sides, and is often referred to as a 12-sided plate. Virtually all of the pieces in this Fenton pattern are plates.

Bowl
Amethyst   160 (1997)
Green also reported

Plate, 9"
Amethyst	90–165	
Blue	125–200	most common color
Green	100–200	
Marigold	85–145	

Three Fruits, Northwood

Northwood's Three Fruits is extraordinarily popular. It's found in both plates and bowls, a variety of edge treatments, several exterior patterns, several base configurations, and many colors. It is also found in a stippled version. The medallion version, with a triple leaf in the center rather than three cherries, is covered under Three Fruits Medallion. Three Fruits is similar to Northwood's own Fruits and Flowers, which has no design in the center. Three Fruits often has wear on the fruit, so check carefully.

Bowl, 8–9", ruffled
Amethyst/purple	65–120	common color
Aqua opal	400–700	scarce color
Green	80–150	common color
Honey amber	225–300	
Horehound	300 (1995)	
Lavender	475 (1996)	smoky
Lime green	525–775	rare color
Marigold	40–70	common color
Pearlized	450 (1997)	
Smoke	425 (1995)	rare color

Bowl, 8–9", pie crust edge
Amethyst/purple	100–175	common color
Amethyst/purple	425 (1998)	smooth back
Green	70–130	scarce color
Lime green	250 (1995)	
Marigold	60–110	common color
Smoke	500 (1995)	

Plate, 9" (most with basketweave exterior)
Amethyst/purple	150–275	common color
Amethyst/purple	225–400	plain back, scarce
Aqua opal	2,000–3,000	rare color
Blue	500–800	scarce color
Blue, electric	800–1,100	
Green	175–350	common color
Green	250–450	plain exterior, scarce
Green, emerald	750 (1998)	
Green	975 (1998)	blue iridescence
Horehound	300–500	rare color
Marigold	125–250	most common color
Marigold	400–650	very dark or pumpkin
Marigold	200–300	plain back, scarce

Three Fruits Medallion, Northwood

Northwood's Three Fruits bowls and plates are also found with a stippled background, bordered by a band near the edge. These pieces are generally valued more highly than the same colors in the nonstippled version.

Bowl, stippled, ruffled

Amethyst/purple	150–250	scarce color
Aqua opal	900–1,800	fairly common color
Blue	225–400	common color
Blue, electric	400–700	
Custard	300–400	pearlized, rare
Green	450–800	scarce color
Ice blue	700–1,200	rare color
Horehound reported		
Lavender	200 (1995)	
Marigold	100–175	common color
Marigold	300–500	dark or pumpkin color
Sapphire	1,000–1,500	rare color
Teal	1,000–1500	rare color
White	250–400	common color

Bowl, stippled, pie crust edge

Amethyst/purple	250–500	scarce color
Blue	400–600	scarce color
Green	600–950	farily common color
Horehound	350 (1997)	
Ice blue	700 (1993)	chips on edge
Marigold	150–200	scarce color
Olive	600 (1994)	ribbed exterior

Plate, stippled, 9"

Amethyst/purple	300–550	very common color
Amethyst/purple	600–800	spectacular examples
Aqua	1,600–2,500	scarce color
Aqua opal	2,000–4,000	relatively common color
Blue	400–650	common color
Blue, electric	650–1,000	
Clambroth	180–300	rare color
Green	2,500–4,000	rare color
Horehound	400–800	rare color
Honey amber	2,400 (1996)	
Ice blue	5,000–7,000	
Ice green, rare		
Lavender	500–800	scarce color
Marigold	200–350	very common color
Marigold	400–700	dark or pumpkin color
Sapphire	1,200–2,000	rare color
Teal	2,500–3,500	rare color
Violet	850 (1997)	

The difference between this version and the regular Three Fruits is the three-leaf medallion in the center rather than the three cherries. Most are seen with the spatula feet and Meander back shown above, but some are found with a dome foot and basketweave or vintage back, or a combination of both (below).

Medallion bowl, dome-footed (scarce)

Amethyst/purple	70–110
Green	85–130
Horehound	80–150
Ice green	250–350
Marigold	70–90
White	150–200

Medallion bowl, spatula-footed, unstippled

Amethyst/purple	90–175	most common color
Aqua opal	450–600	relatively available
Aqua opal	800–1,400	spectacular examples
Custard	400–500	pearlized, rare color
Green	90–170	scarce color
Ice blue	700–1,000	rare color
Ice blue opal	775 (1997)	
Ice green	500–650	rare color
Ice green opal	1,050 (1996)	
Lavender ame.	325 (1998)	
Marigold	80–150	
White	300–500	scarce color

Medallion bowl, spatula footed, stippled

Amethyst/purple	90–160
Aqua opal	450–750
Blue	500–700
Ice blue	1,300 (1997)
Ice green	400–700
Marigold	100–175
White	350–575

Three-in-One, Imperial

Three-in-One has two bands of diamond-filled diamonds (the band near the collar base is barely visible here) on the exterior only. Shown above is the rosebowl version of this pattern. Three-in-One has been reproduced, primarily in the toothpick holder.

Bowl
Marigold	20–40	
Purple	40–60	6–7"
Smoke	40–60	

Plate, 6–7"
Marigold	35–60
Vaseline	55 (1997)

Sauce
Marigold	15–25

Rosebowl
Marigold	35 (1997)

Toothpick holder
Green	20–30	most are probably new

Three Row, Imperial
See Vases

Thumbprint and Ovals, Imperial
See Vases

Tiger Lily, Imperial, Riihimäki

While Tiger Lily was primarily made by Imperial, it was copied by the Finnish firm, Riihimäki. In general, the pieces you see in blue are the Riihimäki version. To make matters more complex, the pitcher and tumbler also were reproduced from the original Imperial molds by several US makers, marked with an "IG" or "LIG."

Water set, 7 piece (all colors scarce)
Blue	550–750	Riihimäki, 5 piece
Aqua/teal	600 (1998)	
Green	300–500	
Marigold	150–250	
Purple sets reported		

Water pitcher
Green	125–235
Marigold	100–160
Teal	175–350

Tumbler
Amber	190–225	rare color
Blue	350 (1995)	Imperial
Blue	100–200	Riihimäki, common color
Blue violet	50 (1995)	
Green	20–35	common color
Helios green	55 (1994)	
Marigold	20–30	most common color
Purple	70–125	common color
Olive	90 (1994)	
Teal	50–90	rare color (if old)

Tiny Hobnail

Shot glass or child's tumbler
Marigold	180–225

Tiny Thumbprint

Breakfast set
Marigold	25–50	with souvenir lettering

Toothpick holder
Marigold	50–70	with souvenir lettering

Tornado, Northwood
See Vases

Town Pump, Northwood
See Vases

Tracery, Millersburg

One of Millersburg's less often seen patterns, Tracery has an interior-only design of floral elements connected by beaded traces. Known only in amethyst and green bonbons.

Bonbon
Amethyst   1,300 (1995)   400 (1998)   oval
Green   900–1,200   square

Tree Bark

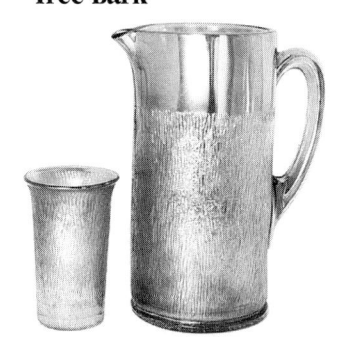

This is a Depression era pattern and as such, holds little interest for most carnival collectors—as must be apparent from the prices it brings. This pitcher, along with eight tumblers, brought just $30 at a 1997 auction.

Water set, 7 piece
Marigold   30–50
Pitcher and tumbler
Marigold   20–35
Water pitcher
Aqua   30 (1996)

Candlesticks
Marigold   15–25

Tree of Life

Curiously, carnival collectors have little interest in the water set pieces for this pattern but seem to like the little baskets. The pitcher and lemonade tumbler above, in light marigold, brought just $15 at a 1997 auction. The Dugan marigold handled basket shown below is six inches tall and brought $30 at the 1995 Great Lakes club auction. Others have sold for as much as $60.

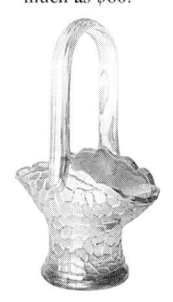

Tree Trunk, Northwood
See Vases

Trefoil Fine Cut, Millersburg

Trefoil Fine Cut is an exterior pattern used on Millersburg's Many Stars bowl. The piece above is a chop plate with a plain front. It is iridized on both sides and is the only one thus far reported. Courtesy of Jerry and Carol Curtis.

Triplets, Dugan

This is another of the several similar patterns with plain interior and flowers extending out from the collar base on the exterior. Others are Daisy Dear and Single Flower. Marigold bowls are worth about $20, peach opal about $30.

Trophy

See Novelties/miniatures

Trout and Fly, Millersburg

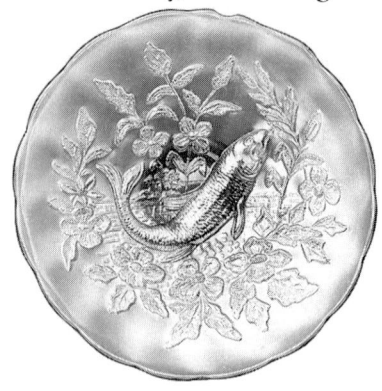

The Trout and Fly is similar to Millersburg's Big Fish but, in this case, the pattern has an insect just beyond the fish's mouth. The above plate, from the collection of Waymon and Nilah Espy, is one of only a few known in green. There are also a couple of plates known in amethyst. Amethyst, green, and marigold appear with approximately equal frequency in the bowls.

Bowl, ruffled
Amethyst	400–700	
Green	350–650	
Horehound	850 (1993)	rare color, chips
Marigold	300–400	

Bowl, 3/1 edge
Amethyst	375–650	
Green	400–700	
Lavender	525–700	rare color
Marigold	225–400	

Bowl, ice cream shape
Amethyst	450–850	
Green	600–1,000	common color
Green	1,500 (1998)	spectacular color
Lavender	750–800	rare color
Marigold	300–475	

Bowl, square or diamond shape
Amethyst	500–800
Green	900–1,200
Marigold	450–750

Tulip and Cane, Imperial

Shown here and in the photo below are the only known carnival shapes in Tulip and Cane (although the pattern was produced in other shapes in crystal—so there could be others in carnival). The above ruffled sauce is courtesy of Carl and Eunice Booker. Below are the goblet (largest), claret (next largest), wine and cordial (smallest).

Water goblet (8 oz.)
Marigold		40–50

Claret goblet (4 oz.)
Marigold		100–150			2 or 3 known

Wine glass (3 oz.)
Marigold		50–65

Cordial, 3⅝" high (1½ oz.)
Marigold		200–350			rare

Sauce, 5"
Smoke		45-60

Tulip, Millersburg

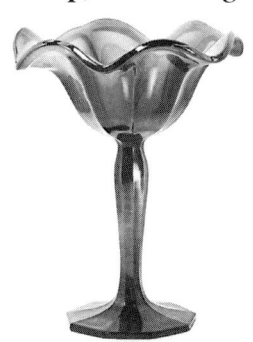

Imagine how many of these have been passed by because they look like any other plain compote with no design on the interior. In reality, this is a rare Millersburg pattern. The only example to sell in recent years was in marigold and brought $675 at the 1997 Lincoln-Land auction. The compote is also known in amethyst.

Tulip Panels

This ginger jar is the only reported example in this pattern. It is marigold and sold in 1994 for $105.

Tulip Scroll
See Vases

Twelve Rings

These marigold candlesticks sold for $70 in 1995.

Twins, Imperial

Another of the many Imperial cut-style patterns, usually found in the small sauce above or a two-piece fruit bowl. This one can be identified by the arch separating the "twin" hobstars.

Small bowl or sauce, about 6"
Blue		350 (1996)			deep
Marigold	15–20

Fruit bowl, 2 piece
Marigold	45–80

Fruit base only
Marigold	5
Smoke		10

Two Flowers, Fenton

There are two *different* kinds of flowers here—a central medallion of one type and a circular band of another. Like its sister pattern, Stag and Holly, Two Flowers was made in both a spatula-footed version and a larger ball-footed one. In addition, it is occasionally found with a collar base.

Bowl, large ball-footed, 10–11", ruffled
Amethyst/purple   85–150   scarce color
Amethyst, black   175 (1997)
Aqua   200–350   scarce color
Blue   110–175   most common color
Green   300 (1997)
Lime green   95–180   rare color
Marigold   65–100   common color
Red, rare
Vaseline   175–250   rare color

Bowl, large ball-footed, ice cream shape
Amethyst, fiery   130 (1995)
Blue   300–400   common color
Blue, smoky   500 (1994)
Lime green   175 (1996)
Marigold   45–85   common color

Chop plate (from large bowl)
Marigold   1,200–2,200

Rosebowl, giant (from large bowl)
Blue   500–900
Marigold   125–200

Bowl, collar base, about 9"
Marigold   85–125

Bowl, small (8–9"), spatula footed
Amberina   900 (1998)

Amethyst   45–70
Blue   45–80
Green   50–75
Lavender   45 (1993)
Marigold   30–50   most common color
Red   1,000–1,800   rare color

Plate, about 9" (from spatula-footed bowl)
Marigold   550–600
Marigold   1,700 (1998)   spectacular example

Rosebowl, small (spatula-footed)
Blue   85–150
Marigold   45–85
Purple   115 (1998)
White known

Sauce, about 6", footed
Amethyst   50–80
Aqua   165 (1997)
Lime green   65–115
Marigold   15–25
Vaseline   95–165

Two Fruits, Fenton

While usually round as in the above example, these two-handled bonbons are sometimes ruffled. There are also examples of similar divided bonbons without the interior pattern.

Divided bonbon
Blue   65–100   most common color
Green   100–175   scarce color
Marigold   35–60

Two Seventy, Westmoreland

Often overlooked because of its small size and plain design, yet good examples bring reasonable prices. Although commonly known as Two Seventy, the original Westmoreland pattern number was 252.

Two Seventy compote, about 6" wide
Amethyst   40–60
Aqua   35 (1998)
Blue opal   90–150
Mar/milk glass   75–125
Peach opal   75 (1994)
Teal   25 (1997)

Valentine, Northwood

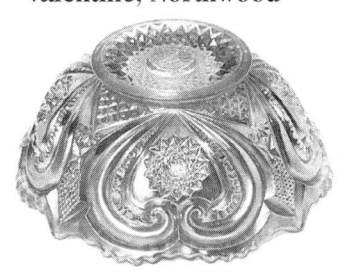

An early Northwood pattern with a smooth interior found in berry sets. This marigold small berry is courtesy of Carl and Eunice Booker.

Venetian, Cambridge/Millersburg

There aren't many of these spectacular pieces around. Usually referred to as rosebowls because they're cupped in, but can also be considered a vase. Although shown in an old Cambridge catalog as the base of an oil lamp, Bob Gallo pointed out several similarities to other Millersburg patterns. The base and stem, for example, are the same as that of the Hobstar and Feather rosebowl. In addition, Bob reported that a Venetian shard had been found in the Millersburg dump. The rosebowl is also found with a scalloped sawtooth top. A creamer and sugar have been reported in marigold.

Rosebowl, giant
Green   900–1,000
Marigold   900 (1996)   base chip

Victorian, Dugan

Most Victorian bowls are found with a ruffled edge rather than the round one shown here. What a pity as the elegant pattern of overlapping circles shows so much better in the rare round bowl. Also known in rare peach opal examples.

Bowl, large round
Purple   275 (1995)   scratch on pattern
Bowl, large ruffled, about 11"
Purple   250–400
Purple   850 (1996)   almost flat

Vineyard, Dugan

Dugan's contribution to the grape theme on water sets has the grapes against a tree bark or rustic texture and is easy to spot for that reason. The purple or amethyst color is much more scarce than marigold.

Water set, 7 piece
Marigold   125–200
Purple   350–525
Pitcher, water
Marigold   80–150
Peach opal 1,200 (1997)
Purple   350–600
Tumbler
Marigold   15–25
Purple   30–50
White, rare

Vintage, Dugan

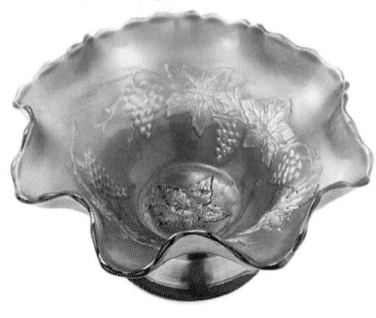

The pattern is very similar to Fenton's Vintage, the main difference being the typical Dugan domed base. The bowl shown is atypical in that it is much deeper than the usual Dugan Vintage bowl. Vintage punch cups go with the Many Fruits punch bowl.

Bowl, ruffled
Amethyst	60–100	
Blue	175 (1995)	
Celeste	900 (1997)	
Green	100–200	
Marigold	30 (1998)	

Plate, 9"
Amethyst	675–725
Lavender	1,000 (1998)

Powder jar
Marigold	40–70	common color
Purple	250–300	
White	225 (1993)	

Vintage, Fenton

Vintage is essentially a Grape and Cable design without the cable—whether it is Fenton or Dugan. Suffice it to say that color and condition will have more effect on value than who made it. Nine-inch plates are very rare in this pattern. They are known in amethyst, blue and marigold, with one aqua opal reported. Vintage is also the interior pattern found on some Wreath of Roses punch sets.

Bonbon or card tray shape
Amethyst	40–60
Blue	35–60
Green	30–55
Marigold	25–40

Small bowl or sauce, 5–6"
Amethyst	10–20	
Aqua opal known in ruffled, round, and ice cream shape		
Blue	20–35	
Blue	25–45	tricorner
Celeste blue	1,000–1,300	rare color
Green	15–25	
Marigold	35–50	
Red	7,750 (1994)	6" cherry red, ruffled

Bowl, medium, 7–8"
Amethyst	20–35	common color
Aqua opal	600–900	rare color
Blue	40–60	common color
Blue, Persian	600–850	rare color
Green	30–50	common color
Marigold	25–40	
Vaseline	75–125	

Bowl, large, 9–10", ruffled, 3/1, candy ribbon
Amethyst	50–80	common color
Aqua opal	1,000–1,800	rare color
Blue	60–100	common color
Blue, Persian	575–750	rare color
Celeste	3,000–4,000	rare color
Green	40–70	common color
Lime	160 (1997)	
Marigold	40–60	common color
Red	1,500–2,500	ruffled
Red	3,000–5,000	3/1 edge
Red	9,000 (1998)	spectacular example, 3/1
Red	1,200–1,700	ice cream shape
Vaseline	125 (1995)	3/1 edge

Plate, small, 6" (all rare)
Amethyst	100–195	
Green	250–400	
Marigold	525 (1994)	6½"

Plate, 7–8"
Amethyst	125–200	common color
Blue	125–200	common color
Green	175–300	most common color
Marigold	150–250	common color

Plate, 9"
Marigold	2,500–4,000
Purple	4,500 (1996)

Chop plate, 10"
Blue	175 (1998)

Compote
Amethyst	25–45	
Blue	50–75	
Green	65–100	most common color
Marigold	25–35	

Fenton made their Vintage epergnes in two sizes, one about 6: high, the other about 4¾" high. The larger has five sets of grapes around the bowl; the smaller, four sets. The larger lily does not fit in the smaller bowl. The smaller epergne is seen most often.

Epergne, 2 piece, small
Amethyst	110–200	
Blue	125–200	
Green	200–350	
Marigold	100–170	most common color

Epergne, 2 piece, large
Amethyst	200–300	
Green	250–350	
Green	230 (1998)	ruffled bowl

Most ferneries are shaped like the one in back but there are a few whimsies including this candy ribbon-edged example in amethyst. Both courtesy of Carl and Ferne Schroeder. Because of the cupped-in shape on the normal fernery, they are sometimes called rosebowls.

Fernery (or rosebowl)
Amberina	400–750	(or reverse amberina), rare
Amethyst	30–50	fairly common color
Amethyst	175–225	whimsey—3/1 edge
Blue	40–70	most common color
Green	50–90	fairly common color
Marigold	20–30	fairly common color
Red	400–650	fairly common color

Wine glass
Amethyst/purple	15–25
Marigold	10–15

Spittoon whimsey
Marigold	6,500 (1994)	one known

Vintage Banded, Dugan

The pattern has a grape and leaf design with a band of diagonal stripes above and below.

Shaving mug
Marigold   20–30

Water pitcher and 6 mugs
Marigold   600 (1993)

Water pitcher, pedestaled
Marigold   350 (1994)

Tumbler
Marigold, very scarce

Vintage Hobnail, Millersburg

The Millersburg Vintage pattern has three bunches of grapes on the interior and hobnails on the reverse. Bowls are known in two sizes, 9½" and a 6" sauce. All are rare. The green sauce shown above is from the John and Lucile Britt collection.

Bowl, ice cream shape (ruffled and 3/1 known)
Green	700 (1997)	cracks
Marigold	500–800	

Sauce, ice cream shape
Known in amethyst and blue
Green	1,000 (1994)	
Marigold	800 (1994)	375 (1998)

Virginia Blackberry

This 4¼" tall child's pitcher is the only iridized example known. It sold most recently for $625 at the 1994 John and Lucile Britt auction (Jim Seeck, auctioneer). Virginia is a US Glass pattern but the blackberries seem to be like those on the Northwood Raspberry pattern.

Vogue, Fostoria
See Novelties/miniatures

Voltec, McKee
Butter, covered, signed Prescut
Purple   65 (1994)

Votive Light
See Novelties/miniatures

Waffle Block, Imperial

Carnival glass collectors are partial to representations of flowers, birds and animals, so the modern-looking Waffle Block design suffers—even though it's a well-done pattern with the theme nicely implemented over the range of shapes.

Basket, handled
Clambroth   20–35
Marigold   35–60   most common color
Purple   55 (1997)
Teal   60–100
Bowl, 7" square
Teal   20–35
Plate, 6"
Marigold   40 (1998)
Breakfast set (creamer and sugar)
Clambroth   50 (1994)   Iron Cross mark
Water pitcher
Clambroth   40–80
Marigold   200 (1994)

The punch bowl and base above are in marigold. The bowl is known in teal, but no bases are known in that color.

Punch set, 8 piece
Marigold   110–200
Punch bowl and base
Clambroth   80–110
Marigold   50–75
Punch cup
Marigold   40–60
Sherbert
Clambroth   15–25

Shown here are a tumbler and a sherbert.
Tumbler
Clambroth   145–160
Marigold   85–150

One certainly wouldn't expect to see the Waffle Block pattern whimsied into a spittoon, but here it is. It is marigold, 9½" wide and 5" high and is in a private collection.

Washboard (Diamond and Fan)
See Diamond and Fan

Water Lily, Fenton

While Water Lily is the traditional name for this pattern, some collectors refer to it as Lotus and Poinsettia, as those are really the flora shown. It is very similar to—and often confused with—other Fenton patterns such as Pond Lily or Waterlily and Cattails. Most bowls and sauces are footed but an occasional collar-base sauce shows up.

Bonbon
Marigold   20–35

Berry set, 7 piece
Marigold   135 (1998)

Bowl, 9–10" (scarce shape)
Amethyst   275 (1998)
Blue   100–180
Green   150–250
Marigold   60–100
Red, two or three examples known
Teal   250 (1996)
Vaseline   275 (1998)

Small bowl or sauce, 5–6"
Amber   85–110   scarce color
Amber slag   450 (1995)
Aqua   100–200   relatively common color
Blue   75–125   common color
Green   125–165   common color
Lime green opal 500–700   scarce color
Marigold   15–25   common color
Red   700–1,200   fairly common color
Rev. amberina   700–1,100   reverse amberina
Rev. amb'a opal 800–1,400   reverse amberina opal
Rev. amb'a opal 2,300 (1998)   spectacular example
Vaseline   75–140   fairly common color

Waterlily and Cattails, Dugan

Yes, Dugan also made Waterlily and Cattails, a pattern usually credited to Fenton and Northwood. The above tumbler and pitcher, in rich marigold, were listed as Dugan in the 1996 auction where they brought $10 and $360, respectively. Generally, marigold tumblers are worth $20 to $35. They differ from the Fenton and Northwood tumblers in that they are smooth near the base—neither basketweave nor short lines.

Waterlily and Cattails, Fenton

Fenton made the bulk of the Waterlily and Cattails pieces—which are almost identical to the Northwood and Dugan. The Fenton water pitcher has a bowled bottom like the Dugan. Toothpick holders whimsied from the small bowls are seen fairly often, but the miniature spittoon whimsey (above) made from a tumbler is very rare. Courtesy of Carl and Ferne Schroeder. Fenton tumblers have a small basketweave pattern near the base.

Water set, 7 piece
Marigold   2,050 (1995)

Pitcher, 1 tumbler
Marigold   250 (1995)

Tumbler
Marigold   25–45

Berry set, 7 piece
Marigold   200 (1998)

Bowl, large
Blue   170 (1994)
Green, rare

Fenton Waterlily and Cattails, continued
Banana bowl
Marigold   140 (1996)
Plate
Marigold   13 (1993)   6½"
Top Hat, whimsey from tumbler
Marigold   300 (1996)
Spittoon, whimsey from tumbler
Marigold   2,350 (1992)
Spittoon, whimsey from bowl (two known)
Marigold   1,000 (1998)   6½" wide

Table set
Marigold   450 (1994)
Toothpick or vase whimsey, from sauce, about 3½" high
Marigold   30–60

Waterlily and Cattails, Northwood

Northwood's Waterlily and Cattails pattern has short lines near the bottom, unlike the clear area on Dugan or basketweave on Fenton. This blue tumbler sold for $450 at the 1998 American convention (Tom Burns). The water pitcher is cone-shaped, unlike the bowled-bottom style of Fenton and Dugan pitchers.

Pitcher, water
Blue   5,500 (1993)   only one known
Marigold   350–650
Tumbler
Blue   450 (1998)
Marigold   35–50
Purple, rare

Weeping Cherries, Dugan

Weeping Cherries is distinguished by its four sets of cherries separated by baseball bat-like shapes on a dome-footed bowl. I know of it only in marigold.

Bowl, dome-footed
Marigold   60–100   ruffled
Marigold   275 (1996)   3/1 edge

Western Thistle, Riihimäki (Finland)

The pattern is noted for the large thistle and the diamond shapes around the base. The above blue set is a good example of the international aspect of carnival. It was made in Finland and found its way to Argentina where is was acquired by Jorge Perri. Perri brought it to the 1996 HOACGA convention and turned it over to Jim Seeck. Jim auctioned off the pieces individually at the 1996 Air Capital club auction. The pitcher brought $250; tumblers from $100 to $250. A blue tumbler sold at the 1996 HOACGA auction for $500; another in blue for $215 at the 1998 HOACGA auction. A blue pitcher sold for $600 in 1997. The other shape in the pattern to sell recently is a 5" marigold vase.

Wheat, Northwood

This rare sweetmeat is similar in design to the Grape and Cable sweetmeat. This purple example is in the collection of Floyd and Cecil Whitley. The purple sherbert cup below is courtesy of Jerry and Carole Curtis.

Wheat Sheath, Cambridge

The Wheat Sheath family includes these cologne bottles in green and marigold, a covered cracker jar in amethyst, and a decanter in green (one known). The colognes are commonly known simply as Cambridge colognes—see that listing for prices.

Wheels, Imperial

Wheels is characterized by large circular medallions appearing on the exterior only. Found in blue and marigold bowls. This blue example is courtesy of Dennis and Denise Harp. A marigold 9¾" bowl sold in 1998 for $145.

Whirling Leaves, Millersburg

Aptly named, Millersburg's Whirling Leaves has a design of four leaves swirling out from the center. The back pattern is Fine Cut Ovals. Known only in bowls, including rare blue examples.

Bowl, 9–10", mostly ruffled or 3/1 edge
Amethyst	175–300	common color
Amethyst	400–500	tricorner, crimped
Amethyst	425–550	square, crimped
Amethyst	450 (1996)	oblong, 3/1 edge, crimped
Blue	4,400 (1997)	
Green	85–150	
Green	400–600	tricorner, crimped
Marigold	75–120	common color
Vaseline	450 (1992)	

Whirling Star, Imperial

An infrequently seen pattern found only in marigold punch set pieces. The bowl measures almost 14" across and stands 13½" high—somewhat larger than an identically named set by US Glass. The punch set was also reproduced, with an IG mark.

Punch bowl and base
Marigold   200–240

Punch set
Marigold   275 (1998)   6 pieces, dark iridescence
Marigold   125   12 pieces

Whirling Star, US Glass

The US Glass version of the Whirling Star punch bowl measures about 11" wide and 8¼" tall. An eight-piece punch set sold for $185 in 1997.

White Oak

Oak leaves and acorns against a rustic background. Known only in marigold, no pitchers have been reported in this pattern. The maker is unknown. These sell for between $100 and $200.

Wickerwork, Sowerby

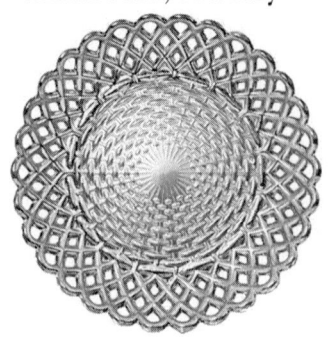

These English plates or low bowls measure about eight inches across and are sometimes found with a separate and uniridized three-footed base. Obviously not intended for ice cream. Quite rare.

Plate or low bowl
Amethyst   350 (1992)
Marigold   120–190

Wide Panel, Northwood

Few pieces of carnival are as dramatic as these large epergnes. Unfortunately, awkwardness in handling has led to considerable damage in the existing examples. The original function was to hold both flowers and fruit.

Epergne, 4 lily
Blue   800 (1995)   one purple lily, damage
Green   800–1,100   most common color
Ice blue known
Ice green known
Marigold   500–800   common color
Purple   825 (1992)
White   1,000–1,800   rare color

Wide Panel, various makers

Most glassmakers made patterns that can be described as Wide Panel, and it is often difficult to distinguish between pieces from different makers. Because Wide Panel is similar to Flute or Colonial, some of the following examples may be those patterns. This list is included only to provide a general idea of shapes and colors available.

Basket, with handle
Ice green   130 (1997)
Marigold   90 (1997)

Bowl, various sizes
Aqua/teal   35–50
Clambroth   5–10
Marigold   5–10   5", 3-footed, pewter trim
Marigold   15–20   12"

Breakfast set (creamer and sugar)
Clambroth   10–20   probably Imperial
Marigold   15–25

Candlestick (single)
Marigold   10–20
Russet   25–40

Candy dish, covered
Ice green   40–60
Celeste   75   etched "1864-1924"
Marigold   20   painted panels
Olive   20
Vaseline   25   with lid

Chop plate, probably Imperial
Clambroth   35–50
Marigold   25–40

Compote
Marigold   10–15   miniature
Marigold   30–50   giant or large size
Smoke   30–50   large
Purple   400   7" tall, flared

Compote, covered
Amethyst, black 100
Celeste   60

Cruet with original stopper
Marigold   75 (1994)   only one known

Goblet, Imperial
Marigold   5–10
Red   200–300

Parfait or mug, probably Imperial
Marigold   15–25

Perfume bottle
Marigold   20–30

Plate, 6", probably Imperial
Marigold   10–15

Plate, 8"
Teal   15–25

Plate, lemon with celluloid fork, original box
Marigold   55

Powder jar
Marigold   15–25

Salt dip, individual, Heisey
Marigold   45

Sherbert
Green   20–35

Spittoon
Red   175

Table set, 4 piece
Marigold   300

Whimsey from tumbler
Marigold   20

Tumbler
Marigold   20–30

Wide Panelled Cherry

This small white carnival pitcher is thought to be Depression era glass by owners Carl and Eunice Booker.

Wide Rib, Dugan

See Vases

Wigwam, Heisey

A rare tumbler, this marigold example is from the collection of John and Lucile Britt. In 1996, one with base damage sold for $290. It sold again in 1998 for $300.

Wild Berry

Rarely seen, these marigold powder jars are sometimes found with souvenir stenciling. The maker is unknown. Prices generally vary between $250 and $400.

Wild Blackberry, Fenton

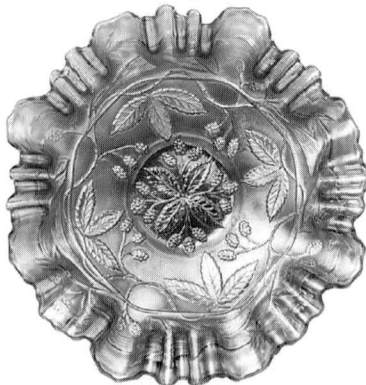

Found in ruffled and three-in-one edge bowls in about equal quantities, Wild Blackberry was also used as an advertising piece with "H. Maday & Sons" molded into the bottom of the base (see Lettered section). Although similarly named, this pattern is quite different from Fenton's and Northwood's Raspberry or Blackberry patterns. The above example in green is courtesy of Galen and Kathi Johnson.

Bowl, about 9"
Amethyst	80–150	ruffled
Blue	250 (1996)	ruffled
Green	125–200	most common color
Marigold	60–85	

Wild Flower, Millersburg

A rare and desirable pattern found only in the cupped jelly compote (shown here), and a flared version. Marie McGee, author and Millersburg expert, says they're known in green and vaseline as well as amethyst and marigold. The amethyst example above sold for $2,500 at the 1996 Heart of America auction (Seeck).

Compote
Amethyst	1,400–2,500
Marigold	1,300 (1996)

Wild Rose, Millersburg
See Lamps and shades

Wild Rose, Northwood

The unique design of the open edge on this pattern makes it memorable. The rose is on the exterior; the interior is plain or has a rayed design. The above nut bowl shape shows the pattern well, but is seen most often as a flared bowl. The rosebowl, with the edges cupped in, is seen occasionally, with one example in sapphire blue. A very flat example in green owned by Jerry and Carole Curtis can only be described as a plate—one of the few known.

Bowl
Amethyst/purple 55–90
Blue   150–200   scarce color
Green   30–55   most common color
Lavender   85 (1997)
Marigold   20–40

Candy dish or nut bowl shape (deep)
Amethyst/purple 45–75
Green   35–60   most common color
Green   525 (1998)   blue iridescence
Horehound   175 (1995)
Marigold   55–110

Rosebowl
Green   75–100
Marigold   165–250
Sapphire blue   5,500 (1997)

Wild Rose, Westmoreland

A true connoisseur's piece, no doubt this syrup jug is passed up many times for seeming unimpressive. The above example, which has a slightly different top than most, brought $825 at a 1996 Tom Burns auction. Usually credited to Westmoreland, some collectors think it is Northwood, others Dugan. Known only in marigold, most sell in the $400 to $650 range.

Wild Strawberry, Northwood

Northwood's Wild Strawberry is almost identical to its Strawberry pattern. The most easily discerned difference is that the Wild Strawberry has a small blossom toward the outer edge of the design—which the Strawberry does not. Most pieces have the basketweave exterior but some have a plain back.

Berry set, 7 piece
Amethyst/purple 400 (1997)

Small bowl or sauce, about 6"
Amethyst/purple 85–130
Marigold   40–60

Bowl, 9–10"
Amethyst/purple 95–170   most common color
Green   400 (1997)   blue iridescence
Ice blue   375 (1992)   chip on edge
Lime green   1,200–1,500   rare color
Marigold   50–80   common color
White   250–400   scarce color

Plate, handgrip, 7–8" (fairly common shape)
Amethyst/purple 150–275   most common color
Green   125–200
Marigold   100–190

Windflower, Dugan

Cleo and Jerry Kudlac, avid Windflower collectors, report six-ruffle, ten-ruffle and ice cream-shaped bowls. There are also two different nappy shapes.

Bowl, 8–9"
Amethyst/purple	50–80	common color
Blue	55–90	fairly common color
Lavender	50–60	scarce color
Marigold	20–35	common color
Marigold	85 (1998)	ice cream shape

Plate, 8–9"
Blue   150–275
Marigold   85–130

Nappy or sauce boat
Amethyst/purple 70–100
Ice green   100–200
Marigold   15–25

Windmill, Imperial

The Windmill pattern is sometimes confused with Imperial's Double Dutch. This pattern, however, has only one windmill. Bowls may be collar-based or footed—with footed bowls worth a bit more. Water sets and bowls have been reproduced.

Small bowl or sauce, about 5" (scarce shape)
Marigold   10–15
Purple   30–50

Bowl, 7–9"
Clambroth	40–70	
Marigold	50–80	
Mar/moon	425–475	round
Purple	100–175	
Smoke	40–60	

Dresser tray (flatter than pickle dish)
Marigold   65–80
Purple   200–350

Pickle dish/relish tray (shown above)
Aqua	50 (1997)	
Green	30–50	common color
Helios green	15–25	
Marigold	15–25	
Purple	85–150	scarce color

Windmill milk pitchers are 6¼" tall.

Pitcher, milk
Green	95–180	
Helios green	85–145	
Marigold	75–125	most common color
Purple	400–650	scarce color
Smoke	150–250	scarce color

Pitcher, mid-size
Marigold	35–60	
Marigold	160 (1994)	gun metal luster

W 253

Water pitcher
Blue/violet   725 (1993)
Purple   850 (1993)   rare, minor flaw
Water set, 7 piece
Marigold   125–225

Tumbler
Green   25 (1994)   marigold interior, nick
Helios green 40 (1996)
Marigold   15–25   most common color
Purple   75–140

Wine and Roses, Fenton

These smallish pitchers are referred to as cider pitchers. The set came with wine-type goblets. Only marigold pitchers were known until 1997 when a blue example turned up in the Pacific Northwest.

Cider set, 7 piece
Marigold   500–700
Cider pitcher
Marigold   400–550

Shown here are a compote and goblet. The compote is ruffled from the goblet and is rare.

Goblet or cider glass
Aqua   80–155   rare color
Blue   55–85
Marigold   15–25   most common color
Vaseline   100 (1994)

Wishbone, Northwood

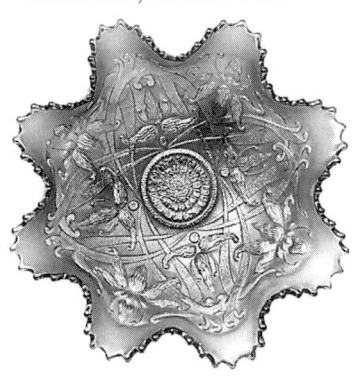

With its overlapping wishbone shapes, this is an easy pattern to spot. There are two bowl molds in Wishbone, the larger one with a collar base and basketweave exterior, the smaller with feet and Ruffles and Rings exterior. Plates were made from each of these molds, the chop plate from the larger. Blue is rare in Wishbone.

Bowl, 9–10", collar base, ruffled edge
Amethyst/purple 100–160   common color
Green   110–200   common color
Marigold   115–145   scarce color
Sapphire   3,500 (1993)
Bowl, 9–10", collar base, pie crust edge
Blue   1,600 (1996)
Blue, electric   2,050 (1995)   chips
Clambroth   400 (1997)
Green   200–350   most common color
Marigold   90–165   common color
Purple   275 (1995)
Smoke known
White   300–425   scarce color

Wishbone, continued

Bowl, 8–9", footed, ruffled

Amethyst/purple	125–200	most common color
Aqua opal known		
Blue	400–600	rare color
Blue, electric	1,200 (1998)	
Marigold, pastel	575 (1997)	
Green	75–135	common color
Horehound	600–700	rare color
Ice blue	800–1,500	scarce color
Ice green	1,100–1,700	rare color
Lavender	110–200	rare color
Lime green known		
Marigold	100–175	common color
White	350–600	scarce color

Plate, 8–9", footed

Amethyst/purple	250–450	most common color
Green	190 (1998)	bruise on back
Marigold	1,200–2,000	

Plate, tricorner whimsey, footed

Amethyst	425 (1994)
Marigold	350–600

Chop plate, basketweave back, 10"

Amethyst/purple	1,600–2,800
Green	3,500 (1994)
Marigold	1,200–2,400

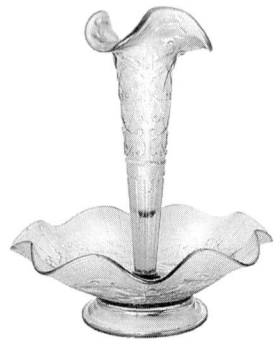

The epergne in the Wishbone pattern, like other epergnes, often suffers from damage around the hole where the lily is inserted. This ice blue example sold at a 1995 auction for $4,000 with a chip on the bottom of the lily.

Epergne, 2 piece

Amethyst/purple	350–500	most common color
Green	450–800	
Ice blue	4,000 (1995)	bottom of lily chipped
Ice green	6,000 (1995)	
Lime green reported		
Marigold	250–400	
White	1,000–1,800	

Epergne, base only

Marigold	85

Epergne, lily only

Green	90
Marigold	40

Water pitcher

Amethyst/purple	1,600–2,000
Green	650 (1998)

Water set, 5 piece

Green	1,500–1,800
Purple	1,300 (1996)

Water set, 7 piece

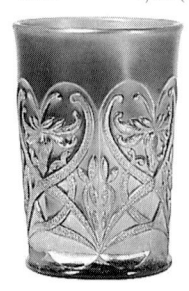

Green	2,400 (1994)

Tumbler

Amethyst/purple	45–80	most common color
Green	100–150	scarce color
Marigold	50–85	common color
Pearlized	2,100 (1995)	one known

Wishbone and Spades, Dugan

Both the 11" chop plate and the 6" small plate shown here are highly desirable. There are no 9" plates in Wishbone and Spaces.

Plate, 6–7"
Peach opal	200–350	
Purple	250–450	most common color
Purple	500–800	exceptional iridescence

Chop plate, 10½–11"
Purple	1,400–2,000

Berry set, 7 piece, ruffled
Purple	700 (1998)

Bowl, banana dish shape (two sides up)
Peach opal	150–300	10"

This peach opal tricorner Wishbone and Spades bowl, made from the same mold as the chop plate, is very rare. Courtesy of Ingrid Spurrier.

Bowl, 9–10", ruffled or ice cream shape
Peach opal	100–200	ruffled
Peach opal	150–250	ice cream shape
Peach opal	250 (1996)	tricorner
Purple	575 (1997)	ruffled

Sauce, about 5", ruffled or round
Peach opal	40–70
Purple	50–90

Wisteria, Northwood

Northwood's Wisteria tankard pitcher and slender, elegantly flared tumbler are among the rarest and most desirable of this company's production. Tumblers resemble Northwood's Grape Arbor, complete with lattice but with wisteria flowers instead of grapes.

Water set, 7 piece
White	4,250 (1994)	two tumblers chipped
White	5,000 (1998)	6 pieces

Water pitcher
Ice blue	1,000 (1992)	crack at handle
White	375 (1995)	crack, epoxy

Shown above is the only known bank whimsey—made from a white Wisteria tumbler. It is owned by Bob and Geneva Leonard.

Tumbler
Ice blue	250–450	most common color
Ice green	500–550	
Lime green	450–550	
White	250–400	

Wreath of Roses, Fenton

The name is pretty descriptive of the pattern but can easily be confused with several other patterns including Fenton's own rare Rose Bouquet bonbon. A very similar design made by Northwood is called Basket of Roses and is also quite rare, so any low bonbons with roses should be checked carefully.

Bonbon, stemmed or without stem
Amethyst	75–125	most common color
Blue	80–150	scarce color
Green	50–85	scarce color
Marigold	20–35	fairly common color
White	250 (1997)	

Wreath of Roses, Fenton, continued

Compote, ruffled
Amethyst/purple 30–45
Blue 35–60
Green 35–60   most common color
Marigold 15–25

Fenton's Wreath of Roses punch set pieces are unusual in that both punch bowls and cups are found with three different interiors: plain, Vintage or Persian Medallion. In addition, the tops of the punch bowls may be ruffled or flared in different ways.

Punch set, 8 piece
Amethyst 525–625 Vintage interior
Amethyst 1,250 (1997) Persian Medallion int.
Blue 475–600 Vintage interior
Green 650 plain bowl int, cups Pers Medal int.
Green 500–600 Vintage interior
Marigold 300–500 Persian Medallion interior

Punch bowl and base
Amethyst 400–700 Persian Medallion interior
Blue 500–800 Persian Medallion interior
Green 650 (1995) square, Vintage interior
Green 600–800
Marigold 250–400 Persian Medallion interior
Marigold 200–350 Vintage interior

Punch bowl top only
Green 375 Vintage interior

Punch base only
Amethyst 50
Marigold 30

Punch cup
Amethyst 25–35 Persian Medallion interior
Amethyst 30–40 Vintage interior
Blue 40–60 Persian Medallion interior
Blue 40–60 Vintage interior
Green 35–50 Persian Medallion interior
Green 25–40 Vintage interior
Marigold 15–25 Persian Medallion interior
Marigold 15–25 Vintage interior

Wreath of Roses, Dugan

Shown above is a one-of-a-kind spittoon shape and the rosebowl shape from which it was made. Both are courtesy of Carl and Ferne Schroeder.

Rosebowl
Amethyst/purple 60–100
Lime green 65 (1997)
Marigold 20–35

Made from the same mold as the small, common rosebowl, the tricorner candy dish doesn't excite much interest—probably because it is fairly common, at least in marigold.

Tricorner candy dish
Amethyst 100 (1996)
Marigold 30–50

W-Z 257

Wreathed Cherry, Dugan

Dugan's Wreathed Cherry, sometimes called Cherry Wreath, has a pattern that is much like Millersburg's Hanging Cherries and somewhat similar to Dugan's own Cherries. In this case, however, the groups of cherries are separated by vertical plumes extending upward from the base. In the berry bowls like those above, the pattern is on both the inside and outside. Bowls are always oval.

Berry set, 5 piece
Amethyst/purple 180–250
White 200–300

Berry set, 7 piece
Amethyst 200–300
Blue 215 (1994)
Marigold 125–200
White 250–400

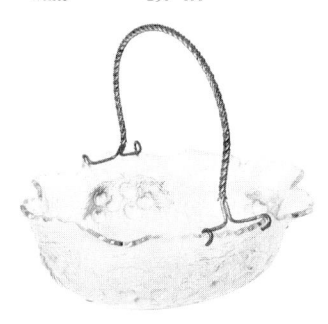

This large bowl in white with an attached metal handle sold for $200 in 1997.

Bowl, large berry (oval)
Amethyst/purple 90–170
Amethyst, black 85 (1997)
Marigold 45–65
White 170–250

Small berry or sauce, about 5" (oval)
Amethyst/purple 40–70
Amethyst, black 35 (1997)
Marigold 15–25
Marigold 60 (1995) with metal holder & spoon
White 45 (1998) red enameled cherries

Table set, 4 piece
White 650 (1997) red enameled cherries
Purple 400 (1998) spooner has smoothed base

Creamer, sugar, spooner
White 600 (1995) red enameled cherries

Creamer
White 50 (1996)

Spooner
White 30 (1996)

Sugar, covered
White 85 (1996) trace of gold decor, bruise

Water set, 5 piece
Amethyst/purple 300 (1994)
Marigold 525 (1995)
White 600 (1997) red enameled cherries

Water set, 7 piece
White 500 (1993)
Marigold 675 (1997)

Water pitcher
Amethyst/purple 325–425
Marigold 200–350
White 350 (1998)

Tumbler
Amethyst/purple 40–65 most common color
Marigold 40–55
White 100–150 red enameled cherries

Zig Zag, Millersburg

Zig Zag has no pattern on the back, unusual for Millersburg. Found only in bowls in the usual range of Millersburg colors.

Bowl, about 9"
Amethyst 250–400 ruffled or 3/1 edge
Amethyst 300–500 ice cream shape
Amethyst 200–400 tricorner, crimped
Amethyst 450–800 square, crimped

258 A Field Guide to Carnival Glass

Zig Zag, Millersburg, continued

Green	175–250	ruffled or 3/1 edge
Green	400–600	tricorner
Marigold	125–200	ruffled or 3/1 edge
Marigold	225–350	square, tight crimp
Marigold	250–400	ice cream shape

Zig Zag, Fenton

This is the pitcher used for many of Fenton's decorated water sets. It is very unusual to find one without the painted flowers. This amethyst example is courtesy of Ed and Cindy Landiss.

Zipper Loop
See Lamps and shades

Zipper Stitch

This cordial set is the only shape found so far in the pattern, thought to have been made in Czechoslovakia. It is from the John and Lucile Britt collection. A marigold tray for such a set sold for $140 at a David Ayers auction in 1998.

Zippered Heart, Imperial

Zippered Heart is an exterior-only pattern, most often seen in the small sauces shown above. It is sometimes confused with Northwood's Valentine— also known primarily in small sauces.

Berry set, 7 piece
Purple   200–250

Bowl, berry or sauce, 5"
Marigold   40 (1997)
Purple   25–40

Whether you call it a rosebowl or a vase, it is a huge piece of glass. These seldom come up for sale and bring good prices when they do. This green example is courtesy of Audrey and Sue Magan. Another in green sold for $1,000 in 1996.

Lettered carnival 259

Lettered carnival glass

Early carnival glassmakers were not about to overlook the lucrative business of providing special orders to commercial firms that used glass as promotional premiums, or to civic organizations for commemorative use.

Most major manufacturers, with the exception of Imperial, provided this service, either modifying existing patterns by adding the appropriate design and text or by creating the design from scratch.

An excellent description of the origins of these pieces is given in John Resnik's book, *The Encyclopedia of Carnival Glass Lettered Pieces*.

Ballard, Northwood

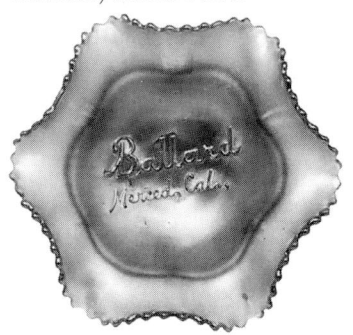

Bowl, ruffled
Amethyst   500–700
Plate
Amethyst   2,200 (1998)

Bernheimer Bros, Millersburg

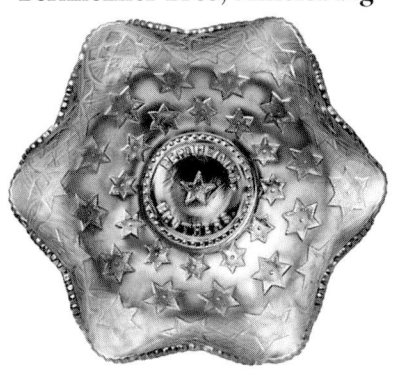

This special order bowl was made from Millersburg's Many Stars pattern. It measures about 10" across. Known only in blue.
Bowl
Blue   2,000–3,000

Birmingham Age Herald

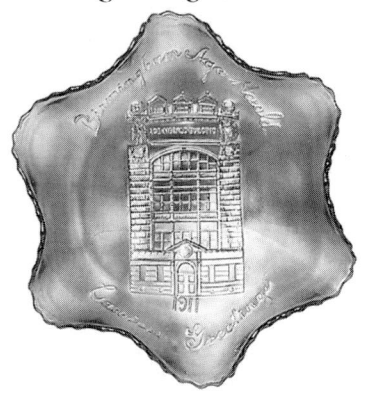

This piece was evidently given to subscribers by newspaper boys as a token of thanks from the Birmingham, Alabama newspaper. The phrase at the bottom reads "Carriers Greetings."
Bowl, 8–9", ruffled or ice cream shape
Amethyst   1,500–2000
Plate
Amethyst   2,000–4,000

Brand, John H., Fenton

The John H. Brand advertising piece has the lettering inside the base of the Open Edge basket and is otherwise similar to the Feldman basket. Only found in marigold, most sell in the $50 to $90 range.

Brazier's Candies, Fenton

Plate, flat or handgrip
Amethyst   400–500
Bowl
Amethyst   650 (1995)   6 ruffles

Broecker's Flour, Northwood

Plate
Amethyst   3,000–4,000

Brooklyn Bridge, Dugan

Brooklyn Bridge lettered bowls are quite readily available, the unlettered examples very rare.
Bowl
Marigold   250–350
Bowl, unlettered (2 or 3 examples known)
Marigold   1,500–2,000

Campbell & Beesley, Millersburg

Plate, handgrip, 1911 Spring Opening, 6"
Amethyst   1,000–1,500

Central Shoe Store, Fenton

Plate, flat or handgrip
Amethyst   900–1,200
Bowl, round
Amethyst   800–1,000

Lettered carnival 261

Cleveland Memorial ashtray, Millersburg

The Cleveland Memorial ashtray is a rare piece and seldom sells at auction. The above example in amethyst (marigold is also known) is courtesy of Floyd and Cecil Whitley.

Cooleemee, J.N. Ledford, Fenton
Rare marigold Heart and Vine plate with "Souvenir of J.N. Ledford Company, Cooleemee, N.C." in center.

Courthouse, Millersburg

The regular bowl has the lettering "Courthouse, Millersburg Ohio" under the building. The unlettered version, which is quite rare, is missing the text under the building. While extremely desirable, the lettered version is hardly rare, with about ten examples selling at auction each year.

Bowl, complete lettering, 7½–8"
Amethyst   700–1,300
Lavender   3,000–3,500

Bowl, unlettered
Amethyst   2,500–3,000

Dandelion, Northwood
Mug, Knights Templar
Ice blue   500–700
Ice green   700–900
Marigold   250–400   most common color

Davidson's Society Chocolates, Northwood

Card tray, 2-sided or handgrip
Amethyst   800–1,200
Lavender   1,000 (1998)

Dorsey and Funkenstein, Fenton

These are quite difficult to find. This six-ruffled example is courtesy of Jack and Eleanor Hamilton.

Plate, handgrip
Amethyst   2,000–2,500

Dreibus Parfait Sweets, Northwood

Bowl
Amethyst   725 (1996)
Plate, double handgrip (2 sides up)
Amethyst   400–800
Plate, single handgrip
Amethyst   700–1,200

Eagle Furniture, Northwood

Plate, flat, 6"
Amethyst   900–1,200
Plate, handgrip
Amethyst   800–900
Plate, 2 sides up
Amethyst   500–700

E.A. Hudson Furniture, Northwood

Plate, flat
Amethyst   1,700–2,000
Plate, handgrip
Amethyst   1,200–1,500

Eat Paradise Sodas

See Paradise Sodas

Elks, Dugan

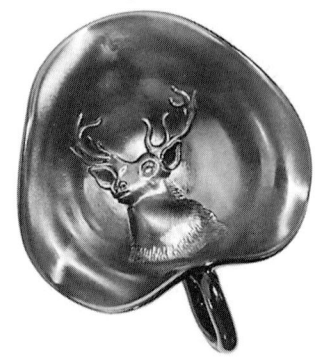

There are only a few of these nappies known, thought to have been prototypes but never produced in quantity. All are in amethyst. The one above most recently sold in 1995 for $7,000. A version with seven ruffles sold in 1993 for $6,500.

Lettered carnival

Elks, Fenton

Fenton made 7" bowls, plates and bells for several B.P.O.E conventions. In the Fenton version, the elk always looks to the right as we view it. Most bowls are ruffled but three-in-one and round bowls are also found. Note that Millersburg also made bowls for the 1910 convention.

Bowl, 1910 Detroit
Amethyst   700–1,000
Blue   800–1,200
Green   600–900
Marigold, rare
Bowl, 1911 Atlantic City
Blue   900–1,500
Plate, 1911 Atlantic City
Blue   1,500–2,300
Plate, 1914 Parkersburg
Blue   1,000–1,700

Bell, 1911 Atlantic City
Blue   1,700–2,500
Bell, 1912 Portland (only one known)
Blue   22,500 (1993)
Bell, 1914 Parkersburg
Blue   2,000–2,700

Elks, Millersburg

The Millersburg version of the Elks pattern faces to the viewer's left and both eyes are seen, thus it is sometimes called the "two-eyed elk." It is found only with the 1910 Detroit date and in amethyst. The paperweight is rare and found only in purple and green. Even damaged examples bring a good price.

Bowl, 1910 Detroit, 7" ice cream shape
Amethyst   2,000–3,000

Paperweight
Amethyst/purple   2,000–3,000
Green   3,000–5,000

Exchange Bank, Fenton

Bowl
Amethyst   600–1,000
Plate
Amethyst   2,300 (1993)
Plate, handgrip
Amethyst   1,550 (1996)

Feldman Brothers, Open Edge, Fenton

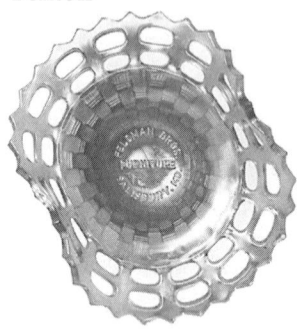

Although these marigold lettered baskets or hat shapes are fairly scarce, they don't attract much interest, bringing between $50 and $90.

Fern Brand Chocolates, Northwood

While this piece uses a pattern much like many other of the six-inch advertising plates and bowls, it is unique. The fern fronds are part of this mold and are not used in any other pattern.

Plate
Amethyst	1,000–1,500	flat
Amethyst	700–800	handgrip, most common
Lavender	725 (1997)	handgrip
Amethyst	500–650	double handgrip

Garden Mums, Fenton

This is the pattern from which Fenton made advertising premiums. Some pieces have enameled lettering—presumably a process that was affordable for shorter manufacturing runs.

Bowl, round
Amethyst   150–300

Plate, 6", flat
Amethyst   400–550
Amethyst   500 (1995)   with enameled lettering

Plate, 6" handgrip
Amethyst   350–500   with enameled lettering

Geo. W. Getts, Pianos, Fenton

The Getts pieces are known in ruffled and ice cream-shaped bowls as well as plates. Note the backward "S" in the word "Forks." It's that way on all known examples. The ice cream-shaped bowl above is courtesy of Tom and Sharon Mordini.

Bowl
Amethyst   600–800

Plate, 6"
Amethyst   2,100 (1995)

Lettered carnival 265

Gevurtz Bros Furniture and Clothing, Fenton

Bowl, 6 ruffles
Amethyst   1,000 (1995)
Plate, flat
Amethyst   2,000–2,500
Plate, handgrip
Amethyst   1,300 (1995)   good detail

Grape and Cable Old Rose Distilling
See Old Rose Distilling

Greengard Furniture Co., Millersburg

Rare advertising piece known in three double handgrip plates, one single handgrip plate, and one ruffled bowl, all amethyst.

H. Maday & Co. 1910, Fenton

The H. Maday lettering is found on the backs of some Fenton Wild Blackberry bowls in amethyst and green. The above green bowl is courtesy of Galen and Kathi Johnson.

Bowl
Amethyst   150–200
Green   375 (1996)

Horlacher Advertising, Fenton

Found on the base of amethyst and green Butterflies bonbons ($75 to $125), seven-inch Peacock Tail in amethyst and green ($75–$100), Thistle nine-inch bowls in amethyst and green ($100 to $175) and Vintage seven-inch bowls in marigold (about $100).

Howard Furniture Co.

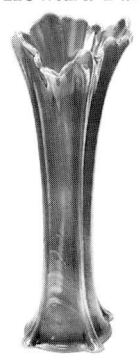

Found in a green Four Pillars vase with "Howard Furniture Co., 109 & 111, Nth Howard St." molded into the bottom of the base. Prices range from $90 to $140.

Illinois Soldiers and Sailors Home, Fenton

These unusual plates are very rare and extraordinarily desirable. This one and the following two patterns all have Fenton's Berry and Leaf Circle back pattern, sometimes called Horse Chestnut. While these plates are expensive and desirable, they are hardly rare, nine having sold in 1997 alone. Marigold outnumber blue by about three to one.

Plate, 7–8"
Blue   1,700–2,500
Marigold   1,500–2,800

Indianapolis Soldiers and Sailors Monument, Fenton

This exceedingly rare blue bowl last sold for $10,000 in 1994.

Indiana Statehouse, Fenton

The above Statehouse of Indiana plate is one of two known in blue. It is from the Rinehart collection.

Plate, 7½–8"
Marigold   16,000 (1994, only one known in marigold)

Isaac Benesch & Sons, Millersburg

Although this bowl has one of the more interesting designs among the advertising pieces, it is relatively easy to come by—which accounts for prices that are much lower than many of the other patterns. A few of these pieces have the word "Benesch" misspelled and are quite a bit more valuable than the examples with correct spelling.

Bowl, 6"
Amethyst   250–450

Bonbon (lettering is on bottom of piece)
Marigold   80–125   front is Holly Sprig pattern

Jockey Club, Northwood

Jockey Club was a perfume according to John Resnik. The pattern is highly collectible—and quite difficult to find.

Bowl, ruffled
Amethyst   1,000–1,500

Plate, 6"
Amethyst   1,050 (1995)   base chip

Plate, handgrip
Amethyst   1,600–2,400

John H. Brand
See Brand

Miller Furniture, Fenton

The Miller Furniture piece, like the John H. Brand, is similar to the Feldman open edge bowls with the advertising on the inside of the base. Prices are a bit higher than the John H. Brand or Feldman pieces—$80 to $120.

Norris H. Smith Real Estate & Insurance, Fenton

The Norris Smith pattern is Fenton's Garden Mums with a configuration similar to other pieces using this basic pattern.

Bowl, 6 ruffles
Amethyst   800–1,000

Ogden Furniture, Fenton

Scarce to rare ruffled and ice cream shaped bowls, handgrip and flat plates. All in amethyst on the Garden Mums type of pattern.

Lettered carnival 267

Old Rose Distilling, Northwood

The back (shown here) of this plate has the lettering "Old Rose Distilling Co., Chicago ILL." on the bottom. The front pattern of this piece is Northwood's Grape and Cable stippled variant. Known only in green.

Plate
Green   500–700

Pacific Coast Mail Order, Fenton

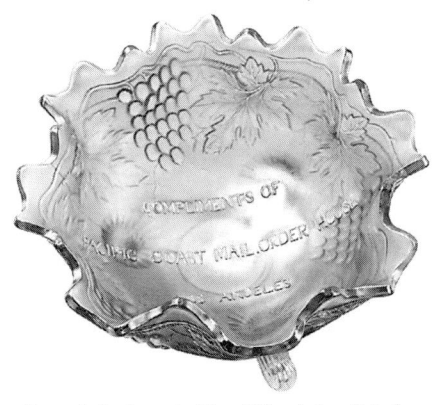

Known in both marigold and blue (a handful of examples of each), these orange bowls have Fenton's Grape and Cable as the exterior.

Bowl
Marigold   2,500–3,000

Paradise Sodas, Seasons Greetings, Fenton

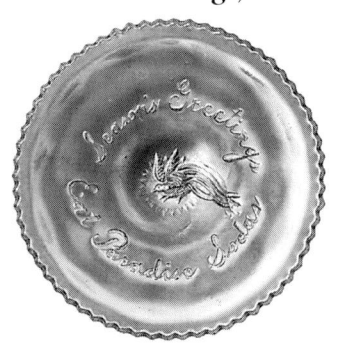

Plate, 5–6"
Amethyst   450–700

Quincy Jewelry, Fenton

A rare pattern. A Peacock Tail hat with molded Quincy Jewelry advertising in green sold for $190 in 1998.

Rood's Chocolates, Fenton

Rood's Chocolates is a very rare pattern, of which only four amethyst plates are known. This example, and the photograph, are courtesy of Dean and Diane Fry. One example sold in 1996 for $4,000, another in 1998 for $3,600.

Spector's Department Store, Fenton

Based on Fenton's Heart and Vine pattern, these marigold plates are about 9" across and bring $800 to $1,200 although one sold for $1,600 in 1996.

Sterling Furniture Co., Fenton

Rare ruffled and ice cream-shaped bowls, handgrip and flat plates, all in amethyst, on the Garden Mums pattern.

Utah Liquor, Fenton

Plate, handgrip or card tray (double handgrip)
Amethyst   700–900

Vases

Carnival glass vases are basically of two types: molded and swung. Swung vases are simply molded vases that, once removed from the pressed-glass mold, have been reheated in the furnace and "swung" on the end of a long rod—the centrifugal force pulling the glass into the elongated shape with which we're familiar. The tops were often flared or ruffled on the swung versions.

A third type is the blow-molded vase. Here, molten glass is attached to the end of a long tube and is "blown" into the mold—much like water pitchers were made. Usually these have a pontil mark on the base where they were temporarily attached to a glass rod during the finishing process.

In recent years, vases have become more popular as collectible carnival glass. As more is written about them, more collectors can identify the vases. With more than 200 patterns alone, there is a great variety to choose from, and with the added variations of color, stunning collections can be formed.

Sizes of vases

While most vases were made in only one base size, some patterns—particularly those that were swung—were made from molds of several different base sizes. Ripples, for example, have a range of five sizes.

Confusion comes when people attempt to describe vase sizes by the height, rather than the base. This is particularly inappropriate with swung vases as they can vary so much in height.

Throughout this section, I use the base diameter as a means of determining sizes.

There are certain terms used to characterize vases. For example, Funeral vases generally have a base diameter of 5–5¼".

Midsize vases generally are in the 4" to 5" base diameter range. Bases in the 4" range are called standard size. If no size is stated, the vase is assumed to be standard size. The exact base diameter measurements for funeral vases, midsize vases, and standard vases vary from one pattern to another.

All this is only useful when there is more than one base size.

Acorn

According to collectors, there are only four Acorn vases known—one each in amethyst, green, marigold, and vaseline. A green example sold for $3,000 in 1994. Definite attribution has yet to be established. Some collectors believe one of the US Glass factories made the pattern—others think Millersburg.

African Shield, Sowerby

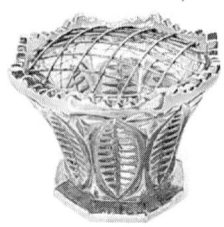

These small vases (about 4¼" high) probably came with the metal flower holder shown, but are seldom found with one. These marigold pieces sell in the $75 to $125 range. Those with a wire flower holder, such as that above, range up to $200.

Apple Tree, Fenton

There are only a few known examples of this vase, all in marigold and all made from the water pitcher mold (note the circular spot, center right, where the handle would have been applied). They have been found with a ruffled top (above) or flared rim.

April Showers, Fenton

April Showers vases were swung to heights from 5 to 15 inches. The base size is always 3½ inches with no pattern on the bottom. Fenton's Peacock Tail pattern is seen on the interior. This pattern is often confused with the similar Fenton Rustic, which has regularly spaced hobs; Fenton Knotted Beads, which has small hobs within circular panels; and Northwood's Tree Trunk, which has crescent-shaped lines around the hobs.

Vase, 8–15"

Amethyst	45–75	common color
Amethyst opal	600 (1996) 1,200 (1998)	
Blue	40–60	common color
Green	45–80	common color
Marigold	20–35	common color
Red	2,300 (1995)	10½", one known
Vaseline	60–100	scarce color
Vaseline	375 (1998)	marigold overlay
White	100–200	scarce color

Vase, squatty (7" or less)

Amethyst	65–100	
Blue	50–75	
Green	75–125	
Marigold	50–80	
White	150–300	scarce color

Basketweave, Westmoreland

This piece is sometimes described as a tub, but it certainly could be used as a vase. It is marigold and 8¼" tall. Worth $30 to $40.

Vases 271

Beaded Bullseye, Imperial

This swung vase features a design of raised circles, each surrounded with beads. The base measures 3⅜" and has a 20-point star in the base. Heights range from about 6" to 12" and the top can be quite widely flared, particularly on some of the shorter examples. Not to be confused with Bullseye and Beads—a Fenton pattern.

Amber	250–300	scarce color
Green	45–85	scarce color
Helios	190 (1998)	
Lime green	85–135	scarce color
Marigold	40–70	most common color
Purple	150–225	common color
Teal	150–200	

Beaded Teardrop

This vase is also known as Frisco. This 6-inch marigold example sold for $110 in 1993.

Beauty Bud, Dugan

Generally seven to ten inches high. Some have twig feet, which doesn't affect the price. What does affect the price is the height. Short examples, five inches or less, are known as Twigs. See Twigs listing. Prices for Beauty Bud run $40 to $70 in amethyst, $30 to $50 in marigold.

Big Basketweave, Dugan

Heights vary from just under 5 inches to about 11. The base is plain and 3¼" in diameter. The short vase above was not swung—it is just as it came out of the mold.

Vase, 7–11"

Amethyst/purple	150–250	common color
Amethyst/purple	400 (1998)	spectacular example, 11"
Blue	80–160	scarce color
Celeste	550 (1996)	10", base chip
Ice blue	350–550	rare color
Horehound	175–300	rare color
Lavender	225–350	rare color
Marigold	30–55	common color
White	90–160	scarce color

Vase, not swung

Amethyst/purple	125–200
Marigold	30–50
White	140–200

Bird and Grapes

This wall pocket is also known as Cockatoo.

Marigold	50–90
Smoke	95 (1995)

Blackberry Bark

Quite an unusual design with a lot of detail, Blackberry Bark has similarities to the Acorn vase which is thought to have been made by either US Glass or Millersburg. This example, one of two known, is amethyst. From a private collection.

Blackberry Open Edge, Fenton

These vases were swung from the Fenton Blackberry Open Edge basket and have a 2½" diameter base. They're mostly seen in marigold, but blue examples crop up every so often.

Vase
Blue   1,400 (1994)
Marigold   1,000–1,800

Boggy Bayou, Fenton

While the squatty version of Boggy Bayou shown here is not necessarily typical in height, it does show the eight loops of the pattern well. Because of these loops, the pattern is often confused with Dugan's Pulled Loop, which has just five loops. This example is lime green opal and 5" tall. It sold for $950 at the 1998 International auction (Jim Seeck).

Vase, 7–11"
Amethyst   35–60   scarce color
Green   75–125   scarce color
Marigold   40–70   most common color

Vase, not swung
Green   85 (1995)   5"
Lime green opal 850 (1995) 950 (1998)   same piece
Lime/marigold   85 (1995)   5½"
Marigold   55–75   most common color

Brocaded patterns, Fostoria

Fostoria made a line of iridized glass that was etched to give it a brocaded look. The pieces were made in many shapes, all in pastel colors. The photo above is of a Brocaded Acorns vase.

Brocaded Acorns
Ice blue   75 (1993)

Brocaded Palms, 11"
Clear   50 (1993)
Ice green   140 (1997)   melon ribbed
Pink   200 (1997)

Broken Branch

This vase was reported as the only one known when it was sold at auction in 1993. It brought $75. The maker is unknown.

Vases 273

Bullseye and Beads, Fenton

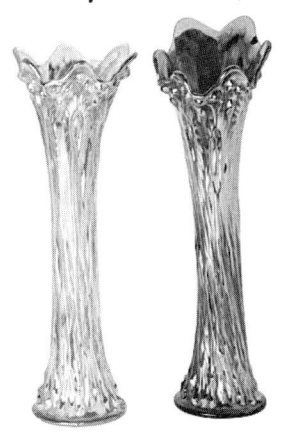

Often confused with Imperial's Beaded Bullseye but less often seen. The design is usually stretched so much that the bullseyes are somewhat difficult to pick out. They are most easily seen on the top one-third of the pattern. Height is generally in the 12 to 14 inch range, and the base size is always 3½".

Amethyst	100–170	scarce color
Blue	175 (1998)	
Marigold	40–70	most common color

Bullseye and Loop, Millersburg

Quite scarce, Bullseye and Loop shows a pattern of loops with alternate loops having a hob (bullseye). The design almost totally disappears when swung. Heights range from about 7" to 11"; base diameter is 3⅜".

Amethyst	350–525
Green	250–450
Marigold, rare	

Butterfly and Berry, Fenton

This is one of the few swung vase patterns that are part of a wider range of shapes. The vases were made from tumbler molds using a different ring cap with flames or scallops. Because the vases were made from such a small mold, they seldom are more than about 9" tall. Most have the pulled-up flames like that on the left, but the crimped top is fairly common. Also known in white.

Vase, with top flames
Amber	100–150	rare color
Amethyst	80–150	scarce color
Blue	50–75	common color
Green	85–150	
Marigold	30–50	common color
Red	1,600–2,200	rare color
Red slag	700–1,000	rare color

Vase, crimped top
Blue	75–100	
Blue	230 (1998)	exceptional example
Marigold	40–60	
Red	425 (1993)	

Cane and Daisy Cut

A curious hybrid, most of the pattern is the result of the molding process but the flowers have been wheel cut. This 10" marigold vase appears to be from the same company that made the Cut Flowers vase, Jenkins. Valued at $85 to $150.

Christmas Holly

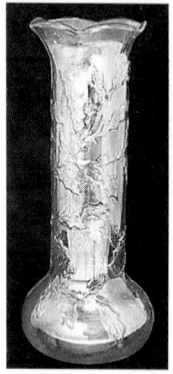

An unusual pattern and the first known example. This 10" tall vase is marigold and has holly encircling both the trunk and the bulbous base. It is a blown vase and sold for $315 at a 1996 Jim Seeck auction. The new owner, Elvis Randell, has identified it as Northwood.

Circle Scroll, Dugan

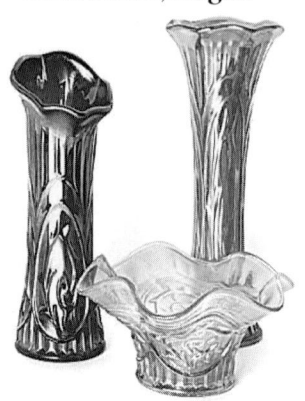

Another of the few vases actually made from a tumbler—which was also used to make the little hat in the foreground. The two vases pretty much fall in the limited size range of 6" to 8", with a 2½" base. Interestingly, the vases are easier to find than the tumblers.

Marigold   95–180
Purple   175–350

Classic Arts

This pattern has a frieze of figures around the top in a green stain; the bottom is marigold. The figures represent various arts. The vase is about 7" tall. A similar design, called Egyptian Queen, has a similar set of figures done in Egyptian style. Classics Arts sell for between $175 and $325.

Cockatoo
See Bird and Grapes

Colonial Lady, Imperial

These vases are about 6½" high and are not to be confused with Rib and Panels, a blown vase.

Marigold   775–1,200   rare color
Purple   500–850   relatively common

Columbia, Imperial

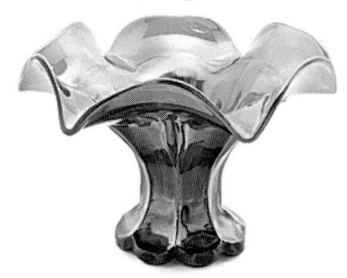

Fashioned from the same mold as the bowls, rare rosebowls, rare plates, and some of the compotes. There is also a stemmed compote.

Marigold   25–45
Purple   150–225
Smoke   50–95

Vases 275

Comet
See Rising Comet

Concave Diamonds, Northwood

This unusual piece is owned by Dick and Jennie Hostetler. Some examples are not ruffled. These vases were fashioned from the pitcher of the guest set (a small pitcher with a tumbler that fits into the top). The usual handle was left off.

Vase
Celeste	155 (1997)
Russet	185 (1997)
Vaseline	250 (1997)

Concave Flute, Westmoreland

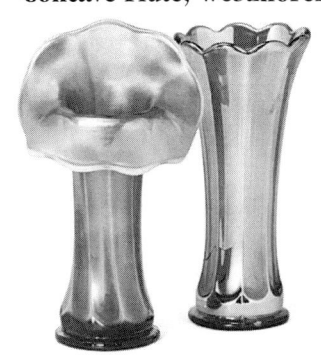

This pattern is the only fluted pattern seen in the jack-in-the-pulpit shape. It has nine flutes or panels and a 3⅛" starred base.

Vase, straight (usually 8–9")
Amethyst	25–45
Green	45–70
Marigold	35–50
Teal	45–70

Vase, jack-in-the-pulpit shape
Amethyst	80–125
Blue opal	250–400
Mar/moonstone	150–200
Teal	115–165

Corinth, Westmoreland

Although this vase has prominent vertical ribs like several other patterns, it's the only one with 12 ribs. The base is 3¼". The vases were made from the same mold that is sometimes seen flattened into a plate or banana dish. Some jack-in-the-pulpit vases have a champagne-colored iridescence.

Corinth vase, straight
Amber	70–90	
Amethyst	25–40	
Blue opal	160–300	
Moonstone	75 (1995)	
Peach opal	50–80	
Teal	60–100	

Vase, jack-in-the-pulpit shape
Amber	75–105	
Amber	190 (1998)	bright, almost yellow
Amethyst	70–100	
Blue opaque	200–300	
Blue opal	200–300	
Marigold	25–50	
Mar/milk glass	80–150	
Teal	125–225	

Corn Vase, Northwood

Among the most desirable of carnival glass shapes, the Corn Vase is known in a wide variety of colors and two different styles: standard and pulled husk (at right). In addition, the standard vases are found with a stalk design in the base (at left) and without.

Corn vase, continued
Pulled husk
Purple	14,000 (1994)	16,000 (1998)

Plain base
Aqua	750–1,000	rare color
Green	500–800	common color
Green, Coke	900 (1994)	Coke bottle green
Green emerald	800 (1997)	
Ice green	250–400	common color
Ice green	700 (1994)	marigold iridescence
Lime green	550–650	rare color
Marigold	800–1,300	scarce color
Purple	350–625	common color
White	200–325	common color

Stalk design in base
Amethyst, black	1,500 (1994)	silvery
Aqua opal	4,000–5,000	very rare
Aqua/marigold	1,100 (1994)	
Green	500–650	scarce color
Green, dark	900 (1994)	
Ice blue	1,300–1,750	rare color
Ice green	300–500	most common color
Lime green	300 (1994)	
Marigold	1,000–1,600	scarce color
Purple	500–800	
Teal	2,000–2,500	rare color
White	250–375	

Cornucopia, Jeanette

Also called Horn of Plenty. Sells for $5 to $15.

Country Kitchen, Millersburg

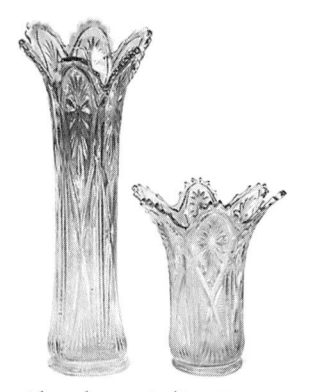

The only vases in this pattern are marigold whimsies made from spooners. Shown above are tall and short versions. There are two known of the tall, one of the short. None have sold recently.

Curled Rib, Imperial

Often confused with, and identified as, Imperial's Morning Glory—a similar pattern with vertical ribs. This one has the vertical ribs curling around with a swirl effect, especially apparent at the top of the jack-in-the-pulpit version. The swirled ribs were not caused by twisting the glass during the finishing process, but are molded into the vase. The jack-in-the-pulpit shapes range from about 6" to 8". Found in smoke as well as marigold and a rare yellow-amber. Whether jack-in-pulpit or straight, the marigold bring $40 to $60, smoke about twice that.

Curved Star, Brockwitz (Germany)

Brockwitz made a number of shapes in blue and marigold (probably in the 1930s) in this pattern including the celery vase which is sometimes called a chalice. This blue vase, one of several sizes known in the pattern, is courtesy of Mark Garrison.

Vases 277

Cut Flowers, Jenkins

Here we have a large cylindrical vase, usually with good color. The flowers are wheel-cut while the rest of the detail is formed by the mold. A similar effect as on the Cane and Daisy Cut vase, which was also probably made by Jenkins. Prices range from about $100 to $175.

Daisy and Drape, Northwood

These popular and desirable vases are found with the top either cupped in or flared out as shown above. Neither is more desirable than the other, but some collectors attempt to find both versions in each color. Aqua opal, uncommon in most patterns, is the most common color here.

Amethyst/purple	800–1,400	scarce color
Aqua opal	400–700	most common color
Aqua/teal	400–600	
Blue	450–650	
Blue, electric	650–950	
Green, rare		
Ice blue	1,700–3,000	rare color
Ice green	3,000–4,000	rare color
Marigold	400–700	scarce color
White	175–300	common color
White	205 (1993)	enameled flowers

Daisy Wreath, Westmoreland

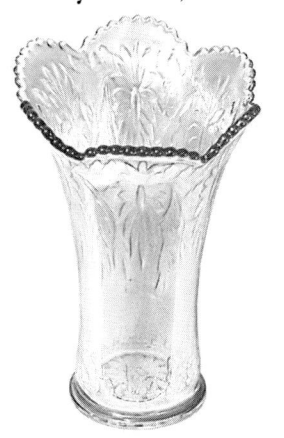

The only such piece uncovered so far, this vase was swung up from a bowl. It is light marigold and brought $1,100 at a 1993 Tom Burns auction.

Dance of the Veils, Fenton

There are perhaps six of these rarities around, all in marigold. Some have a round, rather than ruffled top. The design is of two dancing veiled figures on opposing sides of the vase. Fenton apparently used the mold to make a wide variety of non-carnival shapes as well. This example is from the collection of Waymon and Nilah Espy.

Derby, Sowerby

These vases are also known under the name of Pinwheel, although Derby was the Sowerby name. A wide range of shapes were produced in the Derby pattern. These vases, an 8" marigold and a 7" amethyst, sold for $65 and $225 respectively—in 1993. The pattern was also produced by Inwald.

Vase, 5"
Marigold   85 (1994)

Vase, 6⅜"
Amethyst   175–250
Marigold   75–140
Marigold   475 (1998)

Vase, 9¾", flared
Marigold   120 (1995)

Diamond Cut, Inwald

This marigold 12" tall vase was made by Josef Inwald Company of Czechoslovakia and is patterned after a similar design known in Australia. It sold for $450 at the 1998 Heart of America auction (Jim Seeck).

Diamond Heart

This unusual marigold vase, 5½ inches tall, was probably made in Europe, possibly Czechoslovakia. It sold for $350 at a 1998 David Ayers auction. Several others have been reported.

Diamond Point, Northwood

The heights of these vases range from 6½ to 12" and all have a 3⅜" base. Most have the 12 flame arrangement shown above, but 6-flame variations are occasionally seen.

Vase, 7½–12"
Amethyst/purple	60–90	most common color
Aqua opal	350–550	scarce color
Blue	110–200	scarce color
Green	60–100	common color
Horehound	250 (1995)	
Ice blue	225–400	scarce color
Ice green	150–250	scarce color
Lavender	100–150	rare color
Marigold	40–70	
Sapphire blue	600–1,000	rare color
Smoke	350 (1994)	
Teal blue	475 (1995)	
White	85–125	scarce color

Vase, squatty (6–7½")
Amethyst/purple	60–90	most common color
Aqua	250 (1993)	
Blue	250 (1997)	

Vases 279

Blue, electric	450 (1998)	
Green	45–65	
Ice blue	350–600	scarce color
Ice green	250–450	scarce color
Marigold	100–130	
White	210 (1997)	

Diamond Point Columns, Fenton

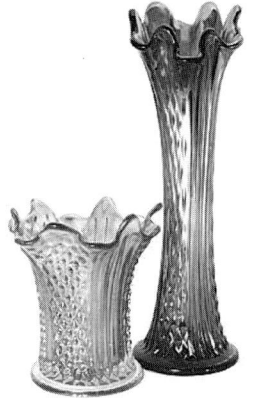

This pattern has alternating panels of vertical ribs and diamond points. All have a 3½" base. Heights normally range between 7 and 12 inches with squatty versions down to 5 inches. Also see Fenton's #916, which has similar alternating panels of ribs and diamond points. These vases were reissued by Fenton in amethyst and perhaps other colors—as well as noniridized colors.

Vase
Amethyst	30–50	common color
Green	35–65	common color
Lime green	40–70	
Marigold	30–50	common color
Marigold	40–70	5–6"
Vaseline	80 (1996)	marigold iridescence

Diamond and Rib, Fenton

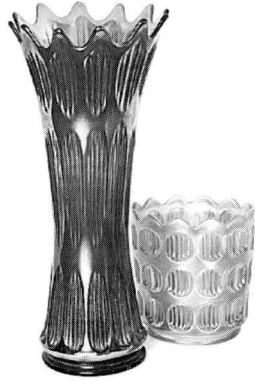

Diamond and Rib is found in two base sizes, the standard and funeral. The standard is found in three base diameters: 3", 3¼" and 3½". In the two funeral-size pieces shown above, the vase has been pulled up to about 17" with an 8" flare. The more rare jardiniere on the right has not been swung at al—it is what the vase looked like before being swung. These jardinieres are also sometimes flared and ruffled. In the standard base size, both tall and squatty vases sell for about the same price.

Funeral size, 5¼" base
Amethyst	1,000–1,500
Green	1,000–1,500
Marigold	3,200 (1998)

Diamond and Rib jardiniere
Green	1,100 (1995)	chips
Marigold	1,250 (1997)	

Base sizes of 3, 3¼ or 3½"
Amethyst	40–70	most common color
Blue	60–100	
Green	30–50	common color
Marigold	25–45	common color
White	65–110	

There are only two of these small Diamond and Rib spittoon-shaped whimsies known, both green. This one is owned by Floyd and Cecil Whitley, the other sold at a Jim Seeck auction in 1996 for $1,700.

Drape, footed

Apparently a blow-molded vase, this one is marigold, about 12" high, and brought $30 at a 1994 auction.

Drapery, Northwood

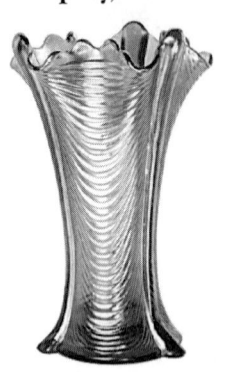

Although the pattern is similar to the Drapery design on Northwood's rosebowls, this one has small feet extending from the collar base. It is actually made from the same mold as the tricorner candy dish. The feet on these vases are quite fragile; most seem to have some sort of damage there. Note that this vase has three vertical ribs, while the similar Drapery variant has four.

Vase, 7–9"
Amethyst	275 (1993)	foot nicks
Aqua	250–450	rare color
Aqua opal	400–500	scarce color
Blue	200–350	rare color
Green	200–350	rare color
Ice blue	250–450	rare color
Ice green	125–200	most common color
Lime green	300–400	scarce color
Marigold	85–150	common color
Sapphire	450–600	
Teal	325 (1992)	
White	85–125	scarce color
White	275 (1994)	squatty–5"

Drapery variant and Drapery footed variant, Northwood

Both these vases show the drapery effect of Northwood's more commonly seen Drapery, but are made from different molds. The Drapery variant on the left lacks toes and has a 2¾" base. The footed variant also has a 2¾" inch base (3¼" across the toes) but has four vertical ribs that extend from the rim to the base to form the toes. The regular Drapery has three ribs and toes (see previous item).

Variant
Amethyst/purple	125–200
Blue	200–350
Marigold	85–155

Footed variant
Blue	100–200
Marigold	70–125

Elephant, Jain

Made by the same Indian company responsible for the Fish and Hand vases. These two views of the same vase show there is less detail than with either of the other vases. Note the ruffle of the top. This one is courtesy of Tom and Sharon Mordini. The only one to sell at auction recently was in 1995 and it brought $400 before being returned as damaged.

Estate, Westmoreland

All the pieces in this pattern—and there aren't many of them—are miniatures, including this bud vase which is about 5" tall.

Blue, smoky	35	souvenir lettering
Lime	130 (1998)	
Smoke	50–90	
Smoke	75	souvenir lettering

Vases 281

Estate, Stippled
See Stippled Estate

Fan and Rib, Imperial

There are a number of similar styles of two-handled fan vases. The marigold coloring in this example appears only on the top half. This example sold at a 1993 auction for $10. See also Two Handle.

Feathers, Northwood

Not a particularly dramatic vase, only the rare colors bring much of a price. And many simply have very weak or irregular iridescence. The pattern is characterized by alternating panels of smooth areas and herringbone-type ribs. The base is 3½"–3¾", some with multipoint stars. Heights vary between seven and eleven inches. Also found in noniridized blue opal.

Green	45–80	common color
Ice blue	300–500	rare color
Marigold	30–55	common color
White	725 (1997)	

Feather Swirl, US Glass

When this marigold vase, with extremely poor iridescence, was sold at auction in 1993, it was listed as the only one known. I'm not sure that's true, but it is the only one I've seen. It sold for $60.

Fenton Panels, Fenton

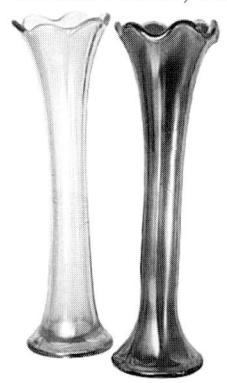

This vase has six subtle panels, terminating at the 3¼" base in even more subtle scallops. Heights are in the 11 to 12 inch range. Generally they're found in marigold, blue, celeste and ice green for between $50 and $200.

Field Thistle, US Glass

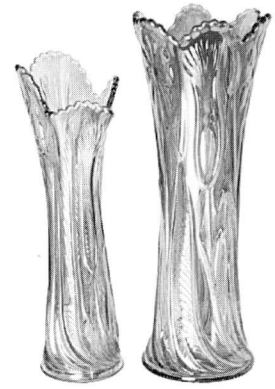

These are quite rare. The smaller of the two shown has a 2¾" base and was pulled up from a spooner. I've seen several of these, but only one of the larger size with a 3¾" inch base.

Marigold	150–225	small, from spooner
Marigold	550 (1994)	large, 3¾" base

File, Imperial

The File vase is a molded vase whimsied from a sugar bowl, according to Carl O. Burns, in his 1996 book on *Imperial Glass*. I've only seen marigold. They sell in a range from $200 to $600, most often about $400. The example above, which is more extremely ruffled than many, sold for $425 at a 1998 Mickey Reichel auction.

Filigree, Dugan

This unusual purple vase is thought to be the first item made in carnival glass by Dugan. It is shown in the 1993 *Dugan-Diamond* book by James Measell. It is the only one known and sold at a 1993 Tom Burns auction for $5,250.

Fine Rib, Fenton

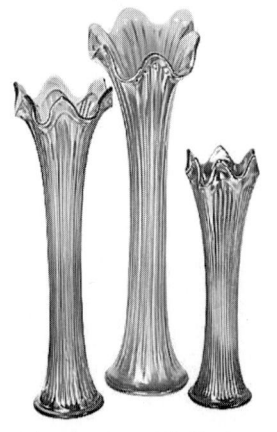

Other than Imperial's Ripple, you'll probably see more Fenton Fine Rib vases than any other pattern.

There is a standard size (base diameter 2½"–2¾"), a large standard size (3"), and a midsize (3¾"). Heights vary from 8 inches to 17 inches but make little difference in the value. The tops are always treated pretty much as shown in the photo. Red is fairly available and almost every auction seems to have one. Other exotic colors such as amber slag, amber opal, and lime green opal have been reported.

Vase, standard size
Amber	50–90	
Amethyst	40–75	scarce color
Amethyst opal	200 (1998)	opal on tips only
Aqua	85–150	scarce color
Aqua opal	450–600	rare color
Blue	30–50	common color
Blue, powder	100 (1998)	
Celeste	700 (1998)	
Green	55–90	scarce color
Lavender	90 (1995)	marigold irid.
Lime	80–150	scarce color
Marigold	20–35	common color
Moonstone	1,050 (1996)	marigold overlay
Red	300–500	common color
Red	600–900	spectacular examples
Sapphire blue	175–300	rare color
Vaseline	55–95	scarce color
Vaseline opal, rare		

Vase, midsize
Blue	60–90
Marigold	40–65
Vaseline	170 (1998)

Fine Rib, Northwood

With an identical name and similar design, this vase is frequently confused with Fenton's. The most obvious distinguishing feature is the plain top edge in contrast to a banded top edge on the Fenton version. There is only one base size in the Northwood, 3½". Some, of course, are marked with the Northwood "N".

Vases

Amethyst/purple	40–70	common color
Blue	75–125	scarce color
Green	35–55	common color
Marigold	24–40	common color
Sapphire	200–300	
White	50–90	

Fine Rib, footed

One of the most confusing vase patterns. Several manufacturers made similar pieces, each shaping the top differently. At one point, the jack-in-the-pulpit version was the only one known, so the pattern became known by that name—although there are a variety of top shapes now known. The piece on the left is Northwood in green and brought $275 at a 1998 Mickey Reichel auction. On the right is the Fenton version in marigold. It sold for $60 at the same auction. In general, marigold vases are worth $70 to $120; green and purple $200 to $300. Note that there is a small Dugan vase, called Thin Panel, that comes in a jack-in-the-pulpit shape, as well as several other top treatments.

Fircone

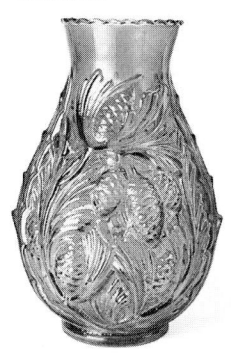

The maker of this rather large and spectacularly colored vase is unknown, although one collector suspects it may have been made in France. There are only a handful known. This one is from the collection of Jeanette Echols.

Fishnet, Imperial

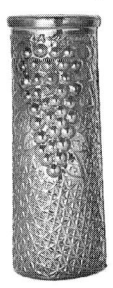

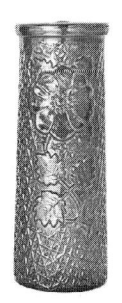

There are three variations of this six-inch tall vase: one with a grape design, one with a rose, and one with a poppy—all on the fishnet background. I've only seen them in red. They are rare and desirable enough to command $550 to $600.

Fish Vase, Jain

As with the Elephant and Hand vases, this one is blown and made by the Indian glassmaker, Jain. They currently sell for between $350 and $425.

Fleur de Lis, Inwald

There are several sizes of these, ranging from about eight inches tall to one reported to be 16 inches tall. Inwald was a Czechoslovakian glassmaker. Valued at between $300 and $400.

Fleur de Lis #5, Imperial

Found in old catalogs listed as No. 5½, in a variety of shapes, this pattern is also seen in carnival bowls. This interesting marigold molded vase came up for auction in 1993. As it sold for just $30, I have to assume someone got a really good deal. There are very few carnival examples known.

Floral Sunburst

This 6⅛" tall vase has two designs repeated around the trunk. The base is 3⅛" with a star indented into it. I have seen two, both blue (but marigold is known). The first sold at a 1993 auction for $500. This one is courtesy of Steve Beranek. I've heard of one other, with the top cupped in like a rosebowl. Believed to be by Brockwitz.

Flower Star

This interesting marigold vase has "Industria Argentina" molded into the side. It was brought from Argentina to the 1996 Heart of America convention by Jorge Perri.

Flute, Fenton

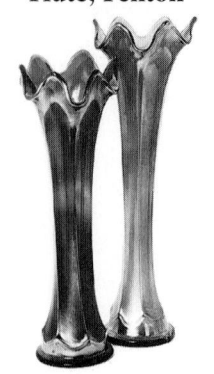

With Fenton Flute, there is one base size: 2½". Heights vary only between about 8 and 11". Seen mostly in marigold. The scarce colors are cobalt, pale smoky blue, green, vaseline, amethyst, red and amber. Prices are contingent on quality of iridescence and condition. For example, a vaseline with poor iridescence or slight damage, will bring $60 to $90 while a perfect one can fetch over $400.

Flute, Imperial

The distinguishing features here are the flat scalloped bands at the bottoms of the flutes, typical of this pattern. Marigold examples are worth $20, lavender $50 to $70, and purple about $35.

Flute, Millersburg

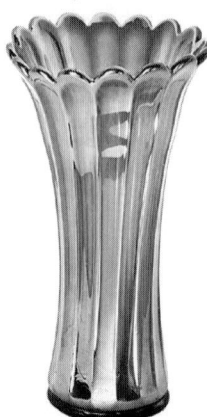

These are fairly large vases with a 4" base. This amethyst example is courtesy of Don Doyle. There is one other known in amethyst and two in blue, one of which sold in 1994 for $2,550.

Vases 285

Flute, Northwood

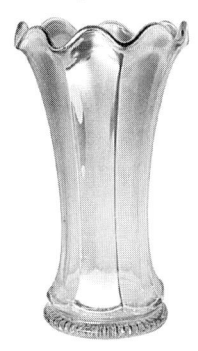

Northwood's Flute has eight wide flutes or panels and a 4¼" multistarred base. Usually seen in green, invariably with heavy marigold iridescence at the top fading at the bottom. Hard to find with good iridescence from top to bottom. This example is just under 10 inches tall, relatively short. They range up to about 17 inches.

Green	75–125	
Marigold	50–80	
Purple	400 (1995)	

Footed Prism Panels

Most often seen in marigold, these 9" tall vases bring $60 to $100 in that color. The blue example shown sold for $400 at the 1998 Heart of American auction (Jim Seeck).

Formal, Dugan

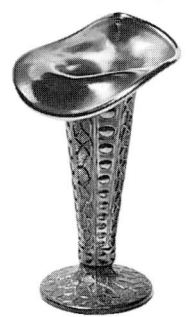

These are flared-out versions of the Formal shape generally considered hatpin holders (but which I think were more likely intended to be a bud vase).

Although there may be other shapes, I've only seen the vases with a jack-in-the-pulpit top.

Marigold	300–450	
Purple	550–850	most common color

Four Pillars

A classic design but still confused with other patterns because of its simplicity. While there are two base sizes—2⅞" and 3⅛"—heights range little, mostly from 9 to 12 inches. For some reason, this piece is particularly susceptible to damage, both on the feet and the top edge. Don't settle for a damaged or inferior example in aqua opal, as this color is widely available. This is also the only vase pattern that has a variant with advertising molded into the base.

Amethyst	70–100	scarce color
Aqua opal	125–200	common color
Black amethyst reported		
Blue	125–200	scarce color
Green	60–100	
Green	90–125	Howard Furniture adv.
Lime green opal	350 (1993)	point chipped
Marigold	15–25	
Mar/custard	2,500 (1993)	rough top
Olive/russet	35–50	common color
Purple	90 (1995)	foot chip
Vaseline	425 (1993)	marigold overlay

Four Seventy Four, Imperial

Unlike most American carnival glass patterns, Imperial's Four Seventy Four has a vase as part of the range. Very few are known. One in marigold, with slight damage, sold for $475 in 1993. This 12½" tall example in green was shown at the 1997 Heart of America club convention by Bob and Geneva Leonard.

Freefold, Imperial

With this vase it is the tops that are the most distinctive, with no two quite the same—yet all strangely attractive and very floral-like. There are two base sizes; 2⅞" with a 12-point star, and 3¼" with a 16-point star. In addition to the colors listed they are found in clambroth and helios.

Lavender	50–100
Marigold	30–50
Purple	70–100
Smoke	80 (1997)

Frosted Block, Imperial

This vase is shown in old Imperial catalogs as available in "Rubigold, Peacock, and Sapphire." This 6¼" example in clambroth sold for $145 at a 1997 Mickey Reichel auction.

Gothic Arches, Imperial

Apparently named for its general design appearance. These are seldom seen, but have been reproduced in ice blue and a pale yellow. Scarce.

| Marigold | 175–300 |
| Smoke | 350–600 |

Graceful, Northwood

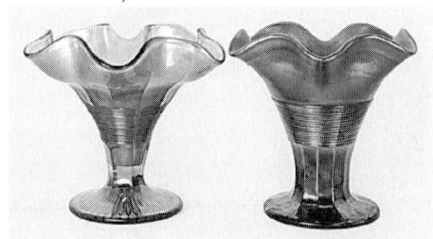

The fine horizontal ribbing around the stem makes this vase unique. As you can see from the photo, there are two slightly differing versions. The one with the narrower stem has a starred base.

Green	35–60
Marigold	25–60
Purple	35–60

Grape and Cable, Northwood

A spectacular piece made from a hatpin holder mold but with a different ring cap. There are three examples known—this one in green and two in amethyst.

Vases 287

Gum Tips, Crown Crystal

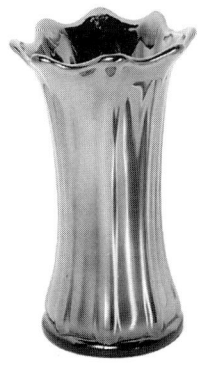

This is an Australian vase, one of the few swung vases made outside the United States. It is eight inches high and in the deep amethyst that was favored by the Australians. Seldom seen in the US. The vase has eight subtle vertical ribs. This one brought $200 at a 1994 auction. Another, a bit taller, in the deep amethyst, sold for $450 at a 1998 David Ayers auction.

Hand vase, JAIN (India)

These are found in both left and right hand version. Note the wrist watch on the tall example on the left. Like the Elephant and Fish vases, this design may have had a ruffled top but the grinding on this tall one suggests it was removed. The tall example in marigold sold for $75 in 1993; in 1997 one brought $650. The miniature version, 5" tall and also in marigold, sold for $575 at the 1998 Heart of America auction.

Heavy Diamond, Imperial

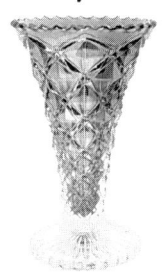

Not too often seen. This Heavy Diamond is smoke and sold in 1995 for $50, although it had some minor damage. Marigold is also known.

Hobstar and Feather, Millersburg

Usually seen in the rosebowl shape, several of these vase whimsies are known—a couple of which have been pulled up so far that the pattern is obliterated. This purple example in a spittoon shape sold for $4,000 in 1995. None of the rare vase whimsies have sold recently.

Hobnail Swirl
See Swirl Hobnail

Honeycomb and Hobstar, Millersburg

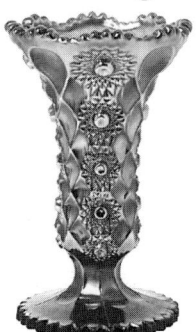

Another Millersburg rarity, few of these exist. This one is amethyst and is courtesy of Don Doyle. Marie McGee, in her 1995 book on Millersburg glass, reports that two are known in amethyst, and one—possibly two—in blue.

Hot Springs

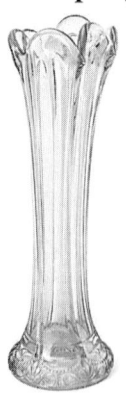

There were a number of vase patterns etched with the Hot Springs lettering. Lightly iridized, they are considered pre-carnival. This one, with nice detail around the base, is courtesy of Carl and Eunice Booker.

Idyll, Fenton

While these 7" tall marigold vases are listed under the name Idyll, they are really part of the Waterlily and Cattails family. Supposedly quite rare, this is the only one I've seen. It was photographed at a 1993 auction where it brought $600. There are a few ruffled examples in amethyst.

Imperial Block

This eight-inch smoke-colored vase was listed as Ranger or Imperial Block at the 1993 auction, where it sold for $45.

Imperial Grape

Yes, yes I know. It's the Imperial Grape water carafe. However, since this shape is described in old ads as a vase, I've included it here.

Green	80–100
Marigold	55–70
Purple	125–200
Smoke	600 (1997)

Inwald vases, Josef Inwald Co.

These vases are typical of those made by Josef Inwald, the Czechoslovakian glass maker. Few of these vase patterns have names so, until they do, I'll simply identify them as Inwald. I came across the vase on the left at the 1996 HOACGA convention. It was brought from Argentina. It is in marigold and measures 11½" high. The vase on the right, also marigold, is almost 8" tall. Courtesy of Gale Eichhorst.

Vases 289

Kittens, Fenton

When these pieces reach the lofty height of 3" or so, they're considered vases rather than toothpick holders. In marigold they're worth $125 to $200, in blue, $225 to $400. This marigold example is courtesy of Carl and Ferne Schroeder.

Knotted Beads, Fenton

Knotted Beads is distinguished by its four rows of six ovals filled with connected beads. Heights range from about 9 to 10½".

Amber	550 (1996)	with tight crimp
Aqua	125 (1997)	
Blue	50–90	common color
Red, rare		
Marigold	20–50	most common color
Vaseline, scarce		

Lattice and Leaves, Brockwitz

Known in marigold and blue, this example is marigold and 9¼ inches high. It sold in 1993 for $105 and again in 1994 for $165.

Lattice and Points, Dugan

This pattern has known at least four names. It is still sometimes called Vining Twigs, one of the two names given it by Marion Hartung. All pieces, including plates and bowls seem to have been made from one shape. Some pieces have a daisy in the inside bottom, some don't. It doesn't seem to make much difference in the price. The short hat-shaped vase above shows the pattern of lattices and grass-like vertical details around the base. Heights range up to just over nine inches.

Amethyst/purple	100–200	scarce color
Blue	150–250	rare color
Marigold	20–40	common color
White	60–90	scarce color

Leaf Columns, Northwood

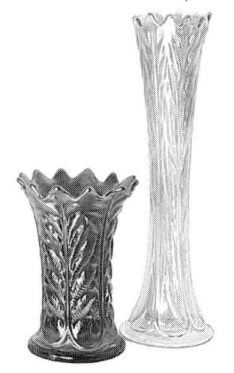

Leaf Columns has a subtle pattern of veined leaves rising in columns around the trunk and is found in heights ranging from six to about 12 inches. The base size is 3½ inches.

Amethyst/purple	70–125	
Green	150–225	
Ice blue	400–550	
Ice green	350–500	scarce color
Marigold	50–80	scarce color
Sapphire blue	500–800	
Teal	250–400	
White	225–400	

290 A Field Guide to Carnival Glass

Leaf Columns, continued
Vase, squatty, 7" tall or less
Amethyst/purple	150–250
Green	175–300
Ice blue	625–750
Marigold	100–150
White	300–450

Lined Lattice, Dugan

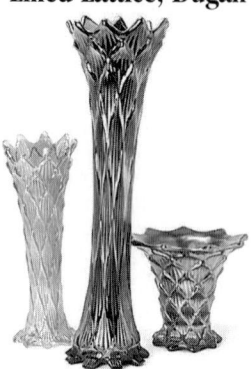

An all-time favorite among the swung carnival vases, the distinct but subtle effect of the lattices is extremely satisfying in this vase. Found in a variety of heights from 5 inches to more than 10. There are two styles of feet: triangular or square toes (the tall example here has the square toes).

Amethyst/purple	150–250	most common color
Amethyst/purple	200–350	5"–6", scarce
Amethyst, black	150–250	scarce color
Lavender	150–250	scarce color
Marigold	60–100	10"–12", scarce color
Marigold	85–125	5"–6"
Peach opal	150–250	5"–6", scarce
White	80–150	

Loganberry, Imperial

These dramatic vases are 10 inches high and have a 3¼-inch diameter base. They have been reproduced; the old vases have a starred base, the new ones have an IG logo on a stippled background. I've also seen them with a plain base—at least some of these are old. See contemporary section.

Amber	450–800	fairly common color
Green	250–400	fairly common color
Helios	200 (1996)	
Marigold	100–200	
Olive	150 (1995)	poor iridescence
Purple	1,300–2,500	fairly common color

Long Thumbprint, Fenton

Pretty much a run-of-the-mill pattern. Often found at flea markets and malls, usually in green. The jack-in-the-pulpit versions are rare, however. There are four rows of thumbprints around trunk. Range in height from about seven to 12 inches. Shorter vases are worth a bit more.

Amethyst	30–50	common color
Amethyst	155 (1997)	JIP
Green	25–40	most common color
Marigold	20–35	common color
Marigold	105 (1997)	JIP
Olive	20–40	

Long Thumbprint Hobnail, Fenton

Usually identified as Fenton's Knotted Beads because of the similarity in design. This one has nine ovals around the vase, with seven regularly placed hobs in each oval. Knotted Beads has six ovals around and connected beads. We think the Long Thumbprint mold was modified to make this vase. Found in the same colors as Long Thumbprint but prices would be in the same range as Knotted Beads.

Vases 291

Lustre Corn, Dugan

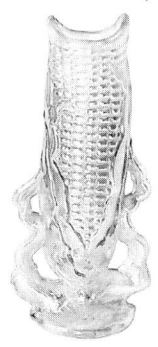

Thought to be the only known example in carnival, this is from the collection of Floyd and Cecil Whitley. However, it is found in opalescent glass and has been reproduced with a flat top.

Maize, Libby

This 7" vase is marigold with blue flashed stalks. It sold at a 1993 auction for $75.

Manhattan, US Glass

This curious vase is the only piece we've seen in the pattern although John and Lucile Britt reported a whiskey set. The vase is also shown in Marion Hartung's tenth book, listed as a souvenir vase. It is about 6½" high and is courtesy of Mike and Linda Cain.

Mary Ann, Dugan

Quite an elaborate design and very desirable. The three-handled versions, called loving cups, are quite rare and bring top dollar.

Vase, two handles
Amethyst   150–250
Marigold   75–125

Loving cup, three handles
Marigold   400–700

Maypole

This light marigold, five-toed vase brought $15 at the 1993 auction where I photographed it. In 1995 a similar six-inch example in purple sold for $140.

Mitered Ovals, Millersburg

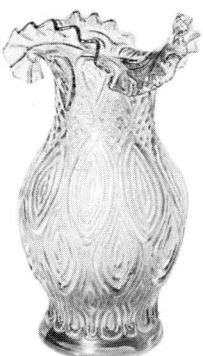

These rare vases, 10" tall with a 4⅛" base, are found in the typical Millersburg colors of marigold, amethyst, and green. They invariably have this three-ruffled top with crimping.

Amethyst   10,100 (1998)
Green   7,000–8,000

Moonprint, Brockwitz (Germany)

Moonprint was made in both this cylindrical shape as well as a pedestalled variety. Only marigold has been reported. This example is from the John and Lucile Britt collection. They are valued from $275 to $400.

Morning Glory, Imperial

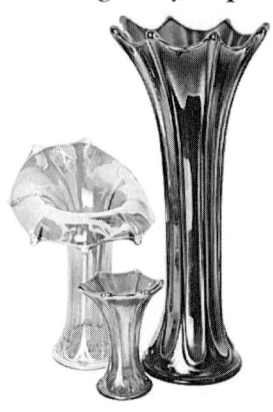

Morning Glory is found with three base sizes. The smallest is 2½" and is referred to as the miniature. The midsize is the rarest, usually seen in a jack-in-the-pulpit shape, with a base diameter of just under four inches. The largest is the funeral, with a base five inches in diameter.

Miniature, 5–8" tall
Purple	75–135	
Clambroth	20–30	
Green	50–90	scarce color
Green	150–200	shortest known, 4"
Helios green	140 (1998)	
Lavender	75 (1997)	
Marigold	40–75	most common color
Marigold	105 (1994)	whimsied top
Smoke	70–130	scarce color

Midsize, jack-in-the-pulpit
Marigold	45–75	

Funeral, 9½–19" tall
Amber	300–425	scarce color
Green	175 (1994)	bad scratch
Marigold	175–300	most common color
Olive	225 (1995)	
Purple	300–500	common color
Smoke	150–200	scarce color

Nautilus, Dugan

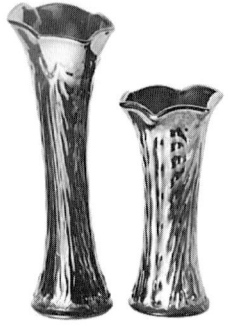

This pattern is rather indistinct because the vase has been swung out. It is made from a tumbler-shaped piece. Interestingly, tumblers are known in non-iridized glass but not in carnival. The base measures about 2½" and heights range from about 6 to 9 inches. Purple is seen most often.

Marigold	150–275
Purple	200–350

Nine Sixteen, Fenton

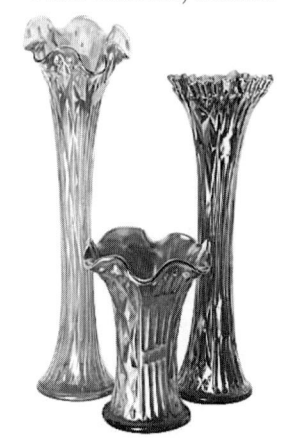

Often confused with another Fenton pattern, Diamond Point Columns, or other similar designs. The shorter version, on which the pattern can be more easily seen, is rare—most are in the 15–16" height range.

Blue	65–100	
Marigold	35–60	most common color

Vases 293

Octagon, Imperial

Imperial seems to have included vases within their patterns more than any of the other carnival glass manufacturers. Still, the Octagon vase is hard to find. I've only seen it in Marigold—selling in the $90 to $150 range. Note that Imperial reproduced this vase in red, calling it Imperial Lace.

Ohio Star, Millersburg

Certainly not as rare as some Millersburg vases but so high on the desirability list that they always bring serious money. Two rare green opal vases sold in 1998, one for $21,000. There also are a handful of examples that have been swung, but these seldom change hands.

Amethyst	1,500–2,500	most common color
Green	2,750 (1997)	
Marigold	2,000–3,250	

Optic, Dugan

One of the simpler vases you'll find, this one has a smooth exterior and 14 subtle interior panels. Usually found in marigold (less than $20), but occasionally seen in scarce amethyst.

Orange Tree, Fenton

Although Fenton made many iridized vases, I doubt if this one was ever listed in their product literature. It is a whimsey, in blue, made from a punch bowl base—one of two reported. It's owned by Ruth Phillips.

Palm Beach, US Glass

The lavender amphora-shaped vase on the left was probably made from a wide mouth version like the one in the middle—but drawn in at the neck. The base diameter is around 3½". In honey amber, it sold for $280 at a 1993 auction. The cylindrical vase was swung out from a spooner. These whimsies are generally in the $250 to $400 range although a marigold version sold at a 1998 Mickey Reichel auction for $725.

Panelled Cane

Not much is known about this vase. It is marigold, 8 inches high, and has a 3¼-inch base. From the John and Lucile Britt collection.

Panelled Diamonds and Bows, Fenton

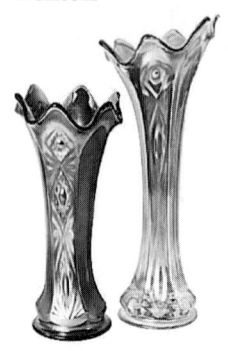

Panelled Diamonds and Bows has six panels with alternating smooth flutes and the diamonds and bows design on the others.

Amethyst	100–150	rare color
Blue	35–60	most common color
Green	80–150	scarce color
Marigold	60–100	scarce color
Red	425 (1993)	very weak irid.

Panelled Treetrunk, Dugan

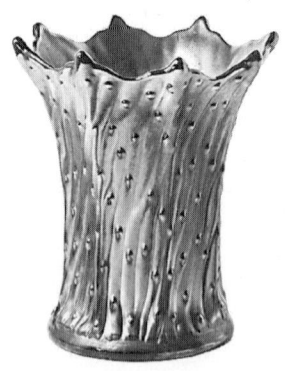

This extraordinary vase is in amethyst, has a base diameter of almost 5", and is 7½" tall. The one shown was the only example reported until another turned up in England in 1997. This one is courtesy of Betty Cloud.

Parlor Panels, Imperial

These have a 3⅜" base with a 16-point star. Frequently found not swung, about 4" high.

Swung, about 6–12"
Green	140 (1996)	
Marigold	60–110	most common color
Purple	125–200	
Smoke	90–150	scarce color

Short, not swung
Blue	1,750 (1993)	two known
Marigold	90–160	
Smoke	100–170	

Peacock Gardens, Fenton

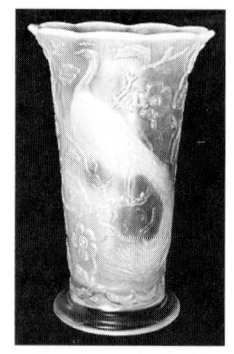

Only a few of these vases have been reported in carnival glass although they are found in greater numbers in noniridized colors. This one is white opalescent and is courtesy of Joe and Dorothy Baur. Blue has been reported. A marigold vase sold for $4,000 in 1993.

Vases 295

Peoples Vase, Millersburg

The most desirable of all carnival glass vases. Apparently made by Millersburg as a tribute to the people of Millersburg, Ohio where the company was located. There are only about 10 known, They include amethyst (all with ruffled tops like the vase on the right), blue, green and marigold. The only two to sell publicly in recent years were amethyst. They were discovered in 1996 and sold at auction that year. A perfect one brought $43,000, a seriously cracked one $13,500. The vases shown here are courtesy of Floyd and Cecil Whitley.

Pinwheel
See Derby

Pinched Swirl, Dugan

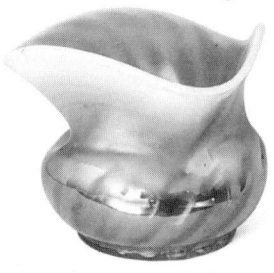

Pinched Swirl is usually found in a pinched-in rosebowl or vase. Above is the seldom-seen spittoon shape with tricorner top, courtesy of Carl and Ferne Schroeder.

Rosebowl
Peach opal   45–80

Tricorner spittoon shape
Peach opal   65–100

Vase, 6½" tall
Peach opal   45–85

Plume Panels, Fenton

This vase has six panels of vertical plumes. Heights seldom vary from the 10"–12" range.

Amethyst	60–110	scarce color
Blue	75–130	scarce color
Green	100–180	common color
Marigold	40–60	scarce color
Olive	50 (1995)	
Red	700–1,000	rare, desirable
Red	1,200–1,700	exceptional examples
Sapphire	475 (1997)	
Vaseline	525 (1997)	

Poppy Show, Imperial

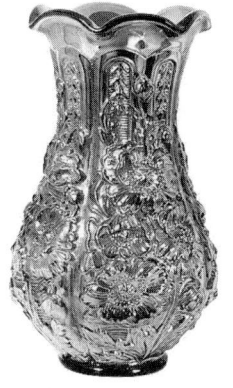

Not the same pattern as Northwood's Poppy Show, which is made only in bowls and plates. This pattern was reproduced by Imperial with those examples having the IG logo in the bottom. Fenton, using the original molds, makes iridized reproductions in non-traditional colors for Singleton Bailey.

Marigold	400–750	most common color
Purple	2,200–2,800	scarce color
Lavender, smoky	800 (1994)	
Smoke	2,400 (1993)	

Princeton, Inwald

This 10-inch tall vase appears in an old catalog of the Czechoslovakian company, Josef Inwald. The edge of the base has a registration number. The vase was named by John Britt.

Prism and Daisy Band

Although pretty, this late marigold vase is not of much value, worth less than $20.

Propeller, Imperial

This vase was made from the compote shape. I have only seen it in marigold but as the compote was made in green, the vase may exist in that color. Vases are valued between $70 and $120.

Pulled Loop, Dugan

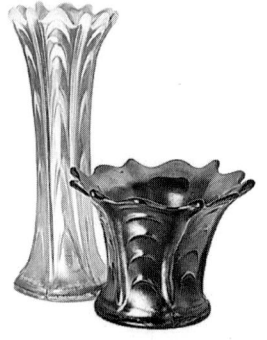

This short version, which is quite rare, shows the pattern of five loops quite well. The pattern is similar to Fenton's Boggy Bayou, which has eight loops or arches in each panel. Most are in the nine to 12" height range. Apparently several molds were used as base diameters range from 3¼" to just under four.

Amethyst/purple	90–150	
Amethyst/purple	275 (1998)	exceptional example
Amethyst/purple	150–250	squatty
Aqua	100–200	rare color
Blue	150–250	rare color
Celeste	600–850	rare color
Green	175 (1998)	
Marigold	25–40	scarce color
Peach opal	50–90	most common color
White	140 (1995)	12"

Rib and Panels

Rib and Panels is a blown vase and has a pontil in the base. In addition to a variety of shapes (the one on the left is more commonly seen) it is found in two base sizes and heights from about 6" to 9". It has been found only in marigold. Because they have been confused with Dugan's rare Colonial Lady vase, Rib and Panels vases sell for somewhat more than their traditional price of $25 to $40. Two sold in 1997 for $55 and $90.

Vases

Rings

Another late carnival vase in marigold. Also blown and measures 8 inches high with a 3¼" base. I have seen a number of these that the owners couldn't dispose of for $15. Don't pay too much.

Ripple, Imperial

Although it's probably the most often seen carnival vase, it's still highly desirable. Because of the variety of base sizes, heights, and available colors, one could make an excellent collection of vases with Ripple alone. There are five different base sizes, heights from five to 18 inches, and a variety of flares and ruffling. The middle base size, three inches, is seen most often. Except at the extreme ends of the range, heights make little difference in price. The largest base size, 4¾", is often referred to as the funeral size and the smallest, 2½", is sometimes called a miniature. By the way, some have been swung in such a way that the ripples have almost disappeared, leaving the vertical interior ribbing the most obvious feature. The second example from the left shows this. Red is the most rare color with one reported example. There is also an enameled Ripple. Blue is very rare, with only a couple of examples in cobalt but quite a few in lighter blue. It should be noted that Ripple was reproduced in smoke and marigold—marked with the IG logo.

Smallest size (2½" base, 5" or shorter are more desirable)

Clambroth	40–60	
Green/helios	35–60	
Marigold	20–40	most common color
Purple	70–100	scarce color
White	40–70	scarce color

"Standard" sizes (3", 3⅜" base)

Amber	70–125	scarce color
Aqua	150–250	scarce color
Blue, medium	250–350	rare color
Blue violet	155 (1996)	10" tall
Helios/green	40–70	common color
Lavender	100–200	scarce color
Lime	55 (1998)	
Marigold	25–40	most common color
Marigold	55 (1998)	5", squatty
Olive	150 (1997)	
Purple	75–125	
Smoke	70–125	scarce color
White	100–150	

Fourth largest size (rarest, 3⅞"-4" base)

Amber	225 (1997)	
Green	50–90	
Marigold	40–80	
Teal	55 (1997)	base cracked

Funeral size (largest, 4¾–5" base)

Green	140 (1993)	12" tall x 9" flare
Marigold	145–325	
Purple	325 (1995)	10" tall

Rising Comet, Inwald

Sometimes called Rising Comet, this marigold vase has a ring of stars toward the top of the piece, each sitting on top of a spiked set of rays. It is known in three sizes, all marigold. This example sold for $95 at a 1996 Tom Burns auction.

Rococco, Imperial

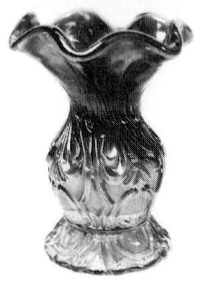

This smallish vase was made from the same mold used for the nut dish and compote—another example of using one mold for multiple shapes. Interestingly, many more vases are seen than all other shapes combined.

Lavender	200–275	scarce color
Marigold	90–160	common color
Smoke	150–225	common color

Rose Columns, Millersburg

As you can tell from the prices, these are indeed desirable vases. In addition to the colors listed, there is an amethyst one with enameled flowers in the collection of Floyd and Cecil Whitley.

Amethyst	3,300 (1994)	
Aqua	7,000 (1996)	may be only one
Blue	12,000 (1996)	two known
Green	3,300–5,280	most common color
Marigold	6,000 (1996)	

Rose Garden, Brockwitz

Made by the German glassmaker Brockwitz and shown in their catalog, Rose Garden is found in both cylindrical and rectangular vases, in both marigold and blue. The rectangular is known in a small and a large size; the cylindrical in three heights—7½", 9¼" and 11". Because of the infrequency with which these sell, prices are difficult to establish. A marigold vase like the one on the left sold at a 1998 Mickey Reichel auction for $900.

Rustic, Fenton

Rustic is similar to Northwood's Tree Trunk and is found in similar sizes. As Tree Trunk is also a hobbed design, there is often confusion between them. Just remember that Rustic has a very regular pattern of hobs without any background design. Illustrated above: a midsize, a funeral and a midsize variant. The midsize variant differs from the regular in that it has eleven rings of hobs with 18 hobs in each ring—except for the top which has nine. The midsize has seven rings of hob with 24 hobs in each ring. The funeral size is often found with a band around the base, sometimes referred to as a plunger base. These are generally more desirable than funeral vases without the plunger.

Standard size (3–3¼" base, 9–15" height)
Amber	400 (1998)	short–7"
Amethyst	40–75	scarce color in this size
Blue	50–80	common color
Green	50–80	
Lime green	950 (1994)	
Lime green opal	1,000–1,300	rare color
Marigold	30–55	
Peach opal	1,250 (1994) 2,400 (1996)	two known
Red	4,200 (1994)	crimped edge
White	50–80	

Midsize (4⅛–4¼" base, 12–17" height)
Amethyst	55–95	
Blue	75–140	
Blue, electric	550 (1995)	
Green	75–120	
Marigold	65–80	
White	100–150	

Midsize variant (4⅛–4¼" base)
Amethyst	70–110	
Blue	80–150	some with crimped top
Green	80–150	
Marigold	70–100	
White	120–175	

Funeral size (approx. 5¼" base, 17–23" height)
Amethyst	700–1,000	no band
Amethyst	1,400–3,600	with band
Blue	500–800	no band
Blue	1,200–1,750	with band
Emerald green	1,600 (1993)	with band
Green	650–900	no band
Green	1,800–1,950	with band
Marigold	400–600	no band
White	450–800	no band

Scroll and Flower Panel, Imperial

There are very few of these around and they were reproduced in the 1960s with an IG logo in the bottom. This one is marigold (purple is thought to exist also) and is from a private collection.

Seagulls, Czechoslovakian

This unusual vase is 11" tall with a 6-inch base. Note the rim, which is similar to that on several other Czechoslovakian vases.

Blue, pastel	175 (1993)	chips on base and top
Marigold	1,550 (1998)	

Smooth Panels, Imperial

These are found in at least five different base sizes, a variety of glass colors (we've even seen one in strong yellow). Always, though, the base has a distinct collar. All are shaped like these two; I've never seen any with ruffling. There are stretch or frosted versions with wheel-cut floral designs.

Small size (2½" base, usually about 5" tall)
Clambroth	10–20	
Marigold	20–35	most common color
Mar/milk glass	145 (1997)	4" tall, 5½" flare
Mar/milk glass	45 (1998)	8¾" tall
Teal	55 (1993)	4½" tall

Larger sizes (up to 12" tall)
Clambroth	15–30	
Marigold	25–70	most common color
Mar/milk glass	30–70	
Smoke/milk glass		170 (1993)
8" tall		
White	100–200	some have Iron Cross mark

Spider Web

I photographed this at a 1993 Jim Seeck auction where it sold for $75. I've not seen another and have no idea who made it. The bulk of the vase is marigold, blending into blue at the neck.

Spiral Diamond and Point Fan

A rare piece; I've seen only a couple and they have all been marigold and are 6" tall. This one sold in 1993 for $80; another in 1998 went for $130. Some attribute it to McKee, others to a European maker. It is also referred to as Diamond Point Spiral.

Spiral Rib, Northwood

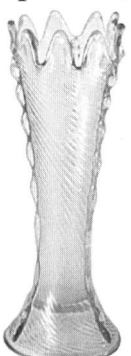

Jim Seeck included this previously unknown white vase in a 1996 auction where it brought $1,500. Jim called it Ribs and Tears. It is marked with the Northwood "N" and stands about eight inches tall.

Spiralex, Dugan

Often confused with twisted examples of Dugan's Wide Panel or the Imperial Curled Rib (all have eight ribs curling one way or the other), Spiralex is usually seen in marigold and is worth about $20.

Standard

These little blown vases in metal holders are all called "Standard." Most are marigold in plain metal holders and are valued in the $15 to $20 range. If they have more elaborate holders like these and particularly if they have patterns in the glass like that on the left, they can fetch up to $70 or $80.

Starbrite

Two of these six-inch green molded vases have sold, one in 1993 for $425 and another in 1994 for $275. I don't know who made them.

Starburst, Riihimäki (Finland)

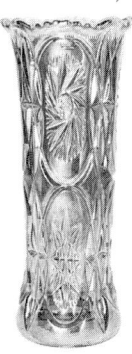

This pattern was made in several shapes and can be found in a 1939 Riihimäki catalog. Vases have turned up in marigold and blue. Other shapes are also known in amber.

Star Medallion, Imperial

These are more properly called celery holders although, of course, they can hold flowers. They're found in marigold and smoke and are worth $40 to $60.

Stippled Estate, Dugan

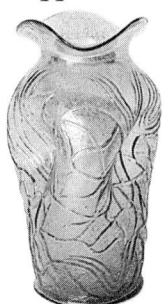

Although the name implies a relationship to the Estate pattern, the vase is quite different. In 1998, Mickey Reichel auctioned vases in amethyst for $225, aqua for $325, marigold for $175, and vaseline for $300.

Stork, Jenkins

At the low end of the collecting spectrum, these Depression era vases are found only in marigold and seldom fetch as much as $20.

Summer Days, Dugan

There is some controversy surrounding this piece; a question of whether it is a vase, the base to Dugan's Stork and Rushes punch set, or both. As a vase the base seems rather oddly shaped. As a punch base, it would seem to be an unstable platform and the flowers are oriented upside down, but every punch bowl I've seen has this base. Either way, they're not too common. This one in amethyst sold in 1996 for $60. Marigold would be worth a little less.

Sunflower and Diamond, Brockwitz

There are three sizes for this vase: a bit over 6" tall, about 7¾" tall, and 9¼" tall. They are shown in a Brockwitz catalog. Eda may have also produced this pattern. In marigold they sell for $75 to $125. Blue examples are valued up to $250.

Superb Drape

A rare and quite beautiful vase with the look of art glass. This one is green; two others are known in aqua opalescent. Courtesy of Elaine Benedict.

Swirl, Imperial

Distinctive but not especially desirable, this vase is seen in marigold and smoke. Either color is worth between $10 and $20 with smoke being the prettier of the two.

Swirl, Northwood

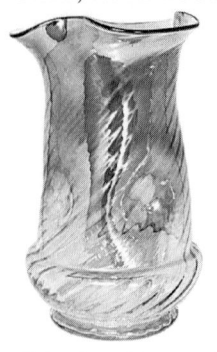

Obviously a whimsey made from the water pitcher sans handle. It is the only one I've seen and is marigold. It sold at a 1997 Mickey Reichel auction for $230.

Swirled Hobnail, Millersburg

One of the more affordable Millersburg vases, these were swung from the same molds used to make the Swirled Hobnail rosebowls and spittoons. Most are in the nine to 11-inch height but range up to 13 inches.

Amethyst	200–350	most common color
Green	200–300	
Marigold	150–250	

Vases

Target, Dugan

Easy to spot; this patterns has six flutes each with a column of five hobs. Apparently there was a long run of these vases as the pattern is found in at least five different base diameters. The squatty flared vases are quite unusual although not rare. This version almost always has base damage. Peach opal is the most common color, blue the least often seen (aside from one-of-a-kind colors).

Vase, 6—12"
Amethyst/purple	50–85	scarce color
Blue	100–150	rare color
Horehound	135 (1997)	
Marigold	20–40	scarce color
Peach opal	60–110	most common color
Lime green opal	400 (1996)	only one known
White	80–100	scarce color

Vase, squatty flared, under 6"
Peach opal	75–125
Purple	200–300
White	100–200

Thin Panel, Dugan

These smallish vases are often confused with others because of their rather plain trunks. However, the tops are found in at least six variations. Peach opal is valued at between $50 and $100; purple examples are worth a bit more.

Thin Rib, Northwood

Northwood Thin Rib vases have nine ribs. Made in prodigious quantities numbers, four different molds were used. The unusual shape on the right is called a jester's cap and, with the exception of a single Tree Trunk, is found only in this pattern. Shorter, squattier vases (under 7" tall) are worth a bit more than the taller ones.

Standard base sizes (3"–3½")
Amethyst/purple	40–70	common color
Aqua/teal	100–200	rare color
Blue	50–90	common color
Blue, electric	400 (1996)	
Custard/nutmeg	200 (1993)	
Green	40–75	common color
Ice blue	150–250	scarce color
Ice blue	325 (1997)	squatty, 7" tall
Ice green	200–300	rare color
Lime green	575 (1997)	squatty, 6" tall
Marigold	30–50	common color
Olive/russet	15–30	
Sapphire blue	300–500	rare color
Vaseline	200–300	scarce color
White	60–90	rare color

Jester's cap top (3½" base)
Amethyst/purple	150–250
Green	125–200
Marigold known	

Northwood Thin Rib, continued

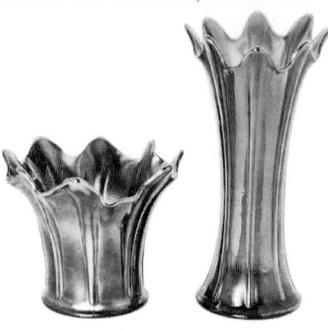

These are the midsize Northwood Thin Rib vases, with a base diameter of 4¾". The vase on the left is 6½" tall and is referred to as a jardiniere. It's in purple and sold for $775 at a 1996 Jim Seeck auction. The vase on the right is green and brought $225 at the same auction.

Midsize (4¾" base)

Amber	1,700 (1994)	
Amethyst/purple	100–200	common color
Aqua opal	1,600 (1993)	
Blue	220 (1998)	
Green	100–200	common color
Ice blue	750 (1997)	
Ice Green	800 (1997)	
Lime green	1,600 (1997)	
Marigold	80–150	common color
Sapphire	700–850	scarce, some with gold trim
Vaseline	700 (1997)	
White	125–250	rare color

Thin Rib and Drape, Imperial

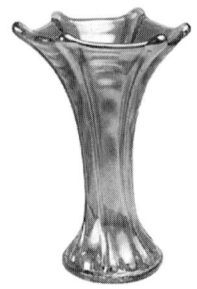

Similar to Imperial's miniature Morning Glory, this one has a subtle drapery effect between the vertical ribs.

Green	200–250	rare color
Marigold	50–90	most common color
Purple	250–350	rare color

Thistle

These vases, about six inches tall, are found only in marigold and are thought to be English. They range in price from $35 to $55.

Three Row, Imperial

This is quite a rare vase; only a handful are known. They measure seven to eight inches tall. The example here is marigold and, with a crack in the base, sold for $75 in 1993. Purple versions sold in 1996 and 1997 for $3,000 each.

Thumbprint and Ovals, Imperial

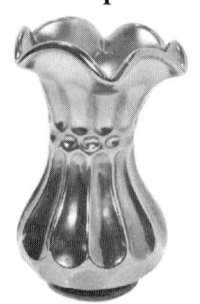

Rather small, this vase has more charm than a photo can show. The vase was reproduced by Fenton in aqua opal as a Lincoln-Land Carnival Club souvenir for their 1995 convention and in peach opal for the 1996 convention. This original, above in purple, sold for $500 in 1993.

Marigold	250–400
Purple	550–900

Vases 305

Tornado, Northwood

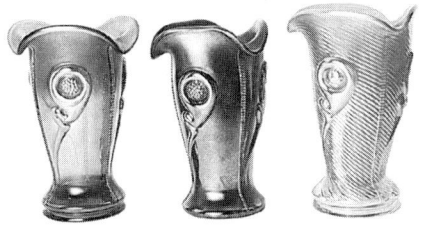

This is an unusual design and is totally unlike any other carnival glass pattern. Oddly, in spite of the relatively small output, there are a number of variants. The basic design is found in two slightly differing sizes—one about six inches tall, the other about one-half inch taller. There is also a style with diagonal ribs (shown on the right, above). In the center is an example without the collar base; a variant that is occasionally found. Whether these are regular vases with the bottom ground off is not known. Not shown is a rare version with a pedestal-type base—thought by some to have been made in Europe. Another rare variant has green tornados attached to a marigold vase. Perhaps the most spectacular are a celeste blue version with whimsied top and an example that is cone shaped.

Small (about 6" tall)
Green	400–900
Marigold	500–800
Purple	500–700

Large (about 6½" tall)
Green	400–700
Purple	400–600

Ribbed, small
Blue (small)	3,050 (1997)	
Marigold	2,000 (1997)	top flared out
Purple	600–1000	

Variants
Marigold	2,100 (1997)	green decorated tornados
Marigold	1,900 (1997)	pedestal-footed variant
Marigold	700	pinched in, flared tricorner

Town Pump, Northwood

A highly desirable pattern known in green ($4,000–$5,000), marigold ($2,000–$3,500), and the comparatively common purple ($700–$1,000).

Tree Trunk, Northwood

Tree Trunk is distinguished by its irregularly placed hobs and short crescent shapes distributed between the hobs. There are four base sizes: 3⅜–3¾" (standard), 3¾" (midsize variant), 4¾" (midsize), and 5¼" (funeral). Shown above are a standard, elephant foot (which is a funeral vase that is less than 15" tall), a funeral, and a midsize. Not shown is the midsize variant that has a band around the foot like the funerals (sometimes called a plunger base).

Standard base size
Amethyst/purple	50–80	most common color
Aqua opal	600–900	scarce color
Blue	125–200	scarce color
Green	50–90	common color
Ice blue	400–600	scarce color
Ice green	300–500	rare color
Marigold	60–100	scarce color
Marigold	2,600 (1997)	Jester's cap (only one)
Sapphire blue	400–700	rare color
White	80–140	

Standard base size, squatty (less than 7" tall)
Amethyst/purple	80–150	very common color
Blue	200–400	rare color
Green	45–80	most common color
Ice blue	400–700	rare color
Marigold	40–70	common color
Marigold	235 (1997)	

Midsize and midsize variant
Amethyst/purple	250–450	common color
Aqua opal	3,000–4,000	about six known
Blue	450–800	
Green	250–450	
Horehound	300–400	rare color
Ice blue	1,000–1,500	scarce color
Ice green	1,200–1,700	rare color
Lime green	900–1,200	rare color
Marigold	300–500	common color
Sapphire blue	900 (1995)	
White	500–800	scarce color

Tree Trunk, continued
Funeral size, 15" or taller
Amethyst/purple 2,000–3,000
Blue 2,000–3,000
Green, few known
Ice blue 24,000–30,000 two known
Marigold 4,000 (1993)
White 4,000 (1994)

Funeral, elephant's foot (shorter than 15")
Amethyst/purple 1,600–2,800
Amethyst/purple 11,000 (1995) exceptional example

Triands, Brockwitz

These marigold vases with bands of large and small vertical ribs occasionally come up for sale—bringing $50 to $70. They are about eight inches tall and are part of an extensive line of shapes in the Niobe pattern.

Tulip Scroll, Millersburg

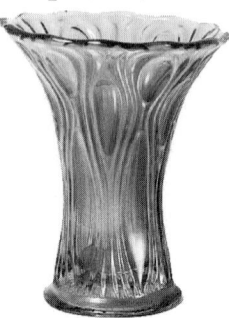

The pattern of thumbprint-type indentations is quite clear in this example of a squatty version of Tulip Scroll. These shorter examples are more numerous than taller ones.

Amethyst 250–450
Green 200–400
Marigold 300–500

Twigs, Dugan

These two pictured are the extremes of the range of top treatments seen in this vase. The vases are short, five inches or less. For taller examples, see Beauty Bud.

Vase, short or mini, with crimping
Purple 600–1,000

Two Handled, Imperial

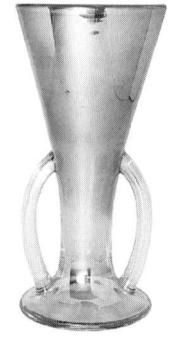

There are several variations on this design, but all have the distinctive arrangement of two opposing handles. In spite of the severity of the pattern, they seem to command fairly good prices. This one brought $70 at a 1998 Mickey Reichel auction.

Waterlily and Cattails
See Idyll

Vases 307

Western Thistle, Riihimäki

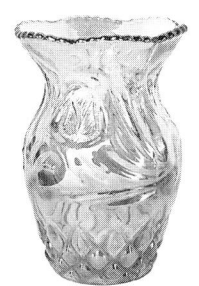

This five-inch tall vase is from the Finnish glassmaker Riihimäki. Found only in marigold so far, prices range from $150 to about $300.

Wide Panel, Northwood

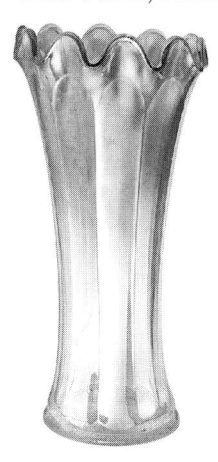

These vases are much like the Flute pattern but have ten panels. Curiously, almost all the green examples have the Northwood Alaskan finish which is a green base glass with marigold iridescence applied to just the top portion. The base size is 4¾" with a 44-point star.

Marigold	60–100
Green	80–110
Vaseline	90–130

Wide Rib, Dugan

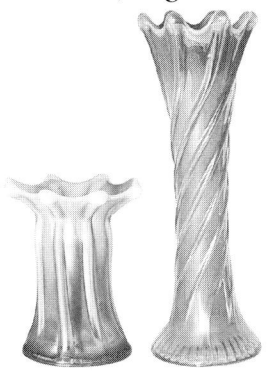

Similar to several other patterns, Dugan's Wide Rib is most easily distinguished from others by the rather bulbous tips and the 3¾" base. As can be seen by the photograph, the vases can be shaped in a number of different ways. Usually in peach opal.

Amethyst	40–75	
Amethyst	100–200	exceptional examples
Peach opal	55–85	
White	45–70	

Woodlands

Woodlands is a fairly scarce vase abut five inches tall and seen mostly in marigold. The design theme is a stalk of foliage and flower.

Vase, 5"

Marigold	175–300
Smoke	210 (1996)

Woodpecker

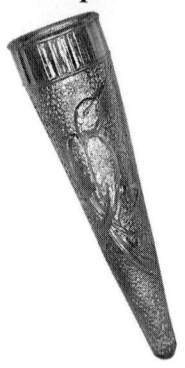

Not often seen, this marigold vase has a built-in hole at the top back so that it can be hung on a wall peg. Normally selling in the $70 to $100 range, one brought the surprising figure of $225 at a 1998 Mickey Reichel auction.

Woodpecker and Ivy

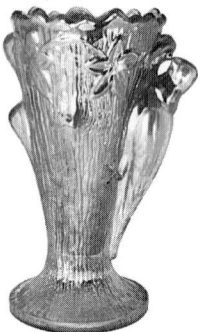

There are only a couple of these known, one in marigold and one in vaseline. Courtesy of Tom and Sharon Mordini.

Novelties and miniatures

Iridized glass tableware was so popular during the early part of the twentieth century that many manufacturers tried making all manner of glass objects using the process. Glassmakers involved in the manufacture of gift items and industrial goods soon added the lustre pieces to their lines. Fortunately, many of these pieces have survived the ravages of time—although many charming pieces must have been discarded simply because they were deemed insignificant.

Unfortunately, few records are left that can tell us just who made these unusual pieces of glass. Nonetheless, collectors are grateful that these anonymous industrialists made the decision to iridize some of their glass.

Arched Flute toothpick holder

Toothpick holder
Celeste   300–400
Ice green   250–300

Atlas E-Z Seal canning jar
A Hazel Atlas half-pint jar in marigold sold at a Tom Burns auction in 1996 for $60.

Auto headlamp lens
A pair of marigold lenses sold for $75 in 1993, then sold again for $25 in 1995.

Baby shoes

From the collection of Carl and Eunice Booker, these marigold baby booties measure four inches long and may have been toothpick holders.

Barrel flask

This marigold oblong bottle surely must have held whiskey. It measures about five inches high and sold at a Gary Cooper auction in 1994 for $300.

Banana

There certainly can be no mistaking this shape, and the satin marigold color really enhances it. The banana is seven inches long and is courtesy of Tom and Sharon Mordini. Values are probably in the $100 to $200 range.

Bathtub

Who knows what this miniature tub was intended for? Candy? Matches? Whatever its purpose, it sold for $65 at auction in 1994. Another had sold for $215 in 1993.

Beaded Compact

Occasionally sells at auction, about $45.

Beaded purse or handbag

Quite a few carnival items were made for milady's wardrobe. Beaded purses were one of the more popular items and came in many styles. Auction prices vary from $30 to more than $100 depending on style, quality, and condition.

Bear bottle

Like most capped bottles, this seven-inch tall bear most likely held candy. It is white and owned by Carl and Eunice Booker.

Beetle ashtray

Among the Argentine pieces of Carnival found in the US is the Beetle ashtray. It measures 5½" across and was made by Christalerias Rigolleau S.A. This example is the only one known in amber glass; blue is the most often seen and marigold has been reported. Courtesy of Tom and Sharon Mordini.

Bellaire Goodwill Tour

These marigold bowls sell in the $30 to $50 range.

Billy Baxter, his ashtray

These marigold ashtrays sell for between $20 and $35.

Bobeche

Bobeches were placed on chandeliers to catch candle wax. Only found in marigold. Courtesy of Jerry and Carol Curtis.

Boot toothpick holder

Footware was a continuously fascinating topic for glassmakers and there are several varieties of these toothpicks. These miniature boots, some with stars on the bottom, bring from $50 to $120. All seem to be marigold.

Novelties/miniatures 311

Boot, with laces
A marigold boot with laces and inscribed "Worlds Fair" sold at a 1997 Jim Seeck auction for $350.

Bride's Basket

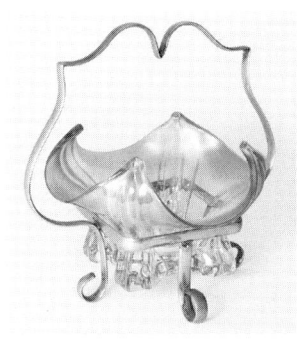

This marigold bowl, pattern unknown, in a silverplate holder sold for $295 at a 1996 auction. The bowl is 5½" wide, the holder 6½" tall.

Bridle Rosettes

These decorative elements, in dark Carnival, were used on horses' bridles. The one on the left has a rose design, that on the right an image of Popeye (with pipe). Courtesy of Carl and Eunice Booker.

Buddha

A rather unexpected object. One wonders just what the intent was. It doesn't seem to be a container or intended for ceremonial use. Perhaps it's a paperweight. The piece is about six inches tall and is courtesy of Bob and Geneva Leonard. A similar item sold at the 1995 HOACGA auction for $2,000.

Butterfly ornaments, Fenton

These are the old Fenton butterfly ornaments. They have a wingspan of three inches and, as can be seen, are much more delicate than the newer ones. It is suggested that they were given away at the factory when a purchase was made. About 40 of these are known in seven colors: aqua, blue, marigold, green, ice blue, ice green and white. The only ones to sell in recent years were marigold and brought $900 and $1,150 in 1993 and $650 and $1,000 in 1998. The two above, in blue and marigold, are courtesy of Jack and Eleanor Hamilton.

Buttons

Buttons can be found in an extraordinary range of sizes and subject matter. Prices, of course, vary depending on subject and quality. Often, groups of buttons are sold on cards. Examples of some of these lots are: 13 buttons, $45; 16 assorted, $160; 44, some figural and scenics, $60; 62, one bird, most plain, $25; 35 sold as lot, $300. Several individual buttons sold in 1997 for $5 each: Hound, Bird and birdhouse, Rip van Winkle. The buttons shown here are from the collection of Carl and Eunice Booker.

Canada Dry bottle

These bottles actually contained the sparkling orange drink and in addition to the marigold iridescence had a surface that emulated orange peel. A clever combination. Bottles without labels sell for $10 to $15 while a bottle with a label in good condition brings $25 or so. In 1997, an example with labels and cap brought $110—an extreme price in my view.

Candelabra

Quite a rare piece, this 4½" tall marigold candelabra is owned by Jack and Eleanor Hamilton. One sold in 1994 for $500.

Canoe

These miniature canoes seem to have been souvenirs as many have names of popular tourists attractions. While these sell in the $25 to $50 range, they have brought as much as $125.

Car Candy Container

This unusual bottle is one of two that were iridized; the remainder of the run being uniridized. It is valued between $150 and $250. Courtesy of Rick and Jackie Kojis.

Cherub toothpick holder

This whimsical toothpick in marigold sold for $190 at a Tom Burns auction in 1994.

Cleopatra bottle

A rather large piece, this marigold bottle with a cork-type top must have held wine. It is 16 inches tall and illustrated in Marion Hartung's book 9. Courtesy of Bob and Geneva Leonard.

Novelties/miniatures

Clock

Yes, this marigold clock does work. It is just over five inches tall and is in the Regal Cane pattern. It brought $800 at the 1998 International Carnival Glass Association auction. An 8¼" tall pitcher in this pattern brought $425 at a 1998 Mickey Reichel auction.

Coal bucket

Most of these have souvenir lettering and were surely intended to hold matches. They sell for $40 to $80 in marigold, somewhat more in green—although a few green examples have sold in the $200 range.

Coca Cola fountain tumbler

Sold at 1996 Pacific Northwest club auction for $85.

Continental whiskey bottle

Valued at $20 to $30.

Corn bottles, Imperial

These small bottles usually have cork stoppers, but occasional examples will have a shaker top.

Green	150–250
Marigold	170–300
Smoke	250–400

Corn cruet

The maker of these small bottles is unknown, but thought to be Dugan or Northwood. It measures 6⅜" tall with a 1¼" base. Two are known, both in white.

Covered Frog

These candy containers are very desirable and quite rare. Ice green examples sold for $450 and $650 in 1996 and 1997. A vaseline example sold at a 1996 auction for $450.

Covered Hen, Little Jessie

Miniature covered dish in marigold sold for $450 at 1998 Heart of American auction.

Cow miniature

Few pieces of carnival have the charm of this marigold cow, which looks like it is smiling. The piece is just 2⅜" long. It is owned by Jack and Eleanor Hamilton.

Crucifix candlestick, Imperial

One of the few ecclesiastical objects in carnival, this candlestick is in marigold and is also found in crystal. A pair of these sold at the Northern California club auction in 1996 for $850 and another pair for $2,000 at a 1997 Jim Seeck auction. A single candlestick brought $700 in 1998.

CR ashtray

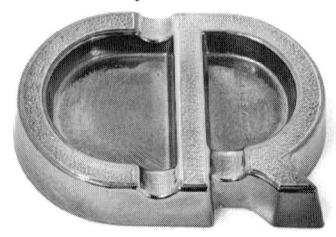

Rarely seen, this ashtray is formed of the letters "C" and "R," which stand for Cristalerias Rigolleau S.A., the Argentine glass manufacturer. This example is blue. A chipped ashtray in amber sold for $60 in 1995.

Daisy Block Rowboat, Sowerby

Known in several sizes in crystal, only one size in carnival. This 12" marigold example sold at a Jim Seeck auction in 1995 for $60. Uniridized supporting stands are known to exist.

Amethyst	135 (1994)	160 (1996)	both chipped
Aqua	200 (1993)		
Marigold	110–200		

Dog candy container

This bottle contains the original candy. Embossed lettering on the side says "SUGAR, STARCH, CORN SYRUP." From the John and Lucile Britt collection. Similar empty pieces have sold for $65 to $150.

Dog, figural

This rather sad looking miniature hound, in marigold, is courtesy of Carl and Eunice Booker.

Dove candleholder

A pair of low marigold miniature candleholders in the shape of doves sold for $55 in 1995.

Novelties/miniatures 315

Egg

Iridized clear carnival, this chicken egg is from the collection of Carl and Eunice Booker.

Egg cup

In a reddish marigold, this honeycomb patterned container could well have served as an egg holder. It might also have been a toothpick or match holder. Courtesy of Dennis and Denise Harp.

Elephant miniature paperweight

About three inches long, this marigold elephant sold for $700 at the 1998 International auction.

Elephant powder jar

Another treasure from the collection of Carl and Eunice Booker.

Encore beer bottle

These marigold bottles are valued at under $10 without labels, about $25 with labels.

Eye cup

Marked "Clasco," marigold, sold for $175, 1997.

Fine Cut and Star

Miniature banana boat in marigold sold for $145 in 1994.

Firestone ashtray

These ashtrays are made with a miniature rubber tire encasing a glass ash holder. A blue example sold for $350 in 1994.

Flower Frogs

These are readily available in carnival. Marigold examples can be found for $5, sometimes less, other colors $10 or a little more.

Frog, covered candy dish

See Covered Frog

Globe bank

A charming bank well worth watching for. This example is courtesy of Carl and Eunice Booker.

Gem Dandy butter churn

Marigold, made by Alabama Manufacturing Co. Sold at a 1994 auction for $500.

Golden Wedding whiskey bottles

Best known of the various carnival whiskey bottles, Golden Wedding is found in five sizes; nip (1/10th pint), 1/2 pint, pint, quart, and two quart. These two have different closures, one with cork style (presumably older) and one with a screw top, both courtesy of Carl and Eunice Booker. Bottles with labels bring more money—the better the label, the better the price. Known only in marigold.

Nip (1/10 pint)	260	with label and contents
Nip (1/10 pint)	60–100	with label
Nip (1/10 pint)	25–50	no label
1/2 pint	15–25	with label
Pint	20–35	
Pint	220 (1997)	original cap and box
Quart	25–50	

Goodyear ashtray

Made in Argentina. A marigold example sold in 1993 for $100, another in 1998 for $110.

Grecian Goddess

This unusual fruit stand has a peacock tail-type green bowl (of the sort that appears to come with the Goddess of Athenia epergne) with a bronze-colored metal figure holding it up. Owner Don Lacock has no idea who made it, and I made up the name.

Hat, miniature

In blue, this hat is 3" long. It is from the collection of Jack and Eleanor Hamilton.

Hawaiian Lei child's sugar, Higbee

This 2¼" high miniature sugar bowl is marigold and courtesy of Jack and Eleanor Hamilton.

Honey pot

Found in a teal as well as marigold flashing, these pieces have two bees and a slot for a honey stick. Because the coloring is coated rather than fired on, they are subject to wear and scratching of the surface. They sell for between $40 and $80.

Horse Shoe shot glass

These marigold shot glasses sell for between $40 and $70.

Novelties/miniatures

Imperial paperweight

The Imperial paperweight is a low eight-sided tray with the Imperial NUCUT, Iron Cross, and NUART marks on the inside. It measure 5½" long by 3¼" wide and is 1¼" thick. Known only in purple, they bring between $600 and $1,000.

Insulators

There are several sizes of these marigold iridized electrical insulators available, including various types of Corning Pyrex. Most sell in the $15 to $25 range. The large ones, called "sombreros," bring $40 to $50.

Jalopy

This marigold miniature was probably a candy container. It is 4½" long and is from the John and Lucile Britt collection.

Jelly jar, covered
Marigold, sold for $50 in 1998.

Joan of Arc
A marigold smelling salts bottle sold for $100 in 1997, but one in 1996 brought only $10.

LBJ hat ashtray

These ashtrays were probably made late in the carnival era—but certainly prior to LBJ himself. They sell in the $20 to $30 range.

Liberty Bell bank

Yet another bank. Like most, it was made later, probably during the Depression and into the 1950s. Generally can be had for $10 to $25, more with a label on the bottom.

Lion miniature paperweight

A realistically rendered piece, this lion was probably intended as a paperweight and is about four inches long. From the John and Lucile Britt collection.

Little Barrels, Imperial

These little bottles probably contained some sort of liquid, perhaps whiskey samples. In 1997, Jim Seeck auctioned a marigold example with a Durer Bros, Cazenovia, Wisc. label for $215. In 1998, a marigold bottle with a printed band circling the middle sold for $260 at a Mickey Reichel auction.

Green	110–200
Marigold	45–80
Smoke	100–175
Teal	130 (1998)

Lucky barrel bank

From the collection of Carl and Eunice Booker. When found, these banks usually sell for between $15 and $25, although one sold at a 1998 Mickey Reichel auction for $65.

Minnesota toothpick holder

A marigold three-handled toothpick holder in this US Glass pattern sold at a 1994 Jim Seeck auction for $155.

Monkey bottle

I didn't see this item and can only assume the name accurately describes it. Listed as marigold and brought $200 at a 1994 auction.

My Lady's powder jar

While this powder jar was probably produced late in the Carnival era (as were many of the figural powder jars), it is of such outstanding design and rarity that it commands a price of around $150.

Narcissus and Ribbon bottle

This marigold bottle is notable for being the actual one that Marion Hartung drew for her book illustration of the pattern. The stopper has a circle of silver in the top. Courtesy of Bob and Geneva Leonard.

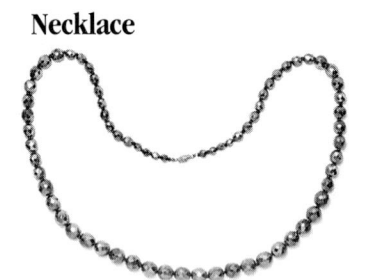

Necklace

I've seen very few single-strand necklaces made of carnival beads. This one sold at a 1996 Jim Seeck auction for $30. A similar one brought $25 and a multi-strand version sold for $25 at the same auction. Other multi-strand necklaces have sold for up to $40 or so.

Novelties/miniatures 319

Nude Lady epergne

What can one say? This has to be one of the most unusual combinations of carnival glass and chrome-plated metal known. The bowls are marigold and it sold at a Mickey Reichel auction in 1995 for $450.

Old Charter

A marigold whiskey bottle brought $30 at a 1995 auction.

Owl, figural

This yellowish marigold owl miniature sold at a 1993 Tom Burns auction for $200.

Pastel Swan

See Swan salt

Penny match holder

In the days when matches were common household objects, such holders were easily found. This example, in purple, is courtesy of Carl and Ferne Schroeder. Similar pieces have sold in the $1,000 range lately.

Perfume atomizers

Most of these perfume atomizers use a spray mechanism patented by Thomas DeVilbiss of Toledo, Ohio in 1922. Bottles were found in glass other than carnival, and some were made in Europe. I have records of sales with prices from $13 to more than $200. The atomizers above, with marigold bottles, sold for $40 (small) and $125 (tall). In 1997 a marigold atomizer listed as Rubicon Tiny Hobnail in its original box sold for $75.

Picture Frame

While this peculiar piece is called "Picture Frame," that's not what it is. Although a picture can be placed behind the hole, there are no fittings to hold it, there is no hanger or stand, and the extremely heavy glass used would not be practical for such a purpose. The piece measures almost eight inches square. This example sold at the 1995 Heart of America auction for $600. At least one other is known, and it has excess glass around the edges that would have later been trimmed. Note that this item has been reproduced as a club souvenir—and should be marked appropriately.

Piggy banks

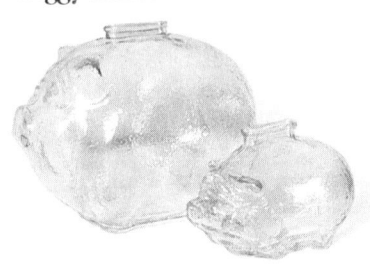

Not in great demand, the larger of these two piggy banks brought $35, the smaller $17.50. Both sold at a Mickey Reichel auction in 1995. I have seen the smaller bank, the most frequently found bank in any pattern, selling at flea markets for less than $10.

Pipe match holder

Few objects could be more appropriate for holding matches than this miniature pipe—although it is sometimes called a toothpick holder. Marigold, usually sells in the $40 to $75 range.

Polo ashtray

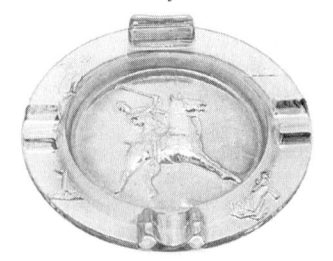

These marigold items usually bring between $15 and $25 at auction.

Poodle powder jar

These late-carnival items are valued at $30 to $50.

Prince Matchabelli

In 1993, a Prince Matchabelli perfume bottle brought $30 at the Heart of America auction.

Rabbit banks

Amazingly similar to the pig banks, but more desirable—probably because of their novelty. Each of these marigold banks sold for $90 at a 1994 auction. I'm not sure how the price was justified, but one of the smaller banks brought $315 at another 1994 auction.

Rexford child's butter, Higbee

Could there have actually been complete table sets in this pattern for children? Such small pieces are very rare. Courtesy of Jack and Eleanor Hamilton.

Novelties/miniatures

Roth Bros. Meat Market ashtray

There was a time when custom glass objects were so cheap to manufacture that many relatively small organizations could afford to give them away. This ashtray was apparently a sales premium for a meat market—or so the lettering on the ashtray implies. Courtesy of Carl and Eunice Booker.

Sandal

So far, this is the only such piece reported. It is marigold and 4½" long. It brought $400 at the John and Lucile Britt auction (Jim Seeck) in 1994.

Scroll Embossed ashtray, Sowerby

It looks a lot like the Imperial design, but this piece was made by the English company, Sowerby. As of this writing none have sold recently although this one, from the collection of Don Kime and the late Roland Kuhn, is due for sale soon.

Shells, Westmoreland

These footed shells are found in two sizes in a variety of colors. The large amethyst above sold for $20, the small marigold for $22.50, both at a 1995 Mickey Reichel Auction. Here are other prices:

Large
Amethyst	10–20	
Blue opal	250 (1997)	
Green	15–25	
Marigold	15–25	
Mar/milk glass	185 (1994)	
Peach opal	250 (1997)	
White	65	damage

Small
Amethyst	25–40
Green	25–45
Marigold	20–30
Teal	35–55

Shinola shoe polish bottle

In 1996 a Shinola shoe polish bottle, described as the small size in clear, sold for $20.

Shoe bottle

Why so much fascination with feet? There seem to be an inordinate number of foot-related novelties in carnival. Perhaps it is the unexpected character that one finds in the combination of feet and glass. This pastel marigold carnival bottle, a shoe with the big toe sticking through, brought $165 at a 1994 auction. What might it have contained? Foot lotion? Gout medicine? Whiskey?

Shoes, miniature

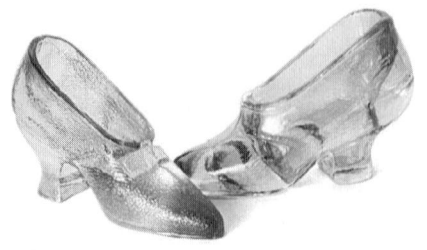

These miniature glass shoes, usually marigold, are very desirable. They are known in several varieties and by several names (Lady Slipper, High Heeled Shoe, Wooden Shoe, etc.). They are valued at $60 to $100, with an occasional example selling up to $150. In 1998 a red Lady Slipper (dated 1938) sold for $225 and a marigold skater's shoe for $225.

Shriner's champagne glasses, Westmoreland

These convention souvenir glasses have long been credited to US Glass. However, in a 1996 book by Chas West Wilson, grandson of the founder of Westmoreland (who was an avid Shriner), evidence is shown that these were actually products of the Westmoreland factory in Grapeville, Pennsylvania.

1908 St. Paul (3rd from left, above)
Ruby flashing   55–95

1908 St. Paul sheath of wheat toothpick or shot glass
Ruby flashing   100–200

1909 Louisville, tobacco leaf (2nd from left)
Clear   70–100   probably most common

1909 Los Angeles toothpick or shot glass
Cranberry   70–120

1910 New Orleans, alligators (far right)
Clear   80–140   fairly common

1911 Rochester, painted camel rider (left)
Clear   75–130   fairly common

1911 Rochester double shot glass
Cranberry   85 (1994)

1917 donkey tumbler
Milk glass   85 (1994)

Slinky Snake

With a dark carnival glass head, $675, 1996.

Star paperweight

Marigold item sold for $1,400 at Tom Burns auction in 1996.

Sun Punch bottle

Apparently soda pop bottlers thought that iridized bottles would make their product more attractive. This lightly iridized marigold Sun Punch bottle, with its unusual shape, sold for $75 at a 1996 auction. While there is a cork in the top, the rim seems to be designed to take a standard metal cap.

Swag and Bracket toothpick

This amethyst toothpick, thought to be old, sold for $195 at an auction in 1996.

Swan, large

This marigold open swan is almost 10 inches long and sold for $95 at the 1997 Heart of America auction. I couldn't determine its age and it has no markings.

Swan paperweight

Miniature item in marigold sold for $145.

Novelties/miniatures

Swan salt, or pastel

These miniature swans are readily available in a range of colors. They were made by a number of companies as indicated by the slightly different designs on the wings and body. They are often called "Pastel Swans." The example shown on the right is typical of the shape. The piece on the left, with the beak resting on its chest, is the only known whimsey. It is teal blue and brought $1,200 at a 1995 Jim Seeck auction. The regular one is amethyst and sold for $175 at the same auction. Note that these have been reproduced.

Amber	200–250	rare color
Amethyst/purple	125–200	scarce color
Aqua/teal	1,200 (1995)	whimsey, one known
Blue opal	50–80	rare color
Celeste blue	30–50	very common color
Green	130 (1994)	
Green opal	50 (1994)	
Ice blue	75 (1995)	
Ice green	40–60	most common color
Lime green	40–70	scarce color
Marigold	150–250	scarce color
Olive green	550 (1994)	
Peach opal	180–325	scarce color
Pink	30–50	common color
Sapphire	550 (1998)	
Vaseline	60–90	
Vaseline opal	185–300	rare color
White	300–450	rare color

Tappan toy creamer

A marigold toy creamer sold for $85 in 1993.

Tiny Hobnail

This child's tumbler in marigold sold for $225 at a Tom Burns auction in 1994.

Telephone

Another unexpected shape, this time in a white carnival telephone that may have held candy (a cardboard cover would have been inserted in the bottom). The piece is 4¼" tall. Courtesy of Carl and Eunice Booker.

Thumbprint and Star

A miniature shot glass in marigold sold at a 1993 Tom Burns auction for $130.

Town Pump, Northwood

See Vases

Trophy toothpick holder

One of many available toothpick holders, this example is marigold with clear handles is 3⅜" high, and a souvenir of Detroit. It sold at a 1995 auction for $280. One with red flashing sold at a 1996 auction for $75.

Vogue, Fostoria

This toothpick holder in marigold sold for $275 at a 1994 Tom Burns auction.

Votive Light, Crystalis Mexico

Shown from both sides, the Votive Light is 4¾" tall. This example is from the collection of the late Bob Gallo. Found only in marigold, an example sold for $325 at a 1994 Jim Seeck auction and another at a 1997 Seeck auction for $800, and a third at the 1998 Texas club auction for $475.

Washtub novelty salt dip

With wood grained texture, a marigold example sold at a 1994 auction.

Welch paperweight
Cobalt/dark   25–40

Wheelbarrow ashtray

A marigold example sold at the 1993 Heart of America auction for $410.

Witch's Pot

Usually with souvenir lettering. Marigold sell in the $200 to $300 range.

Wreathed Cherry in bracket

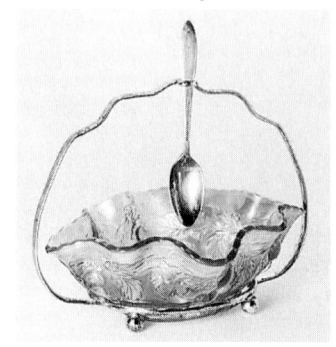

Occasionally a piece of carnival would be combined with a specially made bracket, sometimes silverplate, other times black-painted metal. Whether the glassmaker commissioned the bracket or the package was put together by a third party is unknown. This particular piece, a small Dugan Wreathed Cherry oval ruffled sauce, came complete with a spoon. It sold for $60 at a Jim Seeck auction in 1995.

Decorated carnival glass

Glass was often decorated well before the Carnival era, of course, but it certainly seems to have found a special niche here. The decorated water sets are the most often seen and they are quite dramatic. There were, however, many other shapes that were decorated, including bowls, table sets, and many small individual pieces.

Decorated carnival is sometimes identified by the name of the decor, sometimes by the name of the underlying glass pattern. At times though, when you run across a piece, it may be difficult to identify it at all.

There seems to be little in the way of a general reference for all shapes of enameled pieces but you may want to purchase a copy of Cecil Whitley's book *The World of Enameled Carnival Glass Tumblers*. As of this writing, it is available from her (see the Resources section). The Heart of America Carnival Glass Association Notebook has a section on enameled pitchers. Glen and Stephen Thistlewood have written extensively on enameled patterns in their journal, *Network,* as well as in various club newsletters.

Absentee Grape and Lotus, Fenton

This curious ruffled bowl has no mold-work for the grape part of the pattern. Instead, enameled flowers decorate that portion of the bowl. The glass is blue and the piece sold at a 1993 auction by Tom Burns for $1,450. It was listed as one of two known.

Apple Blossom, Northwood

The decorated flowers are easy to distinguish from other designs as they are the only ones with large overlapping blossoms. These two pieces of Apple Blossom must have set the record for decorated water set pieces. The tumbler brought $255 and the pitcher $1,500 at the 1998 Heart of America auction (Jim Seeck). The pieces are quite rare, these being the only such items to sell in recent years.

326 A Field Guide to Carnival Glass

Apple Blossoms is one of the few enameled patterns to be found on table sets and berry sets. The few known examples are all blue. This spooner sold at a 1996 auction for $125. In 1993, a berry set on blue base glass brought $600.

Barber bottles, decorated

Cranberry	110 (1996)
Gray	70 (1996)
Marigold	100 (1996)

Barley and Hops

In 1998 a beer pitcher in marigold sold for $160 and an accompanying tumbler for $50.

Booker

Carl and Eunice Booker found the first known example of these decorated cider mugs, so Bill Edwards named the pattern for them. The glass is clear, with a delicate marigold overlay and nicely rendered flowers. These pieces sold at a 1994 auction; the pitcher brought $600, the mugs $160 each. Note the unusual shape of the mugs.

Cherries, Dugan

Dugan decorated a number of their patterns with floral themes. In this case it is their widely found Panelled Cherries pattern. It's in peach opal and sold at the 1996 Heart of America auction for $185, several times what the unembellished peach opal bowls bring.

Cherries

This blue tumbler is probably the most frequently seen enameled carnival pattern. According to Cecil Whitley, the pattern is also found on straight-sided tumblers as well as with red-painted cherries—usually the cherries are white. While tumblers usually sell in the $30 to $40 range, particularly nice examples can bring up to $60.

Here the decoration covers a pitcher known as a "cannonball." There are several variations of the Cherries pitcher—Cherries, Cherries and Little Flowers, and Cherries and Blossoms. This pitcher

Decorated carnival

and six tumblers, all blue, sold at a 1998 David Ayers auction.

Water set, 7 piece
Blue 200–300
Water pitcher
Blue 125–200
Tumbler
Blue 20–30

Columbine, Fenton

One of the most frequently seen pitchers, Columbine (it doesn't resemble the flower, but that's the name this pattern has come to be known as) is found in amethyst/purple, marigold, blue and green. This purple example sold for $325 in 1996. A blue pitcher sold for $425 at a 1995 Jim Seeck auction; another in blue sold in 1997 for $350.

Connie

An example of this decorated pitcher in white brought $800 at the 1995 Texas club auction. Five white tumblers brought $175 each at the same time.

Covered jar

This pretty covered jar, in marigold with red flowers, is 4⅝" tall (to the top of the finial). Courtesy of Carl and Eunice Booker.

Crocus

This tumbler shows the typical pattern although there are several variations, some with just one flower. In marigold they sell for $15 to $20, white about $30. A 7-piece water set in marigold sold for $190 in 1994. A white pitcher and two tumblers sold for $200 in 1997, and marigold pitchers sell in the $100 range.

Dahlia, Dugan

Dugan often took advantage of the distinctive flowers in its Dahlia pattern by painting them with red, blue, or gold, and occasionally, red and gold. Most shapes in the pattern can be found so decorated, but are invariably on white carnival. The sugar above has red-decorated flowers and sold for $140 at a 1993 Seeck auction. Here are others:

Berry, large	200 (1996)	red/gold trim
Berry, small	50 (1996)	red/gold trim
Butter, covered	210 (1995)	gold trim
Creamer	135 (1995)	gold trim
Pitcher, water	900 (1997)	gold trim
Tumbler	150 (1995)	blue trim
Tumbler	125–215	gold trim

Daisy and Little Flowers, Northwood

Aside from being part of a water set, tumblers are popular collectibles on their own. This one, in blue, sold at a 1995 Mickey Reichel auction for $50.

Dianthus, Fenton

The pitcher is Dianthus and the tumblers Shasta Daisy on prism band, both by Fenton. The base glass is ice green. The pitcher brought $425, the tumblers $55 each when they sold in 1994. In 1996 another pitcher in ice green brought $400 and in 1998 a white pitcher sold for $175.

Dotted Diamonds and Daisies, Fenton

Distinguished by its small dotted diamonds on both the pitcher and tumbler, this design is found on Fenton's Drapery pitcher. Although seldom seen, the marigold pitcher and four tumblers sold for just $150 in 1998—probably because of a crack near the pitcher's handle.

Double Daisy, Fenton

Daisies were apparently popular flowers, or at least the name was. This deep marigold pitcher sold for $135 at a 1996 Jim Seeck auction. Another by this same name, also in marigold, brought $185 at a 1997 Mickey Reichel auction. The pitcher comes in two styles.

Floral Spray

This beautifully decorated pitcher and tumbler are of clear glass with multicolor iridescence. They are from the collection of John and Lucile Britt who, as far as I know, were never able to determine the maker. The pitcher sold for $375, the tumbler for $30 at a 1998 auction.

Forget-me-not, Fenton

On the Forget-me-not pitcher, the smallish flowers are in two groups above and below the diagonal prism band. On the tumbler, the single flower is largely below the prism band. This pitcher and tumbler in marigold are courtesy of Lee Markley. A blue pitcher and tumbler sold for $425 in 1993. In 1995, a marigold five-piece water set sold for $400, and a marigold seven-piece set sold for $300 in 1996. In 1998, a blue pitcher with three good tumblers and two chipped ones sold for $1,150. Green tumblers sell for $20 to $30, marigold a bit less.

Iris, Fenton

With an exceedingly elegant shape, this decorated diagonal band pitcher and six tumblers sold as a set for $1,300 at the 1995 Air Capital club auction (Jim Seeck). The pieces are green, a scarce color. A marigold seven-piece set sold for $850, also in 1995. That same year an amethyst pitcher brought $700 and a marigold one sold for $800. Blue tumblers sell in the $25 range, amethyst or marigold about twice that. In 1997, an amethyst water set sold for $800.

Lotus, Fenton

Quite a scarce set. The pitcher, which is the cannon-ball drapery shape, has a very large centered lotus in white with green leaves at the sides. Most tumblers have a centered blossom with green leaves on either side connected to the blossom with horizontal stems, although there can be some variation in this arrangement. This water set, in marigold with six tumblers, sold for $165 at a 1993 auction. A green pitcher sold for $600, also in 1993.

Magnolia and Drape, Fenton

The drape part of the pitcher is in the glass. This pitcher, in marigold, brought $175 at a 1995 Mickey Reichel auction; the tumbler $20. Other marigold pitchers have sold in the $100 range; tumblers bring $20 to $40. Berry sets and table sets are also known—all marigold, all rare, and all pedestalled except for the butter dish.

Miscellaneous

A surprising variety of carnival shapes have been decorated, including this miniature rosebowl, miniature syrup, and small mug. All are courtesy of Carl and Eunice Booker.

More decorated pieces from Carl and Eunice Booker, this time a wine glass and two cordials.

Open Edge, Fenton

Fenton decorated an occasional basket. This ice blue one, for example, has gold striping between the pairs of lattice and circling just below the lattices. It brought $500 at a 1994 auction.

Shasta Daisy, Fenton

The Shasta Daisy is found on Fenton's Zig Zag pitcher is found in marigold, white, as well as the ice green shown here, owned by Ed Radcliff. Tumblers can be seen grouped with the Dianthus pitcher on page 328. White pitchers bring $300 to $350, marigold $100 to $150.

Decorated carnival

Silver Queen, Fenton

A bulbous pitcher, the decoration is created with multiple bands of silver containing simple floral designs enameled onto the bands. The iridescence is marigold and this pitcher sold for $25 at a 1994 auction. Silver Queen is also found in more of a tankard style pitcher. Tumblers are valued at $15 to $20.

Ski Star, Dugan

A peach opal handgrip plate with enameled decoration sold for $450 at a 1998 Tom Burns auction.

Stein

In marigold, this stein has a spray of flowers on the drinking side of the glass. The metal is pewter. It sold for $140 at a 1998 Mickey Reichel auction.

Stippled Petals, Dugan

Peach opal seems to make a nice background for painted designs. It's dark enough that white paint shows well, yet vivid colors stand out as well. This bowl, with the usual dome foot, is owned by Carl and Ferne Schroeder. A ruffled bowl in peach opal with decoration sold for $55 in 1998. Dugan Single Flower bowls in peach opal bring $85 to $100 when decorated. Dugan's Stippled Flower bowls are also found with enameled flowers. A number of flower designs can be found on each pattern.

Swallow

A clear water pitcher brought $375 at the International auction in 1998, a clear tumbler $25. Marigold tumblers are worth $35 to $50.

Wreathed Cherry, Dugan

Dugan frequently painted specific parts of its pieces, rather than simply adding flowers to the background. This Wreathed Cherry tumbler in white with red-decorated cherries is a good example. It brought $75 at a 1998 auction (although it had minor damage).

Lamps and shades

Carnival lamps and shades

The classic Carnival glass era of 1907 to 1925 bridged the transition from gas and oil lights to electric lamps, so we have a considerable variety of illuminating devices available in carnival.

In spite of the variety, lamps are not frequently seen and when they are, usually bring a good price. Carnival glass shades, on the other hand, are relatively easy to find—at least the fairly plain marigold ones.

Collecting of the lamps and shades tends to be a pretty specialized subset of carnival collecting itself. It is a rare auction that has more than a couple of related items, and those often go to lamp collectors rather than to carnival glass collectors.

Necessarily, this section presents just an overview of the lamps available. A good source for additional information is Helen Greguire's book, *Carnival in Lights*. It shows many patterns in full color although it does not reflect current prices. Unfortunately, it's a self-published book and is quite hard to find.

Gone with the wind lamps

These huge lamps are characterized by their two glass globes—the lower to hold oil or kerosene and the top covering the chimney. The pattern shown here is Regal Iris and is marigold on milk glass. It sold for $6,500 at a 1997 Jim Seeck auction. Another sold in 1997 for $4,000 and others have brought more than $8,000 in the recent past. Bear in mind that the Regal Iris lamp has been reproduced in aqua opal, cranberry, and red. Other GWTW-style lamps that sell in the above price range are Roses and Ruffles and Sunken Hollyhock.

Table-size oil lamps

Basketweave and Cable
Not truly a miniature but quite small at 7" to the top of the shade. This green lamp brought $750 at the 1994 HOACGA convention auction. It's the only one I've seen.

Hobnail and honeycomb lamps
The hobnail and honeycomb lamps on the left sold in 1994. The hobnail brought $70 and the honeycomb $60. Both are marigold but neither may be old. The hobnail lamp on the right, in green, sold for $175 at the 1998 Heart of America auction. It measures 8½" to the top of the shade, 10½" to top of the chimney.

Diamond Quilted peg lamp
This is an interesting variation of the oil lamp. It's designed to fit into a candlestick—here a swirl candlestick. This one, in marigold, sold for $100 at a 1994 auction with the candlestick.

Little Jewel
This little jewel is exactly that as those words are molded into the side. It measures 3⅜" to the top of the neck and has a 2½" base. Owned by Jack and Eleanor Hamilton.

Grape and Cable
While not exactly common, these miniature lamps made from perfume bottles are occasionally found. I've never heard of any color except purple. They sell in the $400 range—somewhat less than the perfume bottles with stopper.

Lincoln Drape, Daisy Button/Thumbprint
The prices that the miniature lamps bring always surprises me. These two sold at a 1994 auction. The Lincoln Drape (left) in marigold went for $950; the Daisy Button/Thumbprint in marigold on milk glass brought $600.

Lamps and shades

Queen's Lamp
This large green lamp with a pinched-in waist is quite rare. I know of three and have heard that there are several others. This one is courtesy of Lee Markley. An identical one brought $900 at a 1998 Tom Burns auction.

Wreathed Medallion
The auctioneer was unsure of this name at the 1994 auction where this item sold. It is green and has a metal base. The selling price was $125.

Swirl
Also a miniature, the Swirl lamp is seen only in marigold. Sells in the $100 to $200 range.

Zipper Loop, Imperial
Zipper Loop is the most widely available oil lamp in carnival glass. It is found in marigold and smoke in a variety of base diameters and heights. Any of these lamps, in either color, will sell in the $400 to $700 range—depending on condition and the quality of the iridescence. The exception is the finger lamp, shown on the left in the photo above, that brings $900 to $1,500 in marigold and up to $2,400 in smoke. It's worth pointing out that the regular lamp was reproduced by Imperial with an IG mark that is difficult to find (on the side of the inside base). The repros sell for around $100 in marigold and about $150 for smoke.

Wild Rose, Millersburg
This rare lamp is found in three base sizes: 5", 5⅜", and 6⅛"; and in green, amethyst, and marigold. Green is the most commonly seen color and brings $1,100 to $1,700. Marigold and amethyst are in the $2,000 to $3,000 range. The even more rare variation with a Ladies Head medallion sells for more than $4,000 in amethyst and a one-of-a-kind with intaglio rose interior in amethyst brought $5,700 in 1996.

Lamps, electric

Frankly, I'm a little uneasy with many of these electric lamps. They often bring pretty good money, yet the fixtures in many instances are relatively new and simply have an old carnival shade attached. Buyer beware.

Brass desk lamp with August Flower shade
This example sold for $125 at a 1993 auction.

Princess boudoir lamp, US Glass
A lot of controversy surrounds this lamp. The base is known to have been made by US Glass and is found sometimes with a cloth shade. Yet the above version, with a shade made from an inverted Lined Lattice squatty vase, is also widely seen. Lined Lattice was of course made by Dugan. They are highly desirable, selling in the $500 to $900 range with either shade.

Here is a brief listing of other table or desk lamps that have sold in recent years:

Clambroth Leaf Tiers shade on table lamp, $125 (1996)

Two marigold on moonstone ribbed shades on table lamp, $100 (1996)

Two pearlized Laurel shades on table lamp, $105 (1996)

Marigold Coral Shell shade on brass lamp, $110 (1993)

Two marigold Primrose Panel shades on double-neck lamp, $135, (1993)

Two white Buzzsaw shades on double-neck lamp, marble base, $200 (1993)

Marigold shade handpainted with mountain scene on table lamp, $400 (1996)

Marigold shade handpainted with windmill on table lamp, $325 (1993)

Two marigold shades handpainted with castle scene, on brass double-neck lamp, $195 (1993)

Three marigold Fine Panel shades on 21½" brass lamp, $325 (1995)

Brass double-neck lamp with Dragon's Tongue shades
These shades are marigold on moonstone. The lamp sold for $275 in 1993. Another of similar description sold for $550 in 1995.

Panelled floral shade on metal desk lamp
This example, with a marigold shade, brought $250 in 1996.

Lamps and shades 337

Lamp bases

A few patterns are found in large bulbous shapes that are intended as lamp bases—even if they have no electrical fittings or shades attached. Here are two examples:

Lovebirds, Phoenix

This red satin example sold for $110 in 1993. Another, complete as a table lamp, sold in 1995 for $225.

Peacock

These interesting bases are about 11" tall and quite commanding. They are always on frosted white base glass but enameled on the inside to achieve red or purple coloring (or left without enameling for a white effect). Iridescence is applied to the exterior. The base only in purple is worth about $500; wired as a lamp for about $100 more. Red lamps bring $800 to $1,300. White lamp bases are not as dramatic and bring only $200 to $250.

Chandeliers and hanging fixtures

As with table lamps, chandeliers seem to have been designed independently of the shades and may be found with almost any of the patterns. Here is a representative sample of these fixtures:

Hammered Bell chandelier

This five-shade fixture sold for $500 at a 1994 auction.

Pillar and Drape chandelier

Many chandeliers sported five individual lamps, but are also found with other numbers of lights and shades. This five-lamp chandelier with marigold on moonstone shades sold for $600 in 1994.

Here are other chandeliers or hanging fixtures:

Four Dragon's Tongue shades in marigold on milk glass, $375 (1995)

Four painted shades and center dome shade with winter scene, windmill, $800 (1993)

Three Nuart wide panel bell-shaped shades, $105 (1994)

Three smooth panel shades, marigold, $85 (1997)

Two Nuart stippled bell shades, $95 (1994)

Two Nuart etched bell-shaped shades, $115 (1994)

Single cut daisy (intaglio) shade, $45 (1994)

Single enameled cottage scene, $65 (1994)

Single painted shade in marigold: house, trees, lake, $250 (1993)

Shades

There are many patterns of carnival glass shades, some of which are extensions of other pattern lines. Most shades with little patterning sell in the $25 range; more elaborate patterning up to $50 or $60. Below are a few representative shades. Note that the wider shades, with a 4" rim, are intended for gas light fixtures.

Astral

Autumn Oak and Coral Shell

Daisy Chain and Imperial Grape

Pillar and Drape and Wide Panel

Prices for nondecorated shades: The following list provides typical prices for lamp shades. Bear in mind that because carnival shades are relatively scarce, prices can vary widely.

Arterial, 35–40
Astral, 15–20
August Flower, 50–70
Autumn Oak, 30–40
Daisy Chain, 35–55
Diamond Block, 35–45
Dragon's Tongue, marigold on milk glass, 40–65
Etched bell shape, 20
Etched grapes, 20
Frosted Panel, 30–35
Greek Key, 40–50
Hammered Bell, white, 25-40
Imperial Daisy, 25–40
Imperial Grape, 25–40
Leaf Tiers, marigold on milk glass, 35–65
Pillar and Drape, marigold on milk glass, 50–65
Primrose, 25
Ribbed, ruffled, 30
Simplicity, 15–25
Smooth panels (Wide Panel), 25–35
Soutache, swirl interior, 12", 135
Starlyte, 35
Wide Panel, 20–25

Painted shades

These shades are enameled with a variety of scenes ranging from lakes and castles to cottages and forests. Some of these have been found with Czechoslovakian labels.

Castle scene, 70
Mountain scene, 25
Mountain winter scene, 145, 165

Hatpins 339

Carnival Glass Hatpins

Unlike most Carnival shapes, there is little known about the provenance of hatpins. Some are found marked with the word "Geschutzt" which I am told means protected or patented in German. Czechoslovakia is also believed to have been the origin for many.

Something else to bear in mind is that nobody can state with any certainty exactly when most carnival glass hatpins were made. Indeed, there is ample evidence that they continue to be made up to this day.

Nonetheless, these miniature examples of the commercial glassmaker's art exude charm. Some rarities can bring in excess of four figures at auction.

Two books are musts for the hatpin collector:

Alphonse Tvaryanas illustrated examples of hatpins in a book he produced in 1991. Jerry Ferris Reynolds produced a book of hatpin photographs, some in color, in 1994. Both books are listed in the Resources section.

I'd like to thank several carnival collectors who shared their hatpins with me and my camera. In particular, thanks are due to Carl and Eunice Booker (whose collection is included in several other references) and Barton and Sue Dooley—who seem to find many unusual hatpins.

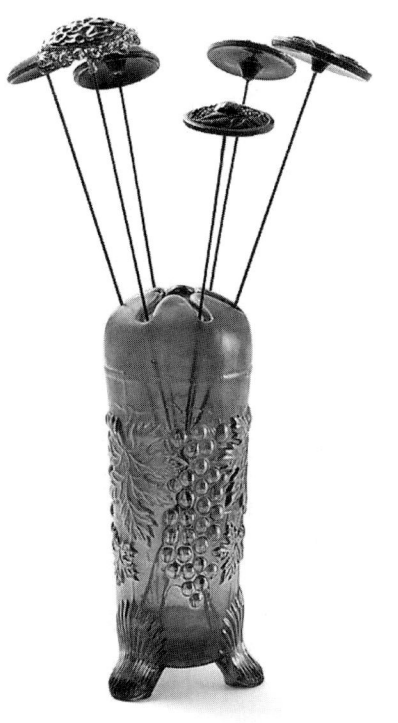

At the turn of the twentieth century, every lady used hatpins to keep her hat attached to her often voluminous hair. The hatpins, of course, had to be stored and displayed somehow, so hatpin holders were made for this market, some in carnival. Most often seen are the Northwood Grape and Cable (above) and Fenton's Butterfly and Berry and Orange Tree.

Banded Berry Cluster

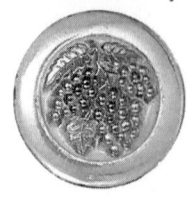

This pattern is also known by several other names including Grape Cluster. I've only heard of it in lavender and purple. Priced at $100 to $150 for the lavender, a bit less for the purple.

Banded Criss Cross

Relatively scarce, but because of the rather ordinary design it doesn't bring much as hatpins go. Worth $90 to $140.

Banded Flower

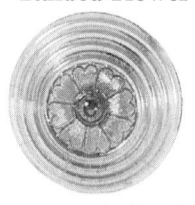

For want of a formal name, I've named this one Banded Flower. It's the only example I've seen and is lavender—and sold for $85 at a 1993 auction.

Bars and Beads

A straightforward design seen only in dark glass. It sells in the $80 to $100 range.

Basketflower

Also known as Sunflower Basket, this hatpin has been found in fairly large quantities and always in dark glass with bluish iridescence. It is currently selling for $40 to $60.

Basketweave

The basketweave theme is popular throughout carnival glass and there are several other hatpin patterns with the design. This one, always in dark glass, is in the $80 to $110 price range.

Beaded Fringe

I've never seen one of these although Tvaryanas illustrates one in his book; it has the typical slight dome covered with beads that continue down to make a fringe. A hatpin by this name, with multicolor beads, sold in 1994 for $255.

Beaded Pinwheel

A rather pleasing design and quite rare. I've never seen one for sale.

Bee on Flower

A very pretty hatpin with a naturalistic design. Known only in dark or purple glass and sells for $550 to $600.

Bee on Honeycomb

This is the only one of these I've seen. It was listed as amber and sold at auction in 1994 for $150. An amber example sold for $125 in 1998.

Belle

Not many of these around. Two sold in 1995 for $220 and $375; another in 1997 for $75. Go figure.

Big Butterfly

These oval hatpins are sometimes called Scarab or Egyptian Butterfly. They're an interesting design although pretty common. Always dark in color and sell in the $40 to $60 range.

Hatpins 341

Bird of Paradise

A rare hatpin in a private collection. The design is basically on dark glass with the center bead an amethyst color.

Border Path

Often called Squares and Triangles or Garden Path, this piece is always dark and sells for between $60 and $100.

Border Path variant

Very rare, this one is in a private collection.

Diamond Sphere, Bullet, and Oval Sphere

Diamond Sphere (left) has sold for as much as $375 although the most recent price was $210. Bullet (center) is in the $100 range; Oval Sphere (right) brings $50 to $90.

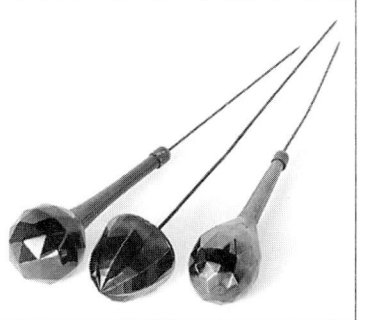

Bubbles

This dark hatpin sold for $450 at auction in 1995.

Bumblebee
See Dragonflies

Butler's Mirror

Some call this pattern Greek Key because of the design around the edge. Always dark in color and sells for $25 to $50.

Cane

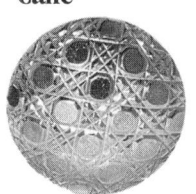

This is not the official name; but then I don't know that there is one—so this will have to do. In a private collection.

Cattails
See Six Plums

Cherries

These are smallish and have hanging fruit. Two sold in 1997—for $325 and $375, and another in 1998 for $250.

Concentric Circles

This lavender hatpin sold at a 1995 auction for $185.

Coolie Hat

When viewed from the side these hatpins appear shaped like the traditional Chinese headgear—thus the name. Only known in purple and bring $40 to $60.

Daisy and Button

I've not seen this pattern but a dark one sold for $110 in 1997.

Diamond and Oval

This pattern has a diamond superimposed over an oval base. It's in a private collection.

Dimples and Brilliants

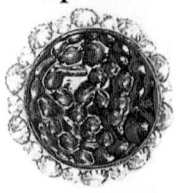

These fairly common hatpins have a circle of rhinestones (brilliants) around a dimpled dark center. They sell in the $60 to $80 range.

Dinner Ring

This is the only one of these I've seen. It was named by the owner after a similar button.

Dogwood

There are several similar designs called Dogwood and have sold at auction for $220 to $490. This particular one has gold decoration between the groups of flowers and is in a private collection.

Double Crown

These brownish hatpins seldom bring as much as $40 at auction.

Dragonflies

An intriguing design but, unfortunately, very common. In the $25 to $35 range.

Elegance

Often seen with a bright blue iridescence, these dark hatpins are found in two sizes. The large are worth $150 to $250, the small about 30% less.

Embroidered Circles

An obvious name, these dark or purple hatpins sell for between $100 and $200.

Faceted Butterfly

A really elegant design in black, or dark, glass. It is in a private collection.

Faceted Dome

A dark hatpin of average availability and desirability. Worth $60 to $100.

Faceted Oval

Although I have seen these rather simple hatpins sell for more than $100, they are realistically in the $40 to $50 range.

Fancy Beetle

These hatpins have the word "Geschutzt" on the back. Sell for $400 to $500.

Ferris Wheel

Not many of these around. This dark example sold for $500 at auction in 1995.

Hatpins 343

Floral Spray

Quite unusual with two flowers and bracket devices arranged around the hatpin. It is amethyst and was sold as the Two Flowers pattern when it brought $235 in 1993. A hatpin named Floral Spray sold for $125 in 1998.

Flower Arcs

Also called Garden Path, this dark hatpin brought $145 at a 1995 auction.

Flower and Jewel
See Orchid

Flower Petals

I've not seen this hatpin, but a dark example sold for $350 in 1998 at the Texas club auction.

Flying Bat

In my book, the best designed hatpin, bar none. Marvelous execution of the theme, and with a striking shape. Iridescence is usually quite good, too. Purple or dark glass. Generally sell in the $100 to $160 range.

Four of Hearts
See Hearts and Cross

Fuchsia Basket

Fairly large, measuring 2 inches in height. This example, in aqua blue, sold for the princely sum of $2,100 in 1995. It's also known in green.

Garden Path
See Flower Arcs

Grape

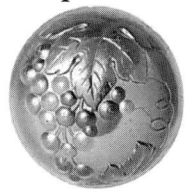

I've not seen other examples of this pattern nor can I find any in my sales listings. This one is lavender and privately owned.

Hearts and Cross

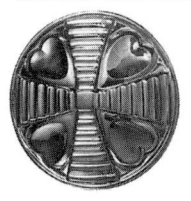

Also known as Four of Hearts. This example sold for $325 in 1995, another for $135, also in 1995, and a third in 1998 for $200.

Hex Dome

Examples of hatpins by this name sell for $35 to $65.

Horsefly

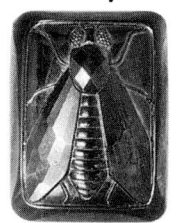

A very unusual shape for a hatpin—and a wonderful insect. Insects seemed to be popular, although one wonders why a lady would like such a thing in her hair. This one is from a private collection.

Jute Braid

Known also by the alternate name of Basketweave variant. These sell normally in the $80 to $150 range although one sold for $400 in 1995.

Laurel Jewel

This is the only example of this dark glass hatpin I've seen and none have sold in recent years. It's from a private collection.

Leaf and Veil

Sometimes listed as Leaf and Veiling, two examples sold in 1995—one for $75 and the other for $675. I have no idea as to why the difference.

Looped Buckle

Dark and quite a rare item. One of these sold in 1997 for $155.

Lots of Diamonds

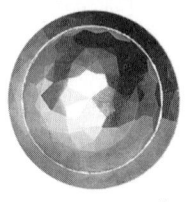

From a private collection, this dark hatpin is similar to many with the word "faceted" in the name.

Marvelous

Rhinestones in a gold setting surrounding a dark five-petal pin make up this unusual piece. This one sold for $500 in 1995.

Metal framed

Interesting, although I'm hard pressed to call these truly carnival. The design is in metal that overlays a flat iridescent disk. Eight of these sold as a lot at a 1995 auction for $105 each. In 1998, five similar items sold for $10 to $25.

Moiré Beetle

Sometimes called Moiré Scarab or Moiré Taffeta because it looks like the fabric. The word Moiré is pronounced moray, thus you'll sometimes see them listed as Moray Beetle hatpins. Always dark and sell for $25 to $35.

Nautical

I've suggested this name as the metal frame looks like rope as does the design around the edge of the glass. There are five anchor-type objects radiating from the center. The color was listed as clambroth at the 1993 auction where it sold for $235.

Orchid

Also called Flower and Jewel. This example is from a private collection but one sold in 1997 for $550 and another in 1994 for $850.

Oval Diamond Cut

A pin by this name sold at a 1998 auction for $155.

Owl

Owls were favorite subjects for carnival hatpins and several varieties are found. The most common are these pastel pieces found in green and lavender ($1,000 to $1,200), and marigold ($2,000).

Owl, Horned

Even more rare is the horned version (just above the eye feathers). One of these sold in 1997 for $1,800.

Hatpins 345

Owl, metal frame

This example, in a private collection, is secured to a metal frame (note the edge).

Owl, Tiny

Somewhat smaller than other owl hatpins. Such an item sold in 1995 for $350.

Paisley

A lavender example sold in 1998 for $30.

Penstar

These usually have a very attractive blue iridescence on dark glass and have been selling for $200 to $400. In late 1997, however, it was reported that this pattern is currently being made in the Czech Republic. One of these sold in early 1998 for $180.

Pheasant

See Top o' The Morning

Piazza

A rather busy design that brings $400 to $500 at auction.

Propeller

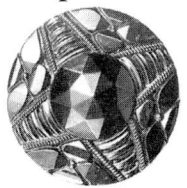

This is the only example of this pattern I've seen. It is dark and sold for $700 in 1995.

Rectangular Diamonds

An unusually shaped hatpin in a private collection.

Ribbon Triangle

Not many around. One of these sold in 1996 for $400.

Rooster

These hatpins are found in a variety of colors and paint schemes. This one is lavender with the background painted black and the rooster's comb painted red (the dark area on his back is a shadow from where the pin is attached). The other colors are amber, aqua/teal, blue, celeste, green, ice blue, red, sapphire, and white. All sell for $40 to $80 although, depending on the condition, paint combination, and auction dynamics, they can sell for as little as $35 or as much as $180.

Scarab

There are a number of hatpins based on the scarab motif. The one most often identified as Scarab, however, is actually Big Butterfly.

Scarab Shell

In blue, this hatpin sold for $1,200 at a 1995 auction. Other colors such as green and purple sell for $350 to $500.

Scarab, Stylized

Fairly rare. This example is green and brought $190 at a 1994 auction. In 1995 a green pin sold for $250. An amethyst example was reported for $160 in 1996, a green one for $130 the same year, and another green one in 1997 for $105. In 1998 an amethyst example sold for $95.

Scroll and Diamonds

Lavender example sold for $375 in 1998.

Six Plums

Just about the most common hatpin you'll find, these dark pins sometimes are found with just the plums iridized, sometimes only the other parts. Can be bought for about $30. It is also called Cattails.

Snake

A hatpin described as the head of a snake sold in 1997 for $500. It was listed as the only one.

Spider

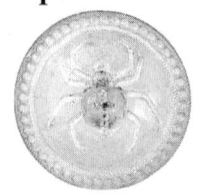

There are several spider hatpin designs, but this one with the beads around the edge seems to be the most common. The example here is light marigold and brought $160 in 1993. At the same auction an amber Spider sold for $85. The same year an ice green Spider brought $225.

Spider, King

Sometimes called Big Spider, in this version the spider's legs extend to the edge of the pin—which is almost two inches across. They are known only in dark glass. This example sold for $900 in 1995.

Spinner

A simple design, this marigold on milk glass example sold for $175 in 1993. I have no records of any having sold since.

Spiral Dance

Similar to many faceted hatpins, this one has the facets arranged in a spiral—thus the name. This is a $40 hatpin although they have sold for as much as $100.

Star Center

There are two sizes of this hatpin that were reported in late 1997 as currently being made in the Czech Republic. They are found in dark color with bluish iridescence. In 1998, a large example brought $130, a small one $70.

Star and Flower

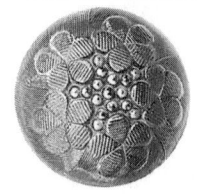

This example, in a beautiful blue, sold for $1,000 at a 1995 auction.

Star of David and Baguettes

Rare hatpin from a private collection.

Hatpins 347

Stork

This hatpin, in powder blue, has the distinction of being the most expensive hatpin sold at auction. It brought $2,600 in 1995.

Strawberry

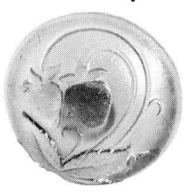

A very desirable hatpin usually seen in green. In that color they bring $400 to $700 although they have auctioned for as much as $1,500. An amber example sold for $1,100 in 1995.

Sunflower

While the design looks more like a daisy than a sunflower, it is always seen in white and brings $70 to $90.

Sun's Up

A rooster crowing as the sun rises. Found in lavender and purple, this pin sells for $150 to $225.

Swirley Taffeta

In early 1998, a purple hatpin by this name sold for $185.

Throw Pillow

A dark hatpin with an indentation in the center, Throw Pillow sells for $50 to $80.

Top O' the Morning

Referred to alternately as Pheasant (which is what it appears to be), this pin is sometimes seen with brilliant multi-color iridescence.

Triad

A good pin for starting a collection. Triad sells for $25 to $35.

True Scarab

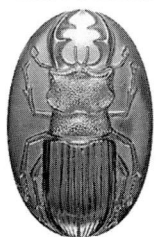

As with most insect hatpins, very desirable. This one sold for $1,000 in 1995, another in 1997 for $700.

Tufted Throw Pillow

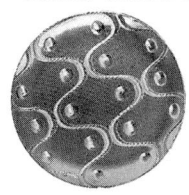

Readily available and a must for every collection, this dark hatpin can be found for $40 or $50.

Turban

A dark colored hatpin, Turban can be had for $80 or $100.

Twin Gators

I haven't been able to photograph one of these but as you'd expect, there are two opposed alligators (although they look more like salamanders to me). One sold in 1997 for $1,400.

Two Flowers

This design is one of several that are called Two Flowers. Some sell in the $200 range. Some collectors say similar designs were made in West Germany in the 1950s.

348 A Field Guide to Carnival Glass

Ugly Bug

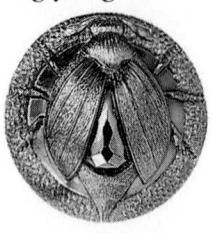

Apparently with carnival glass hatpins the uglier the bug, the better. This one sold for $1,650 in 1997. Another sold for $1,700 the same year.

Unknown pattern

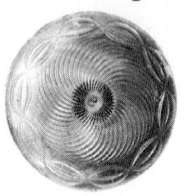

This unlisted geometric pattern with a swirl center and a cable design around the edge sold for $220 in 1994. It is a sort of yellow-marigold color.

Veiling

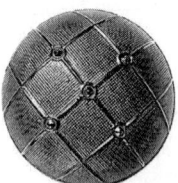

Sometimes called Veiling and Beads, this is a pleasing pin that sells in the $40 to $50 range.

Waves

Usually seen in chocolate colored glass that sells in the $100 range. Also reported in blue ($300), green ($200 to $400) and purple ($280).

Zig Zag

This amber hatpin is in a private collection.

Contemporary iridized glass

Now we come to one of the most confusing and contentious aspects of carnival glass: recently produced iridized glass.

We're now within striking distance of the 100th anniversary of the start of carnival glass in 1907. There has been a continual production of iridized glass since then. The value of carnival glass is greatly affected by its availability and when newer glass mimics the old it causes great concern among all collectors.

Yet much of the newer glass has become quite collectible itself, and prices of several hundred dollars and more are not unheard of.

How does the serious collector resolve these differences? The place to start is learning the old patterns, the new patterns, and what's been reproduced. That's a tall order. This book is intended to help you with that, although its focus is on the classic glass. New glass and reproductions are a large and complex topic, more than can be adequately covered here (my personal opinion is that there have been more patterns made in contemporary carnival glass than there were in the classic era). Nonetheless, I feel it important to provide a basis for understanding glass that has been produced since the 1960s.

This includes some of the patterns that were reissued during the 1960s, 1970s, 1980s and 1990s by a few of the original makers of carnival; reproductions by companies that bought the molds when the original companies went out of business; and fakes that continue to plague collectors.

A word about trademarks. While little of the classic carnival was trademarked—aside from Northwood—much of the newer glass is. Although it would be nice to offer a compendium of such marks here, it would likely take a whole chapter in itself—especially when one considers that something of a company history is necessary to provide accurate information.

There is excellent information on these marks on the Woodsland/www. cga website (see Carnival glass clubs in back of this book).

Bear in mind that quite a number of companies have produced newer carnival glass, and many continue to do so—some from molds used in original carnival production. The state of the business is in flux, so collectors will no doubt need to remain vigilant about new patterns as well as fakes.

One more thing: collectors of contemporary carnival often assign different names to patterns produced during the classic era. In addition, there are new patterns that have been given the same names as the classic ones. Confusion reigns.

Acanthus

This is a celeste blue Acanthus bowl made by Fenton from the original mold. It was made as a souvenir for the 1995 International Carnival Glass Association convention held in Dallas. It is also known with slightly different ruffling. There is an unrelated contemporary pattern also called Acanthus known in four-footed bowls and in other shapes with the pattern on the exterior.

Apple Tree, Fenton

Apple Tree water sets were reissued in red in 1995. Tumblers are also known in green.

Butterfly and Berry, Fenton

In addition to the fairly well-known amethyst tumblers by Fenton, there are other shapes lying in wait for the unwary collector. The above large bowl, in white, could easily be mistaken for the extremely rare original in this color. It is sold by A & A Imports who also have a purple version. Fenton also produced a vase/spittoon shape whimsey from tumblers in aqua or green opal. All Fenton pieces should be signed with their logo.

Butterfly, Fenton

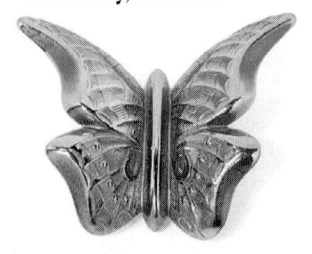

Called Fenton's #5170 Butterfly, this piece differs considerably from the original Fenton butterfly (see Novelties/miniatures).

Butterfly tray, Jeannette

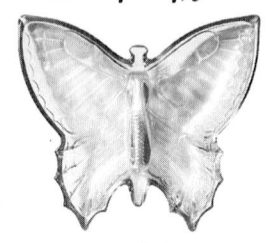

Sometimes called pin trays or mint dishes, these butterflies are occasionally found in sets of five—one large and four small, so they were probably intended for use as nut or candy dishes. Known in marigold, smoky blue, and aqua/teal.

Carolina Dogwood, Fenton

Fenton apparently acquired the Westmoreland Carolina Dogwood mold. I don't know of it being used to make pieces that could be confused with the original bowls and plates. This basket has one-of-a-kind decoration and is in red base glass. The flowers were handpainted by Jenni Cunningham. The basket was provided by Fenton to the Lincoln-Land club for their 1997 convention whimsey auction where it brought $475.

Contemporary iridized glass 351

Checkerboard, Westmoreland

Checkerboard water set reproductions were made from the original mold of the pitcher—while the new tumblers are taller. Although none of the original Checkerboard sets was made in blue, as was the one shown above, amethyst was made in both eras. Westmoreland also reissued the set in honey, lime green, and ice blue.

Cherry and Cable, Mosser

While this child's punch set was not made in the old carnival, it's good enough to fool some folks into thinking it might be old. It is in green and has a bowl that is 5¼" tall and cups that are 1½" tall. I expect that other colors are around. Amethyst cups have also been used as table favors by at least one carnival club.

Cherry and Cable, Westmoreland

Westmoreland is said to have made cracker jars in this pattern during the 1970s in cobalt, ice blue, lime, purple and turquoise.

Cherry Chain, Fenton

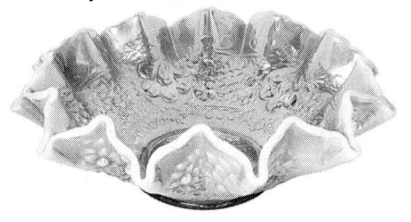

Fenton reissued Cherry Chain in a number of shapes and colors—including this aqua opal ruffled bowl.

It has an Orange Tree exterior and is also known in red. Round bowls in black amethyst, chop plates in aqua opal, and an 8" rosebowl in reddish amethyst are also known. As Fenton usually made pieces in a number of colors and shapes when it reissued patterns, there are no doubt several others.

Cherry and Lattice, Mosser

Although it is not a pattern found in the original carnival issue, it certainly could be confused with the older glass. Made by Mosser in 1978, this three-piece table set in purple has an "M" inside the sugar bowl.

Chessie, Fenton

Fenton first made these 9" tall candy jars showing a sleeping cat's head for the Chesapeake and Ohio Railroad in 1970. They were intended as gifts for friends and VIPs. In 1995 Fenton reissued the piece in a limited edition of 800 in celeste blue.

Christmas Compote

In 1997, the original molds for this treasured compote were uncovered. Dave Richardson has reissued this compote in three Fenton colors: ruby, topaz and green opalescent.

Chrysanthemum, Imperial

If this pattern looks like the old Chrysanthemum chop plate, you're right. It's the same size as the old and should have the IG logo as well as a stippled base if it's a reissue. Made in marigold, smoke, white, and ice blue from 1965–1970.

Covered Hen, Fenton

Covered hens have long been favorites among glassmakers—and collectors. This is Fenton's late version in black amethyst. It's 8 3/8" long and sold at a 1997 Mickey Reichel auction for $100. Several other companies have also made carnival covered hens in various sizes. They are quite different from the older butter dishes made by Sowerby.

Covered Swan

In the foreground is the newer covered swan. Note that the beak touches the neck and the opening thus formed is filled with glass. On the older swan, background, the neck curves differently and the space between the neck and body is open.

Daisy, Imperial

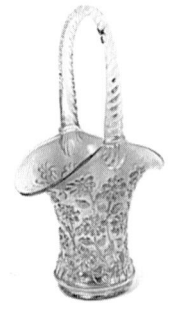

This 9½" high basket was made from the same mold as the original and reissued in marigold, smoke, ice blue, amber, and helios green. Again, new items should have the IG logo.

Daisy Wreath, Westmoreland

Westmoreland is said to have reproduced plates in plum opal in the early 1980s.

Dahlia, Westmoreland

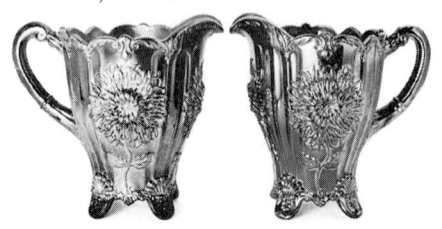

This is one of the most confusing situations in carnival collecting. In 1977, L. G. Wright had Westmoreland make Dahlia pitchers using the original molds in amethyst/purple and white—both of which had been used in the original production—and ice blue. It is virtually impossible to tell the difference. In the above photo, the new one is on the right, in purple like the older one on the left. In the newer one the iridescence is an artificial-looking purple—although not all are like this. With the old examples, the underneath of the base was not iridized, so pieces with an iridized base are most likely new.

Contemporary iridized glass 353

Although Dahlia tumblers were also reproduced, they are easier to differentiate as they have three flowers around the trunk—rather than four as in the old. The older tumblers also have a many-rayed star in the base, the new ones are plain and iridized. I've been told that Mosser is currently producing the pattern from the old molds.

Diamond Point Columns, Fenton

Fenton reissued the Diamond Point Columns vase in amethyst as well as noniridized colors. The base size of the new one is 4¼", somewhat larger than the original.

Drapery, Fenton

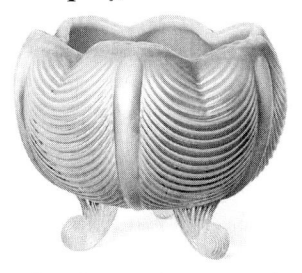

If you don't see the Fenton mark and forget that Northwood's version had no feet, you could make an expensive mistake with this piece. The example you see here is very nicely done in aqua opal and is said to date from 1978. Other versions are known in plum opal and the rosebowl has been whimsied up into a bud vase in aqua opal. The pattern is sometimes referred to as Curtain by collectors of newer carnival.

Fancy Flowers, Imperial

This large compote was reproduced in marigold and smoke.

Fantail, Fenton

I've seen both blue and red 9" bowls in the Fantail pattern. As with the original examples, there is a Butterfly and Berry exterior. Apparently made from the old molds with the Fenton logo added.

Farmyard

The original Farmyard bowls were made by Dugan in purple and green with one peach opal bowl known. It is said that the molds for the new versions are not the same, however, as used in the originals. Apparently the new set has passed through several owners including a couple who commissioned pieces with their logo, MIMI, on the bottom. Subsequently, Singleton Bailey acquired the molds and has commissioned Fenton to make various shapes and colors with his signature, DBs. Bailey continues to reissue these pieces in plates and bowls in a variety of contemporary colors.

Fenton's Flowers, Fenton

These reissued rosebowls are called Leaf & Orange Tree by Dorothy Taylor, who reports them made in amethyst in 1970 and marigold in 1971.

Fieldflower, Imperial

Fieldflower water sets were reissued from the same molds as the originals, so there is no way to tell between old and new except for the IG or LIG mark. The new sets are known in amethyst (or purple), blue, sapphire blue, ice blue, red and perhaps other colors. Interestingly, some of these sets have become quite valuable, selling for between $100 and $200.

File and Fan, Westmoreland

Using the same mold from which its classic era compote was made, Westmoreland made miniature punch sets in a huge variety of colors. It is unlikely they could be confused with the old glass, but it is worth mentioning anyway.

Fine Cut and Grape, Fenton

Were it not for the Fenton logo on the bottom, the casual observer might think this an old Northwood Fine Cut & Roses at first glance. The pattern, shape, and size are similar but this pattern has grapes rather than roses. Note the Fenton label.

Floral and Grape, L.G. Wright

Water sets in this pattern were made in purple in the 1970s by Westmoreland for L.G. Wright. Tumblers are marked with the Wright "W" trademark that appears to be an "N" with a short line attached to the left side. This is probably the result of a law suit against Wright for infringing the Northwood mark.

Four Seventy Four, Imperial

Imperial reissued the pattern in 1970-1971 in water sets, a mug and a compote. Collectors of newer carnival sometimes identify the pattern by other names. Joan Westerfield had Imperial make 250 water sets in blue in 1977. Imperial also reproduced the pattern in shapes not known in the old—a differently shaped vase, a covered box, salt and pepper shakers, and a sugar shaker.

Frolicking Bears

While not the exact pattern found in the old Frolicking bears tumbler, the similarity could trick someone into thinking they are rare variations. In reality, this spooner/tumbler and spittoon are convention souvenirs for carnival clubs.

Fruits and Flowers, L.G. Wright

You won't easily forget these huge chop plates, which measure almost 14" across. This one is in black amethyst and has a logo that could be mistaken for the Northwood "N." Wright is also said to have made a bowl from the same mold. Courtesy of Jeri Vincent.

Fruits and Flowers, unknown

Owen Loudon showed this stemmed bonbon at a 1995 convention and reported that he got it from a woman who claimed to have gotten it at the Fenton factory. We have not heard that Fenton had the mold for this piece, although it is certainly possible. It has the look, however, of a straight ripoff—with mirror-like iridescence and extra glass in the openings of the handles. This example is purple.

Contemporary iridized glass 355

God and Home, Westmoreland

Beginning in 1972, L. G. Wright had Westmoreland make water sets in the pattern's original molds, in a variety of colors—amethyst, green, ice green and red, some of which carry the "W" in a circle trademark. It was reissued in ice blue for Levay in 1976. The old sets (c. 1912) were made only in blue.

Good Luck, Fenton

As part of its 1991 limited edition offering, Fenton produced ruffled bowls in light amethyst. While the pattern has the same horseshoe and lettering as the Northwood, other details differ. It should, of course, be marked with the Fenton logo. Also known in green and perhaps other colors.

Good Luck, unknown

Bowls in this pattern have been produced in Korea or Taiwan. Colors are said to be marigold, blue, and green. The iridescence is harsh and metallic. There is an "N" in a circle but it is oversized compared with the authentic Northwood mark. These have turned up in England and Australia as well as the US.

Gothic Arches, Imperial

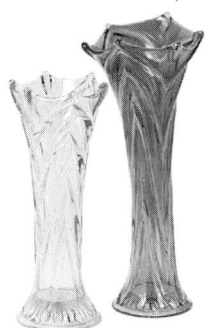

Imperial reproduced their Gothic Arches vase in ice blue (on left) and yellow. As neither has a trademark, it is easy to assume these are from the classic era. On the right is an example of the marigold Gothic Arches in the original glass. It is also found in several shades of smoke.

Grape and Cable, Fenton

I've seen these Fenton bowls (apparently made from the mold used for the base of the original humidor) in several colors and rufflings as well as a spittoon in peach opal. In 1991 Fenton produced a punch set in light amethyst that they called Panelled Grape. It could also be called Grape and Cable or Vintage.

This decorated basket was probably made from the same mold as the above bowl. It's in blue with an attached twisted handle. Fenton provided this one-of-a-kind piece to the Lincoln-Land club for their 1997 whimsey auction where it brought $450.

In 1969, Rose Presznick, a collector and early author of books on carnival, had Fenton make these Grape and Cable humidors. They are amethyst and marked on the base with the Fenton logo and words about Presznick's Carnival Glass Museum. The lid is also marked.

Grape and Cable, Mosser

In Mosser's version of the Grape and Cable covered butter, the cover is almost identical to the original. The base, however, is quite different, with a wide panel design and scalloped edge rather than the beaded or sawtooth edge of the old. Mosser made it in amber, ice blue, and cobalt.

Grape and Cable, Wetzel

Sherman Hand, the early carnival glass researcher, commissioned Wetzel Glass to make small electric lamps in green and blue in the Grape and Cable pattern.

Grape and Cable, fake

I can't claim to have actually seen one, but fake Grape and Cable hatpin holders have been reported in green. The report I saw said there was a sticker saying it was made in China. There may be other colors. I have seen uniridized examples of this shape in red and blue.

Grape Delight, fake

At least two rip-offs of this pattern are known in the nut bowl shape shown here. None have been spotted of the cupped-in rosebowl, but there may be some. Mosser is known to have made the nut bowls in amber and ice blue. Some have an "N" in a circle which is obviously fraudulent as Northwood did not make the Grape Delight pattern.

Grapevine Lattice, L.G. Wright

Wright commissioned the reissue of the Grapevine Lattice water sets in amethyst in 1978. Reissues should be signed with a "W" with an underline all enclosed in a circle.

Hanging Cherries, Fenton

Fenton made a creamer and sugar in 1974 in a pattern very similar to the Millersburg Hanging Cherries pattern. No info on colors.

Hansen glass

The brothers Robert and Ron Hansen began iridizing glass made by other manufacturers in the 1960s. Their early glass was not signed but after splitting up, each began signing their work on the base. The above pieces are typical of the work of Robert, the more prolific of the two. The violin bottle is in teal (and shown here somewhat smaller than it really is in comparison with the other two pieces), a Santa Claus fairy lamp in red (I've seen two of these sell in the $1,000 range), and an Eyewinker tumbler in red. Needless, to say, work of the Hansen brothers has become very collectible.

Hearts and Flowers, Fenton

It doesn't look much like the Northwood pattern but still could fool the newer collector. Notice the dome foot, which Northwood did not employ with the pattern. I've seen red and amberina in addition to the pictured 11" bowl in amethyst. All examples, of course, should have the Fenton logo.

Contemporary iridized glass 357

Harvest Flower

This was a surprise to me. I wasn't aware that the pattern had been reproduced until I saw a tumbler in blue opal at a 1998 auction of new glass.

Heavy Grape, Fenton

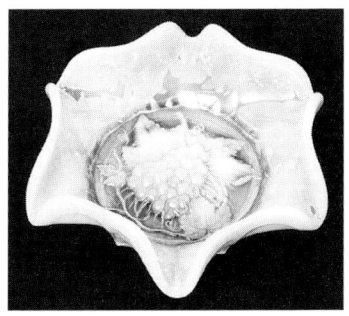

Another case where Fenton seems to have come into possession of original Imperial molds. This is the one from the small mold and is 7½" wide.
In aqua opal, this was made as a 1996 convention souvenir for the Southern California club.

Heavy Iris, Westmoreland

In 1979, Westmoreland made amethyst water sets in this pattern from the old Dugan molds for L.G. Wright. The new pitchers are taller, with a plain two-inch band just below the ruffled top. I've seen tumblers in aqua opal, cobalt and vaseline opal.

Hex Optic, Jeanette

The iridized examples of this Depression pattern are from the late 1950s and early 1960s. This pitcher and tumbler are from a water set that sold in 1997 for $15. You might find them at the local mall for $25 a set. Note the ice lip—not seen in the older glass.

Hobstar

I've seen quite a few of these covered cracker jars, mostly in green, with the IG. Punch sets were also reissued by Imperial and I am told that Smith now has the molds.

Holly, Fenton

While this example is in aqua opal, amethyst is also reported for these bowls apparently made from the original molds. This one sold for $20 at a 1997 Mickey Reichel auction.

Holly, Joe St. Clair

Joe St. Clair was another craftsman who iridized glass made by others. The 4¾" high creamer in aqua, above, along with a similar handled mug, are probably the most often seen of St. Clair's work.

Holly Band, Joe St. Clair

A very deceptive tumbler. As some are not signed, many folks could think they're old. I once saw half a dozen of these being offered at a high price as Millersburg. This one is blue-violet and they've been reported in white, amberina, marigold, ice blue and cobalt. Sometimes called Panelled Holly.

Homestead, Imperial

One of the most desirable of the chop plates in the original production, Homestead was reissued in ice blue, smoke, white, marigold, and pink. All except the pink should be marked with the IG logo; the pink with LIG. I hear that Summit now has the mold and is producing pieces with the IG logo still in place. The old Homestead chop plates have a ribbed back and a smooth base. The new ones have a plain back and a stippled base with the logo in the center (unless it has been ground off).

Imperial Grape, Imperial

Imperial reissued their Grape pattern in many shapes and colors beginning in the 1960s. Many are quite well done and sometimes sell for comparatively good prices. Also found in the water carafe, goblet, salt and pepper, cruet, wine set, a footed creamer and sugar, small bowls, footed juice glasses, and about a dozen other shapes. Mostly seen in marigold, smoke, and a few in helios green, as well as most of the other 60s–70s colors.

Indian Head toothpick holder

This head-shaped toothpick was not produced in classic carnival although the mold dates back to the 1880s. Joe St. Clair used the mold to make carnival pieces and it was sold to Summit Glass in 1978 who produced carnival in a variety of colors. (Thanks to Glen and Stephen Thistlewood for the info.)

Imperial Lace, Imperial

This pattern was called Octagon during the classic Carnival era. This red 8" vase is one of the more frequently seen pieces. See Octagon in this section.

Contemporary iridized glass 359

Inverted Fan and Feather

In the classic era of carnival, this motif was used only as the exterior of only a couple of Dugan patterns. It is widely used, however, by many of the contemporary glass makers and is found in a variety of shapes and colors.

Inverted Feather
Tumblers have been reproduced in ice blue. They should have an "M" inside the base.

Inverted Strawberry

To the best of my knowledge, none of the classic era Inverted Strawberry pieces has been reissued. There are, however, many pieces with this general design in contemporary carnival glass. The miniature punch can be easily found and the pedestalled creamer, in purple slag, was made as a souvenir for the 1996 American Carnival Glass Association convention. Other table set pieces as well as a spittoon were made for other ACGA conventions.

Inverted Thistle
Linda Heaton reports pieces by L.G. Wright and water sets and table sets in pink and ice blue by Mosser.

La Bella Rose, Imperial

This marigold 6¼" vase turns up fairly often and can be mistaken for old glass even though the pattern is not known to have been made in the early era. It has the IG mark. Also made in smoke and red.

Lions, Fenton

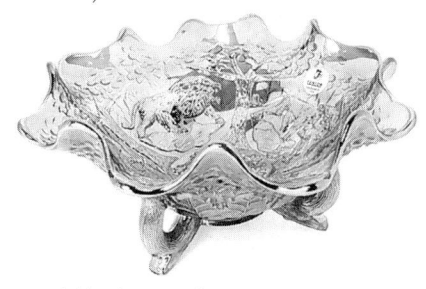

Much like the original Lions pattern in some respects, the new Lions has the three twig feet and Orange Tree exterior of the Fenton's Flowers rosebowl. This one is in green and all should have the Fenton logo.

Loganberry, Imperial

These are the vases made from the molds of the well known and highly desirable original Loganberry vases. The Imperial number was #356. Shown are pink (marked LIG), green (IG), and ice green (LIG). The tops of the new vases are ruffled—the old are not. Imperial also offered a contemporary vase they called Loganberry (#109), a somewhat smaller and more slender piece.

Lombardi, Jeanette-McKee

This piece has collected a lot of innocent buyers. Glen and Stephen Thistlewood report that it was made by Jeanette-McKee in the 1960s and 1970s. It has been reported in milk glass, two-tone blue/green, two-tone red/orange, and uniridized. This one is marigold.

Lustre Rose, Open Rose

Lustre Rose and Open Rose were reproduced by Imperial, its successor companies, and others. Water sets, table sets, bowls, and plates have been reported. Mostly the colors will be in the standard Imperial repro colors of marigold, smoke, green or helios. The crimped bowl above is teal, the round one is blue as is the table set below (marked AIG).

Marbles

Marbles can be found in a variety of colors, many quite attractive. I've seen big barrels of them at flea markets and have been told that they are being made today. I know of no way to determine whether they are old. Worth a dollar or two each. I've seen large marbles with advertising imprinted on them and have been told by marble collectors that they are relatively recent.

Maple Leaf

This pattern has been reproduced by Westmoreland for L.G. Wright. Reported in water sets and table sets in amethyst and red. I spotted a tumbler in ice green at an auction of new glass.

Millersburg souvenir, Imperial

A nicely done tumbler in blue. It was made by Imperial for the 1971 Millersburg, Ohio festival.

Nautilus

Toothpick holders are currently being made by Summit according to Glen and Stephen Thistlewood. The shape was not made in the classic period.

Nugget (or Nugate), Pilgrim

These small pitchers (4"–5" tall) are found in a large variety of shapes. Usually on blue base glass

Contemporary iridized glass 361

with marigold fluted handles applied after the glass had been blow molded. According to Glen and Stephen Thistlewood, writing in their journal, *Network*, the pitchers were produced by Pilgrim Glass of Ceredo, West Virginia, between 1968 and 1973.

Octagon, Imperial

Among the numerous shapes Imperial reissued in its Octagon pattern (which they called Imperial Lace), the small compote (in blue) and toothpick (in green, though other colors are common as well) are the most often seen. I've seen the large bowls in blue and green.

Ohio Star

I list this vase under the name "Ohio Star" because that is how it's known by collectors of new glass. It was *not* made from the same mold as the classic era vase of this name by Millersburg. In the Millersburg, the central star is a rayed version, not the whirling one shown here. Many other details are different, the most telling being the base which is sawtoothed here and smooth on the old ones.

Open Edge, Fenton

Fenton's popular open edge baskets were reproduced in amethyst in 1970–73 and in marigold in 1976–77. Note also that Fenton made red baskets for the Canadian Carnival Collectors Association in 1990. The Fenton logo is on the basketweave part, not the base and the club lettering is enameled in white—and easy to remove. Buyer beware.

Owls, Imperial

These are relatively recent Imperial products not found in the older glass. The covered jar on the left is blue and signed ALIG. The double-faced owl toothpick holder is also blue and is signed IG.

Pansy, Imperial

According to Linda Heaton, Imperial reissued the pattern in nappies and pickle dishes in a variety of old colors in the late 1960s. Sugars and creamers have also been reissued.

Pansy plate, fake

Beware of Pansy pattern plates that look like the Imperial pattern but have the Northwood "N" mark. According to Tom Mordini, these are fakes and have been reported in custard.

Peacock Garden, Fenton

Peacock Garden vases are very rare in the original Carnival, thus one must be very careful about the 8" reissues. This example is in black amethyst and I've seen them in amethyst.

Peacocks, fakes

These two Peacocks bowls are copies of Northwood's original designs. Probably made in far East. The most obvious differences are the extremely mirror-like iridescence and the base which is a solid disk of glass—not the typical collar base. The "N" mark is also much larger than the original. Known in marigold, blue, and green.

Persian Medallion, Fenton

Fenton has gotten a lot of mileage out of their Persian Medallion molds. Their production of items includes bowls, plates, stemmed rosebowls, compotes, baskets made from bowls with attached handles, and goblets or chalices in a number of colors. No doubt these and other shapes will continue to appear.

Picture Frame

The smaller new versions were modeled after the original rarity (see Novelties/miniatures) and offered as convention souvenirs for the International Carnival Glass Association.

Pony, Westmoreland

The pony bowls are particularly difficult to tell from the early pieces as they were made from the original molds and not marked. Sometimes, as in the example shown here, the iridescence is extremely shiny and metallic looking.

Poppy Show

Originally part of the Imperial line, the Poppy Show vase is still being produced by Fenton, from the original mold, for Singleton Bailey (including the blue one above). These vases are highly collectible and are found in contemporary carnival colors.

Contemporary iridized glass 363

Presznick Museum souvenir

Dated 1972, this mug or handled tumbler is in celeste blue and was apparently a souvenir of Rose Presznick's carnival glass museum.

Rambler Rose, Westmoreland

In 1977 Westmoreland began producing water sets from their original molds for L.G. Wright. I've only seen them in amethyst but other colors could be out there.

Ripple, Imperial

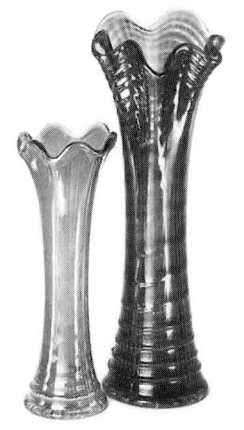

Yes, the Ripple vases were reissued—from the original molds. The swinging and workmanship are excellent and were it not for the IG mark on the bottom, these could pass for old. Two base sizes are known—2⅞" and 3⅞". Both sizes come in marigold and smoke.

Robin, Imperial

Imperial reissued Robin in both the mug and water set. This mug is red and is also known in pink. Reissued water sets are found in cobalt, white, green, and red. A white 7-piece water set sold for $85 in 1998.

Scroll Embossed, Imperial

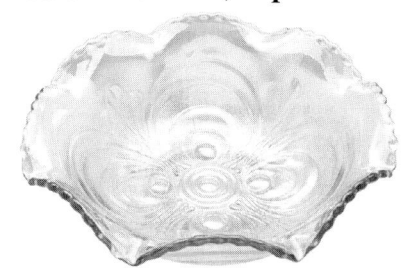

Often with excellent iridizing, these 9" bowls are found in ice blue, ice green, pink and possibly amethyst. The examples I've seen are marked LIG, but the mark is so faint that it's more easily felt than seen.

Scroll and Flower Panels, Imperial

These vases (also see vase section) were originally made in marigold and, I suspect, purple. The newer ones have an IG on the inside bottom. According to John Valentine, they were made in smoke and marigold with two types of tops—cupped in as shown here, or flared out.

Singing Birds

When this tumbler sold at auction, it was described as blue opal. I'd have to call it ice blue as the color is very light and any opalescence is quite subtle. The maker is unknown. I've seen others in blue and amethyst that were identified as being by Summit.

Stag and Holly

With such a popular pattern as Stag and Holly, it's not surprising that there be ripoffs. There are at least two known fake versions. One of them was brought to us by A & A Importing in the same colors as they did the Butterfly and Berry fakes—white opal and purple. Frank M. Fenton states that Fenton's pieces show the tongue of the stag, others do not. Some collectors point out that the fakes also have round eyes; the older ones more oval shaped. There are other differences, such as the number and placement of the berries in the holly sprigs.

Star and File, Imperial

Among the many patterns Imperial reissued is the one called Star and File—found in this wine set. It is seen in marigold and a hard-to-find smoke. Imperial used the name Peacock for this 60s–70s smoke iridescence.

Star Medallion, Imperial

The Star Medallion and Star and File patterns are often confused—and they are similar. Both are also found in the original glass and both should have the IG mark on the reissues. Star Medallion has the medallion design element repeated against a background of buttons. This ice blue compote is typical of the reissues and has also been reported in marigold, smoke, helios, and amber.

Stork and Rushes, L.G. Wright

Wright reproduced many carnival patterns from the original molds or similar ones. Most were marked with the Wright logo. The new Stork and Rushes table set (shown here) never had a butter dish as did the old, and the tops of the sugars are significantly different (with a terraced effect on the old). This set is in purple. Water sets are reported in marigold and purple, and a purple 7-piece berry set sold at a recent auction.

Strutting Peacocks, Westmoreland

Using their old molds, Westmoreland is said to have reproduced the creamer, sugar, and spooner in red and amethyst in 1979.

Contemporary iridized glass 365

Swan mug, Fenton

While this cobalt swan mug looks like one of the older patterns, it was not made during the classic carnival era. I've been told that it is still being produced by Fenton and, of course, has their logo.

Swan salt

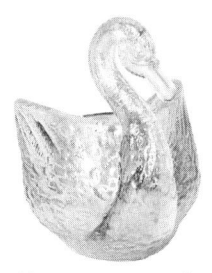

This swan is a reproduction of the popular pastel swan salts seen in classic carnival. Note the twist of the neck in this ice green example, which means it is a reproduction—although not all repros have such shaping. Bear in mind that old swan salts in the most frequently seen colors of celeste, ice green, and pink seldom sell for more than $50. Imperial is said to have made their version of these swan repros in red, blue, and white.

Thistle goblet, St. Clair

Joe St. Clair iridized several goblet patterns not known in classic carnival. As far as I know none were marked, so there is always the possibility of someone coming across these and paying too much because they think they've found a rarity.

Three-in-One toothpick, Imperial

These toothpick holders are found in both new and old versions. Carl O. Burns, in his book on Imperial glass, says he has seen new examples without the IG logo. Both are found in green, the new one also in ice blue.

Tiger Lily, Imperial

Imperial reissued this set in several colors including ice blue, marigold, pink, and white. Some are signed IG, others LIG—as is this ice green set.

Unspecified pattern

This is undoubtedly the Imperial bowl shown in their reissue catalogs from the 1971–1972 era. It is number 1152 in white and described as a 3-toed 10" bowl.

Windmill, Imperial/Lenox

This water set, called sueded, has frosted panels of uniridized glass on the sections with the windmills and marigold iridescence elsewhere. The pattern, but without the frosted panelling, is also known in water sets and bowls in marigold, smoke, and pink as well as blue plates.

Zipper Loop lamps, Imperial

Imperial reissued their large size lamps in marigold and smoke in the late 1960s. They should be marked with the IG logo but I am told that the logo appears on the inside part of the base, difficult to see. It may be easier to feel. Still, for lamp collectors, these are worth watching for as they're valued in the $100 range (the old average around $500).

Index to color pages

Index to color pages, 153–184

Acorn Burrs, 180
Apple Blossom Twigs, 158, 169
Apple Tree, 170, 180
Australian Banded Diamonds, 182
Australian Butterfly Bush, 159
Australian Swan, 169
Beaded Basket, 159
Beaded Cable, 158, 175
Beaded Shell, 180
Beaded Spears, 182
Bernheimer Bros, 170
Big Butterfly, 182
Birds and Cherries, 159
Blackberry Spray, 178
Boggy Bayou, 178
Bouquet, 182
Bushel Basket, Northwood, 171
Butterfly and Berry, 180
Butterfly and Fern, 180
Cape Cod, 182
Captive Rose, 164
Cherries, Dugan, 153
Colors
    amber, 164
    amberina, 174, 179
    amethyst, 168–169
    amethyst, black, 169
    amethyst, fiery, 169
    aqua, 171
    aqua opal, 176–177
    blue, 170
    blue opal, 178
    blue milk glass, 179
    blue slag, 179
    celeste, 171
    clambroth, 165
    cobalt opal, 178
    custard, 179
    green, 172–173
    green opal, 179
    helios, 173
    honey amber, 164
    ice blue, 170
    ice green, 173
    lavender, 169
    lime green, 173
    lime green opal, 178
    marigold, 162–164
    moonstone, 179
    peach opalescent, 175
    Persian blue, 179
    powder blue opal, 178
    powder blue slag, 179
    purple, 168–169
    red, 174
    red opal, 178
    Renninger blue, 171
    sapphire, 171
    smoke, 166
    teal, 171
    vaseline, 173
    white, 167
Corn vases, 153
Cosmos and Cane, 164, 182
Cut Cosmos, 182
Dahlia, 182
Daisy and Drape, 170
Daisy and Plume, 158
Dandelion, 182
Diamond Lace, 180
Diamonds, Millersburg, 180
Dogwood Sprays, 168
Double Stem Rose, 178
Dragon and Lotus, 157
Drapery, 171
Fan, 175
Fans, 182
Farmyard, 156
Fashion, 160, 165, 166
Fenton's Flowers, 158
File and Fan, 175
File, 180
Fine Cut and Roses, 158
Fine Rib, 177
Fishnet epergne, 158
Fleur de Lis, Millersburg, 168
Four Seventy Four, 160
Frolicking Bears, 182
Frosted Block, 165
Fuchsia, 159
Gay Nineties, 182
God and Home, 170, 183
Good Luck, 169, 176
Gothic Arches, 166
Grape and Cable, 179
Grape and Cable, Fenton, 178
Grape and Cable, Northwood, 157, 158, 160, 177
Grape Arbor, 181
Greek Key, 160
Hanging Cherries, 183
Harvest Flower, 183
Hearts and Flowers, 163, 170, 178
Heavy Grape, 161
Heavy Iris, 181
Hobnail, 183
Hobstar and Feather, 167
Hobstar and Flower, 173
Hobstar Shield, 183
Holly, Fenton, 176
Homestead, 164
Horse Medallion, 171
Imperial Grape, 159, 169, 173
Inverted Coin Dot, 181
Inverted Feather, 173
Inverted Thistle, 183
Jewelled Heart, 181
Lattice and Daisy, 181
Lattice and Grape, 181
Leaf and Beads, 171, 176
Leaf Chain, 167, 176

Leaf Rays, 159
Lightning Flower, 164
Lily of the Valley, 183
Lotus and Grape, 179
Louisa, 158
Lucile, 183
Lustre Rose (Imperial Rose), 170, 174
Maple Leaf, 181
Marilyn, 183
Mayan, 161
Memphis, 173
Milady, 181
MiniRib, 177
Nesting Swan, 172
Octagon, 160
Ohio Star, 178
Oklahoma, 183
Omnibus, 183
Open Edge, 159
Open Rose (Imperial Rose), 171
Orange Tree, 174, 177, 181
Oriental Poppy, 181
Peacock and Grape, 175
Peacock and Urn, Fenton, 174, 184
Peacock and Urn, Millersburg, 184
Peacock and Urn, Northwood, 165, 177, 184
Peacock at the Fountain, 158, 167, 172, 177
Peacock at the Fountain, Dugan, 181
Peacock Tail, 168
Peacock, Millersburg, 184
Peacocks, Northwood, 163, 166, 170, 179
Perfection, 183
Persian Garden, 158
Plums and Cherries, 183
Pond Lily, 179
Pressed glass mold, 154
Quill, 183
Ragged Robin, 172
Rambler Rose, 181
Raspberry, 173
Ripple, 162
Rising Sun, 183
Rose Show, 172
Roundup, 167
Scales, Westmoreland, 178
Scroll Embossed, 169
Shell, Imperial, 166
Singing Birds, 169
Springtime, 160
Strawberry Wreath, Millersburg, 168, 173
Ten Mums, 181
Thin Rib, 177
Thistle, 158
Tree Trunk, 177, 179
Vintage, Fenton, 157
Waffle Block, 159
Water Lily, 179
Waterlily and Cattails, 181
White Oak, 183
Windmill, 165, 181
Wishbone and Spades, 159
Wishbone, 176
Wreathed Cherry, 181

Resources

Carnival glass resources

As with all hobbies, information is crucial to the understanding of carnival. The following resources provide excellent material to help the collector learn more about carnival glass.

Of general interest

Network
Independent quarterly newsletter. Discusses patterns, origins, and other relevant material in tightly edited 6" x 8½" format of 24 pages. Occasional use of color. Glen (Mrs.) and Stephen Thistlewood of England bring many years of study and collecting of carnival to readers, often providing news and insights not found in club newsletters. US subscriptions, $20 yearly. PageWorks, PO Box 2385, Mt. Pleasant, SC 29465. Elsewhere in the universe, contact the Thistlewoods at PO Box 83, Alton, Hants GU34 4YN, England.

Carnival Glass Auction Prices
Listing of more than 5,000 auction prices. Updated yearly. The best source for accurate, up-to-date individual sale prices. $10 postpaid, US and Canada (add $3 per copy for overseas shipment). Tom and Sharon Mordini, 36 N. Mernitz, Freeport, Illinois 61032. 815 235-4407.

Heart of America Carnival Glass Association Pattern Notebook
Compiled over fourteen years, this three-ring binder of hundreds of color photos is divided into sections by shape: water sets, rosebowls, plates, compotes, punch sets, vases, etc. An invaluable resource for the serious student and collector. $150 for complete binder plus $5 for shipping and handling. Individual sections also available.

Heart of America Carnival Glass Association Educational Series
Three books (Series I, II, and III) that are mainly reprints of articles that appeared in the HOACGA bulletin. The articles touch on many of the nuances, wonders, and idiosyncrasies of carnival glass. Series I is general information, Series II is entirely tumblers, Series III covers bonbons, bowls, drinking vessels, rosebowls, novelties, and table sets. All photos in black and white. Series I is $17.50, Series II and III are $20 each, all including postage.

Marion Hartung Carnival Glass Series
Series of 10 books with sketches of patterns. Marion Hartung was an early collector and writer who first described and named most of the carnival patterns. Each of the 10 books covers 100 patterns. Entire set is $60 plus $6 s/h. Published by Heart of America Carnival Glass Association

Note: The above books and series published by Heart of America Carnival Glass Association are available from them. To order these books, you must be a member of that association (because of Kansas sales tax restrictions on not-for-profit organizations).

Carnival Glass: The Magic and Mystery
Glen and Stephen Thistlewood
A thoroughly researched work with much new information, particularly on non-US carnival glass. Schiffer Publishing, 1998 publication date.

Standard Encyclopedia of Carnival Glass, 6th edition
Bill Edwards
The name says it all. 406 pages, all in color, 8½" x 11", 1997. Published by Collector Books.

Books on carnival glass makers

Dugan/Diamond: The Story of Indiana, Pennsylvania Glass
William Heacock, James Measell, Berry Wiggins
An in-depth look at the history and production of this pioneering glassmaker. Many patterns correctly identified for the first time. 212 pages, 48 in color, 8½" x 11, 1993. Antique Publications, (800) 533-3433.

Fenton Glass: The First Twenty-five Years
William Heacock
This is one of the best books available on early Fenton carnival glass as well as other lines. Shows patterns and colors as well as catalog reprints and displays of vintage advertisements. 144 pages, 72 in color, 8½" x 11, 1978. (also available are subsequent books in the series, The Second Twenty-five years, The Third Twenty-five years, and The 1980s Decade). Antique Publications, (800) 533-3433.

Fenton Art Glass: 1907–1939
Margaret and Ken Whitmyer
Covers Fenton carnival patterns (as well as other styles) with color photos in alphabetical order. Values listed adjacent to photos. 1996, 320 pages, 8½" x 11", 1996. Published by Collector Books.

Imperial Carnival Glass
Carl O. Burns
An essential reference for this Bellaire, Ohio company. Covers Imperial colors, patterns, trademarks, and Imperial reissues. 184 pages, most in color, 8½" x 11". Order from Carl O. Burns, 60 Rumford Center Rd, Andover, ME 04216.

Harry Northwood, The Wheeling Years, 1901-1925
William Heacock, James Measell, Berry Wiggins
Extensive coverage of Northwood carnival. 207 pages, 64 in color, 8½" x 11". Antique Publications, (800) 533-3433.

Millersburg Glass
Marie McGee
The only book around that adequately covers the intricacies of Millersburg carnival—by an author who is one of the premier experts on this fabled glass. 128 pages, 48 in color, 8½" x 11". Antique Publications, (800) 533-3433.

Westmoreland Glass
Chas West Wilson
Wilson is the grandson of the founder of Westmoreland Glass and provides some interesting insights. Unfortunately the coverage of their carnival is rather brief, but the company didn't make much carnival either. 335 pages, in color. 8½" x 11". Collector Books.

Books focusing on special aspects of carnival glass

The Encyclopedia of Carnival Glass Lettered Pieces
John Resnik
Shows, with black and white and color photos, all known carnival patterns with molded-in lettering for advertising premiums and commemoratives on the front of the piece. 102 pages, 5½" x 8½". $15.95 plus $2.50 postage in USA. Order from John Resnik, 235 Walnut St, Statesville, NC 28787. 704 872-7075

The world of Enameled Carnival Glass Tumblers
Cecil Whitley
Shows photos and includes descriptions of 60 decorated tumblers. 26 pages, 6" x 9", 1985. $10, postage included in USA. Cecil Whitley, 1041 Cheshire Lane, Houston, TX 77018.

Carnival Glass Hatpin Patterns
Alphonse Tvaryanas
Sixty-six pages of beautiful drawings in black and white, by a professional illustrator, of 48 common and rare hatpins. 5½" x 8½". $15 plus $3 postage in USA. Order from Alphonse Tvaryanas, 284 Clearstream Rd, Jackson, NJ 08527.

Iridescent Hatpins and Holders of the Carnival Glass Era
Jerry Ferris Reynolds
Shows 78 hatpins in black and white and color as well as hatpin holders. 160 pages, 5½" x 8½". $16.50 plus $3.25 s/h, priority mail in USA. Order from Jerry Reynolds, 1305 N Highland Pkwy, Tacoma, WA 98406.

Carnival glass clubs

It is very difficult to learn about carnival without some contact with other collectors. Joining clubs is one of the best ways to do this, and to see what other folks find interesting and important. I'd suggest a local club and one of the larger groups with national presence for a start. For the electronically inclined, the www.cga group on the Internet is a truly great source. Most clubs have newsletters, some quite informative.

While listing the clubs is important, the trick is providing the contact names. The clubs are all run by volunteers and those in charge of memberships often change from year to year. In addition, the issue of privacy arises; many do not want their names printed in a book as widely distributed as this one. However, if you are interested in finding out more about a club and have access to the Internet, check the Woodsland (www.cga) site listed below. You'll find many clubs listed there.

Internet

www.cga
no charge
Includes daily e-mail bulletin, many pages of photos of carnival, educational sections, links to other sites, listing of auctions, chat room, and more.
www.woodsland.com/woodsland/carnivalglass

International scope

American Carnival Glass Association
$15 yearly. Quarterly newsletter. Convention in July usually in eastern half of US.

International Carnival Glass Association
$20 yearly. Quarterly newsletter, convention in July, generally in midwest.

West coast, USA

Pacific Northwest Carnival Glass Club
$10 yearly, meet three times a year, convention in August

Northern California Carnival Club
$10 yearly, meet three times a year in Modesto

Southern California Carnival Glass Club
$18 yearly, meet four times a year in Long Beach

San Joaquin Valley Carnival Glass Club
$5 yearly
Meet three times a year in Fresno

San Diego County Carnival Glass Club
$18 yearly, includes excellent quarterly newsletter of more than 60 pages with actual color photos tipped onto the pages. Meet four times a year with convention in March

Midwest, USA

Air Capitol Carnival Glass Club
$15 yearly. Meet in Wichita, Kansas area, October convention.

Heart of America Carnival Glass Association
$25 yearly. Includes monthly newsletter, considered one of the best. Convention in April draws collectors from around the world.

Texas Carnival Glass Club
$20 yearly. Meet four times a year. Convention in Houston during February.

Gateway Carnival Glass Club
$5 yearly, meet in St. Louis, Missouri area.

Lincoln-Land Carnival Glass Club
$15 yearly. Includes six-times per year newsletter, monthly glass for-sale bulletin, convention in Milwaukee during early June.

Great Lakes Carnival Glass Club
$5 yearly, meet three time a year. Convention in Michigan in November.

Hoosier Carnival Glass Association
$10 yearly, meet monthly in Indiana except February, July, August.

Eastern US

Keystone Carnival Glass Club
$10 per year, meet monthly in Lititz, PA. Convention in May.

Mid-Atlantic Carnival Glass Club
Yearly Jamboree in Hagerstown, MD during October.

Western New York Carnival Glass Club
$5 yearly, meet monthly Sept–June, Churchville NY

New England Carnival Glass Club
$15 yearly, meet 5 times yearly in Southbridge, MA, convention in September

Sunshine State Carnival Glass Association
$25 yearly, bimonthly newsletter, convention in February.

Tampa Bay Carnival Glass Club
$7.50 yearly, meet monthly except June, July, August, convention in February.

Canada

L'Association du Verre Carnaval du Quebec
$20 yearly (Canadian). Bilingual newsletter. Meetings announced in newsletter.

Canadian Carnival Glass Association
$12 yearly, meet 6 to 8 times per year, convention in October.

Carnival Companions
$7.50 yearly donation, five to six meetings per year.

United Kingdom

The Carnival Glass Society Ltd
15 pounds for overseas members yearly, convention in August.

Australia

Australian Carnival Enthusiasts Association, Inc.
$12 yearly, $15 overseas. Quarterly meetings.

Buying carnival glass at auction

Other than carnival conventions, the best way to hone your glass knowledge is at auctions. There are 30 to 40 auctions held around the country each year, some at conventions. The typical auction has 300 to 400 lots for sale—a great way to see a lot of glass in one place.

All auctioneers allow ample time prior to an auction for buyers to check out the glass, occasionally extending the preview to day before. You'll have to register to get a bidding number, but there's no charge for this. If you aren't successful in any of your bids, there's nothing to pay.

Auctioneers announce the ground rules prior to the auction and mention any pieces for which significant damage has been uncovered. Most, but not all, auctioneers will describe damage in their auction catalogs. The auctioneer will also state his policy about allowing return of pieces that are discovered to have damage after purchase.

Where you sit makes little difference, but some buyers prefer the back of the room where they can view the other bidders, others prefer the front so they are forced to ignore the action in back of them. This sometimes happens when people have friends in the crowd and don't want to be aware of whom they're bidding against.

The auctioneer will sell the pieces in the order listed in the catalog. Each auctioneer has his own style of call, but all will call an auction slowly enough that everyone can pick up the bids.

Most auctioneers will start the bidding at the price they think the piece will bring. Then, to get things going, offer it at a significantly lower price. The bids move up in increments appropriate to the value of the piece—a low price piece may move in $5 increments, a valuable piece in $100 increments.

When your piece comes up and you feel comfortable with the progress of the bids, wave your bidding card to get the auctioneer's attention. He'll point to you to acknowledge your bid and then look for other bids. Bid only up to your predetermined high point. Disciplince is the key to successful bidding.

Occasionally a group of similar items will be offered for "choice." That means that the high bidder get his or her choice from the lot—and may take as many pieces as they want at that price. The bidding then starts over with the highest bidder picking from what's left and so on.

Jim Seeck calls a bid while assistants show the glass.

In most carnival glass auctions, the piece you bought will be handed to you. It is then your responsibility and you'll need to pack it to keep it out of harm's way. If you are planning on making several purchases, bring lots of wrapping and a box sufficient to hold the pieces.

The auctioneer's staff makes immediate record of the item and buyer number. When you present you buyer's card, they will tally your purchases and give you a total. It should be consistent with your own tally. If an auction service has a buyer's premium, that—along with any sales tax—will be added to the total. Most auction houses accept checks if the buyer is known to them.

If you cannot attend an auction but still wish to bid on some items, auctioneers will accept mail or phone bids. If you do this, the auction house will want to know your highest bid, and they will do the bidding for you. If you're successful with an absentee bid, you'll be notified about how much you paid. They'll send your purchase when your check has cleared.

While absentee bidding can cut your travel expenses, there is a downside. You don't get to see the glass itself before you commit to it. I've seen lots of good pieces go to mail bidders simply because nobody at the auction was interested. On the other hand, I've seen pieces with poor iridescence or flaws go to mail bidders because nobody at the auction wanted them.

Attending auctions can be a lot of fun. Often the action can be riveting—especially when the bidding on important pieces reaches into the stratosphere. And every auction has bargains. This book should prepare you to recognize them.

Below are a few of the better known auction services that specialize in carnival glass.

Ayers Auction Service
Conducts auctions in central Illinois (Peoria area)
PO Box 320, Tremont, IL 61568-0320
309 925-3115
ayers@dpc.net

Burns Auction Service
Conducts auctions mostly in eastern US and several club auctions around the country.
PO Box 608, Bath, NY 14810
607 776-7942   330 757-4917
brnzauctsv@aol.com

J & J Auction and Appraisal Service
7939 Main, Horatio-Greenville, OH 45331
914 831-6825   937 447-8909

Bill Payne Auctions
PO Box 178
10 Maddox Lane, Amissville, VA 20106
540 937-4142
bpa@tidalwave.net

Mickcy Reichel Auction Company
Conducts auctions from own auction center in Boonville, Missouri (central part of state)
516 Third St, Boonville, MO 65233-1536
660 882-5292
mreichel@undata.com

Seeck Auctions
Conducts auctions in St. Louis, Missouri, Mason City, Iowa areas, as well as for several of the clubs around the country.
PO Box 377, Mason City, IA 50402
515 424-1116
www.willowtree.com/~seeckauction
seeckauction@willowtree.com

How this book came to be

Rather than the usual "about the author" material that appears in most books, I thought it would be more interesting to describe the process involved in putting together a work such as this.

After attending auctions and conventions for several years, I realized that nobody was systematically recording the marvelous and unusual pieces of carnival glass to be found at every carnival gathering. In early 1993 I began taking photos of carnival at conventions and auctions. While the first photos were essentially snapshots, I soon began setting up a small table at the back of the auction room or in my hotel room. With a simple background of white paper or black cloth I was able show each piece to full advantage without the distractions of other pieces sitting around it.

As my photos of the unusual pieces accumulated, I started looking for an interesting way to share the photos with collectors. In 1994 and 1995, my wife Joan and I published appointment calendars illustrated with some of the color photos. Although we received a lot of support and encouragement, it was clear that the expense of producing such elaborate booklets on a limited basis could not be justified.

Casting around for another way to use the photos, it occurred to me that what collectors really need—especially newer ones—was something portable that showed a greater range of shapes for each pattern than is usually found in books, and would be accompanied by prices based on actual sales. As I had also been cataloging auction sale prices in my computer database, I realized I had the raw material to begin a book such as this.

After exploring several potential formats, I settled on the arrangement you see in this book. I began by electronically assembling the photo scans, information, and prices on a page layout program in my computer. This gave me the ability to easily alter or add photos and prices—and to build the book as I went along, so to speak.

When I had the book at the stage where I knew I could complete it, complex as it was, I contacted Dave Richardson at The Glass Press. The Glass Press had published several landmark books on carnival including Marie McGee's book on Millersburg, the book on Dugan/Diamond, and a series of Fenton books, *The First Twenty-five Years,* and so on. After a period of discussion about the potential for this book, we arrived at a contractual arrangement and a deadline.

The deadline gave me roughly ten months to pull the book together. Over the six next months or so I revised the book several times, adding new photos, checking data with collectors, and reviewing and adjusting prices. At Dave Richardson's suggestion, I added the color section. When the book was substantially complete, I turned it over to Joan for a final check.

For the next three months, Joan reviewed every word, questioned many hypotheses, removed much of the editorializing to which I am given, and in general made substantial improvements and corrections. The editorial quality of the book is largely due to her knowledge and thoroughness.

As the book took final form, I shipped sections to The Glass Press on computer disk. They reviewed it again, checked the content, and prepared it for film from which the printing plates would be made. Proofs from the film were returned to me for yet another checking. When everything was in order, The Glass Press sent the film to their printer for final completion of this long process.